ZAPOTEC CIVILIZATION

How Urban Society Evolved in Mexico's Oaxaca Valley

NEW ASPECTS OF ANTIQUITY

General Editor: COLIN RENFREW

Consulting Editor for the Americas: JEREMY A. SABLOFF

JOYCE MARCUS • KENT V. FLANNERY

ZAPOTEC CIVILIZATION

How Urban Society Evolved in Mexico's Oaxaca Valley

With 302 illustrations, 16 in color

THAMES AND HUDSON

for Manuel Esparza and
María de los Angeles Romero Frizzi
whose unfailing support made possible
much of the research reported here

© 1996 Thames and Hudson Ltd, London

First published in the United States of America in 1996 by Thames and Hudson Inc., 500 Fifth Avenue, New York, New York 10110

Library of Congress Catalog Card Number 95-60561
ISBN 0-500-05078-3

Printed and bound in Slovenia

Contents

Foreword from the Editors

Long-term excavation at a single archaeological site is an established scholarly tradition worldwide, while short-term settlement surveys of extensive areas have been rising in popularity with the advent of new technological aids, from computerized theodolites to satellite images. But ongoing, well-planned and coordinated projects of regional scope that combine detailed survey and meticulous excavations are much less frequent. However, it has become clear in recent years that only through the latter type of research, with its depth and breadth, can crucial anthropological questions about the development of cultural complexity over long periods of time be adequately answered.

Archaeological research over the past 25 years in the Valley of Oaxaca in southern Mexico has revolutionized scholarly understanding of the rise and growth of civilization in ancient Mexico and has become an oft-cited model of combined regional survey and excavation. In this stimulating volume, the renowned archaeologists Joyce Marcus and Kent V. Flannery offer a superb synthesis of this remarkable research. Dr Marcus, who is Professor of Anthropology and Curator of Latin American Archaeology in the Museum of Anthropology, and Dr Flannery, who is the James B. Griffin Distinguished Professor of Anthropology and Curator of Environmental Archaeology in the Museum of Anthropology, both at the University of Michigan, have had extensive archaeological experience in Oaxaca and elsewhere, as is clearly in evidence in *Zapotec Civilization*.

The authors walk the reader through approximately 10,000 years of Pre-Columbian history in the Valley of Oaxaca from the earliest human occupation of the valley, to the domestication of plants, to the beginnings of settled village life, to the rise of social, economic, and political complexity, to the establishment of Monte Albán, the first city in ancient Mesoamerica, to the growth and ascendancy of the Zapotec state. If the volume merely described the cultural developments in Oaxaca, it would be of great interest, because it offers an expert overview of one of the best-known cultural sequences in the Americas. But this book does so much more. With clear, incisive prose, wit, and insight, Professors Marcus and Flannery not only show how new archaeological research has enabled them to infer *what* happened in the valley, but they further offer carefully reasoned inferences about *how* and *why* such events may have occurred.

Readers may be surprised at how the authors organize their presentation, particularly as regards their explanations for the major changes in the Oaxacan sequence. Those familiar with discussions of long-term cultural trajectories in the archaeological literature of recent decades will still find some examination of the transitions from chiefdoms to states or from ranked to stratified societies. In their final chapter, however, the authors eschew evolutionary stages and emphasize instead a systemic view of culture as illuminated by an anthropological theory known as "action theory." Their interpretations abound with insights into the relationships between individuals ("actors") and institutions.

Although Joyce Marcus and Kent Flannery's book will obviously be of great interest to people who are interested in the great Pre-Columbian civilizations of Mexico, their detailed depiction of the extended development of urban society in the Valley of Oaxaca should also stimulate the attention of readers whose studies have previously been devoted to other civilizations throughout the ancient world, or who are generally interested in the comparative growth of civilizations. No matter what their geographic focus, they are certain to find much food for thought in *Zapotec Civilization* and are urged to partake of the intellectual banquet that is presented in the pages that follow.

Jeremy A. Sabloff
Colin Renfrew

The Zapotec and the Valley of Oaxaca

"Draw me a map of New Spain," said his majesty Carlos V. Across the table from him sat Hernán Cortés, conqueror of Mexico, who had returned in 1528 for a royal audience in Toledo. In a few months' time the Spanish king would reward Cortés with a title of his own choosing: Marquis of the Valley of Oaxaca. Now he was curious to see where that *marquesado* would lie.

Legend has it that Cortés picked up a piece of paper, crumpled it between his hands, and dropped it to the table. In the yellow light from the window the wrinkled paper had become a series of tiny barrancas and mountain ranges, the jagged peaks and canyons of a miniature sierra. "That," Cortés is said to have replied, "is a map of New Spain."

Cortés might well have identified the crumpled paper as a map of Oaxaca, the Mexican state whose largest valley he received as his reward. Some 400 km south of Mexico City, the eastern and western branches of the Sierra Madre flow together to form the Mesa del Sur. "There is little level land in this rugged mountain mass," geographer Robert C. West once wrote. "The hundreds of small torrential streams that drain the highlands have carved deep V-shaped valleys into the surface, creating a land of precipitous slopes and knife-edged ridges."[1] The high point, a dormant volcano named Zempoaltepec, rises 3390 m above sea level. Countless other ranges crest at 2500 m or higher, stealing rain from the canyons and valleys below.

Mountains dominate Oaxaca. One cannot appreciate the region's history without understanding how isolated the mountains left the occupants of the tiniest valleys, and how powerful and envied they left the occupants of the largest. Oaxaca's Central Valley System, shaped by a downfaulted trench some 95 km long and 25 km wide, was home to one of Mexico's earliest civilizations. The rest of the Mesa del Sur, perhaps because of its fragmentation and isolation, had given rise to no fewer than twelve different languages by the time of the Spanish Conquest.[2] The majority belong to Otomanguean, the language family that scholars believe has the longest time depth in Mexico. Proto-Otomanguean, the ancestral tongue from which all those later languages arose, was spoken somewhere in southern Mexico before agriculture and village life began.

The greatest expanse of level land in highland Oaxaca can be found in the Central Valley System at an average elevation of 1500 m. Here the Atoyac River and its tributary, the Río Salado, have produced a Y-shaped valley covering more than 2000 km² and surrounded by forested mountains rising to 3000 m. The climate is temperate and semi-arid, with 550 mm of annual rain. Rain falls

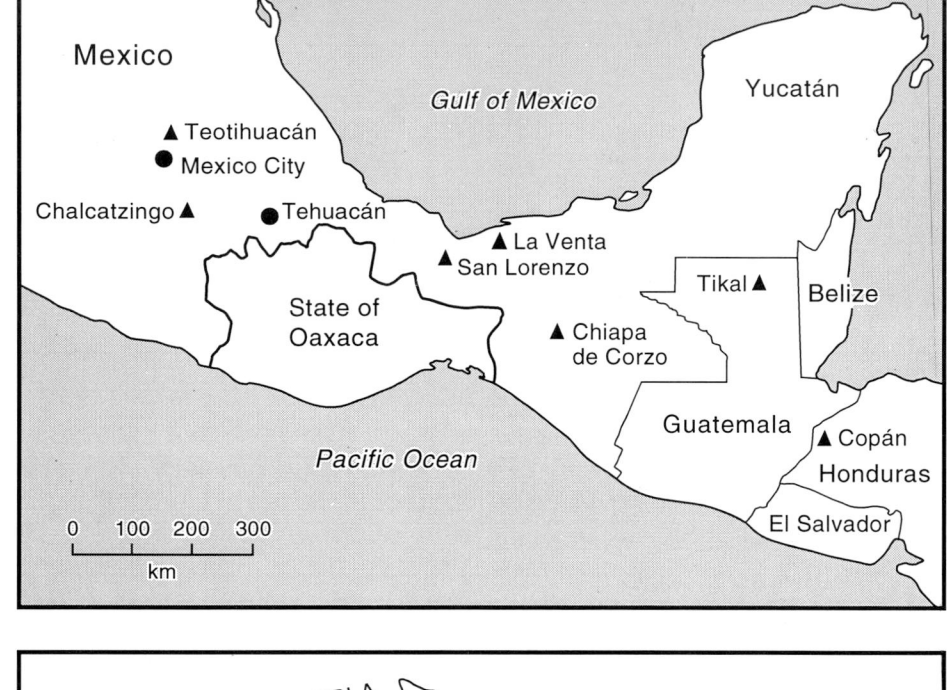

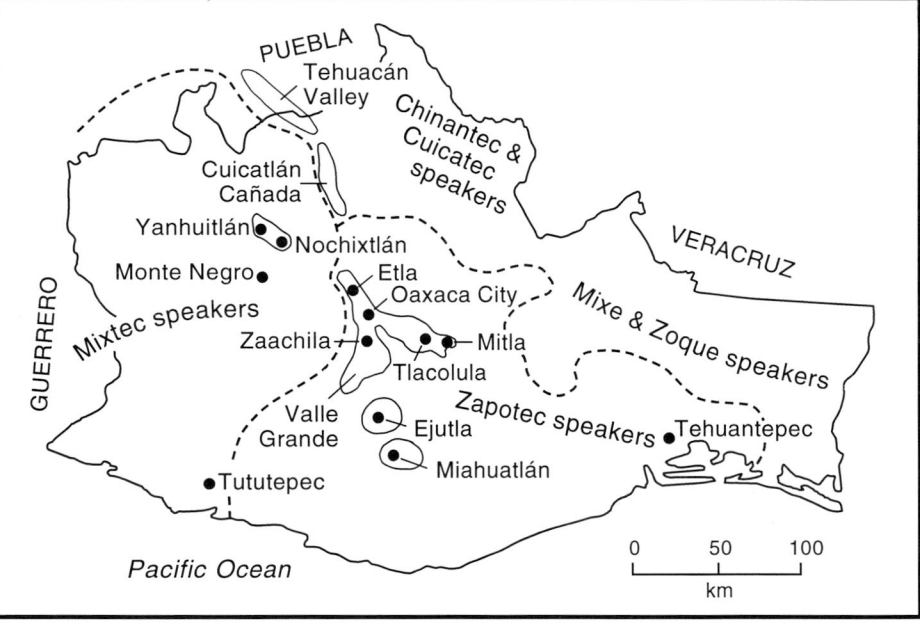

1 (*Above*) The State of Oaxaca within Mexico and Mesoamerica. (*Below*) Zapotec speakers currently occupy Oaxaca's Central Valley System and part of the mountainous region surrounding it.

mostly between May and September, creating a seasonal burst of green that fades to yellow between November and March.

Geographers classify the valley system as an area of "permanent drought," one in which precipitation throughout the year is less than potential evapotranspiration.[3] Despite these conditions, agriculture is today the principal means of livelihood, and more than 2700 archaeological sites testify to its success in the past.

The three subvalleys producing the Y, or three-pointed star, are known collectively as the Valley of Oaxaca. On the northwest is the Etla subvalley, narrowest and highest of the three, where the Atoyac River begins. On the east is the

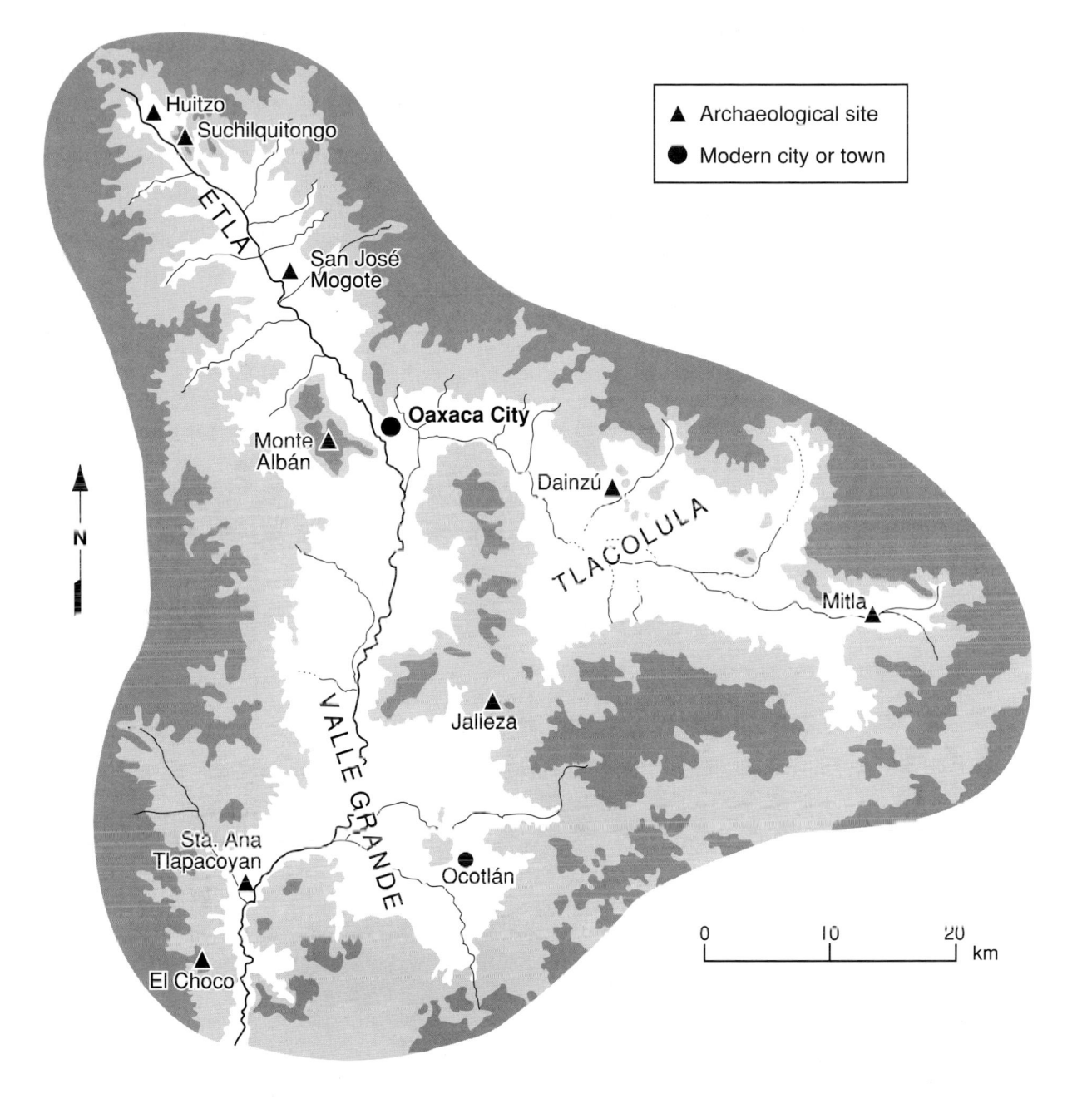

Tlacolula subvalley, broader but drier, the product of the Río Salado. To the south lies the still broader Valle Grande, where the combined waters of the Atoyac and Salado flow on their way to the Pacific Ocean. Not far to the south-east are two more components of the Central Valley System, the Valleys of Ejutla and Miahuatlán, both on tributaries of the Atoyac and politically tied to the Valley of Oaxaca through much of their history.

When the Spaniards conquered the Valley of Oaxaca in AD 1521, the main language spoken there was Zapotec, one of the dominant members of the Otomanguean family. Mixtec, another Otomanguean language, was spoken by some communities in the Etla region and Valle Grande. Archaeological and eth-

2 The Valley of Oaxaca is composed of three subvalleys: Etla, Tlacolula, and Valle Grande.

nohistoric research reveals that the Zapotec were the original occupants of the Valley of Oaxaca while the Mixtec speakers entered later, often through arranged marriages with Zapotec nobles. Most Mixtec speakers lived in the mountain valleys north and west of Etla.

Though less intensively studied than the Aztec or Maya, the Zapotec produced one of the first civilizations of ancient Mexico. They were among the first native Americans to build astronomically oriented public buildings; to use adobes, stone masonry, and lime plaster; to carve hieroglyphic inscriptions; and to achieve urban status. The cradle of Zapotec civilization was the Valley of Oaxaca, but the frontiers of that civilization extended far beyond the Central Valley System. The Zapotec affected many other parts of Mesoamerica, that region of ancient high cultures comprising central and southern Mexico, Guatemala, Belize, and parts of Honduras and El Salvador.

In the case of Oaxaca, "cradle of civilization" is more than a phrase. It implies a period of infancy, then youth, a rapid spurt of adolescent growth, and finally maturity. That image of growth is appropriate, since the Zapotec did not spring into being civilized. They reached civilization only after thousands of years of social evolution.

Our purpose in writing this book is to present the Zapotec as a case study of how early civilizations arose. We will begin, however, by describing the Zapotec as they were on the eve of their conquest in AD 1521. That description, in turn, will help us to interpret the archaeological evidence for their emergence as an ethnic group.

The Sixteenth-Century Zapotec

When Cortés arrived in Mexico, the Zapotec had recently endured a series of bloody encounters with Aztec armies from the Basin of Mexico. At that time the mightiest of several Zapotec kings was Cociyoeza, "Lightning Creator," who is thought to have lived between AD 1487 and 1529. Although heir to the Zaachila dynasty of the Valley of Oaxaca, Cociyoeza had been forced by Aztec military pressure to move his headquarters to a fortified mountain near the Pacific Coast. His son Cociyopii (AD 1502–1563), the last member of the dynasty, survived to be questioned by Spanish priests about his "idolatrous" religious practices. He was eventually baptized with the Christian name "don Juan Cortés."[4]

Such interrogations by the Spaniards give us much of what we know about the Zapotec at the time of the Conquest. Dutifully written down and sent back to archives in Spain, these accounts by Zapotec nobles of their own past, or *ethnohistory*, are an invaluable source for reconstructing their culture. A series of questionnaires, filled out between 1578 and 1581 at the request of the Spanish crown, tell us about the political systems, religious beliefs, subsistence practices, and military conflicts of Zapotec towns in what is today the Mexican state of Oaxaca.[5]

A great deal of this ethnohistory has been synthesized by Joseph W. Whitecotton in his book *The Zapotecs: Princes, Priests, and Peasants*.[6] Other scholars who have contributed to Zapotec ethnohistory include Alfonso Caso, Ignacio Bernal, John Paddock, John Chance, and Judith Zeitlin. We ourselves have read as many Spanish accounts of the Zapotec as we could get our hands on.

We will never know exactly how many speakers of Zapotec there were when the Spaniards arrived; accurate censuses did not exist. The Settlement Pattern

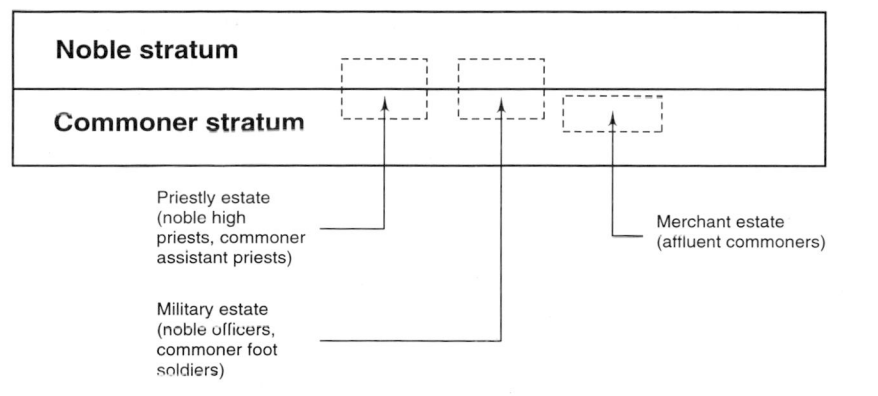

3 Zapotec society consisted of two social strata, crosscut by "estates" or special-function groups such as the priesthood or the military.

4 (*Below*) A Zapotec *quihuitào* or "beautiful royal palace," consisting of a dozen rooms around an interior patio.

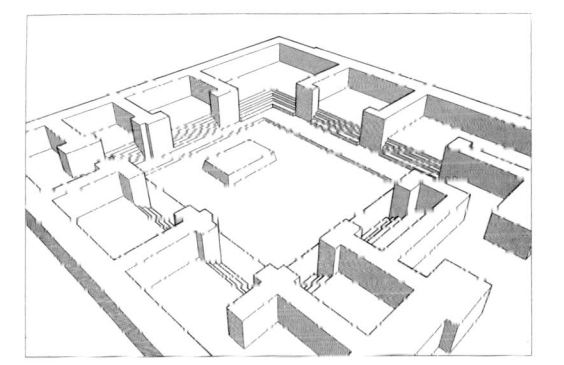

Project, a group of archaeologists who surveyed the Valley of Oaxaca in detail, estimates its final prehispanic population at more than 160,000 persons.[7] The Province of Coyolapan, a much larger region which included the entire Central Valley System and its surrounding mountains, has been estimated as having 350,000–367,000 Zapotec speakers.[8] We would thus not be surprised to learn that there were once more than 500,000 Zapotec. They were decimated during the Colonial period by introduced Old World diseases, European exploitation, and the Spanish Inquisition; 20th-century medicine and Mexican democracy have helped them rebound to more than 300,000.

Social Stratification

On the basis of Spanish accounts we know that Zapotec society was divided into two strata kept separate by *class endogamy*, the custom of each individual marrying within his or her stratum. The upper stratum, or hereditary nobility, was headed by a male ruler, the *coquì*, and his principal wife, the *xonàxi*. Various suffixes attached to those terms were used to distinguish individuals such as a *coquitào* ("great lord" or "king") or *coquihualào* ("prince").

Within the upper stratum of Zapotec society there were many ranks or levels of nobility, but since nobles of all levels could marry each other, these ranks did not qualify as separate social classes. The Spaniards, in fact, saw parallels between the Zapotec levels of nobility and the European ranking of nobles as princes, dukes, earls, and barons.

Among the Zapotec there were lineages called *tija coquì*, those of the greatest hereditary lords; *tija joàna*, lineages of lesser nobles reminiscent of Spanish *caballeros*; and *tija joánahuini*, lineages of still lesser nobles reminiscent of Spanish *hidalgos*. Elaborate residences were often associated with such nobles. A *coquì*, for example, lived in a *yòho quèhui*, "royal house," while a *coquitào* lived in a *quihuitào*, "beautiful royal palace." Such palaces were usually built of adobe brick over a stone foundation.

The other stratum of Zapotec society consisted of free commoners, serfs, and slaves. There were numerous differences of rank, prestige, and wealth among commoners, but since commoners of all levels could intermarry they also did not qualify as separate social classes. Even slaves did not constitute a separate class; many were simply commoners from other ethnic groups who had been captured in war. In Mesoamerican societies it was not unusual for slaves to earn their freedom, to marry free commoners, or to be taken as concubines by nobles.

5 Pottery sculptures of a Zapotec nobleman (*left*) and noblewoman (*right*) wearing jade necklaces and earspools. Height of male figure, 15 cm.

Collectively, free commoners were referred to as belonging to *tija pèniquéche*, "lineages of townspeople," and they lived in simple houses known as *yòho*. Sixteenth-century Zapotec dictionaries, such as that written by the Spanish friar Juan de Córdova,[9] give many occupations for commoners. Whitecotton has found words for day laborer, free servant, weaver, dancer, musician, sculptor, painter, interpreter, diviner, curer, merchant, and peddler among others.[10]

A question frequently asked is whether Mesoamerican societies, such as the Zapotec, had a "middle class." The answer is "no," at least not in the sense of a third class-endogamous stratum interposed between hereditary nobles and commoners. There were, of course, people who were intermediate in "wealth" in Mesoamerican societies, but socially those people were either wealthy commoners or lower-ranking members of the nobility.[11]

We should bear in mind that "commoner" does not mean "impoverished." Many commoners were wealthy merchants or master craftsmen who lived almost as well as minor nobles. They differed from the latter, however, in that they were ineligible for high office or noble marriage despite their wealth.

The key differences between nobles and commoners involved hereditary privileges. Nobles wore bright cotton mantles and loincloths, while commoners wore agave fiber mantles and loincloths. Nobles could also wear feather mantles, feather headdresses, jade necklaces, and jade lip plugs or ear ornaments; commoners could not. The nobles conducted hunts during which commoners were allowed to drive deer toward the huntsmen by beating the brush; nobles got the venison, while the commoners settled for rabbits, lizards, wood rats, and other small game. Nobles also went into battle protected by quilted cotton armor; the footsoldiers were commoners dressed in loincloths.

Nobles had access to a range of foods not permitted to commoners, including chocolate grown in the nearby lowlands. Commoners ate a lot of beans and prickly pear cactus. Nobles were addressed in reverential terms equivalent to "your grace" or "your lordship," and some male nobles had as many as 15–20 wives. (Commoners were allowed to have more than one wife, but only the wealthiest could afford this.) Anyone who appeared before the *coquì* had to remove his sandals and keep his head bowed during the whole encounter.

Zapotec Religion

Religion permeated all levels of Zapotec society, but our best Spanish descriptions are of the state religion, run by full-time priests. Church and state were not really separate, since the highest-ranking priests were recruited from noble families, and the Zapotec lord himself underwent religious training before taking office. Rulers accumulated the wealth and manpower to build temples called *yohopèe*, or "house of the vital force."

Such temples were manned by priests who had their own hierarchy. Among the lower-level priests were the *bigaña*, who are described as virtually never leaving the *yohopèe*. Temples usually had two rooms, an outer (less sacred) chamber to which worshipers could come and an inner (more sacred) chamber in which the priests performed their rites. Those rites included the burning of incense and the sacrifice of animals and humans. The animals could be quail, turkeys, or dogs; the humans could be infants, slaves, or captives taken in war.

Priests also performed autosacrifice, offering their own blood by perforating

6 The building occupied by the high priest at Mitla featured a long, narrow outer room fronting on a courtyard; behind this was an elegant "papal apartment."

their tongue, earlobes, or other fleshy parts of their body with stingray spines, obsidian blades, or agave spines. Some rituals involved the use of drugs like jimson weed (*Datura*), hallucinogenic mushrooms (*Psilocybe*), or very strong wild tobacco (*Nicotiana*); others required the drinking of *pulque*, the fermented sap of the agave or century plant.

Some aspects of Zapotec religion could be described as mind-altering, with the celebrants trying to break through to another plane of consciousness. A series of Spanish accounts written in 1580 describe Zapotec townspeople sacrificing children, drinking, and dancing at night;[12] fasting for periods of 40 or 80 days, while taking tobacco every four days; drawing blood from their tongue and ears, dancing, and becoming intoxicated;[13] or sacrificing dogs and slaves, followed by dancing and eating hallucinogenic mushrooms "so that they saw many visions and frightful figures."[14]

At the top of the Zapotec religious hierarchy was a high priest described by one sixteenth-century Spaniard as "like our pope."[15] In late prehispanic times that high priest (known as the *uija-tào* or "great seer") resided at Mitla, a town

7 The inner court of the high priest's "papal apartment," decorated with intricate geometric mosaic designs in volcanic tuff.

8 Now cleared of its original forests after thousands of years of agriculture, the Valley of Oaxaca features a flat, alluvial valley floor, an irrigable piedmont, and a zone of high mountains.

in the eastern Tlacolula subvalley, which served the Zapotec as a kind of Vatican City. The building in which he lived is still above ground and beautifully preserved; in many ways, it represents the ultimate elaboration of the Zapotec two-room temple. Two large pillars flank the doorway to the outer room, whose roof was supported by six huge columns of volcanic tuff. From this more public room, a narrow L-shaped corridor leads back to the private quarters of the *uija-tào*, a magnificent set of four rooms around a central court. The Zapotec architects had converted the inner room of the temple, in which priests had traditionally lived, into a "papal apartment" whose walls were decorated with intricate geometric mosaics in volcanic tuff.

Ethnohistoric sources suggest that while high priests were of noble birth, many lower-ranking priests were trained commoners. This placement of commoners in powerful ritual positions conflicts with our notions of a hierarchy based on inherited rank. Whitecotton gets around this conflict by dividing Zapotec society into three "estates" – the hereditary nobility, the commoners, and the priesthood. The priestly "estate" would thus include both nobles and commoners.[16]

Subsistence Practices

Zapotec civilization was supported by maize agriculture, and it is a tribute to the ingenuity of the Zapotec that they were successful agriculturalists in a land of rugged topography and permanent water deficit. The sources of water for agriculture in the Valley of Oaxaca include rainfall, springs, small streams and rivers, and the subsurface water table. It is best characterized as a region in which a variety of water-control techniques could be practiced, but no single source of water was large enough to encourage centralized control by a prehispanic government.[17-19]

There are at least three physiographic zones in the Valley of Oaxaca: a flat, alluvial valley floor; a piedmont that varies from gently to steeply sloping, often cut by stream canyons; and a zone of high mountains. The valley floor has the best soil, but also the highest rate of evaporation; the mountains have the lowest evaporation rate, but also the stoniest soils. On these three zones the Zapotec practiced at least five types of agriculture: rainfall farming, well irrigation, canal irrigation, floodwater farming, and hillside terracing.

In addition to growing crops such as maize, beans, squash, avocados, chile peppers, tomatoes, agaves, and prickly pear cactus, the Zapotec raised both dogs and turkeys for food. They collected wild plants like acorns, piñon nuts, mesquite pods, organ cactus fruits, berries of different kinds, and a variety of herbs such as *Crotalaria*, *Chenopodium*, *Amaranthus*, and *Portulaca* which were used to flavor food. They also hunted deer, peccary, rabbits, raccoons, opossums,

9 Even the drier and stonier parts of the Tlacolula subvalley provide edible wild plants, such as cactus fruits and legume seeds.

gophers, wood rats, quail, doves, turtles, lizards, and other small game. Because of the high human population, however, not all members of society had access to the more prestigious animals; as we have seen, deer meat was virtually restricted to nobles.

Tribute and Warfare

In addition to agriculture, hunting, and plant collecting, the Zapotec state was supported by tribute from neighboring peoples whom they had either subdued militarily or dominated politically. At the time of the Spanish Conquest there was no single Zapotec army, but a series of armies assembled by the rulers of important communities. Zapotec armies consisted of officers, who were members of the nobility, and footsoldiers, who were commoners rounded up as needed. Warriors who distinguished themselves were rewarded with special animal costumes identifying them as members of respected military orders. Their weapons were bow and arrow, lance, sling, the *atlatl* or spearthrower, and the *macana* or wooden broadsword, edged with sharp obsidian blades.

The Zapotec conducted auguries before combat and are described by the Spaniards as going into battle singing, beating a wooden drum, and carrying an "idol." While the first prisoner taken was sacrificed to the idol, the rest were brought home as slaves to be put to work, sold, or sacrificed on special holidays. According to one account, a priest cut open the chest of the sacrificial victim and removed his still-beating heart; the idols were bathed with his blood; the victim's body might then be quartered, cooked, and eaten.[20] The Zapotec were especially pleased when they captured a tasty noble officer from the opposing army.

In spite of their fortifications, weaponry, military orders, and terror tactics (which included cannibalism, torture, and mutilation), the Zapotec were more famous for their diplomatic strategy than their pitched battles. Time and again they settled disputes with alliances, secret agreements, or even tribute payments to their enemies.

Not long before Cortés' arrival in Mexico, the Zapotec ruler Cociyoeza was engaged in conflict with the Aztec ruler Ahuitzotl.[21] Cociyoeza formed an alliance with the Mixtec ruler of Achiutla, a town north of the Valley of Oaxaca, to attack the Aztec army while it was in the tropical lowlands of Tehuantepec. After a siege of seven months, the Aztec and Zapotec agreed to a truce, one condition of which was that Ahuitzotl's daughter would marry Cociyoeza. The Aztec were also entitled to place a small garrison of soldiers in the Valley of Oaxaca and receive a "courtesy" tribute each year. As for the Mixtec of Achiutla, who had been promised land at Tehuantepec in return for their military assistance, they were "rewarded" with some of the least desirable land at Tehuantepec. Such was the Zapotec talent for combining limited warfare with skilled diplomacy, royal marriage alliance, and clever dissimulation.

The Ancient Zapotec Mind

The preceding description of the sixteenth-century Zapotec covers their kings and queens, their priests, their commoners, their warfare, their subsistence, and many other aspects of their ancient life. A few decades ago, such a description would have been seen as an adequate model to guide archaeological research into the more distant past. Many of today's archaeologists, however, demand more:

they want the model to include cosmology, religion, ideology, and other products of the ancient mind.[22,23] Such aspects of Zapotec cognition are much harder to glean from ethnohistoric documents because they were poorly understood by the *conquistadores* who wrote them down. Nevertheless, the broad outlines of the cognitive system are there to be discovered.[24]

Like all high cultures of Mesoamerica, the Zapotec believed that the universe was divided into four great world quarters, each associated with a color (red, black, yellow, or white). In turn, the center of the world was associated with blue-green, which the Zapotec considered a single color. The main axis along which their world was divided was the east–west path of the sun.

Zapotec religion was animatistic. They recognized a supreme being who was without beginning or end, "who created everything but was not himself created," a being so infinite and incorporeal that no images were made of him and no mortal came in direct contact with him. The forces and beings with whom the Zapotec *did* come into contact include ones we would consider "natural" and ones we would consider "supernatural." All were equally "real " to the Zapotec.

Most powerful and sacred of those forces was *Cociyo* or Lightning, whose companions included Clouds (*Zaa*), Rain (*Niça Quiye*), Wind (*Pèe*), and Hail (*Quiezabi*). Lightning was the spectacular and angry face of Sky, one of the great divisions of the Zapotec cosmos. The other division was Earth, whose spectacular and angry face was Xòo, Earthquake. Sometimes the two concepts were joined, as in the Zapotec expression for thunder: *Xòo Cociyo*, "Lightning's Earthquake."

In Zapotec cosmology, everything alive was deserving of respect. Living things were distinguished from inanimate matter through their possession of a vital force called *pèe*, "wind," "breath," or "spirit." *Pèe* made things move, and the movement showed that they were alive: a bolt of lightning, clouds sweeping across the sky, the earth moving beneath one's feet during a tremor, the beating of a heart, the wind in one's hair, even the foam on a cup of *pulque* or chocolate.

Inanimate things could be manipulated with technology, but objects with *pèe* had to be approached through ritual and reciprocity. The Zapotec hunter apologized to the deer for the necessity of killing it, then offered the deer's heart to the great natural forces to whom it belonged. The greatest sacrifice one could offer to Lightning was something alive, like a heart still beating and hence infused with *pèe*.

The Zapotec had two words for blood, *rini* and *tini*. *Rini* was dried blood; *tini* was flowing blood, still moving, still alive, such as that drawn from one's own body with an obsidian blade, agave thorn, or stingray spine.

Even time was alive. The Zapotec, like other Indians of Mexico, believed that time was cyclical rather than linear and that given days returned over and over again. To keep track of the cycle they had two calendars – one solar, one ritual.[25] The solar year had 18 "months" of 20 days, plus 5 extra days to bring it to 365. The ritual calendar or *piye* was composed of 20 hieroglyphs or "day signs" which combined with 13 numbers to produce a cycle of 260 days (Table 1). As its name implies, the ritual calendar had *pèe*; sacred time moved and was alive. The fourfold division of the universe was reiterated by the fact that each quarter of the *piye* was called a *cociyo* or "lightning," and a specific "lightning" was assigned to each of the four world quarters.

19 Pottery sculpture of *Cociyo* or Lightning, with four receptacles for his companions Clouds, Rain, Wind, and Hail. Height 15 cm.

11 Pottery sculpture of a young Zapotec lord, inscribed with two hieroglyphs taken from the 260-day calendar. The date on his chest is "13 Flint"; the date on his headgear is "13 Water."

12 Zapotec funerary urn depicting a bundled corpse with jade earspools, possibly a noble ancestor. Height 13 cm.

Table 1
Day Names of the Zapotec *Piye*, or 260-day Calendar

Zapotec Day Name	*Possible Translation (Depending on Tone)*
Chilla, Chiylla	crocodile, reptilian monster, divining bean
Laa, Quiy, Guiy	live coal, fire, wind?
Guela, Ela	night
Gueche, Quichi, Achi	frog, iguana
Zee, Ziy, Cee, Ziye	misfortune, serpent, young corn
Lana, Laana	soot, rabbit
China, Chiyña	deer
Lapa, Laba	divide into pieces, crown, garland
Niça, Queça	water
Tela, Tella	face down, dog
Loo, Goloo	monkey
Piya	twisted, turned
Quiy, Laa, Niy	reed
Gueche, Eche, Ache	fierce animal, jaguar
Naa, Na, Ñaa	mother
Guiloo, Loo	raven, crow, owl, eye
Xòo	earthquake
Opa, Gopa, Oppa	dew, vapor from the earth, stone
Appe, Ape	clouded, cloudy
Lao, Loo	eye, face

Each Zapotec was supposed to be named for the day of the 260-day calendar on which he or she was born. However, certain days were considered luckier than others; therefore many persons (especially nobles) were named for auspicious days that fell near their actual birthday. Names such as "8 Deer" or "5 Flower" were typical for nobles, and many also had nicknames such as "Lightning Creator" or "Great Eagle."[26]

One aspect of Zapotec religion that the 16th-century Spaniards misunderstood was royal ancestor worship. After Zapotec lords or royal married couples died, they were often venerated as beings who could intercede on behalf of their people with great supernatural forces like Lightning. Indeed, deceased rulers were thought to metamorphose into clouds, and even today some Zapotec speakers refer to their ancestors as *binigulaza*, "old people of the clouds."

The Spaniards recorded dozens and dozens of alleged "gods" in sixteenth-century communities, but when one translates the actual names of these "gods" it appears that most are venerated royal ancestors. Many have names taken from the 260-day calendar, and some names even include royal titles like *coquì* or *xonàxi*. Add the fact that there is almost no overlap in names from one community's list to another, and it appears that each town was venerating its own deceased rulers – *not* a pantheon of Zapotec "gods."[27] In fact, had the Spaniards described these heroic ancestors as "saints" rather than "gods," they would have been closer to the mark.

A Colonial document from Ocelotepec, a Zapotec town in the mountains south of the Valley of Oaxaca, speaks of a renowned *coqui* named Petela, "4 Dog," who died shortly before the Spanish Conquest. After his death, Zapotec nobles "commemorated him as a god . . . and sacrificed to him as a god."[28] The Spanish administrator Bartolomé de Piza searched for Lord Petela's mortal remains, which he discovered "buried dry and embalmed," then burned them to discourage what he considered a heathen practice. When a plague hit Ocelotepec six months later, killing more than 1200 persons, the Zapotec nobles "went back to making sacrifices to Petela over the ashes of the bones which de Piza had burned, for he [Petela] was an interceder with [the deity] whom they wanted to call off the plague."

The Zapotec divided animals (*mani*) into several broad categories, including those walking on four legs, those flying, and those swimming. Many names for animals began with a *pe* or *pi* syllable (*pichina*, deer; *pella*, fish), perhaps an animal classifier but also a reflection of the fact that animals had *pèe*. Wild animals were *mani quijxi*, "animals of the wilderness." (The adjective *quijxi* could mean "wild," "not eaten," or "belonging to the wilderness," and was also used to refer to wild plants.) The Zapotec had a single word, *yàga*, that could mean "plant," "tree," or "wood." Adjectives could be added to specify a particular plant, such as *yàga queti*, "pine tree," or *yàga pichij*, "organ cactus." A major distinction was made between plants that could be harvested and eaten by man, and those that were simply part of the native wild vegetation.[29]

The Zapotec also had their own system of weights and measures, vestiges of which can be glimpsed in the markets of monolingual Zapotec towns. One unit that can be detected archaeologically was the *yaguén*. This was the length of one's forearm, between elbow and wrist – about 26–27 cm on an average Zapotec male.[30] Several carved stone monuments at Monte Albán were cut to multiples of *yaguén*.

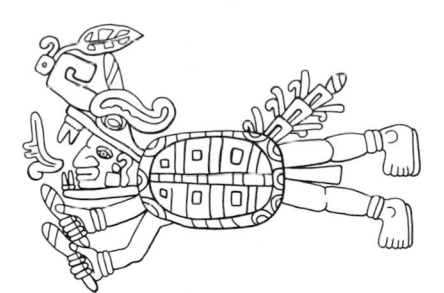

13 Zapotec nobles often pictured their "Cloud Ancestors" as flying turtles, perhaps because cumulonimbus clouds reminded them of turtle carapaces.

Ideology

Having looked briefly at Zapotec cosmology, let us now examine political ideology. Zapotec society was extremely hierarchical, with the ruler's will communicated to the commoners through several levels of nobles. No one at any level doubted that this was the way the world should be, because the Zapotec believed that nobles and commoners had had separate origins far back in time.

Commoners were born of commoners. They lived; they worked; they died; their immediate ancestors were important only to those who had actually known them; their distant ancestors were nameless. In contrast, the royal family had descended from venerated ancestors who were now "Cloud People," living in proximity to Lightning. They ruled on earth for a while, did great deeds, built temples, went to war and returned with captives, and finally were placed in a royal tomb, from which they ascended to the sky and metamorphosed into "Cloud People." Then it became their subjects' and their noble descendants' duty to keep them as happy as possible, so that they would intercede on their people's behalf with the great supernatural forces who ran the world.

Under ideal conditions, a Zapotec ruler would be succeeded on the throne by the first-born son of his first wife. Rules of birth order were so important that among the hieroglyphs used by the Zapotec were hand glyphs with fingers extended. If only the thumb was extended, the glyph signified first-born; if the

Table 2

Zapotec Ordinal Numbers Used Both for Fingers and for Male Birth Order

Right hand	Left hand	Birth order, sons
yobi (thumb)	*yobijye* (thumb)	*yobi* (first)
tini (index finger)	*teije* (index finger)	*tini* (second)
texi (third finger)	*texije* (third finger)	*tixi* (third)
payo (fourth finger)	*xayoyye* (fourth finger)	*payo* (fourth)
yee (fifth finger)	*pijye* (fifth finger)	*yopije* (fifth)
		teyye (sixth)
		texiye (seventh)

index finger was extended, it signified second-born; and so on.[31] The hieroglyph of an extended thumb corresponded to the Zapotec word *yobi*, which is both the ordinal number "first" and the term for "first-born son" (Table 2).

Even having the proper credentials for accession to the throne, however, was not enough. The Zapotec ruler-elect was supposed to perform a number of pre-inaugural acts to prove himself worthy. Those acts could include: (1) taking captives for sacrifice at his inauguration; (2) offering a small amount of his own royal blood; (3) sponsoring a major new building; (4) commissioning a monument to one of his royal ancestors; and (5) obtaining the support and approval of neighboring rulers.

There were tensions and contradictions in this ideological system whenever the order of succession was in doubt. When a ruler had two sons, would his throne really go to the first-born, or would the second son wrest it from him? If he had fathered only daughters, would he be succeeded by a princess, or would one of his daughters strategically marry one of her father's rivals? Would a usurper conspire with others to alter royal genealogical records, putting himself in line for a throne he did not deserve? Would a strategic marriage to a Mixtec princess assure an ambitious Zapotec lord of Mixtec allies if it came to war? In Zapotec ideology the rules of the game were clear, but how far one went depended on how the game was played.

While their nobles jockeyed for positions of power, important titles, advantageous marriages, and access to tribute, life for the commoners went on unchanged. Farmers, potters, masons, shellworkers, lapidaries, weavers, and woodcutters pursued their occupations and looked forward to the drinking and dancing of the next religious holiday. For them the ruler – a being so powerful that his face could not even be gazed upon directly – was the epitome of wisdom, generosity, and magnanimity.

Ethnogenesis and Social Evolution

One of the most pleasant spots in the Valley of Oaxaca today is the balcony bar of the Hotel Victoria. From a hill above the city of Oaxaca it overlooks the confluence of the Valle Grande, Etla, and Tlacolula regions.

The visitor who sits here, sipping a cold margarita, looks out over the urban sprawl of the city and the more distant carpet of maize and alfalfa that stretches to the base of the mountains. Far to the east, one can just make out the range of volcanic tuffs behind the famous ruins of Mitla. Hard by on the west, the prehispanic city of Monte Albán runs along the summit of a 400-m mountain. Off to the south an occasional aircraft, bound for Oaxaca's main airport in the Valle Grande, flies in over the massive archaeological mound of Zaachila.

Visitors know that Oaxaca has ancient ruins and a climate of eternal spring. What they may not realize is that the valley is also a laboratory for the study of social evolution. Paleontologists return repeatedly to the Permian Basin of Texas, which holds beneath its surface the fossils of countless extinct animals. Archaeologists return again and again to the Valley of Oaxaca, which holds beneath its surface the fossils of countless extinct societies.

Ten thousand years ago the Valley of Oaxaca was not the open expanse of cornfields the visitor sees today. Then it was forested from the tops of its mountains to the floodplains of its rivers. Those forests have been cleared, but their fossil pollen survives. The small groups of hunters and gatherers who moved through the forests are also gone, but some of their camps and tools are still there below the surface. And in caves in the mountains, the bones of the wild animals they hunted and the dried remains of the wild plants they gathered are still preserved.

These early Indians lived in groups of 25 persons or less. Their society had no hereditary differences in rank and their leadership was ephemeral, based on individual differences in charisma and skill. At the turn of this century, our world still contained many peoples of that kind. Anthropologists usually refer to them as "hunting and gathering bands."

Five thousand years ago there were tiny clearings in the Oaxaca forest where the Indians had begun to plant gourds, squash, beans, and maize. Thirty-three hundred years ago the clearings had grown to accommodate whole villages of farmers. The floors of the farmers' houses, the holes where they set their upright posts, the piles of debris where men and women worked, the structures where rituals were carried out, are preserved below the surface. And sometimes the men and women themselves are still there, buried beside their homes.

Table 3
Archaeological Periods of the Valley of Oaxaca

Period	Approximate Date
Spaniards arrive in Oaxaca	AD 1521
Late Monte Albán V	AD 1300–1521
Early Monte Albán V	roughly AD 1000–1300
Monte Albán IV	AD 700/750 to 950/1000
Monte Albán IIIb	roughly AD 500 to 700/750
Monte Albán IIIa	roughly AD 200–500
Monte Albán II	from 150/100 BC to AD 200
Monte Albán Ic	300 to c. 150/100 BC
Monte Albán Ia	500–300 BC
Rosario phase	700–500 BC
Guadalupe phase	850–700 BC (in the Etla subvalley)
San José phase	1150–850 BC
Tierras Largas phase	1400–1150 BC
Espiridión complex	somewhere between 1900 and 1400 BC
Archaic	c. 8000 to 2000 BC
Late Ice Age	15,000 (or before) to c. 8000 BC

The Indians in those early villages still displayed no hereditary differences in rank. Much of the integration of their society, now based in settlements of 50–150 persons, was accomplished through two mechanisms. One was a belief in descent from a common ancestor. The other was membership in fraternal orders to which one had to be initiated. Leaders were self-selected, ambitious individuals who knew how to accumulate resources and organize public projects. Anthropologist Robert Carneiro has called such groups "autonomous village societies."[1,2]

Twenty-seven hundred years ago the clearing of Oaxaca's forests was further accelerated, carried out with stone axes by a society with a chiefly elite. The adobe houses in which community leaders lived can still be found below the surface. Even the leaders themselves – their skulls artificially deformed as a sign of elite ancestry, their corpses adorned with jade – are buried there. The white-washed temples they commissioned have collapsed, but the temple floors and the great platforms below them survive. So do the skeletons of sacrificed enemies, left as offerings in the platform.

Anthropologists have provided us with several terms for groups of this type. The most inclusive is "rank society," which refers to the fact that there were now inherited differences in rank among individuals. Our world had many such societies at the beginning of this century, but Carneiro points out that they could be divided into two categories.[3] Some rank societies, like the Northwest Coast Indians of Canada and the United States, had hereditary differences in rank, but their villages had not lost their autonomy. In other rank societies, like those of the Pacific Islands of Tonga, Tahiti, and Hawaii, small villages had lost their autonomy and came under the command of high-ranking leaders at large villages. The latter rank societies are usually called "chiefdoms."

14 (*Opposite, above*) The prehispanic city of Monte Albán, seen here as it looked during Alfonso Caso's excavations, occupies the summit of a 400-m mountain. In the background lies the city of Oaxaca.

15 (*Opposite, below*) The town of Zaachila is dominated by a huge archaeological mound, rising more than 20 m above the floodplain and covering 2500 years of prehistory.

Two thousand years ago, the descendants of Oaxaca's early chiefdoms had built a city on the summit of a mountain. Their rulers recorded their conquests on stone monuments, using hieroglyphs to name the places that defined the limits of their realm. The monuments are still there, and the skeletons of many rulers are still in elegant tombs beneath the patios of their palaces. The floors and lower walls of their colonnaded temples survive, as do the sacred offerings below the floors, and the incense burners and sacrificial knives used in ritual. Adobe houses contoured to hillside terraces, kilns and chipping debris left by artisans, irrigation canals dug to increase corn production, are all there below the surface. So are the forts built on the frontiers of a great militaristic state, and the burned villages of conquered foreigners, and the craft workshops of less powerful neighbors, drawn into the economic network of an expanding civilization.

This urban polity of 2000 years ago had a stratified society with a professional ruling class. It had kings, queens, princes, minor nobles, commoners, and slaves. In the ground plans of its public buildings we recognize many institutions of the historic Zapotec, and in its icons we recognize the supernatural forces worshiped at the time of the Spanish Conquest. It therefore provides us with evidence for two processes of interest to anthropologists: the *origins of the state* and *ethnogenesis*.

States are among the most powerful societies that have ever evolved, and they come in several types. Most states in the modern world, called "nation states," have elected governments with presidents, premiers, prime ministers, governors, and the like. On the other hand, most states in the ancient world – sometimes called "archaic states" – were run by members of hereditary royal families.

Archaic states were highly centralized polities whose kings were drawn from a stratum of hereditary nobles. While these nobles knew in detail their genealogical relationship to the ruler, they did not consider themselves closely related to the stratum of commoners. In many Mesoamerican states, nobles were seen as having descended from supernatural beings, while commoners had arisen from mud.[4]

Archaic states were extremely diversified internally, with residential patterns – especially in urban areas – often based on shared professions, or a combination of profession and kinship. Rulers also expected individual citizens to forego violence, while the state could wage war, conscript soldiers, levy taxes, and exact tribute.

Archaic states usually had populations numbering into the tens of thousands, hundreds of thousands, or even millions. Not all of those people were engaged in production of food; many were full-time artisans living in urban residential wards, or in the case of the Zapotec, in villages with a craft specialty. Such societies attained a high level of artistic and "scientific" achievement, often because of the state's support of (and constant demands upon) artisans of all kinds.

Archaic states had public buildings, works, and services of various kinds, usually implemented through professional architects, engineers, masons, and other specialists. These public buildings included temples, staffed by full-time priests who knew the esoteric ritual of state religion and patronized by kings who wished to be admired for their piety. Early states could also be bureaucratized, but the Zapotec state did not have as many bureaucratic positions as other Mesoamerican states, like the Aztec or Tarascan.

16 The ancient city of Monte Albán, seen here in an artist's reconstruction, once covered 6 km² of terraced mountaintops.

As for *ethnogenesis*, it is a term used for that point in an archaeological (or historical) record when a known ethnic group becomes recognizable for the first time. We believe that the occupants of the Valley of Oaxaca became recognizably "Zapotec" sometime between 400 BC and AD 100.

1920–1960: The Study of Ethnogenesis

The first archaeologists to work in Oaxaca were not overly concerned with social evolution. They were, however, fascinated by ethnogenesis. Aware that both Zapotec and Mixtec had occupied the valley in the sixteenth century, they were determined to identify the accomplishments of each ethnic group.

In the course of their travels, many nineteenth-century visitors to the Valley of Oaxaca found carved stones bearing undeciphered hieroglyphs. These glyphs attracted attention because they were different from those of the better-known Maya, yet seemed to involve some similarities, like a numerical system in which a dot stood for one and a bar for five.

During the 1920s a brilliant young Mexican anthropologist, Alfonso Caso, identified these hieroglyphs as Zapotec and began their systematic study.[5] Caso noted the differences between Zapotec writing and that of other regions, and he began to suspect that the Zapotec calendar and writing system might be more ancient than those of the Maya. It is a measure of Caso's scholarship that all subsequent studies of Zapotec glyphs are based on his pioneering efforts.[6,7]

Caso decided that the key site for understanding Zapotec writing and civilization was Monte Albán, and in 1931 he began excavating there. Caso's excavations continued for eighteen field seasons, at times directed by his student Ignacio Bernal or his colleague Jorge Acosta. Caso, Bernal, and Acosta established the first chronological sequence for the Valley of Oaxaca, spanning the

17 Jorge Acosta's excavations near the South Platform of Monte Albán's main ceremonial plaza, 1946.

period from 500 BC to the Spanish Conquest.[8] They revealed that Monte Albán was one of Mexico's first cities, the capital of Zapotec civilization for more than 1000 years.

With Caso's retirement from excavation, the torch passed to Ignacio Bernal. Charming, erudite, and generous, a man of global vision with a keen sense of humor, Bernal envisioned a survey of the entire Valley of Oaxaca. Such a survey would put Monte Albán into perspective and answer many of the questions raised by the excavations there. Monte Albán had sprung into being at 500 BC, already urban, and with no known antecedents. It had declined by AD 800 for unknown reasons. From whence had its founders come, and why did it decline? What role might its neighbors, the Mixtec, have played in the demise of Zapotec civilization? How large an area might Monte Albán have ruled at its peak?

For at least 40 years, until his death in 1992, Bernal was the undisputed dean of Oaxaca archaeology. He located 280 sites with one or more archaeological mounds, often joking that it would be "simpler to list those places in the Valley of Oaxaca that *lacked* surface potsherds, than to list those that had them." Many of the sites he found, including San José Mogote, Huitzo, Tierras Largas, Tomaltepec, and Abasolo, are now known to predate Monte Albán. Others he surveyed, such as San Luis Beltrán, Cuilapan, Noriega, Yagul, Mitla, and Macuilxochitl, were excavated by Bernal in an effort to clarify Monte Albán's decline during the period AD 700–1000. Bernal's last excavations were at Dainzú, a site in the Tlacolula region that rose to prominence just as Monte Albán was becoming the capital of a state (Chapter 13).

Bernal's work at sites like Yagul and Mitla was carried on by his dedicated student, John Paddock, who has himself spent 40 years studying the genesis and interaction of Zapotec and Mixtec.[9] In the course of his excavations, Paddock taught Oaxaca archaeology to a number of students still working there. Kent Flannery and James Neely worked with Paddock at Yagul; Stephen Kowalewski worked with Paddock at Lambityeco. Richard Blanton and Charles Spencer then studied with Flannery; Gary Feinman and Laura Finsten, in turn, studied with Blanton. Most recent to arrive is Feinman's student Andrew Balkansky, a member of the seventh generation of Oaxaca archaeologists to descend in an unbroken lineage from Alfonso Caso.

By the 1960s, the focus of archaeology in the Valley of Oaxaca had begun to shift away from ethnogenesis and toward the study of social evolution. Everyone by then agreed that the Monte Albán state was Zapotec. Concern now shifted to discovering how and why it had arisen.

Three research projects of the last 30 years were designed to shed light on the rise of Zapotec civilization. The first of these was the project "Prehistory and Human Ecology of the Valley of Oaxaca" (hereafter Human Ecology Project), begun by Kent Flannery in 1964 and projected to last into the next century. Flannery's original interest had been the origins of agriculture and village life, but he expanded his goals when he saw that Oaxaca had an uninterrupted sequence leading to urban civilization.

No civilization can be understood without a broad regional perspective on its network of cities, towns, and villages. Flannery therefore urged Richard Blanton, a settlement pattern specialist, to survey the entire Valley of Oaxaca. In 1971 Blanton began the project "Prehistoric Settlement Patterns of the Valley of Oaxaca" (hereafter Settlement Pattern Project). He was joined, in alphabetical order, by Gary Feinman, Laura Finsten, Stephen Kowalewski, and Linda Nicholas.

Between 1971 and 1973, the Settlement Pattern Project surveyed the 6-km² city of Monte Albán.[10] Their second task was to survey the 2150-km² Valley of Oaxaca, which they did between 1974 and 1980.[11] In addition, Feinman and Nicholas have surveyed the Ejutla Valley,[12,13] and Donald Brockington and Charles Markman have surveyed the Miahuatlán Valley,[14,15] completing the entire Central Valley System. Surveys currently in progress will extend outward from the Zapotec region to the Mixtec-speaking valleys of northern Oaxaca.

By 1971 Flannery was convinced that one source of information on Zapotec civilization – the hieroglyphic texts studied earlier by Caso – had fallen into neglect. He therefore urged Joyce Marcus, an archaeologist working with the Maya epigrapher Tatiana Proskouriakoff, to study the Zapotec writing system. Marcus immediately began the ongoing project "Zapotec Monuments and Political History" (hereafter Zapotec Monuments Project), recording over 600 monuments between 1972 and 1982.[16,17] Since 1973, she has been co-director of the Human Ecology Project as well.

All three of these projects have worked in concert for more than two decades, yielding better results through collaboration than they could have alone. To be sure, there are occasional conflicts between various sets of data. Population estimates for certain ancient communities, calculated from surface remains by the Settlement Pattern Project, do not always match the estimates calculated from excavations by the Human Ecology Project. Pottery types seen by excavators as "most typical of a period" are not always the types seen by survey teams as "most recognizable on the surface." Despite these conflicts – inevitable when multiple lines of evidence are used to attack a common research problem – all three projects described above are in agreement 90 percent of the time.

All archaeologists who study the evolution of society from hunting-gathering bands to archaic states do so within the framework of a theory. The twin purposes of that theory are to account for the archaeological evidence, and to provide testable explanations for why society evolved. Since no theory of social

1960–1990: The Study of Social Evolution

The Theoretical Frameworks Used in this Book

evolution has so far proven universally satisfactory, over the years archaeologists have worked steadily to improve their frameworks – keeping what seems to work, rejecting or modifying what does not.

Most theories of social evolution come from anthropology, and it is easy to explain why. Anthropologists have studied living bands of hunters and gatherers, autonomous village societies, chiefly societies, and states of various types. They control rich and intimate details about living groups, details that no archaeologist could know about the extinct societies he or she studies. On the other hand, archaeologists can study changes over thousands of years, long-term processes difficult to document in living societies. In a way, therefore, archaeology can serve as a kind of "proving ground" for anthropological theory.

That statement is particularly true for a theoretical framework that arose during the 1980s. It has been called "practice theory," "praxis," or "action theory," and it comes in several versions. We will refer to it as "action theory," since the term "praxis" sets our teeth on edge. We will also limit ourselves to the version thoughtfully described by anthropologist Sherry Ortner a decade ago.[18] This version is significant because it has awakened in anthropologists a greater interest in history than they had previously. Anything that can awaken an interest in history should also be good for archaeology.

Evolutionist Anthropology

Anthropology entered the 1960s with what Ortner describes as "three major, and somewhat exhausted, paradigms": British structural-functionalism, American cultural and psychological anthropology, and American evolutionist anthropology. A "somewhat exhausted paradigm" is a theoretical framework which has been used so long and hard that it has reached the point of diminishing returns.

Evolutionist anthropology was rejuvenated in the 1960s by Marshall Sahlins, Elman Service, Morton Fried, and Robert Carneiro.[19-22] Over two decades, drawing on information from hundreds of societies (and responding to lots of criticism from their colleagues), they began to define the stages of evolution we refer to in this book: bands, egalitarian village societies, rank societies, chiefdoms, and states.

Like all theoretical frameworks that are heavily used, this rejuvenated evolutionary paradigm had itself become "somewhat exhausted" by the end of the 1970s. Most archaeologists who used it had learned as much from it as they could, given their limited data. Those who did not use it were simply tired of hearing about it, so much so that some wanted to abolish evolutionary stages entirely.

This would have been foolish, as theoretical archaeologists like Charles Spencer have pointed out.[23] Just as paleontologists would find it difficult to study biological evolution without stages like "fish," "amphibian," "reptile," and "mammal," archaeologists would find it difficult to study social evolution if hunting-gathering bands, chiefdoms, and archaic states were simply lumped together as "prehistoric societies."

Nevertheless, by 1990 it was clear that evolutionary anthropology (as well as archaeology) needed further rejuvenation. The most frequently heard complaint was that explanations of prehistoric change had become too deterministic, relying too heavily on ecological pressures and too little on human decisions. A framework was needed that would give individual humans, or "actors," a greater role to play in social change. Action theory offers that kind of framework.

The Rise of Action Theory

Ortner describes action theory as arising, in part, as a reaction against some of the more static and formal frameworks used by anthropologists during the 1960s and 1970s. Like some of the "ecological-functionalist" archaeology of the same era, these frameworks seemed to leave little room for humans to be more than cogs in a machine.

Modern action theory "seeks to explain the relationship(s) that obtain between human action, on the one hand, and some global entity which we may call 'the system' on the other."[24] This "system" includes not only the natural environment in which humans find themselves, but their own culture – that set of beliefs, cosmologies, ideologies, customs, and traditions that shape their goals. It also has a prior history, whose trajectory was determined not simply by factors beyond the control of humans, but also by decisions made of their own free will.

Interacting with this system are "actors" who are conceived of as essentially individualistic, self-interested, rational, and pragmatic. These actors go after what they want, and what they want are things that are materially and politically useful for them, given the cultural and historical situations in which they find themselves. Since these cultural and historical situations are partly the product of the "system," the latter has a role to play in shaping human action. Aggressive actors, however, can change the system, and many of the changes they bring about can have unintended long-term consequences. We will see examples of such consequences in this book.

How does the actor change the system? Marshall Sahlins, a major contributor to action theory, suggests that it is not usually through revolutionary moves that promote wholesale overthrow of the system. Rather, it is likely to be through a self-interested change in the meaning of existing relations, a change whose full implications may not be felt until much later.[25] We will see examples of these changes as well.

Here, then, after decades of archaeological models in which some aspect of the "system" – population pressure, environmental deterioration, class struggle – was seen as driving human societies to a new evolutionary stage, comes a model in which many changes can take place through the actors' own decisions.

In fact, change can originate either in the system or in the actor. Emphasizing this point, Clifford Geertz has drawn a useful distinction between *strain* and *interest* in action theory.[26] In "strain models" the burden of explanation falls on the system, which is seen as producing a problem the actor must solve. In "interest models" the burden of explanation falls on the actor, whose self-interested actions change the system. This interplay of system and actor over time, Ortner argues, shifts anthropology away from "static, synchronic analyses" toward "diachronic, processual ones." In this book we shall see how both "strain" and "interest" contributed to diachronic process.

Field Methods and Bridging Arguments

Whatever their theoretical framework, all archaeologists studying social evolution must decide on a set of field methods and bridging arguments. Field methods are the means by which raw archaeological data are collected. Bridging arguments connect these data to the theoretical framework being used.

The raw archaeological data presented in this book include the results of surface surveys and excavations: patterns of settlement, ground plans of houses and public buildings, burials, plant and animal remains, and artifacts of many kinds. Our main bridging arguments are drawn from ethnographic analogy and the direct historical approach.

The direct historical approach was pioneered by North American archaeologists of the 1930s like William A. Ritchie, William Duncan Strong, and Waldo R. Wedel.[27-30] It is a way of working back in time from the known to the unknown, using anthropological or historical data to interpret prehistoric sites. In the case of the Zapotec, for example, one can use Spanish eyewitness accounts of the sixteenth-century Indians to interpret remains left before the Spaniards arrived.

Obviously, the direct historical approach works best when one can show continuity from the archaeological past into the historical present. Archaeological sites less than 2000 years old, occupied by societies clearly recognizable as Zapotec, are most appropriate for this kind of bridging argument. As one moves farther back in time, one encounters societies so different from the sixteenth-century Zapotec that such arguments become less appropriate.

For these older societies, our bridging argument of choice is ethnographic analogy. Over the years ethnographers, or social anthropologists, have studied thousands of living groups all over the world. Large numbers of those groups share widespread patterns, a fact that has allowed anthropologists to group them into categories like hunting-gathering band, autonomous village society, and chiefdom.

Many of those patterns are also shared by the ancient societies of the Valley of Oaxaca, both before and after the emergence of recognizably Zapotec culture. This fortunate circumstance helps us to interpret prehistoric behaviors of 10,000 years ago, 5000 years ago, and 3000 years ago.

For much of this case study, therefore, we employ two kinds of bridging arguments. The older the society, the more heavily we rely on the widespread patterns of ethnographic analogy. The younger the society, the more heavily we rely on the specific patterns of the historic Zapotec.

An Invitation

Since 1930, as we have seen, seven academic generations of archaeologists have labored in the Valley of Oaxaca. Many of those scholars passed up bigger regions with larger cities, taller pyramids, richer tombs, and greater name recognition. They came because the preservation of architectural features, plants, animals, artifacts, and human skeletal remains makes the Central Valley System a rewarding place in which to test ideas about the evolution of human society.

One thing all seven generations shared is that they were field workers, rather than armchair archaeologists. They believed that many of the answers they sought lay buried in the earth, and they were prepared to dig as deep as it took to get them. On their behalf, we now invite you to climb into our battered field vehicle and travel along with us through one of the great fossil beds of prehistory.

I Jade pectoral with marine shell eyes and teeth, found with a sacrificial burial at Monte Albán. The upper part is the mask of a giant bat (17.5 cm high). Monte Albán II period (100 BC–AD 200). Painting by John Klausmeyer.

II The mountaintop Zapotec city of Monte Albán, with its North Platform acropolis on the left.

III Building K, a temple pyramid at Monte Albán, seen from the south at dusk. The hilltop ruins of Atzompa, Monte Albán's northernmost urban ward, appear in the background.

IV Building J in the Main Plaza of Monte Albán, with the North Platform in the background. II–IV courtesy of Dr Colin McEwan.

III

IV

V The alluvial floor of the Valley of Oaxaca, now cleared of its ancient mesquite forest by 5000 years of maize farming.

VI Flint points for the *atlatl*, or spearthrower, used by the hunting-and-gathering peoples who occupied Oaxaca 8000–5000 years ago. Length of point at far left, 8.3 cm. Painting by John Klausmeyer.

VII

VII Monument 3 of San José Mogote, a carved stone showing a sacrificed prisoner. Length 1.45 m. Late Rosario phase (sixth century BC).

VIII Structures 1 and 2 of San José Mogote, a set of terraced platforms and stairways for public buildings of the San José phase (1150–850 BC).

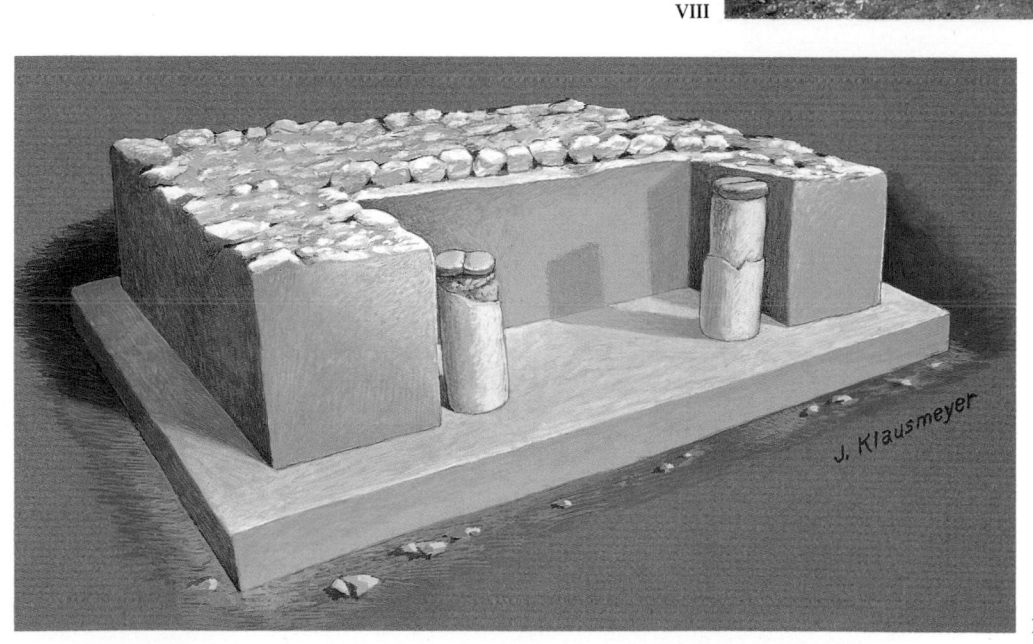

VIII

IX The Yellow Temple of Dainzú, built during the transition from Monte Albán I to II, reflects an early stage in the evolution of the Zapotec temple (first or second century BC). Width of doorway, 3 m.

IX

X

X Effigy incense brazier covered with vermilion pigment, buried beneath a temple at San José Mogote. Monte Albán II period (100 BC–AD 200). Height 55 cm. Painting by John Klausmeyer.

XI Figurine of the Guadalupe phase (850–700 BC). Height 14.7 cm.

XII Four figurines arranged in a ritual scene, buried beneath the floor of House 16 at San José Mogote (1150–850 BC). Height of tallest figurine, 15 cm.

XIII A Rosario phase ritual cache, featuring examples of "resist" white-on-gray pottery and a vessel carved from a giant limpet (length 14.5 cm). 700–500 BC.

XIV Elite drinking vessel of the Rosario phase. Height 17.4 cm.

XV Pottery of the San José phase (1150–850 BC). XIV–XV painted by John Klausmeyer.

XI

XII

XIII

XIV

XV

J. Klausmeyer

XVI Jade statue buried beneath the floor of a Zapotec temple (Structure 35 of San José Mogote). Monte Albán II period (100 BC–AD 200). Height 49 cm. Painting by John Klausmeyer.

The Late Ice Age and the Strategy of High Mobility

Archaeologists believe that the ancestors of the American Indians entered the New World via the Bering Strait. All agree that these migrations took place late in the Pleistocene, or "Ice Age," when lowered sea levels had exposed a land bridge between Siberia and Alaska. There is no agreement on the date of the first arrivals, with estimates ranging from 15,000 BC to before 20,000 BC.

While parts of North America would have been covered with glaciers during the Ice Age, some immigrants moved south through ice-free corridors to forage in what are today the states of Texas, New Mexico, and Arizona in the United States, and Sonora, Chihuahua, and Coahuila in northern Mexico.

Today geographers assign much of that region to two major environments: the Sonoran Life Zone on the west, and the Chihuahuan Life Zone on the east. Both zones are arid. The Sonoran is characterized by rugged mountains and deserts

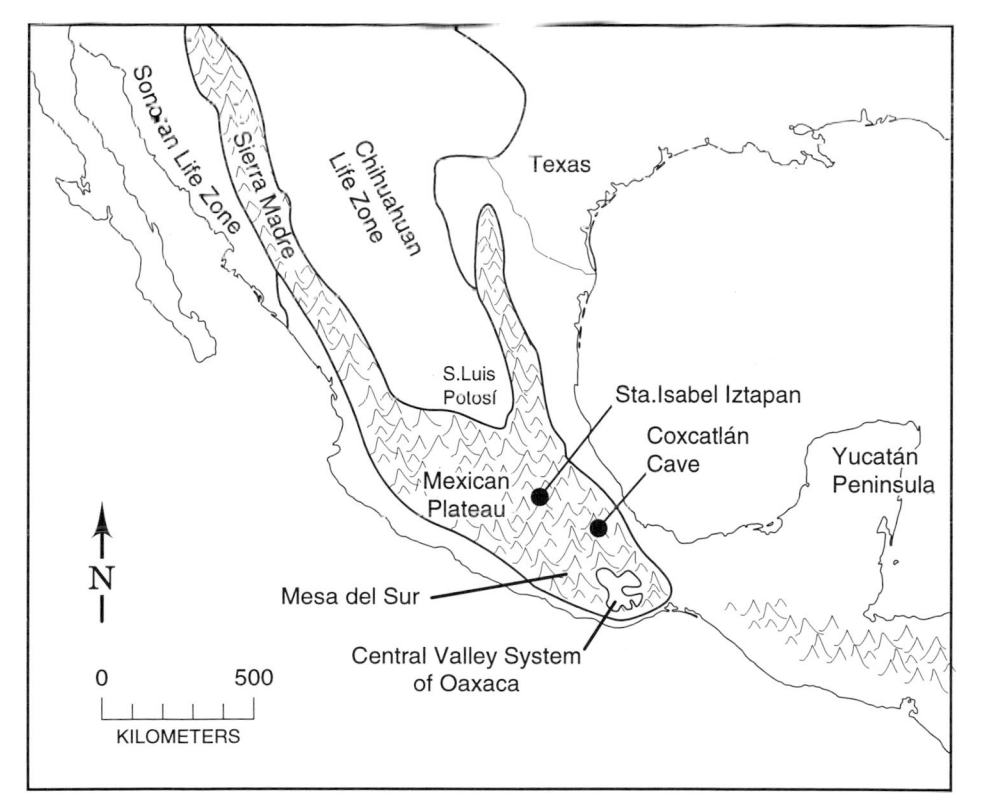

18 Today the Mexican Plateau lies to the south of the Chihuahuan Life Zone. Under the cooler conditions of the late Ice Age, however, some Chihuahuan species lived as far south as Oaxaca.

19 The Chihuahuan Life Zone is typified by treeless plains.

20 The pronghorn antelope (*Antilocapra americana*).

21 The Texas gopher tortoise (*Gopherus berlandieri*).

with organ cactus. The Chihuahuan has rolling plains with yucca and prickly pear. These zones were a kind of "proving ground" for the Indians who eventually colonized the Mexican highlands to the south. Unless they could learn how to survive under Sonoran or Chihuahuan conditions, they were never going to make it south to areas like Oaxaca, Puebla, or the Basin of Mexico. They not only survived, but brought to central and southern Mexico much of the technology they had developed in the Sonoran and Chihuahuan zones.

To be sure, the geographic limits of the Sonoran and Chihuahuan zones would have been different during the late Ice Age, since the world's climate was colder then. Scholars believe that the lowered temperatures of the Late Pleistocene caused vegetation belts to shift farther south. That means that Chihuahuan species might once have extended farther south into Mexico than they do today. This reconstruction is supported by fossil pollen grains in Late Pleistocene lake bed deposits, by small rodent skeletons left behind in ancient caves, and by a wide variety of other paleoenvironmental studies.[1]

For example, pollen grains and animal remains indicate that the Late Pleistocene climate of the central Mexican highlands was cooler and drier than today's.[2,3] Paleoclimatic specialist Geoffrey Spaulding has produced a computer model to explain this phenomenon.[4] According to Spaulding's model, differences in solar radiation during the Late Pleistocene led to colder winters, and to a suppression of the summer rainy season of the Mexican highlands. Winter rain may have been more important than summer rain during the peak of the last Ice Age. The shift to today's pattern of summer-rain dominance probably took place when the Pleistocene ended around 8000 BC.

Some typically Chihuahuan animals were indeed found far to the south of their present ranges during the late Ice Age. For example, the pronghorn antelope lived as far south as Mexico's Tehuacán Valley, and the Texas gopher tortoise has been found still farther to the south, in the Valley of Oaxaca.[5–7] All this strengthens our suspicion that the first people to reach Oaxaca must have brought with them a whole range of skills learned in the Chihuahuan Life Zone.

Compared to later periods of Mexican prehistory, we know little about the first inhabitants of the central and southern highlands, known as the Mexican Plateau. We infer that their population numbers were very low — well below one person per 100 km² – and that they lived by hunting wild game and collecting wild plants. Given a technology that had no ground stone tools and no evidence of containers for boiling, there were probably many plants they could not fully utilize.

Since they had survived the Chihuahuan zone, these people probably knew how to roast succulent plants such as agaves, yuccas, and sotol (*Dasylirion* spp.) in earth ovens. Their hunting tools included the lance and the *atlatl* or spearthrower (ill. 22). The spears, or "darts," for their atlatls had a long main-shaft and a shorter, detachable foreshaft. This foreshaft was tipped with a point of flint, chert, silicified volcanic tuff, or a volcanic glass called obsidian. The bow and arrow had not yet reached Mexico, and would not arrive until long after the period covered by this book.

Most of the archaeological sites of the Late Pleistocene – referred to by archaeologists as the Paleoindian period – fall into two categories. Some appear to be "base camps" at which groups of up to 25 persons lived for a week to a month. Other sites appear to be places where a single animal was killed and cut up. We presume that these "kill" or "butchering" sites were brief occupations made by people who came from, and eventually returned to, a base camp.

Two of the more exciting kill sites of this era were found at Santa Isabel Iztapan in the Basin of Mexico. The animals butchered were imperial mammoths (*Mammuthus imperator*), Pleistocene elephants native to the New World

Pleistocene Lifeways of the Mexican Plateau

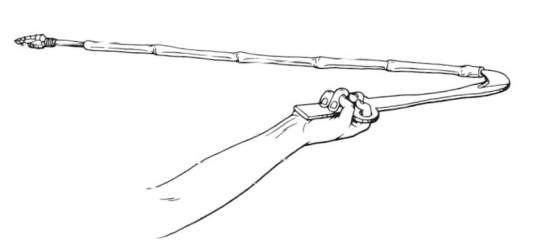

22 The *atlatl*, a wooden device that served as an extension of the human arm, increased the force with which a spear could be thrown.

23 Artist's reconstruction of the imperial mammoth (*Mammuthus imperator*).

24 The excavation of Mammoth 1 at Santa Isabel Iztapan, Basin of Mexico, 1952.

Mammoth 1

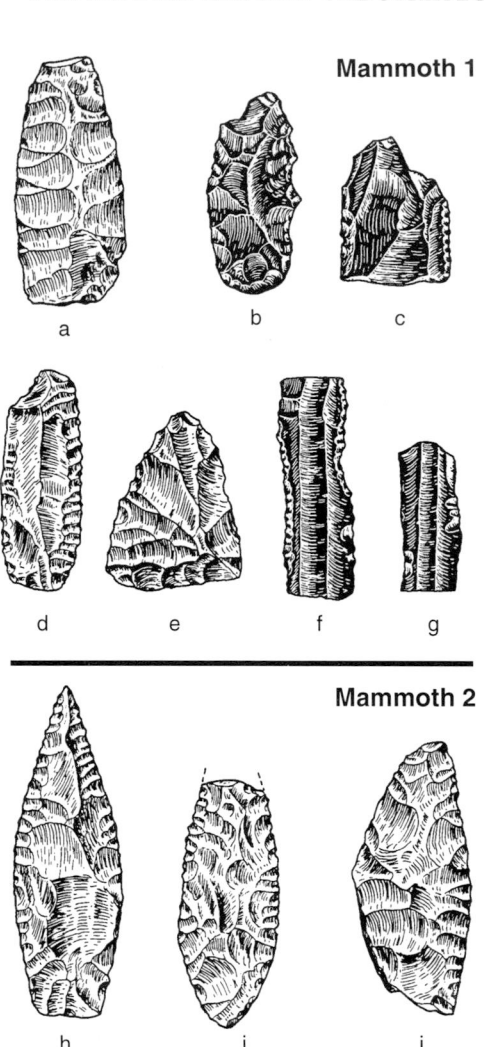

Mammoth 2

25 Stone tools found with Mammoths 1 and 2 at Santa Isabel Iztapan.
(*a*) Scottsbluff spear point of gray flint; (*b*) obsidian spokeshave; (*c*) two-edged obsidian sidescraper; (*d*) retouched blade of gray flint; (*e*) triangular scraper of clear gray flint; (*f*) retouched obsidian blade; (*g*) obsidian blade; (*h*) Angostura spear point of red volcanic stone; (*i*) Lerma spear point of light brown chert; (*j*) bifacial knife of light brown chert. Length of (*h*) 80.2 mm.

but extinct since the Ice Age. Both mammoths had either been chased into the muck around the edge of a Pleistocene lake, or had become mired there on their own, reducing their mobility and allowing the hunters to spear them.[8,9]

As interesting as the mammoths themselves were the tools found with them. All 10 (7 with one animal, 3 with another) appear to be finished artifacts, made elsewhere and brought to the site; no debris from tool manufacture was found with either mammoth. Included were 3 spear or atlatl points, 2 scrapers, and several retouched blades. Some of the tools appear to have been resharpened after breakage, suggesting that they might have been kept and used for some time.

Several tools were made of raw material whose sources occur outside the Basin of Mexico. One spear point is believed to have been made of red volcanic stone from Guanajuato or San Luis Potosí, perhaps 300 km to the north.[10] Such use, curation, and resharpening of tools from distant sources was not unusual in Late Pleistocene North America. Ancient bison hunters are known to have converged on the Lindenmeier Site in Colorado, bringing obsidian from as far away as Yellowstone Park (600 km to the northwest) and Jemez, New Mexico (550 km to the south).[11] This phenomenon is thought to be characteristic of highly nomadic bands of foragers who travel enormous distances, coming together periodically to hunt, collect plants, and exchange artifacts with other groups.

In the excitement that followed the discovery of the Iztapan mammoths, many archaeologists began to speak of the Paleoindians as "big-game hunters," implying that this was the primary focus of their subsistence. Balance was restored to our picture of these Late Pleistocene hunter-gatherers, however, by Richard S. MacNeish's excavation of Coxcatlán Cave in the Tehuacán Valley.[12,13]

The deepest four levels of that cave were "living floors" from a series of camps, probably made between 12,000 and 9000 BC. The campers, belonging

26 Coxcatlán Cave in the Tehuacán Valley.

to a period known as Early Ajuereado, had left behind 1200 identifiable bones from fifteen species of mammals, reptiles, and birds. There were remains of extinct Pleistocene horse; pronghorn antelope, red fox, and Texas gopher tortoise, none of which live in the area today; more than 700 bones of rabbits; and abundant smaller species such as skunk, ground squirrel, wood rat, quail, and others. Not a single mammoth bone was found.[14]

In particular, the debris of Level 26 provided insight into the life of the Early Ajuereado hunters: it appears they may have taken jackrabbits by means of communal drives, like those of North America's Great Basin Indians. On that living floor were nearly 400 rabbit bones, many from the trimmed-off feet of at least 40 individuals, seemingly butchered at a single sitting.[15,16]

There are several reasons why jackrabbits can profitably be taken by communal drives. Jackrabbits are creatures of open environments, relying on speed for defense. They do not dig burrows, but live in "forms," or semi-nests of grass on the surface. The Indians of the Great Basin soon learned that by beating the weeds as they moved across an open plain, they could rout hundreds of jackrabbits out of their forms and keep them moving into a blind canyon, temporary fence, or long net where they could be clubbed. Masses of dead rabbits were then skinned, butchered, and cut into strips for preservation by drying. It would appear that the hunters of the Early Ajuereado phase had learned this technique – not surprisingly, since in order to reach the Tehuacán Valley their ancestors would have to have crossed thousands of kilometers of Chihuahuan jackrabbit country.

27 Jackrabbits (*Lepus* spp.).

Paleoindian spear or atlatl points can occasionally be found on the surface of the Valley of Oaxaca, in spite of the fact that the Ice Age land surface is often deeply buried. For example, a point referred to as the Scottsbluff type was found on the slopes of a mesa west of Mitla, near a chert quarry used throughout prehistory. A similar point was found with one of the Iztapan mammoths (ill. 25).

In a cornfield near San Juan Guelavía in the Tlacolula subvalley, members of the Settlement Pattern Project found the important fluted point shown in ill. 28. Made of yellowish chert, the point has been thinned (presumably for hafting) by having a long, narrow "channel flake" removed along its long axis.[17] Similar fluted points occur at Late Pleistocene sites in North America and northern Mexico.

Near Mitla, at the eastern limits of the Tlacolula subvalley, the landscape is dominated by high mountains, rocky canyons, and isolated mesas of volcanic tuff. There are numerous rock shelters in these uplands, as well as veins of silicified tuff that can be chipped as easily as most flint. Cueva Blanca, a cave covering 165 m² in the side of a canyon, may have been visited briefly by some of Oaxaca's late Ice Age inhabitants.

The oldest deposit in Cueva Blanca, called Level F, is a layer of fine particles weathered from the walls of the cave. In it are lenses of Late Pleistocene animal bones whose closest similarities are to the Early Ajuereado fauna from Coxcatlán Cave. The Texas gopher tortoise is there, as well as the same red fox seen in Early Ajuereado times; there are also deer, cottontails, jackrabbits, and wood rats. Significantly, many bones show signs of burning and deliberate fracture.

Paleoindian Sites in the Valley of Oaxaca

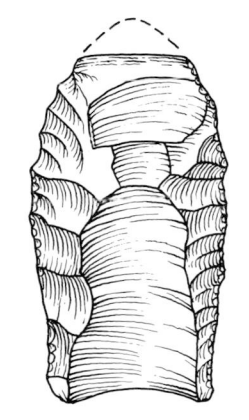

28 Fluted spear point of yellowish chert from San Juan Guelavía, Valley of Oaxaca. Length (broken) 35 mm.

29 Cueva Blanca lies in a piedmont canyon in the eastern Valley of Oaxaca.

According to botanist James Schoenwetter, pollen grains from Level F may reflect a Late Pleistocene climate somewhat cooler than today's.[18] Pine pollen dominates the sample, and there are occasional grains of spruce, fir, and elm. Pollen of mesquite, organ cacti, agaves, and other plants, however, is common enough to suggest the presence of a thorn forest on the slopes below the pines.

Perhaps because of the small area covered by the lenses in Level F, no associated artifacts were found. This lack of tools is disappointing, but not too surprising when one considers that only eleven artifacts were found with the 1200 identifiable animal bones in the lower four levels of Coxcatlán Cave.[19] We suspect that the main occupation of Level F may have been farther out near the mouth of the cave, an area unfortunately disturbed by later occupants.

The Paleoindian Lifeway

Archaeologist Richard Gould has defined two contrasting strategies for hunter-gatherers living in arid regions.[20] One strategy, which he calls "drought escape," amounts to a flight from one's own resource-depleted territory to a region of temporarily abundant food. This means migration over long distances, followed by the sharing of resources with people one may not even know well. It requires a network of relationships with distant acquaintances, perhaps reinforced by gift-giving.

Gould's second strategy, which we propose to call "drought buffering," requires that a group solve its problems within its own territory. It involves the use of a wider range of resources, including ones previously ignored – some useful in dry years, some useful in wet years. A series of short moves, rather than long migrations, are combined with new technologies for more efficient foraging.

While the two strategies are not mutually exclusive, we believe that "drought escape" best characterizes the Paleoindian period. The spearpoint of Guanajuato/San Luis Potosí stone found with the Iztapan mammoth, like the Jemez and Yellowstone obsidians found at Lindenmeier, suggests that Paleoindian hunters traveled hundreds of kilometers and exchanged gifts when they met. Moreover, two of the major resources of the Chihuahuan Life Zone, the pronghorn antelope and the jackrabbit, are well suited to a strategy of migrations to places where communal hunts can be held.

Pronghorns are animals of treeless temperate steppe who travel widely in times of drought. They are also very social, with males and females living together in massive herds. What this meant to the Paleoindian hunter is that there would be long periods with no antelope in sight, followed by news of a herd of 50 or 100. Such herds could best be hunted by communal drives, with scattered groups of hunters migrating in from a wide area to share in the large meat supply.

Jackrabbits, too, are best hunted by communal drives because they are subject to wide population swings over time. For reasons which are still not completely known, certain areas may have too few jackrabbits one year and a superabundance some years later. The number of rabbits available during population upswings can be astonishing. In December of 1981, jackrabbit populations exploded on the rural landscape near Mud Lake in eastern Idaho. Local farmers, worried about the destruction of their crops, held three rabbit drives that killed more than 28,000 animals.[21] Such moments of superabundance provided a reason for the migration of Paleoindian groups from distant regions to share in the hunt.

Compared to the Archaic foragers who followed them (Chapter 4), we envision the Paleoindians of the Mexican Plateau traveling longer distances and exploiting a narrower range of resources. One reason lay in their technology. There were many plants in their environment that could have been rendered edible by the use of grinding stones, but the Paleoindians lacked such tools. Still other plants could have been eaten after prolonged soaking or boiling, but the Paleoindians lacked pottery. Our evidence suggests that they usually roasted foods over an open fire or in earth ovens, limiting the range of foods that could be used and making it more difficult to buffer drought on a local basis. Hence our suspicion that they relied heavily on "drought escape."

The Early Ajuereado and Cueva Blanca F peoples present us with the baseline from which subsequent societies on the Mexican Plateau evolved. So meagre are our data that we must rely on ethnographic analogies with the antelope- and jackrabbit-hunting peoples of western North America. The latter lived in loosely structured bands and had an egalitarian ethic which permitted only ephemeral leadership. For example, communal hunts among some Great Basin groups in the western United States required the election of a Hunt Leader – a respected individual who, for a brief period, was given authority over the members of several groups. The position was important because the leader's skill could make the hunt a success, but it was only a temporary post.

Our Ice Age data from Tehuacán and Oaxaca contribute to the demise of an old stereotype: the notion that these people were "mammoth hunters" who belonged to a "big-game hunting phase." When they had the chance to camp for some time in a region, as for example following a rabbit drive, the Early Ajuereado people hunted or trapped a wide range of animals – creatures as large as deer, pronghorn, and Pleistocene horse, and those as small as cottontail rabbit, ground squirrel, wood rat, and quail. To be sure, they occasionally came together to hunt very big game, but this activity must be kept in perspective. "Probably," Richard MacNeish has suggested, "they killed a mammoth once in their lifetime and never stopped talking about it."

30 White-tailed deer (*Odocoileus virginianus*).

Coping with Risk at the Local Level

Sometime around 8000 BC the climatic regime of the Ice Age came to an end. With temperatures increasing worldwide, continental glaciers melted back across North America and returned the water to a rising sea. Air circulation patterns changed, the Chihuahuan Life Zone drew back to northern Mexico, and the present-day climatic pattern established itself in the Mexican highlands. This is a pattern of cool, dry winters and warm, rainy summers.

We suspect that for areas like the Tehuacán Valley, the environmental changes were profound. Ice Age Tehuacán is thought to have been a relatively open steppe with pronghorn antelope, jackrabbit, and Texas gopher tortoise. Rising temperatures and the establishment of monsoonal summer rains turned it into a thorn forest of leguminous trees, dense brush, and tall columnar cacti. The antelope, gopher tortoise, and many jackrabbit species withdrew to the north. What took their places were white-tailed deer, cottontail rabbits, collared peccaries, and mud turtles.[1]

31 Cottontail rabbits (*Sylvilagus* spp.).

In the Valley of Oaxaca, pine forest on the mountains gave way to a mixed forest of oak, pine, manzanita, and madroño. The piedmont below these mountains would have been thorn-scrub-cactus forest with leguminous trees, prickly pear, organ cactus, yucca, and agaves. On the alluvial valley floor, there would have been a woodland of mesquite and acacia trees. Along the course of the Atoyac River and its major tributaries there would have been gallery forest of baldcypress, alder, willow, and fig.[2] Like the Tehuacán Valley, this too would have been an environment for white-tailed deer, peccaries, cottontails, doves, quail, and mud turtles. The Mexican Plateau now had its own distinct mixture of temperate and semitropical species, separated from the Chihuahuan Life Zone by 1000 km.

32 Collared peccary (*Dicotyles tajacu*).

In terms of action theory, the transition from Pleistocene to Holocene environments would be an example of the larger system changing, presenting the actors with a problem to solve. Fortunately the transition was gradual rather than abrupt, and some genera of plants and animals persisted after the changeover.

One of the Indians' biggest adjustments must have been to a reduction in the two animals most suited to communal hunting drives: jackrabbit and pronghorn antelope. White-tailed deer, moving singly or in small herds through the forest, are best pursued by small groups of hunters who knew the country well. Cottontail rabbits, since they live in the underbrush and dig burrows for escape, are poorly suited to communal drives; a better strategy is to set traps within their

33 Mud turtle (*Kinosternon integrum*).

34 Thorn-scrub-cactus forest on the Valley of Oaxaca piedmont.

Opposite

35 Woodland of mesquite and acacia trees on the Valley of Oaxaca floor.

36 Baldcypress trees (*Taxodium* sp.) on a tributary of the Atoyac River.

home ranges. Hunting parties seem to have been much smaller in the Early Holocene, judged by remains in caves and rockshelters.[3]

Because of the warmer temperatures and greater rainfall after 8000 BC, edible species of plants were more varied and abundant. One could now find what he or she needed without the long migrations of the Ice Age. However, those plants were also dependent on a rainfall regime with a great deal of unpredictable annual variation. In the Valley of Oaxaca, for example, the summer rains bring an average of 550 mm of precipitation to the region. In a dry year, however, less than 300 mm will fall; in a wet year, the figure can be more than 800 mm. Recent rainfall figures suggest that wet, dry, and average years occur in unpredictable order, so that any given year can produce a bumper crop or a drought.[4,5] Learning how to deal with this variation without abandoning the region was a second major adjustment for the Indians.

This chapter deals with the period from 8000 to 2000 BC, a time known as the Archaic. During that period, the hunters and gatherers of Oaxaca and Tehuacán learned how to deal with risk in an unpredictable but potentially productive environment. Some of their decisions changed the course of Mexican prehistory forever.

Archaic Settlement Patterns

Lewis Binford has suggested that most hunting-gathering societies occupy a position along a continuum from "foraging" to "collecting."[6] Foragers, the most mobile, travel to where the food is, and their pattern of settlement becomes dispersed or aggregated as resources become dispersed or aggregated. Collectors,

Organ cactus
(fruits, Feb–March)

Mesquite groves
(pods, May–Aug)

Chert quarry

37 Surrounded by many of the same wild resources their ancestors used, a group of Zapotec workmen excavate the Martínez Rockshelter (1966).

the most nearly sedentary, tend to remain in one favored locality while smaller task groups go out and bring back resources for the larger encampment.

Pauline Wiessner has suggested a similar continuum of "risk acceptance."[7] At one end of her continuum are hunter-gatherers who accept risk at the level of the local group, through pooling and widespread sharing of resources among the families encamped together. At the other end are societies in which risk is accepted at the level of the individual or the nuclear family, with fewer opportunities to use pooling to even out differential success at foraging.

While the Early Archaic occupants of the Valley of Oaxaca did not lie at the extreme of either continuum, they can be described as "foragers" because they changed residence several times during the year, traveling to where the resources were most abundant. They also spent parts of the year in "microbands" of 4–6 persons, made up of both men and women.[8] These small groups were probably analogous to the family collecting bands of the Paiute and Shoshone Indians of the western United States, who accepted risk at the family level.[9]

At certain times, however, these dispersed family bands came together to form larger "macroband" camps of 15–25 persons. Since the antelopes and jackrabbits of the late Ice Age were no longer abundant, these larger camps were not made for communal hunting drives. Instead, they were made for harvesting seasonally abundant plants found in the denser post-Pleistocene vegetation. The archaeological record does not yet tell us whether these Archaic people pooled and shared resources at their larger camps, but they may have. We also do not know whether they sent out smaller task groups to collect specific resources for

Agave (heart
can be roasted)

Prickly pear
(young stems and
fruits, June–Oct)

the macroband, but there are suggestions that this practice may have been in use by the Late Archaic (see below).

The periods when up to 25 persons camped together must have been exciting for families who had spent much of the year dispersed in the wilderness. At one such macroband camp in Oaxaca, called Gheo-Shih, we have found evidence for ritual activity and ornament manufacture on a scale not seen in microband camps. This suggests that some activities, such as group ritual, gift-giving, exchange, and perhaps even initiation and courtship, were deferred until the moment when all the foragers living in a region came together.

Because Archaic sites are ephemeral compared with those of later periods, it is difficult to estimate the population of the Valley of Oaxaca. Judged by the known sites, there might have been no more than 75–150 persons in the entire valley system.[10] On the other hand, we may have underestimated the Archaic population because their sites are so inconspicuous on survey. Perhaps fifteen open-air scatters of flint tools have been recorded in the least-alluviated parts of the valley, and there are another half-dozen finds of isolated Archaic atlatl (spearthrower) points on the surface.[11]

It is in the caves and rockshelters of the surrounding mountains that we get our best glimpse of the Archaic, for it is here that the preservation of artifacts, plants, and animal bones is richest. So low was the Archaic population, however, that only 8–10 caves out of the 70 so far surveyed had remains of that period. Three of the best known are Guilá Naquitz, Cueva Blanca, and the Martínez Rockshelter.

Guilá Naquitz Cave

In the Archaic period, much of the alluvial floor of the Valley of Oaxaca was covered by a woodland of mesquite (*Prosopis* sp.), whose syrup-filled pods came ripe during the May-September rainy season. Also available during this season were the small yellow fruits of the hackberry (*Celtis* sp.). As the availability of these foods began to diminish in late summer, Archaic foragers turned their attention to the thorn forest of the upper piedmont, whose resources reached their peak in the autumn.

An occasional camping place for these foragers was Guilá Naquitz, a small cave at 1926 m elevation in the mountains west of Mitla.[12] Because Guilá Naquitz was a dry cave, in which ancient plants were preserved by desiccation, we can reconstruct many activities of the foragers whose debris produced Level D of the cave. They were members of an Early Archaic microband, perhaps a family of 4–6 people; this suggests that conditions during the occupation of Level D favored dispersal into small groups.

Three of the family's first acts were to collect masses of oak leaves for use as bedding in the cave; to excavate at least one storage pit in the cave floor; and to prepare a shallow hearth near the center of the cave. By so doing they had begun a conceptual division of the cave floor into men's and women's work areas. An

38 Guilá Naquitz Cave during excavation.

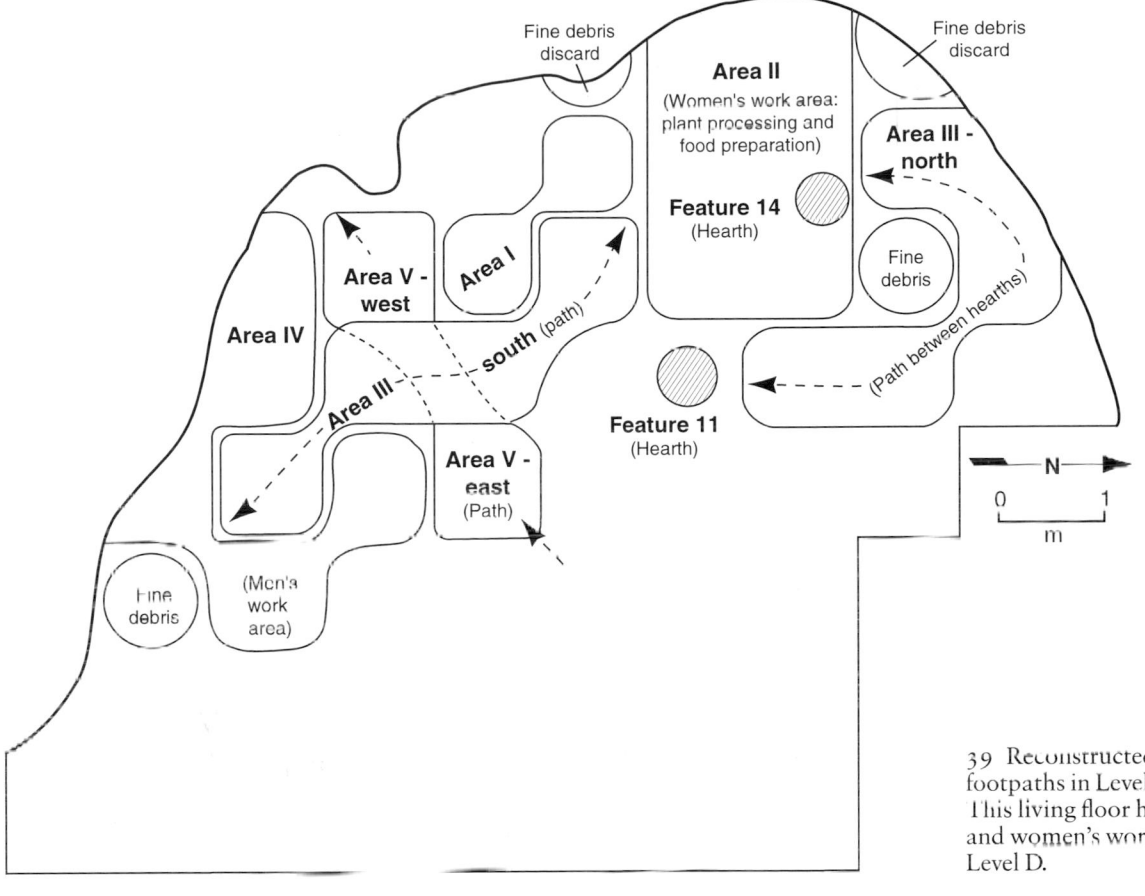

Fine debris discard

Fine debris discard

Area II
(Women's work area: plant processing and food preparation)

Area III - north

Feature 14
(Hearth)

Fine debris

Area V - west

Area I

(Path between hearths)

Area IV

Area III

south (path)

Feature 11 (Hearth)

Fine debris

Area V - east
(Path)

Fine debris

(Men's work area)

Feature 11
(Hearth)

N

0   1
m

39 Reconstructed activity areas and footpaths in Level B1 of Guilá Naquitz. This living floor had a division into men's and women's work areas similar to that of Level D.

area for women to process plant foods and cook meals appeared near the hearth, while a footpath began to develop between the hearth and the storage pit. Mesquite pods brought from the valley floor were stored in the pit, prior to having their edible syrup removed. At least two people, perhaps women, sat eating hackberries and spitting out the seeds into discrete piles on the cave floor.

A work area for men developed along the south wall of the cave. Here the bones from at least one juvenile deer, some cottontails, and a mud turtle were discarded, along with a flint biface that may have been the "blank" for making an atlatl point.

Late summer or early autumn is a good time for collecting the ripe fruits and tender young stem sections of the prickly pear cactus (*Opuntia* spp.). The stem sections had their spines removed and were roasted over the hearth on wooden skewers. Both men and women ate the ripe fruits, with piles of leftovers indicating that they had collected more than they could eat. They also ate fruits of the West Indian cherry (*Malpighia* sp.), whose seeds they spat out in some quantity around the hearth.

Late autumn ripened the products of the piedmont and lower mountains. At this point, the storage capacity of the cave was tripled by the digging of two more storage pits. This was done in anticipation of the acorn harvest, an activity of enormous importance. One can only imagine how many thousands of acorns

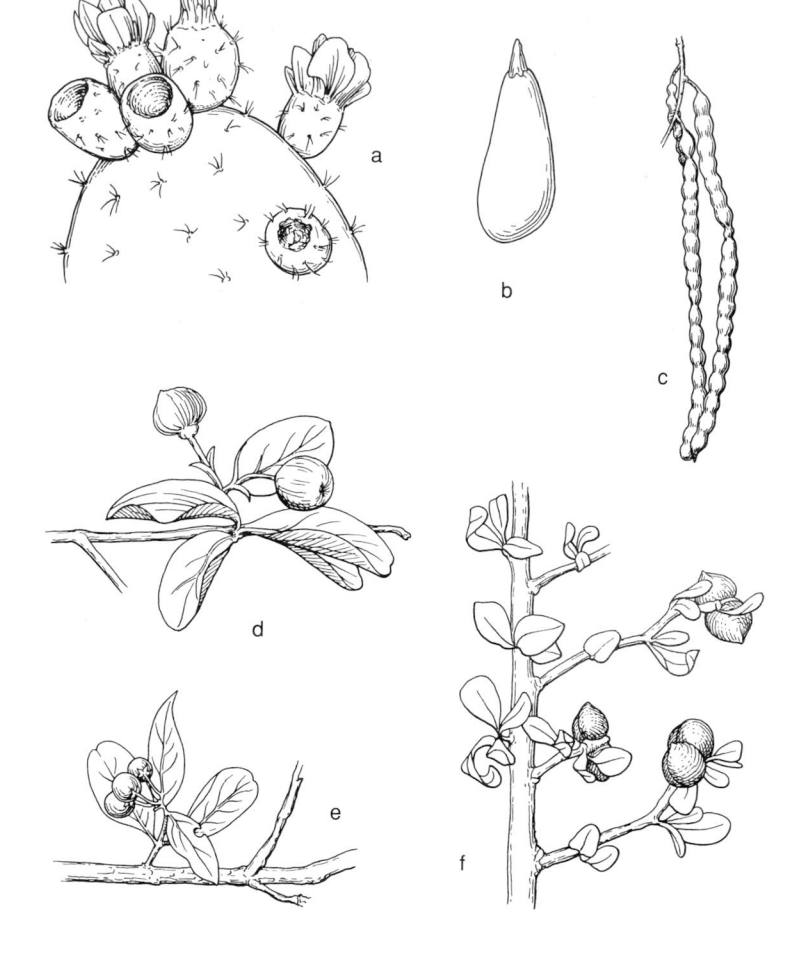

40 Edible wild plants of the Guilá Naquitz area. (*a*) Fruits of prickly pear cactus (*Opuntia* spp.); (*b*) wild avocado (*Diospyros* sp.); (*c*) pods of mesquite (*Prosopis juliflora*); (*d*) West Indian cherry (*Malpighia* sp.); (*e*) fruits of the hackberry (*Celtis* sp.); (*f*) nuts of *yak susí* (*Jatropha neodioica*).

the family collected, since more than 3000 were left behind uneaten in Level D. Judging by the grinding stones in the cave, thousands more were milled into acorn flour.

Piñon pines grew among the oaks or upslope from them, and judging by the places where hulls were discarded, their nuts were collected along with the acorns. Other foods of the thorn forest, such as the nuts of the *susí* bush (*Jatropha neodioica*) and the seeds of guaje trees (*Lysiloma* sp. and *Leucaena* sp.) were also harvested. The foragers of Guilá Naquitz made trips to nearby springs and stream areas to collect bulbs of the wild onion (*Allium* sp.) as flavoring for their meals.

Late autumn is also good deer-hunting season, since white-tailed deer are attracted to acorns, oak twig tips, and buds. The occupants of Layer D killed at least one buck, one collared peccary, and a series of cottontail rabbits.

One of the most important food plants of the November-to-April season must have been the agave or century plant (*Agave* spp.). The agave, a hardy member of the amaryllis family, survives the winter drought by storing water in the heart of the plant. At a time when few other plants are available, the agave can be dug up, its leaves trimmed off, and its heart cooked for 24–72 hours in an earth oven. The heart can then be cut into pieces which taste like fudge; those pieces from

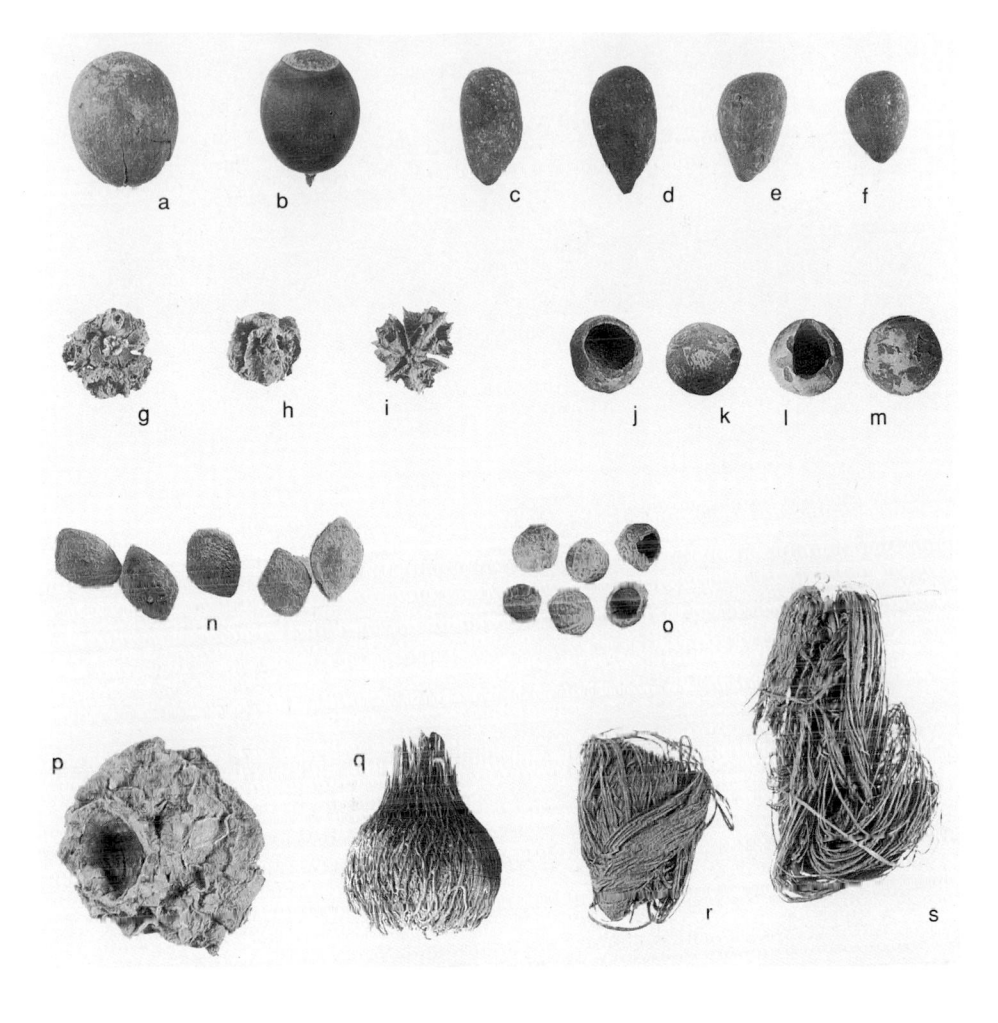

41 Wild plants harvested by the Archaic foragers at Guilá Naquitz and preserved by the aridity of the cave. (*a,b*) Acorns; (*c–f*) piñon nuts, (*g–i*) seeds of West Indian cherry; (*j–m*) hulls of *yak susi;* (*n*) seeds of mesquite; (*o*) seeds of hackberry; (*p*) dried fruit of prickly pear cactus; (*q*) wild onion bulb; (*r,s*) quids of chewed agave fiber. Length of (*q*) 18 mm

near the leaf bases, however, contain inedible fiber which must be expectorated after considerable chewing. Nearly 50 "quids" of chewed agave fiber had been left on the Level D living floor. The foragers also left behind flint flakes whose edges show the characteristic polish or "sheen" of a tool used to trim off the tough leaves of the century plant.

Eventually, as the dry winter wore on, the plant resources of the thorn forest became scarce and the family decided to move on. Evidently they had departed by February, as not a single fruit of *Myrtillocactus* sp. – an organ cactus which bears up to 900 fruits per plant in February and March – was present in the cave. We do not know where the family went, but we suspect that they ascended to the more humid forests of the higher mountains, just as deer do during the dry season. Not only did they leave behind hundreds of uneaten plants, they evidently left their campfire smouldering, since it later ignited many of the oak leaves they had used as bedding.

Gheo-Shih

When the first rains of May turned the floor of the Valley of Oaxaca green again, foragers made their annual return to lower elevations. By July the mesquite trees

42 Archaeologists examine the surface of the Gheo-Shih site for artifacts.

43 One of the unusual features of Gheo-Shih was the boulder-lined area in the foreground. In the background is a dense scatter of rocks and flints which may indicate the presence of a shelter or windbreak.

were heavy with pods, the hackberries were in fruit, and deer and cottontail rabbits were abundant in the alluvial woodland. In a rainier than average year, with resources in excess of the amount a single family could harvest before the season ended, groups of up to 25 persons might come together in the groves of mesquite.

We believe that this happened several times at a place the Zapotec call Gheo-Shih, "River of the Gourd Trees." Gheo-Shih is an open-air Archaic camp site on an exposure of ancient alluvium near the Río Mitla, a tributary of the Río Salado. Occupying an area of roughly 1.5 ha, its surface was littered with grinding stones, flint bifaces, steep denticulate scrapers, and atlatl points when archaeologists first discovered it.[13]

Excavation of Gheo-Shih by Frank Hole revealed an unusual feature: two parallel lines of boulders stretching for 20 m and spaced 7 m apart. The 140-m² enclosed space had been swept clean of artifacts; to either side of the feature, however, artifacts were abundant. What the boulder-lined feature most resembles is a cleared dance ground, like the ones laid out by some Indians of western North America at their macroband camps.

Outside the boulder-lined feature, Gheo-Shih had oval concentrations of flints and fire-cracked rocks, suggesting that small temporary shelters or windbreaks were built at the camp. There were areas with high concentrations of grinding stones, other places with abundant atlatl points and scrapers, even an area where stream pebbles had been drilled to make ornaments.

No similar ornament-making area has been found at any of the smaller sites of the Archaic. Like the boulder-lined "dance ground," this area for ornament manufacture implies that when temporary abundance allowed Archaic foragers to get together in camps of 15–25 persons, they engaged in social, ritual, and craft activities not carried out at smaller camps. Time limits to such macroband camps, however, would have been set by the shrinking resources of the alluvial woodland at the end of the rainy season.

44 The occupants of Gheo-Shih drilled stream pebbles for use as ornaments. Diameter of lower specimen, 3.5 cm.

Cueva Blanca

Cueva Blanca, whose Late Pleistocene deposits were mentioned in Chapter 3, was also visited during the Archaic. These Archaic foragers left behind larger samples of flint tools and animal bones than the occupants of Guilá Naquitz; but conditions at Cueva Blanca were unfortunately not good for the preservation of plants.

Because of the larger numbers of tools at Cueva Blanca, computer scientist Robert Reynolds was able to find statistically significant associations among tool

45 Cueva Blanca lies in a volcanic tuff cliff surrounded by thorn forest.

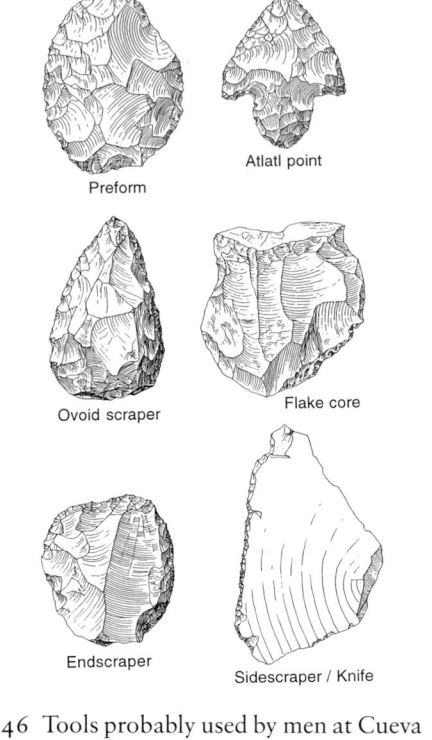

Preform Atlatl point

Ovoid scraper Flake core

Endscraper Sidescraper / Knife

46 Tools probably used by men at Cueva Blanca. Length of preform, 9 cm.

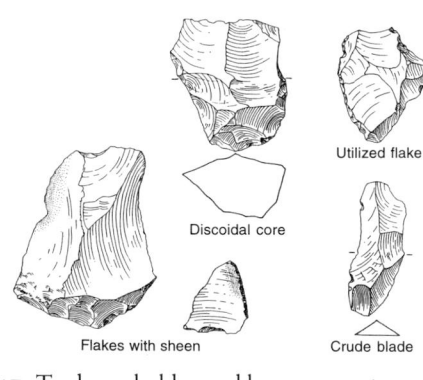

Utilized flake

Discoidal core

Flakes with sheen Crude blade

47 Tools probably used by women at Cueva Blanca. Areas of stipple indicate sheen. Length of crude blade, 5.8 cm.

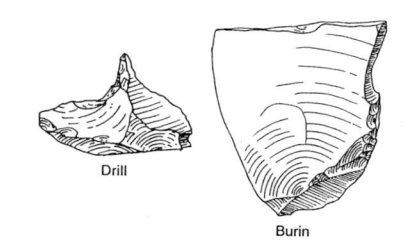

Drill

Burin

48 Tools not strongly associated with either men's or women's activity areas at Cueva Blanca. We do not know who used these "tools to make other tools." Length of burin, 5.2 cm.

The Search for Men's and Women's Tool Kits

Cueva Blanca was excavated by a grid of 1 × 1 m squares. Robert Reynolds reasoned that tools used together might be discarded in the same square. He used a common statistical measure of association: if Tool A and Tool B were always discarded in the same square, they had a positive association of +1.0. If they were never discarded in the same square, they had a negative association of −1.0. Most pairs of tools had less than perfect associations, such as +0.8, or −0.4.

Reynolds began with the assumption that atlatl points were men's hunting tools, and looked to see which other tools were discarded with them. On most of Cueva Blanca's Archaic living floors, points were *positively* associated with the bifacial "quarry blanks" from which they were made, as well as with steep scrapers, end scrapers, side scrapers, and ovoid scrapers. They were *negatively* associated with choppers, burins (engraving tools), and drills; on some living floors they were also *negatively* associated with crude blades and flakes with sheen.

Since flakes with sheen had been associated with the trimming of leaves from agave hearts at Guilá Naquitz, Reynolds considers it possible that they were tools used often (though not exclusively) by women. Over most Archaic living floors at Cueva Blanca, flakes with sheen were *positively* associated with discoidal flint cores and crude blades. Flakes with sheen were *negatively* associated with such men's tools as "blanks" for atlatl points – reinforcing our suspicion that women often struck off their own flakes, then used them to cut tough plant material until the edges developed a sheen.

types, leading to the discovery of men's and women's tool kits.[14] What Reynolds did was to determine which tools tended to be discarded together on the same small area of the cave floor. He reasoned that tools discarded together had probably been used by the same person (see Box).

Reynolds' results increase our information on division of labor in the Archaic. He found that men's tool kits included atlatl points; the oval blanks or "preforms" from which the points were chipped; and a whole series of scrapers that were probably used for working animal hides. Women's tools included discoidal cores from which flakes had been struck; the flakes themselves; crude blades; and flakes with "sheen" or "edge polish" that probably resulted from the repeated cutting of coarse plant material like agave leaves. One of the most interesting implications was that men and women may have used somewhat different cores, or flint nuclei, from which they struck the flakes that would later be made into tools.

"Drop Zones" and "Toss Zones"

On all three Archaic living floors at Cueva Blanca, there were areas of relatively dense flint and bone debris, and areas of lighter debris. When one draws maps connecting the areas with the densest debris, as has been done in ill. 49, they

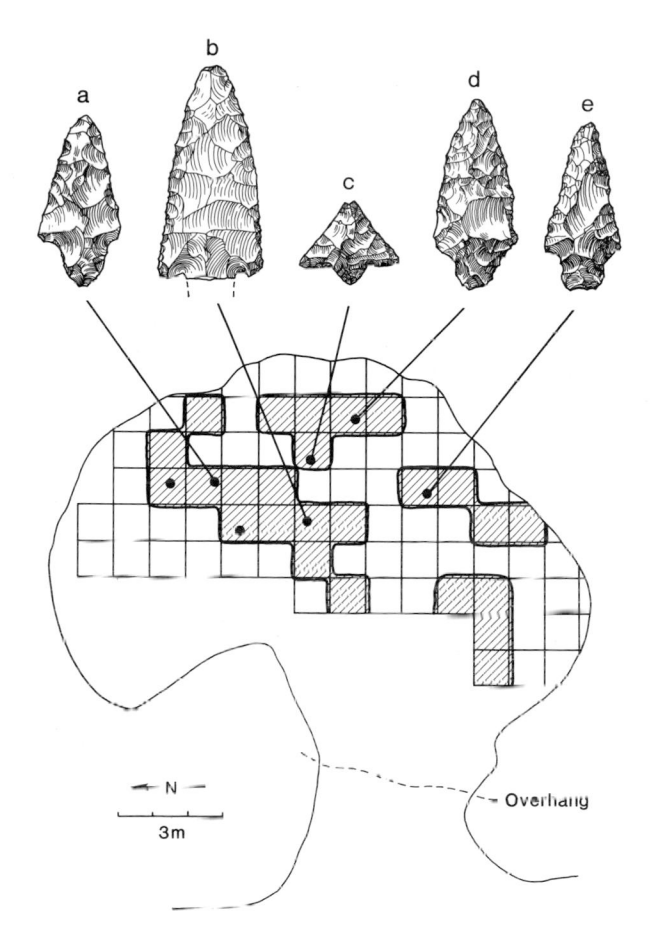

49 Level C of Cueva Blanca had discrete areas of dense debris (hachured). Almost all *atlatl* points (black dots) had been left in such areas. Some of the more complete points were of San Nicolás type (*a, d*), Coxcatlán type (*c*), and La Mina type (*e*). Point (*b*) is unclassified.

resemble what Lewis Binford has called "drop zones" – areas where one or more of the cave's occupants set tools down nearby as he or she worked. The areas of lighter debris resemble Binford's "toss zones" – areas farther away, where discarded tools were tossed.[15]

The Shift from Foraging to Collecting

Small family groups, containing both men and women, seem to have been responsible for creating the earliest Archaic living floors at Cueva Blanca. Level C, the living floor illustrated in ill. 49, is different from earlier encampments. Dating to the Late Archaic (perhaps 3000–2000 BC), it may have been an all-male deer-hunting camp at which the usual evidence for women's activities and tool kits is missing or ambiguous. Unless future analyses contradict this view, Level C could turn out to be our first hint of a new strategy for the Late Archaic.

Level C may indicate that the Indians of the Valley of Oaxaca were now shifting away from "foraging" (traveling to where the plants were) and toward "collecting" (leaving most of the group at a large base camp, while sending smaller "task groups" out to collect and bring back a specific resource). The deer-hunters who lived on the Level C floor might represent a small group of men, sent out from a larger base camp to procure venison. For reasons discussed below, this could represent a significant change in strategy.

The Egalitarian Ethic

One more insight into the hunter-gatherers of the Late Archaic emerges from the distribution of their atlatl points. In contrast to some Archaic hunters of North America, who used only one or two styles of points during a prehistoric time period, the Late Archaic hunters of Oaxaca used a great variety: as many as six or seven point types might be used by the same microband. Such variety suggests a society in which each hunter made his own distinctive type of point. Some hunting bands of the recent past did this because it was important for them to know whose projectile had killed the animal. Such information could affect the distribution of meat among the hunters.

If this were the case at Cueva Blanca, one might expect that each type of atlatl point would cluster in the "drop zone" of a particular hunter. A glance at ill. 49, our map of Level C, shows that this is not the case. For example, points of San Nicolás type occur in two different "drop zones," often in association with other types.

We may, therefore, have a situation similar to that of the !Kung Bushmen of Botswana, Africa, studied 30 years ago by Richard Lee. Although each !Kung hunter made his own distinctive arrows, they were widely exchanged with hunting partners. In 1964, Lee made an inventory of the quivers of four !Kung hunters. All but one had arrows made by 4–6 different men, and "two of the four men had no arrows *of their own* in their quivers."[16]

According to Lee, such widespread exchange of arrows reinforced the !Kung egalitarian ethic by diffusing the responsibility for meat distribution, and spreading around the prestige of having one's own arrow kill the prey. Without such exchange, the most skilled hunters could become an envied meritocracy. We suspect the hunters of the Oaxaca Archaic may have had an equally strong egalitarian ethic.

Over how wide an area might Archaic hunters have exchanged atlatl points with their friends and relatives? The point of Coxcatlán type marked *c* in ill. 49 may have come from as far away as the Tehuacán Valley, 160 km to the northwest of Cueva Blanca. A nearby sea shell from the Pacific Ocean, perforated as an ornament, probably came from just as far away to the southeast. Such distances, however, pale by comparison with those traveled by some of the spear points of the preceding Paleoindian period (Chapter 3).

50 Occasional sea shells, like this one from Level C of Cueva Blanca, reached the Valley of Oaxaca during the Late Archaic. Length 26 mm.

The Archaic Lifeway: Implications for the Future

It would be easy to see the Archaic strategy of the southern Mexican highlands as a simple response to climatic change. The Chihuahuan Life Zone withdrew to the north at the end of the Ice Age. With it went a whole set of plants and animals, ending a lifeway based on "drought escape" through long-distance migration and communal game drives.

Taking the place of the Chihuahuan steppe was a complex mosaic of temperate and semitropical thorn forests and mesquite woodlands. Now foragers could solve their problems at the local level by knowing just when to move to dense seasonal stands of edible plants, just when to disperse in family bands, and just when to come together in groups of 15–25. A technology that now included grinding stones made greater numbers of species edible. Storage lengthened the plants' season of availability. The buffering of drought was achieved through shorter, scheduled moves instead of long, unscheduled migrations.

Such an ecological-functionalist explanation, however, leaves out the decisions made by human actors. The decision to accept risk at the level of the family for part of the year was not forced on our actors by climatic change. The decision to reinforce their egalitarian ethic by exchanging atlatl points was not forced on them by the white-tailed deer population. The decision to divide labor along the lines of gender, resulting in men's and women's tool kits, was not forced on them either. All those decisions were choices made by people who perceived them to be in their best interests.

In 1986 Robert Reynolds produced a computer simulation of foraging at Guilá Naquitz.[17] The simulation was like a computer game, in which an imaginary microband tried to stay alive in a world of wild vegetation just like that within walking distance of the cave. The foragers were allowed to make their own decisions about what plants to collect. Their only instructions were to remember what they had tried in the past, and to use as little effort as possible in supplying each member of the band with 2000 kilocalories and 40 g of protein per day.

After a long period of trial and error, the rank ordering of plant species used by the imaginary foragers was very like that of Level D of Guilá Naquitz. When Reynolds looked back through the computer data to examine the foragers' decisions, he found the following. (1) They had chosen to make longer trips to denser plant stands, rather than shorter trips to sparser stands. (2) They had concentrated on high-calorie plants, always getting their 2000 kilocalories even if it meant falling short on protein. (3) They had developed two strategies – a more conservative one for drought years, and a more experimental one for wet years. (4) Many crucial improvements in foraging efficiency had been made in wet years, then expanded to dry years as they proved useful over time. One of the important implications of Reynolds' simulation is that when actors are allowed to make their own decisions, and have long periods of time to consider the results, they can bring off successful strategies which do not need to be explained through environmental determinism.

Another of the decisions of Late Archaic peoples, hinted at in Level C of Cueva Blanca, may have been to move farther from the "foraging" end of the continuum and closer to the "collecting" end. This move had implications for the origins of the village. It is difficult to see how the highly mobile Ice Age hunters, or even the foraging microbands of the Early Archaic, could provide a context out of which permanent settlements could arise. However, once a pattern of establishing longer-term macroband camps had taken hold, one can imagine a number of scenarios leading to village life.

Archaic hunters probably looked forward to living in macroband camps like Gheo-Shih, because of the more intense social and ritual life they provided. What the foragers lacked was a resource that could be harvested in abundance and stored all year at such large camps, eliminating the necessity to move. By the Late Archaic it was becoming clearer what that resource would be.

5

Agriculture as an Extension of Foraging Strategy

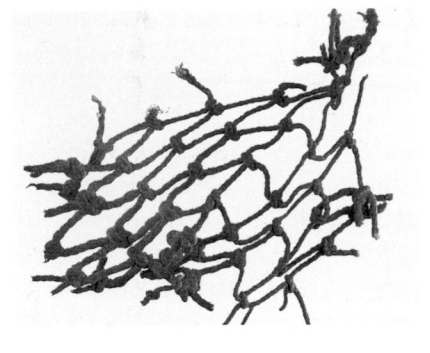

51 (*Right*) Net bags were used by Archaic foragers to carry food back to the campsite. This fragment of net was found in Guilá Naquitz Cave. Size 4.5 by 5 cm.

Over the millennia of the Archaic, the Indians of the southern Mexican highlands continued to improve their ability to deal with risk and adapt to drought. Coping with an unpredictable succession of wet, dry, and average years, they had developed a technology of snares, nets, fire-making drills, baskets, and food storage that became a legacy for later periods. They learned how to roast the agave to make it edible; how to make tongs for picking the fruits of the prickly pear; how to singe the spines off those fruits and split them for sun-drying; how to grind acorns into flour; how to extract syrup from the pod of the mesquite; how to leach tannic acid from the acorn; how to find wild bean and onion flowers in the underbrush; and how to predict from such flowers when the edible parts would be ready to harvest.

The flexible social structure of these foragers allowed them to split into family groups and spread out over the landscape during lean seasons, then come together with other families to form larger groups when resources were abundant. Some of the plants they ate were tough, coarse, and fibrous, but nutritional studies by John Robson and Joel Elias show that the occupants of Guilá Naquitz probably had little trouble getting 2000 kilocalories and 40 g of protein a day during the time they lived at the cave.[1]

We have described these Archaic foragers as "buffering" rather than "escaping" drought; accepting risk at the level of the nuclear family; dividing labor along gender lines; and pursuing an egalitarian ethic. By the Late Archaic, they had added another strategy to their foraging repertoire: artificially increasing the density and availability of certain plants by planting them near their camps.

Cucurbits and Beans

52 (*Above*) Archaic foragers made fire by rotating a hard wooden drill in a "hearth" made of softer wood until it ignited. This "hearth," made of agave inflorescence, was found in Guilá Naquitz Cave. Length 20.7 cm.

We suspect that the first plant domesticated in Mexico was the bottle gourd, *Lagenaria siceraria*. Bottle gourds would have been among the most important portable containers for drinking water available to mobile hunter-gatherers. We do not know where gourds were first domesticated, but we do know that *Lagenaria* is better adapted to moist, humid conditions than to arid, cool environments.[2] Hunter-gatherers of highland Mexico must have crossed many cool, arid regions where they encountered no bottle gourds. At some point it appears that they began carrying gourd seeds with them, to plant where there had been none. Desiccated rinds of *Lagenaria* suggest that this had occurred by the time Guilá Naquitz was occupied. Thus it is possible that the Archaic foragers' first attempts at cultivation were aimed more at providing themselves with water bottles than with food.

But *Lagenaria* belongs to the botanical family Cucurbitaceae, the family of gourds, squashes, and pumpkins. Once gourds had been successfully cultivated, Archaic foragers must have recognized their other cucurbit relatives as potentially cultivable.

Dozens of species of squash grow wild in Mexico. Most have small fruits the size of an orange and are useful only for their edible seeds, since their flesh is bitter to nonexistent. Archaic foragers surely regarded squash seeds as tasty, simple to dry and store, light to transport, and easy to carry from camp to camp. What they did not realize was that squash seeds were also higher in protein than almost any other plant available to them.[3] The growing of squash, therefore, had the potential to improve a diet that usually concentrated on high-calorie plants.

We suspect that Archaic foragers eventually began growing squash right along with their bottle gourds. Squashes are notorious "camp followers," weedy plants that do well in habitats disturbed by humans. It might even have been possible to grow them on the disturbed talus slope below an occupied cave, or on a nearby stream floodplain. By so doing, foragers could decrease their search time by producing a relatively dense stand of an edible plant at a predictable locality.

Two species of squash appear in the Archaic refuse of Guilá Naquitz. One is a tiny yellowish-brown squash, possibly a distant relative of today's pumpkin (*Cucurbita pepo*); it is represented by seeds, stems, and rinds. Local Zapotec speakers refer to this plant simply as *giht*, their generic term for "squash." The other squash from the cave is *Apodanthera*, the wild coyote melon; it is represented only by its edible seeds, since its fruit is both bad-tasting and bad smelling. It is referred to as *giht lahn*, "stinking squash," by the local Zapotec.[4]

Large samples of Archaic pumpkins had previously been found by Richard MacNeish at caves in Tamaulipas, northern Mexico.[5] Still other species of squash (*Cucurbita mixta* and *C. moschata*) had been found in Late Archaic levels at Coxcatlán Cave in the Tehuacán Valley. These early races of squash are very primitive compared to today's, and since we do not know the full morphological variation of their seeds and stems, all claims of domestication to date should be treated as tentative.

Also native to the forested uplands of Mexico are dozens of species of wild beans. Many have seeds so small that only their edible root is used today; this is the case with the wild bean *Phaseolus heterophyllus*, which still grows near Guilá Naquitz. Local Zapotec speakers refer to it simply as *gužehl*, "small tuber."

In the Archaic refuse at Guilá Naquitz there were more than 100 small black seeds of a runner bean that has not yet been identified to species. So numerous were these beans that their density might have been artificially increased by planting them near the cave. If such were the case, however, it was an attempt at cultivation that was ultimately abandoned, since this particular species of runner bean has left no domestic descendants.[6]

Today's Zapotec still grow small black beans, which they call *bisya lăs*. The species they grow today, however, is the common bean *Phaseolus vulgaris*. Thus it is possible that as time went on, certain early domestic beans outperformed their relatives so thoroughly that attempts to cultivate the latter were dropped. This probably happened because, within the gene pool of some species, there were occasional mutant genes that made the plant bigger, tastier, easier to

53 Remains of gourds and squashes from Guilá Naquitz Cave. (*a*–*c*) Fragments of gourd rind; (*d*) base of squash stem; (*e*) seed of wild coyote melon (*Apodanthera* sp.); (*f*) squash seed. Length of (*c*) 1 cm.

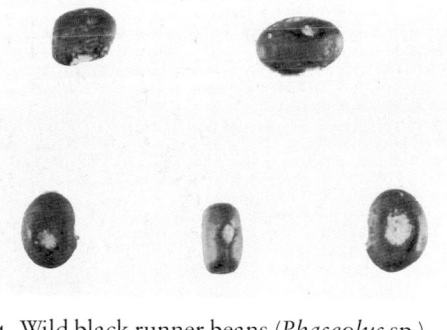

54 Wild black runner beans (*Phaseolus* sp.) from Guilá Naquitz Cave. Length of lower left specimen, 5 mm.

process, or all three. Seeds from mutant individuals could then be selected for planting, increasing their frequency in the next generation.

Agriculture may have begun simply as one of a number of Archaic strategies, designed to give foragers more kilograms of food with less travel and harvest time. Eventually, however, selection led to domestic varieties of squash that were larger, produced more seeds, and had good-tasting flesh. It also led to beans that had larger and more water-soluble seeds, as well as tough, limp pods – much easier to harvest than the explosive, corkscrew pods of the wild bean, which can shatter on contact and scatter the seeds.

Eventually agriculture became an almost irreversible process, since the newly created domestic races could not survive without human assistance, and the humans in turn were beginning to rely more and more on the domestic races. In time, the increased effort put into agriculture took time away from the collecting of certain wild plants. As the use of squash and beans increased near Guilá Naquitz, for example, the use of mesquite pods also increased, while the use of acorns, piñon nuts, *susí* nuts, and hackberry declined.[7] We suspect that these changes took place because Late Archaic families were increasing the time they spent on the mesquite-rich valley floor alluvium – the best agricultural land in the valley – and reducing the time they spent in the pine-oak forest above.

The Domestication of Maize

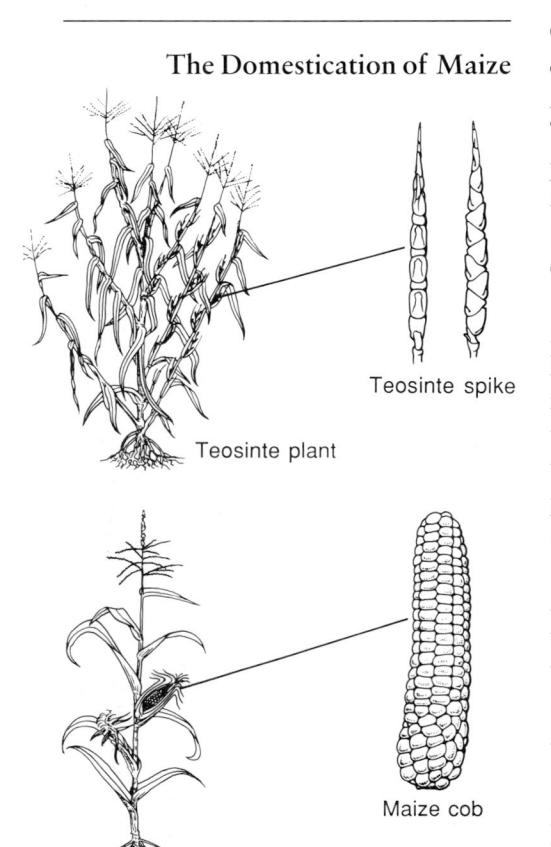

Teosinte spike

Teosinte plant

Maize cob

Maize plant

55 A comparison of teosinte and maize.

Gourds, squashes, and beans were only the first of many plants that came to be cultivated by the Archaic foragers of central and southern Mexico. By the Late Archaic, chile peppers (*Capsicum annuum*) show up in dry caves of the Tehuacán Valley, and carbonized seeds of the cherry tomato (*Physalis* sp.) are present at a macroband camp on Lake Chalco in the Basin of Mexico.[8] Both the aforementioned regions also used grain amaranths (*Amaranthus* spp.). Cotton (*Gossypium hirsutum*), whose domestication provided fiber for string, nets, and early textiles, may have been grown in the Tehuacán Valley by the Late Archaic.[9]

Of all of Mexico's Archaic crops, however, none had a greater impact than maize or Indian corn (*Zea mays*). From its humble beginning as a wild grass with hard-to-process and relatively unappetizing seeds, maize was eventually transformed into the staple crop of Mexican civilization. In the words of Nobel-Prize-winning botanist George Beadle, Mexico's Archaic foragers "can be credited with having produced the greatest morphological change of any cultivated plant" and "with having adapted corn to the widest geographical range of any major crop plant."[10]

Most botanists now believe that the wild ancestor of maize was a grass the Aztec called *teocentli*, "maize of the gods."[11,12] Now hispanicized as *teosinte*, this wild grass grows in a variety of races from the Mexican state of Chihuahua to the Guatemalan-Honduran border.[13] Exactly where in this vast range it was first domesticated is not known with certainty, but some botanists are now focusing on the *parviglumis* race of teosinte from west-central Mexico.[14]

To the casual observer, a stand of teosinte looks very much like a stand of maize. One must be very close to see the difference: instead of an ear, teosinte has a spike of 7–12 seeds set in a single row, each seed enclosed in a rock-hard fruit case. This fruit case will not allow the seed to sprout until persistently soaked by rain, a natural defense in times of drought. How the Archaic foragers even determined that teosinte was edible is a good question; they may have dis-

56 A massive stand of teosinte, growing on a fallow field in the mountains 120 km southwest of the Basin of Mexico.

covered that it "pops" like popcorn when heated over a fire. Otherwise one would have to spend hours crushing the fruit cases in a mortar.

Annual teosinte is a weedy, pioneer plant that colonizes natural scars in the landscape. In some areas of west-central Mexico, foragers who cleared a camp in the thorn forest might return the next year to discover that their former campsite had turned into a teosinte field. Wild runner beans and squash can also occur in such secondary growth, with the beans twining around the teosinte stalks. It may be no accident, therefore, that the Indians of Mexico eventually came to grow maize, beans, and squash together in their cultivated fields: nature may have provided the model.

We do not know when Archaic foragers first began eating teosinte. Its carbonized seeds have been found in Middle Archaic levels in a macroband camp in the Basin of Mexico.[15] No comparable seeds have been found in Archaic sites in Oaxaca, but pollen grains resembling those of teosinte have been found in Archaic refuse at Guilá Naquitz, Gheo-Shih, and Cueva Blanca.[16]

Even deliberately cultivated teosinte could not have been a very appetizing food; the secret of its success lay in its genetic plasticity. For example, a single gene locus called *tga1* controls a key difference between teosinte and maize – the difference between the hard fruit case of the teosinte seed and the exposed kernel of maize.[17] We do not know how many such mutations had to take place before teosinte became maize; Beadle once estimated that only five "significant independently inherited gene differences" lie between the two forms. Whatever the steps involved, it appears that the single-rowed spike of teosinte, with its hard fruit cases, was eventually converted by mutation and human selection into a maize ear with multiple rows of kernels held in soft cupules.

The oldest known cobs of domestic maize come from two dry rockshelters in the Tehuacán Valley – Coxcatlán Cave and San Marcos Cave.[18] These tiny, primitive maize cobs are not much longer than a cigarette filter (19–25 mm) and have only 4–8 rows of small kernels. The kernels are held by glumes that show signs of teosinte ancestry. Although the earliest maize may have had more ears per

57 Wild runner beans twining around a stalk of teosinte.

plant than modern maize, those ears were so small that the yield may have been only 60–80 kg/ha.[19] Moreover, since the maize cob had lost its seed-dispersal mechanism when it lost the teosinte spike's ability to shatter, it was now a genetic monstrosity dependent on humans for survival.

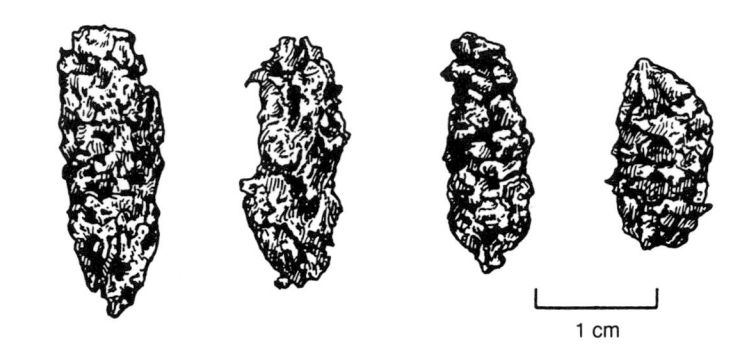

58 Four of the earliest maize cobs from San Marcos Cave in the Tehuacán Valley.

1 cm

Absolute Dates for Early Agriculture

We have put off discussion of the absolute dates for Archaic agriculture until the end of this chapter because, at this writing, the whole chronology of the Mexican Archaic is undergoing re-evaluation.

Until recently, virtually all absolute dates for the dry caves of the Tehuacán and Oaxaca Valleys came from samples of charcoal, radiocarbon-dated during the 1960s. Those samples of charcoal were presumed to date the living floors on which various early domestic plants – gourds, squash, beans, maize, chiles, tomatoes, and so on – had been found. Archaeologists knew that they might find an occasional living floor where the charcoal, the desiccated plants, or both, were intrusive from another level. They hoped that this had happened infrequently, so that if they obtained a large enough set of dates the overall pattern would be clear.

The 1960s dates suggested that bottle gourds might have been domesticated by 7000 BC. A few squash seeds from 7000–6000 BC in Oaxaca, and a larger sample from 5000–3000 BC in Tehuacán, appeared domesticated. Wild runner beans were present in Oaxaca by 8000–7000 BC, and early domestic beans showed up in Tehuacán caves between 4000 and 2000 BC. The earliest cobs of domestic maize appeared in levels of the Coxcatlán phase in the Tehuacán Valley. Charcoal samples from those levels suggested that this phase dated to 5000–3500 BC.

Since the 1960s, an alternative to traditional radiocarbon dating of charcoal has been developed. This is accelerator mass spectrometric (or AMS) dating, and it can be performed directly on uncarbonized material such as desiccated maize cobs. In 1989, a team of geophysicists and botanists subjected twelve of the oldest maize cobs from Tehuacán to AMS dating, and obtained dates 1500 years younger than expected.[20] The AMS dates place the oldest maize, from Level F of San Marcos Cave, in the 3640–3360 BC range, near the end of the Coxcatlán phase as defined in the 1960s. Some of the cobs from Level XIII of Coxcatlán Cave produced even more recent dates, well into the third millennium BC.

What are we to make of these new dates? While some archaeologists are already scrambling to explain the difference between the 1960s radiocarbon dates and the 1980s AMS dates, we recommend patience. Over the next decade many more AMS dates will be run, and when they are combined with traditional radiocarbon dating we may one day have a consensus on the absolute date for early agriculture in Oaxaca and Tehuacán. Right now we have no proof that either set of dates is "correct" in an absolute sense, and we can only create speculative scenarios about why they do not agree.

Even if it were to turn out that the Coxcatlán phase dated to 3500–2500 BC rather than 5000–3500 BC, it would not change the context of early agriculture. After a long period of using the wild ancestors of corn, beans, and squash, the semi-nomadic hunter-gatherers of Tehuacán and Oaxaca began to cultivate them. Agriculture was here to stay by the Late Archaic, whatever its absolute date. With time and patience, with careful saving of the best and largest seeds for each year's planting, and with the encouragement of every favorable mutation once it had appeared, the Indians of the Mexican Plateau gradually produced a set of crops that could support a civilization.

Atoyac River

River overflow

Site 5-8-128

59 The Atoyac River in flood near Site 5-8-128 (Santa Inés Yatzeche) in the Valle Grande, 1970. The strip of permanently humid alluvium along the river is called *yuh kohp* in Zapotec.

Learning to Live in Villages

The oldest type of farming in the Valleys of Tehuacán and Oaxaca, the type practiced in the Late Archaic, was likely based on rainfall. Even today, rainfall farming of maize is the most common type of agriculture in the Valley of Oaxaca; it is also the most risky. The valley receives an annual mean of 550 mm of rain, but this is only enough to support one maize crop in an average year.[1] Three years out of ten, rainfall is likely to dip below 500 mm, threatening crop failure.

Along the main rivers of the Valley of Oaxaca, however, runs a strip of land where the water table is so close to the surface that it creates a zone of permanently humid alluvium. When maize is planted in this zone – called *yuh kohp* in Zapotec – the roots of the plant can extract water continuously by capillary action, helping the maize to survive between rains. Zapotec farmers also conserve water in the soil by careful weeding, so that no moisture will be lost to competing plants. In areas still planted with the ancient digging stick, farmers make shallow basins for each seed and disturb the rest of the surface as little as possible.

This strip of high water table was essential to the establishment of sedentary life in the Valley of Oaxaca. Virtually all the earliest villages in the valley (1700–1200 BC) lie adjacent to this type of land. Because *yuh kohp* occurs on less than 10 percent of the valley floor, early village sites must have been chosen with care, and were spaced widely to minimize competition for this prized resource. Even Gheo-Shih, the Archaic macroband camp described in Chapter 4, was located near a strip of *yuh kohp* along the Río Mitla.

We do not know when the Indians of Oaxaca decided to make maize farming their most important economic activity – a decision that changed both settlement patterns and social institutions forever. Their decision, however, might have been based on the growing productivity of maize as its cob size increased during centuries of human selection.

Field studies by geographer Anne Kirkby show that Zapotec farmers do not consider land clearance and cultivation to be worth the effort unless a yield of 200–250 kg/ha of shelled maize can be expected.[2,3] Kirkby also discovered a statistical relationship between average maize cob length and yield. By her calculations, the earliest maize from Tehuacán might only have yielded 60–80 kg/ha. That yield would hardly make it worth clearing away mesquite trees (which themselves produce 160–180 kg/ha of pods) in order to plant maize.[4] By 1700–1500 BC, however, maize cobs had increased in size under human selec-

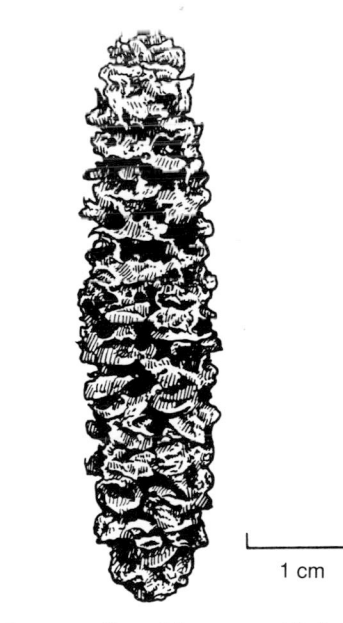

1 cm

60 By the time village life was established on the Mexican Plateau, maize cobs had reached the size of this specimen from a dry cave near Tehuacán.

61 Wattle-and-daub houses with thatched roofs, resembling those of 1500–1000 BC, are still used in parts of the Valley of Oaxaca.

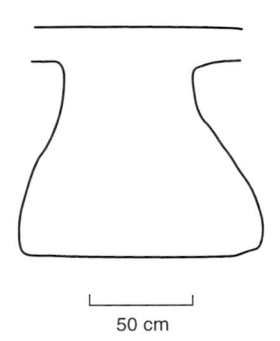

50 cm

62 Storage pits used by Oaxaca's earliest villagers were bottle-shaped in cross-section.

63 Bedrock below one of Oaxaca's earliest villages. The smaller holes are for house posts; the larger ones are storage pits or earth ovens.

tion to the point where they might have yielded 200–250 kg/ha. This is remarkably close to the date by which the Indians of Oaxaca had made a commitment to living in permanent villages near the best farm land.

What are the implications of this commitment? Evidently our prehistoric actors had decided that (1) clearing trees from the *yuh kohp*; (2) planting maize, beans, and squash with a digging stick; (3) weeding; (4) harvesting; and (5) storing seeds was a better strategy than foraging over thousands of square kilometers in search of food. To be sure, they continued to hunt wild game and collect wild plants, but those activities were now done by small "task groups" sent out from the village.

On the site chosen for the village, individual families built houses for themselves. These houses were made of pine posts brought down from the mountains, and had roofs thatched with reeds or grasses. The walls were constructed of bundles of canes lashed together, then plastered over with clay in the architectural style called "wattle and-daub." Over the simple, stamped-earth floor went a layer of river sand to provide a dry surface, and perhaps a reed mat or two to sleep on. Near the house, each family dug storage pits for its harvested maize. Larger than the pits seen at Guilá Naquitz, these storage units could have held up to a metric ton of shelled corn, or a year's supply for a family of 4–5.

Living in Larger Settlements

One of the unintended consequences of sedentism was that people were now living permanently in larger groups. Some early villages had 50–100 persons, far exceeding the macroband camps of the Archaic. The human population was growing. One likely reason is that successful agriculture on humid alluvium was raising the valley's capacity to support people. A less obvious reason is that the process of becoming sedentary, all by itself, can increase population. Migrating hunter-gatherers often suffer travel-related infant mortality, and may space out the births of their children over many years because it is stressful to carry infants on long trips. Once encouraged to become sedentary in villages, some previously nomadic hunter-gatherers have seen their populations rise, partly because of lowered infant mortality and partly because of shorter spacing between births.[5]

Whatever the case, by 1700–1200 BC the occupants of the Valley of Oaxaca were living in larger settlements than ever before. Throughout the Archaic, any social conflicts could have been resolved by splitting up the camp, with annoyed or unwelcome families "voting with their feet." Now quarreling families had to stay because they were tied to a strip of humid bottomland, perhaps a hectare or two of which had been set aside for their use. They had also invested labor in a house and a set of storage pits which they were reluctant to abandon.

A major challenge facing the villagers of the period 1700–1200 BC, therefore, was to find ways to integrate larger communities and resolve conflict without fissioning. Another challenge was to defend the area of good land on which they had settled, protecting their autonomy from envious neighbors. Both challenges led to social institutions not known from previous periods.

We have been led to expect those institutions from our reading of ethnographic data and social evolutionary theory. As we shall see in later chapters, however, detecting them in the archaeological record requires some work.

The Origins of the Village

No one is sure how the transition to village life took place. It may have been an erratic process, with various Archaic groups approaching sedentism in good years, backing away from it in drought years, then approaching it again. Increased reliance on domestic plants provides a centripetal pull to remain on the best land, and the difficulty of transporting a metric ton of maize discourages migration. On the other hand, a year with only 200 mm of rainfall could provide a strong centrifugal pull to disperse into family microbands again.

At Tlapacoya, on the shores of Lake Chalco in the southern Basin of Mexico, Christine Niederberger excavated the remains of an Archaic group who she believes had already established "prolonged or permanent residency in the same

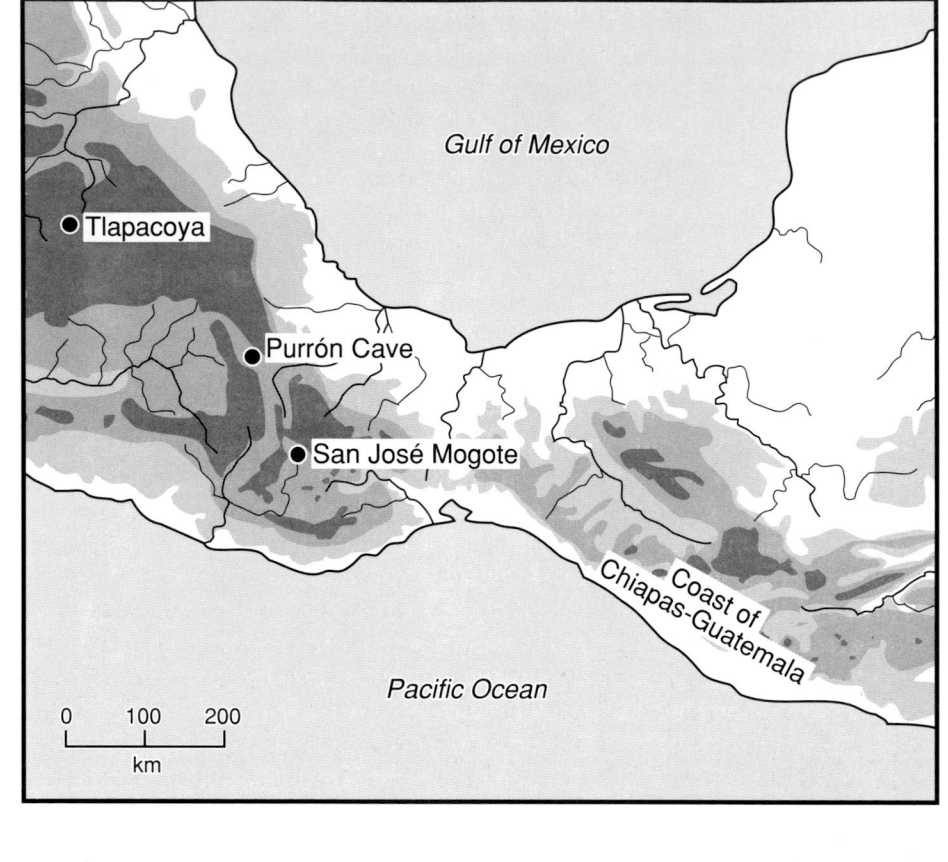

64 Some of the localities where archaeologists now seek the origins of sedentary life and pottery making in Mesoamerica.

site."[6] Her argument is that the unusually rich environment of the Chalco lakeshore might have provided year-round food. No permanent houses were found at the site, however. And while plants and animals from the rainy season and the dry season were present in the refuse, the same was true at Guilá Naquitz. All that is necessary to collect them is for a group to arrive in August (late rainy season) and stay until January (mid-dry season).

Whatever the case, Niederberger's data remind us that the Mexican Plateau was a mosaic of rich and poor environments. Some rich environments, like the shore of Lake Chalco, might have provided enough supplementary wild food to keep early farmers together in a macroband camp (or incipient village) during years of poor maize yields.

Hints of increasing sedentism can be found in the emergence of crafts that are more common in a village than a temporary camp. Pottery making is one of these. Pottery has advantages over gourds, since it can be made into much larger vessels and placed directly over cooking fires. Such larger and heavier containers are, in turn, the last thing a forager would want to drag over 50 km of mountain trails. In a village, the 10-liter water jar becomes a permanent fixture in the corner of the thatched hut, with a smaller gourd bowl becoming its dipper.

The Purrón and Espiridión Complexes

Some time between 1900 and 1400 BC, the Indians of the Tehuacán and Oaxaca Valleys began to make undecorated buff-to-brown pottery in a few simple shapes: hemispherical bowls, globular jars with necks, globular jars without necks. Most of the shapes look like pottery imitations of gourd vessels. Our sample of this early pottery is limited to 389 broken fragments from two archaeological sites. The older sample, 127 fragments, comes from Purrón Cave in the Tehuacán Valley, and has been called the Purrón Complex.[7] A younger sample, 262 fragments, comes from San José Mogote on the Atoyac River in the Valley of Oaxaca.[8] The latter sample, called the Espiridión Complex, was associated with the remains of a wattle-and-daub house in what was apparently a village. The Purrón sample, which came from two living floors in a rockshelter, could have been left by a "task group" sent out from an undiscovered village somewhere nearby.

So meagre is our evidence from this period that we cannot reconstruct its pattern of settlement and subsistence, much less its social organization. The most we can say is that the first permanent village now overlooked the humid alluvium of the Atoyac River in the Valley of Oaxaca.

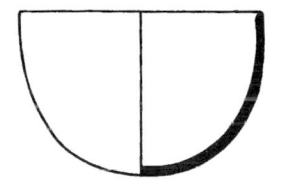

65 Some of Mexico's earliest pottery vessels imitated the shape of a gourd bowl.

66 A gourd bowl (*above*) compared with an early hemispherical pottery bowl from Oaxaca (*below*). Note that the pottery vessel even has "dimples" on the rim where the gourd vessel has its stem scars. Diameter of gourd vessel, 13.5 cm.

67 (*Left, above*) Some of Mexico's earliest pottery was found at Purrón Cave in the arid Tehuacán Valley.

68 (*Left, below*) San José Mogote, an open-air site in the less arid Valley of Oaxaca, has also produced early pottery.

Creating Prestige in Egalitarian Society

One of the most misunderstood words in evolutionary theory is "egalitarian." Nearly all hunting-gathering societies are described as egalitarian; so are most autonomous village societies.[1]

Ask ten archaeologists to define an egalitarian society, however, and five will reply, "a society in which everyone is equal in prestige or status." That answer is wrong, since there is no society in which everyone is equal in prestige or status. The skilled man selected as Hunt Leader during a Great Basin antelope drive has greater prestige than the average hunter-gatherer.[2] The Chimbu entrepreneur who accumulates the resources to build a Men's House for his village has greater prestige than the average New Guinea tribesman.[3]

The ethnologists who refer to hunting-gathering and autonomous-village societies as "egalitarian" do not mean to imply that such societies are lacking in status differences. They mean that any status differences are *achieved, not inherited*. Individuals in egalitarian societies can acquire prestige through advanced age, personal accomplishment, or the accumulation of valued goods. But they do not *inherit* high status, as happens in societies with chiefly lineages or a stratum of nobles.

Unfortunately, many archaeologists have taken "egalitarian" to mean "homogeneous." They assume that people in such societies are as alike as coins made at the same mint, and when – as inevitably happens – they find evidence for heterogeneity, they wrongly conclude that they have discovered a "chiefdom."

With increasing frequency, we see phrases like "complex food-collectors" or "precocious complexity" in the archaeological literature. The adjectives are superfluous. They tell us only that some of our colleagues expected a simplicity and homogeneity in egalitarian society that never was there to begin with. To cry "rank society," some archaeologists need only find a few burials with shell artifacts – as if members of egalitarian societies never wore ornaments.

Prestige in Egalitarian Societies

For an example of heterogeneity in egalitarian society, we can turn to the Pueblo Indians of the Southwestern United States. Their villages may be autonomous, but their society is filled with status differences. Among the Tewa, for example, there are three levels of "being" on earth and three more in the spirit world.[4]

At the top of the earthly ladder are the *patowa* or Made People, whose years of skilled community service have made them ritual leaders. They have ascended to their position through a hierarchy of fraternal orders, beginning with the "scalp" society and rising through the "hunt," "warm clown," and "bear medicine" societies. At the bottom of the ladder are Dry Food People, common Tewa who occupy no official position in the political or ritual system. On a regular basis, the Made People may select ritual assistants or *towa é* from among the Dry Food People, but after a period of service these assistants return to the Dry Food pool. While serving, the *towa é* mediate between the Made People and the Dry Food People; the Made People, on the other hand, mediate between the human world and the spirit world.

The Tewa tell us a great deal about the institutions of autonomous village society. The village is divided into groups of related families and the groups are linked by fraternal orders which draw members from both units. The basis for belonging to one of these orders is ritual and community service. The focal point of ritual is a special structure (called a *kiva* in the Tewa case), and the rituals involve special costumes, artifacts, and paraphernalia. While there is no hereditary ranking – all members of the village are theoretically born equal – great differences in prestige exist among adults, because some have the skill and ambition to ascend the ritual ladder while others do not. Significantly, more prestigious individuals are thought to have a closer relationship with the spirit world.

Still another set of autonomous village societies can be found in the New Guinea highlands.[5-8] Once again, in the absence of hereditary ranking, the ritual system bears the burden of producing differences in achieved status – what Raymond Kelly has called "a hierarchy of virtue."[9]

Among the Chimbu there are *yomba pondo*, "Big Men," who are prominent and vocal in clan meetings, participate widely in interregional exchange, and have ties outside their own community.[10] Below them are "Prominent Men" who are more productive than average, have two or more wives, and claim some dependents and followers. "Ordinary Men" produce enough for their families, but have few aspirations to prominence. At the bottom of the ladder are *yogo*, "Nothing Men" or "Rubbish Men," who fail to keep a wife, produce little, and participate only marginally in exchange.

Chimbu Big Men become leaders solely through their own ambition and achievements in food production, group activities, intervillage warfare, and ceremony. According to Paula Brown, "They propose enterprises and attract followers, but they cannot punish those who fail to follow."[11] Big Men sponsor feasts, brag, threaten, assassinate, and lead raids against other groups to avenge insults or attacks on their followers. They also assemble the resources and manpower to build the Men's House which, like the Tewa *kiva*, is the focal point of ritual activity.

Fredrik Barth has given us a fascinating look at such Men's Houses, or thatched-roof "temples," among New Guinea's Mountain Ok.[12] One type, the *katiam*, is a temple for curating hunting trophies and making sacrifices to increase agricultural yields. Miscellaneous bones of the ancestors may also be kept there. Access to the *katiam* depends on whether a man is uninitiated, partly initiated, or fully initiated into the ritual system. At one Ok village, 11 fully initiated men were found living in the *katiam*; 15 partly initiated men had attended rituals there; and 128 uninitiated men had never been allowed inside. Secret hunts were planned there by full initiates, then carried out with the assistance of partial initiates. After the hunt, some animals were offered to the ancestors by consuming them around one of several sacred fires.

A second type of Ok temple, the *yolam* or "Ancestor House," is a non-residential structure for agricultural increase and warfare rituals. The *yolam* may contain two sacred fires, as well as multiple skulls of ancestors from many different clans. Only fully-initiated men can enter to make prayers and offerings; most members of the village are excluded. Here raids on enemy villages are planned, and rituals to make them successful are carried out. Not surprisingly, such temples are often the first structures burned when a village is attacked.

Our New Guinea examples reveal a few more of the institutions of autonomous village society: (1) It is very important to keep one's ancestors around. An individual is integrated into a large group of relatives by shared descent; the spirits of the ancestors are invited to take part in descendants' activities; the continued presence of the ancestors, either as burials or curated skeletal parts, makes farming and warfare successful, reinforcing one's right to a particular plot of land. (2) Men's and women's ritual takes place in different places – the men's in the Men's House, the women's in the home. (3) In spite of egalitarian ideology, the focal point of men's ritual is a house one cannot enter until he has achieved a certain level of prestige. (4) The building of the Men's House is likely to have been directed by a major entrepreneur – a man who can accumulate surplus, carry out trade, give feasts, feed workmen, direct labor, and lead a raid.

Settlement Choices in the Tierras Largas Phase

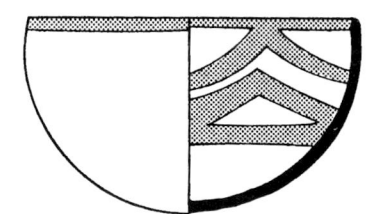

69 Hemispherical bowls of the Tierras Largas phase frequently bore stripes or chevrons of red paint.

Let us now look at the first period in the prehistory of the Valley of Oaxaca for which the institutions of the autonomous village are detectable. That period is the Tierras Largas phase (1400–1150 BC). It is also the first phase whose pottery is decorated in such a way as to make it instantly recognizable on survey. That decoration – featuring bands, stripes, and chevrons of red paint – has made it possible for the Settlement Pattern Project to locate at least nineteen permanent settlements of the Tierras Largas phase.[13]

Examination of Tierras Largas phase settlement patterns reveals several kinds of heterogeneity. All but one of the nineteen permanent settlements are hamlets of less than 3 ha. Most, in fact, are no more than a hectare, or about the size of Gheo-Shih. That means that the smallest known Tierras Largas phase hamlet was about as big as the largest known Archaic camp.

The remaining Tierras Largas phase settlement is a horseshoe-shaped cluster of nine discrete residential areas, totaling roughly 7 ha. This loosely aggregated village, San José Mogote, is perhaps three times as large as the second largest site of its period, and seven times the size of a typical hamlet. It also has features not found in any smaller community, suggesting that more than size was involved.

There are several ways to estimate the population of the valley during the Tierras Largas phase. The Settlement Pattern Project used William T. Sanders' "Compact Low-Density Village" coefficient of 10–25 persons/ha;[14] this coefficient yields estimates ranging from 185 to 463 persons, with a mean of 325. We, on the other hand, based our estimates on excavations at the hamlet of Tierras Largas (the type site for the phase), which suggest that one hectare of settlement might have had five to ten households, or 25–50 persons.[15] This approach produces estimates for the valley ranging from 463 to 925 persons, with a mean of 693. The Settlement Pattern Project estimates San José Mogote, the largest community in the valley, to have had 71–186 persons. Our estimate, based on exca-

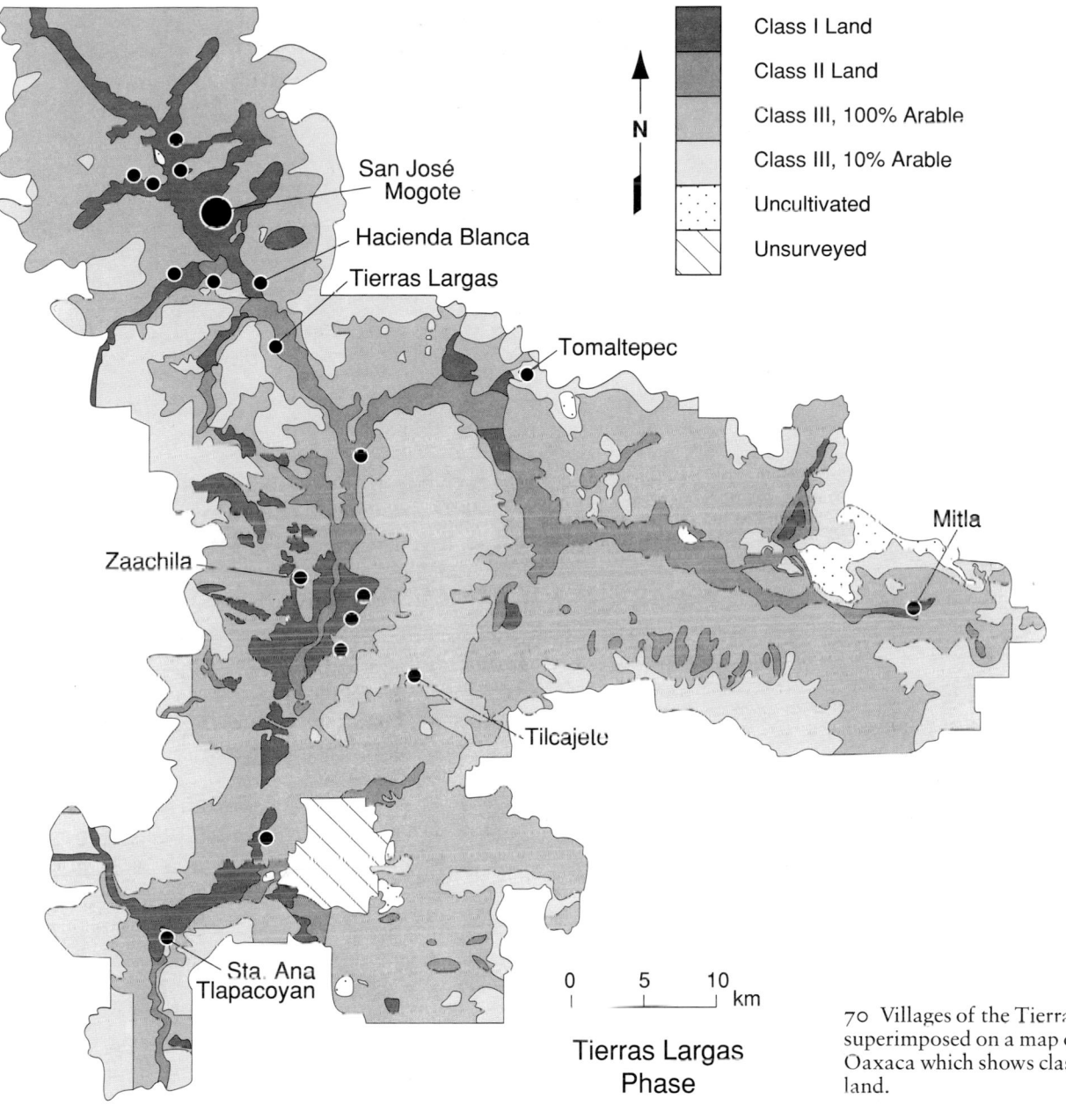

Class I Land
Class II Land
Class III, 100% Arable
Class III, 10% Arable
Uncultivated
Unsurveyed

N

San José Mogote
Hacienda Blanca
Tierras Largas
Tomaltepec
Mitla
Zaachila
Tilcajete
Sta. Ana Tlapacoyan

0   5   10 km

Tierras Largas Phase

70 Villages of the Tierras Largas phase, superimposed on a map of the Valley of Oaxaca which shows classes of agricultural land.

vation, would be 170–340 persons. In spite of the different methods used, these estimates overlap in the 170–186 person range.

Now consider another source of heterogeneity: Tierras Largas phase hamlets were not distributed evenly over the valley. More than 50 percent of the estimated Tierras Largas population lived at nine communities in the Etla region, the smallest of the valley's three arms. A group of four hamlets were clustered in the center of the Valle Grande, but otherwise that largest arm of the valley was sparsely settled. Sparsest of all was settlement in the Tlacolula subvalley.

Atoyac River

Site 1-1-16

Hacienda Blanca

71 Site 1-1-16, near Hacienda Blanca in the Etla subvalley, shows a typical pattern for Tierras Largas phase villages. The site covers a low spur of piedmont surrounded by Class I land (the alluvial plain of the Atoyac River). View to the south (1970 photo).

Why should the Etla subvalley have attracted so many people? The answer, we believe, lies in the differential distribution of Class I land, a highly prized zone which today has yields of more than 2 metric tons of maize per hectare (see Box). According to a study by Linda Nicholas, of the 12,740 ha of Class I land in the Valley of Oaxaca, 5117 ha can be found in the Etla subvalley.[16] Another 3345 ha occur in the northern Valle Grande, the area with the second largest number of Tierras Largas hamlets. No other part of the valley comes close, with the eastern Tlacolula region having less than 400 ha. When one superimposes all Tierras Largas phase communities on Nicholas' land use map of the valley, sixteen of nineteen sites are adjacent to Class I land.

The Classification of Agricultural Land in the Valley of Oaxaca

In 1973, cultural geographer Anne Kirkby divided farm land in the Valley of Oaxaca into six categories, based on how it was used:

1. Water Table Farming
2. Marginal Water Table Farming
3. Canal Irrigation
4. Good Floodwater Farming
5. Poor Floodwater Farming
6. Dry Farming

In 1989, archaeologist Linda Nicholas consolidated Kirkby's six categories into three classes, based on maize yields:

I   *Class I Land* consists of "water table" and "canal irrigable land" that produces the highest and most dependable yields (usually more than 2 metric tons of maize per hectare with today's races of maize).

II   *Class II Land* consists of "marginal water table" and "good floodwater farming" land, which usually produces 1.2–2.0 metric tons of maize per hectare with today's races of maize

III   *Class III Land* consists of "poor floodwater farming" and "dry farming" land, which usually produces less than 1.2 metric tons of maize per hectare with today's races of maize.

For valley-wide plotting of archaeological sites on land types, Nicholas' land use areas are more convenient because they are larger and less mosaic than Kirkby's. For certain early periods, however, one must sometimes use Kirkby's more fine-grained classification, because it separates water table farming (which was important by 1300 BC) from canal irrigation (which may have evolved later).

We conclude that, with a few unexplained exceptions, Tierras Largas families were building their houses on low, non-flooding slopes immediately overlooking Class I land (usually *yuh kohp*, or humid alluvium). Not only did the Etla region have more of this land, it was also the narrowest arm of the valley. Etla farmers, therefore, had the shortest trip to the forested mountains that provided them with deer, wild plants, fuel, and wood for construction. Those environmental factors may help to explain the differences in population among various arms of the valley, but they fall short of explaining the disproportionately large size of San José Mogote.

Tierras Largas Phase Agriculture

Exposed as they are to the elements, early villages lack the rich plant remains of dry caves. One can get carbonized vegetation to float to the surface, however, by submerging ashy debris in water.[17] The carbonized plants from early farming communities in the Valley of Oaxaca include cereals, legumes and other vegetables, condiments, and even tree crops. Although there were later additions to the inventory, most of the basic staples of later Zapotec civilization were present by 1500–500 BC.

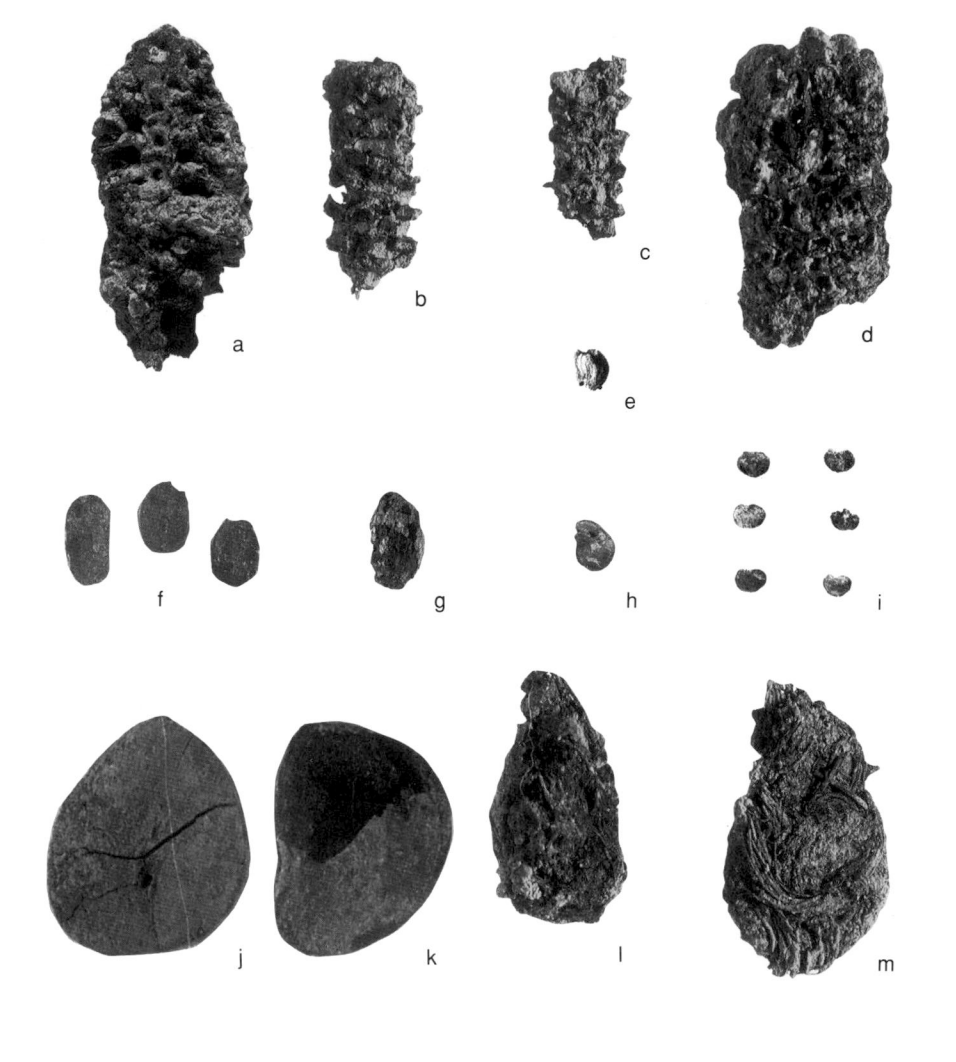

72 Carbonized plants from villages of 1500–500 BC in the Valley of Oaxaca. (*a*) Partial maize cob, Tierras Largas phase; (*b,c*) small maize cobs with indurated glumes (the result of crossing with teosinte), San José phase; (*d*) fragment of maize cob, San José phase; (*e*) fruit case of teosinte, San José phase; (*f*) common beans, Guadalupe phase; (*g*) squash seed, San José phase; (*h*) seed from prickly pear cactus fruit, Tierras Largas phase; (*i*) chile pepper seeds, San José phase; (*j,k*) avocado seeds, Guadalupe phase; (*l,m*) quids of chewed agave fiber, Rosario phase. Length of (*a*) 3.2 cm.

During the latter millennium, of which the Tierras Largas phase was but the opening chapter, Oaxaca villagers grew maize related to Nal-Tel and Chapalote, two ancient races still found in Mexico and Central America. Teosinte evidently grew alongside maize, either as a field weed or a deliberate crop; maize acquires drought resistance and hybrid vigor when the two plants cross. Squashes and common beans were also planted, perhaps right among the corn. Chile peppers added flavor and vitamins to the diet, and avocados had become the first tree crop. Both agaves and prickly pear were eaten, but since both plants are propagated vegetatively, it is hard to tell if the carbonized remains were wild or domestic.

Villagers continued to collect some wild plants from the piedmont and mountains, such as black walnuts, pods from relatives of the acacia, and the fruits of the hackberry and organ cactus. With carbohydrates provided by maize and baked agave, protein from beans and venison, fats from avocados and game, and vitamins from fruits and chile peppers, Tierras Largas villagers had access to a varied diet. Moreover, given the size and productivity of Tierras Largas phase maize cobs, we suspect that the Valley of Oaxaca could have supported even more people than those for which we have evidence.[18]

These early farmers continued to hunt deer and peccary, but their hunting strategy had changed: it apparently no longer involved flint-tipped atlatl darts, since flint points are virtually absent in their refuse. It is not clear what this change means. It could reflect a shift to larger hunting parties, who used fire-hardened wooden spears and long nets stretched between two or more hunters; such strategies were known in Chiapas, to the south of Oaxaca.[19]

Tierras Largas phase villagers also trapped rabbits, doves, quail, and other small game, dug up pocket gophers from their cornfields, and collected mud turtles from river backwaters. Domestic dogs – thought to have been introduced to the Mexican Plateau from North America between 2500 and 1500 BC – flourished in Tierras Largas phase villages, and were regularly eaten. So far as we can tell, every household had access to venison. This egalitarian situation would change in later periods, when the population had grown so large that there would not be enough deer for all.

Life in a Tierras Largas Phase Hamlet

For a glimpse of life in a hamlet of the Tierras Largas phase, we can turn to the "type site" for which the period is named. Situated on a piedmont spur like the one shown in ill. 71, Tierras Largas overlooks the Atoyac River floodplain in the southern part of the Etla subvalley. Although Tierras Largas technically overlooks Class II land (see Box), the locale is very close to the 2000 kg/ha minimum for Class I land.

During the Tierras Largas phase, this site was a hamlet of 5–10 households covering an area of 1.58–2.24 ha.[20] Each household seems to have consisted of one house, a dooryard for outdoor activities, and a series of nearby storage pits. Household LTL-1 of the late Tierras Largas phase can serve as an example. The wattle-and-daub house, whitewashed with a solution of lime, covered about 4 × 6 m; a set of storage pits with an average capacity of 1.5 m³ lay in the dooryard to the west.

This family of perhaps 4–5 persons had engaged in agriculture (as shown by carbonized maize kernels and avocado seeds), food preparation (as shown by fourteen fragments of grinding stones), hunting and trapping (as shown by the bones of deer, cottontail, jackrabbit, gopher, and mud turtle), and sewing (as indicated by bone needles). There were also clues to ritual and social life. In one storage pit were the wing bones of *Ara militaris*, a blue-green macaw widely used

73 Artist's reconstruction of Household LTL-1 at Tierras Largas.

for its feathers. Another pit produced fragments of a turtle-shell drum made from the lowland species *Dermatemys mawii*.

Both the macaw and drum were imported from tropical regions outside the Valley of Oaxaca. As we mentioned earlier, autonomous village societies engage in a great deal of ritual, much of it involving food, drink, music, and costumes made from animal parts, feathers, and marine shell. Clearly, someone in Tierras Largas society was negotiating for ritual paraphernalia from other regions of Mexico, made more valuable by the distance from which it had come.

Since the Late Archaic at Cueva Blanca, the occupants of the valley had received small numbers of sea shells from the coast. Now, with escalating ritual needs and a population estimated at five to ten times that of the Archaic, the trickle of shell was becoming a steady stream. Mother-of-pearl (*Pinctada* sp.), spiny oyster (*Spondylus* sp.), and estuary snails from the Pacific Coast were imported by late Tierras Largas phase communities.

It appears that during the occupation of Household LTL-1, several family members had died and were buried near the house. One woman, 20–30 years of age, had been buried in the dooryard to the west; another adult woman had been buried in a storage pit, perhaps because it was conveniently open and unused at the time of her death.

In another storage pit, a man over 40 years of age had been buried fully extended, face up. It is significant that the fill of that pit included more than 70 burned fragments of cane-impressed daub from the walls of a house. It is possible that this man was a senior household head, after whose death the house was deliberately burned and its remains buried with him. Alternatively, he and his house might have been the victims of a raid.

Death and the Ancestors

The ancestors played several important roles in Tierras Largas phase society. One of the ways that autonomous villages are integrated is by having large groups of people claim descent from a common ancestor. Also, by burying their ancestors in graves or cemeteries in the settlement, villagers demonstrate to themselves and their neighbors that they have hereditary rights to a particular piece of the world.

The mountains and piedmont of the Valley of Oaxaca were still an "outfield" of undeveloped wilderness – *quijxi*, as today's Zapotec call it. Most likely this outfield was shared amicably, since all villagers needed access to pine poles, flint, lime, hematite pigment, game, and salt. But around each village there was now an "infield," improved by the building of houses, the digging of pits, the clearing of *yuh kohp*, and the burial of the ancestors. It is a virtual certainty that this infield was defended from outsiders.[21,22]

The way the ancestors were buried tells us that Tierras Largas phase society still lacked many of the later institutions of the historic Zapotec. None of the burials found so far show any sign of sumptuary goods. We have no cases of husband-wife burial; everyone, male or female, was treated as an individual. Burial positions were unstandardized. While most people were laid out in the extended position, they could be prone or supine; have their arms at their sides, or folded on their chest; and face almost any direction.

Three burials from the late Tierras Largas phase (one from Tierras Largas and two from San José Mogote) stand out as different. All are middle-aged men

74 Workmen at San José Mogote excavate the burial of a seated male.

75 (*Below*) Burial 29 of San José Mogote, a man more than 40 years of age, buried in a seated position.

Red-on-buff hemispherical bowl

and all are buried in the seated position, so tightly flexed as to suggest they were in tightly-wrapped bundles. For various reasons we suspect that these were individuals of high *achieved* status, perhaps analogous to the "fully initiated" men of highland New Guinea or the Made People who had passed through all levels of Pueblo society. We are influenced in this regard by the importance of seated burials in later Mexican and Central American societies (Chapter 8). We stress, however, that nothing found with these Tierras Largas phase burials implies *inherited* status.

Another clue to the importance of the ancestors in village life may be found in the human figurines of the Tierras Largas phase. Made of the same fired clay

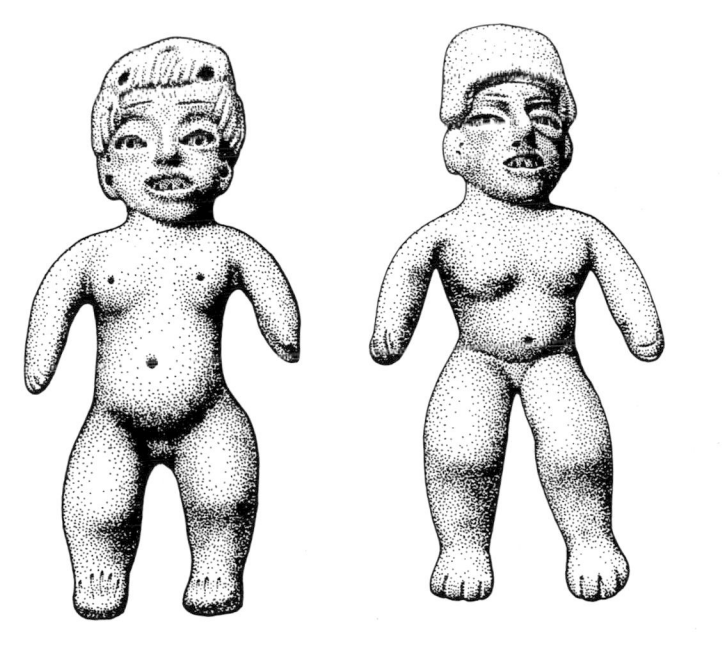

76,77 Tierras Largas phase figurines. (*Left*) female; (*right*) male.

78 Aerial view of San José Mogote, on a piedmont spur surrounded by Class I land in the Etla subvalley. The earliest part of the site lies nearest the Atoyac River. South is at the top of the photo.

as the pottery vessels, they increased in frequency over the course of the period. The majority represent women, and all occur in households or household refuse.[23] They are never found in and around the small public buildings to be described below, which we consider analogous to the Men's Houses or "initiates' temples" of autonomous villages. We consider most of these figurines to represent female ancestors, and to be part of a woman's ritual complex centered in the home. We believe that there was a separate men's ritual complex, focused on Men's Houses at some distance from the household.

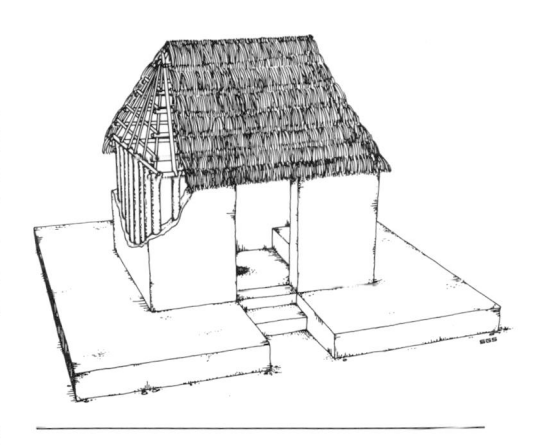

Life in the Valley's Largest Village

As we saw earlier, San José Mogote was the largest community in the Valley of Oaxaca by several orders of magnitude. The site is dispersed at the household level, but clustered relative to the rest of the Etla region. It consists of nine discrete residential areas – each virtually as large as a hamlet elsewhere in the valley – occupying 7 ha of a piedmont spur on the left bank of the Atoyac River. The spur is surrounded on three sides by Class I land, but that fact alone is not sufficient to explain its unusual size and configuration. Someone, or some institution, was holding together an unprecedented number of people.

Essential to understanding the site, we believe, is the westernmost residential area, where 300 m² was given over to non-residential architecture. At any given moment in the phase, this area was dominated by a one-room building which we regard as analogous to the *yolam* of the Mountain Ok or the *kiva* of a Southwestern Pueblo. Periodically each such building was razed, and a new one was built on virtually the same spot. Measuring no more than 4 × 6 m, these buildings could only have accommodated a fraction of the community. Given their small size we believe they were restricted to the equivalent of "full initiates," that is, a subgroup of the men in the village.

While these buildings had wattle-and-daub walls, they differed from ordinary residences in several ways: (1) They were oriented roughly 8 degrees west of true north, an orientation shared by later religious buildings in Oaxaca. (2) They contained 2–3 times as many pine posts as ordinary houses. (3) Their floors and walls (inside and out) were given multiple coats of true lime plaster, making them pure white. (4) The buildings themselves were set on rectangular platforms up to 40 cm high and lime-plastered; access to the door was by small steps inset in the platform. (5) Some of these buildings had a centrally placed, lime-plastered storage pit incorporated into the floor.

When discovered intact, the aforementioned pits were filled with powdered lime, perhaps stored for use with a ritual plant such as wild tobacco (*quèeza* in Zapotec), jimson weed (*nocuàna còhui*), or morning glory. At the time of the Spanish Conquest, both the Zapotec and the Mixtec used wild tobacco mixed with lime during their rituals.[24-26] The Zapotec believed that it had curative powers and could increase physical strength,[27] making it an appropriate drug to use before raids.[28]

We do not believe that anyone actually lived in these buildings, which were swept virtually clean. Thus they cannot be compared to buildings like the New Guinea *katiam*, where some senior males actually reside. We see them as limited-access structures where a small number of fully initiated men could assemble to plan raids or hunts, carry out agricultural rituals, smoke or ingest sacred plants, and/or communicate with the spirits. While no bones or relics of the ancestors

79 (*Above*) Artist's reconstruction of a Tierras Largas phase "Men's House."

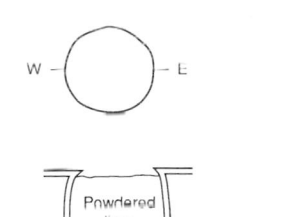

80 Plan and cross-section of a lime-filled pit from a Tierras Largas phase "Men's House."

81 Workmen build a protective wall around the lime-plastered floor of Structure 6, a Tierras Largas phase "Men's House" at San José Mogote. The centrally placed pit for powdered lime is clearly visible.

were found in these small white buildings, it is perhaps significant that two of our seated burials of middle-aged men were found nearby.

Who built such buildings? First, there is no suggestion, either in the labor effort or the raw materials involved, that anyone outside San José Mogote was involved. Despite its size, we have no evidence that this one village had overcome the autonomy of nearby hamlets. Second, an actor-centered approach forces us to recognize that someone planned the construction of each of these buildings, organized and fed the labor force, directed the work, and took credit for it. San José Mogote must therefore have had a succession of self-selected, socially ambitious leaders who knew how to turn their hard-won agricultural surplus into prestigious public works. Such men, the ethnographic record tells us, accumulate more than their share of wives, kinsmen, and affines, as well as a body of followers who do their bidding in return for favors and reflected glory. It was probably this kind of leadership, and not simply Class I land, that attracted nine clusters of families to San José Mogote during the Tierras Largas phase.

Now let us consider for a moment how the "system" may have shaped the Tierras Largas phase actors. Think back to Wiessner's dichotomy between: (1) risk pooled at the group level; and (2) risk accepted at the family level.[29] As far back as the Archaic, Oaxaca peoples had begun to accept risk at the family level. In the hamlets of the Tierras Largas phase, the nuclear family of 4–5 persons still appears to have been an important unit of residence, planting, storage, and risk acceptance, separated by 20–40 m from its nearest neighbor.

In a system based on private storage, the potential is always there for one family to plant more, work harder, and accumulate more agricultural surplus than its neighbors. Eventually the head of such a family can support more spouses, attract more followers, engage in more trade, and underwrite the construction of more public buildings than can other families. Potentially this might violate an egalitarian ethic, but there can be mitigating circumstances. In some societies, agricultural success is attributed to supernatural assistance from the spirit world, and the building of a Men's House is seen as public-spirited. With hard work, conspicuous generosity, and a bit of help from the spirit world, great differences in prestige can be created in egalitarian society.

The Wider Context of the Tierras Largas Phase

The social changes of the Tierras Largas phase, of course, did not take place in a vacuum. Despite the rugged mountains surrounding the Valley of Oaxaca, the villagers of the Tierras Largas phase were in contact with societies undergoing similar changes.

Widely-shared styles of decorating pottery link the Valley of Oaxaca to many other regions. For example, the Tierras Largas phase shares a complex of red-on-buff bowls, bottles, and jars with communities in the Basin of Mexico, the Tehuacán Valley of Puebla, the Nochixtlán Valley of northern Oaxaca, and the Cuicatlán Cañada. This highland "red-on-buff" sphere fades out as one reaches the lowlands of Tehuantepec, where it is replaced by a pottery sphere linking Chiapas and southern Veracruz.[30]

From various other regions, perhaps through the strategy of establishing "trading partners," Tierras Largas households received foreign products. Some, like obsidian, apparently reached families even in the smallest hamlets. Others, like glossy black pottery made on non-local clay, seem only to have reached San

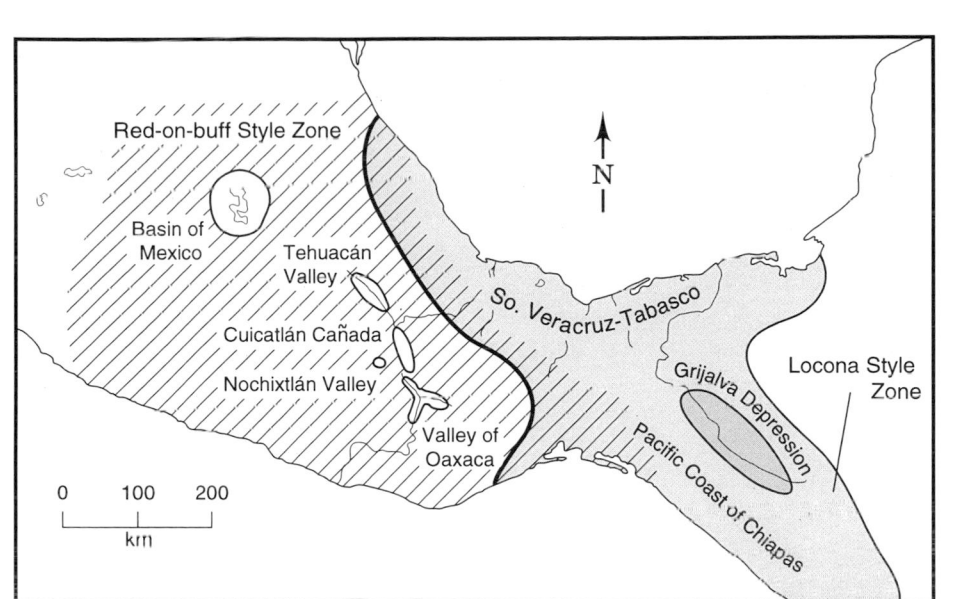

82 Approximate limits of the "red-on-buff" pottery style zone to which the Valley of Oaxaca belonged during the Tierras Largas phase. To the east lay the Locona pottery style zone.

José Mogote. Still other products, like marine shells, reached San José Mogote in larger amounts than those seen at small hamlets. This could mean that the same Big Men who attracted so many followers to San José Mogote were also heavily involved in exchange.

Some of the mechanisms of this exchange can be deduced by tracing the movement of gray obsidian from a source near Otumba in the Basin of Mexico. A study by Jane Pires-Ferreira shows that the farther a village lay from Otumba, the less obsidian it received from that source.[31] Villages within 40 km of Otumba (a 1–2-day trip) received nearly all their obsidian from that source; villages 245–390 km away (an 8–12-day trip) received perhaps a third of their obsidian from Otumba. This pattern suggests that Otumba obsidian passed slowly from villages in the Basin of Mexico, to villages in Tehuacán, and on to villages in Oaxaca, with each village keeping part of what it received and passing the rest "down the line."[32]

Just as interesting was the heterogeneity of use once obsidian had reached villages like Tierras Largas.[33] It appears that all households had some access to obsidian, but the sources and amounts used varied greatly from house to house. Household LTL-1 (the one described earlier in this chapter) received 84 percent of its obsidian from a source 100 km north of Tehuacán. A nearby household received 70 percent of its obsidian from Otumba. Some houses had as many as 25 pieces of obsidian, others as few as one. This is the pattern one would expect if each household procured its obsidian on its own. It is a pattern typical of autonomous village societies, in which each family may have trading partners – in-laws, friends, or fictive kinsmen – in neighboring regions.

We believe that this kind of exchange, negotiated by individual families with their trading partners and presumably reciprocal, was the dominant "trade" of the Tierras Largas phase. Only at San José Mogote do we see hints that more elaborate trade, perhaps negotiated by the same Big Men who directed the building of Men's Houses, was beginning to emerge. Such trade may have extended beyond the red-on-buff sphere, linking Oaxaca to more distant regions.

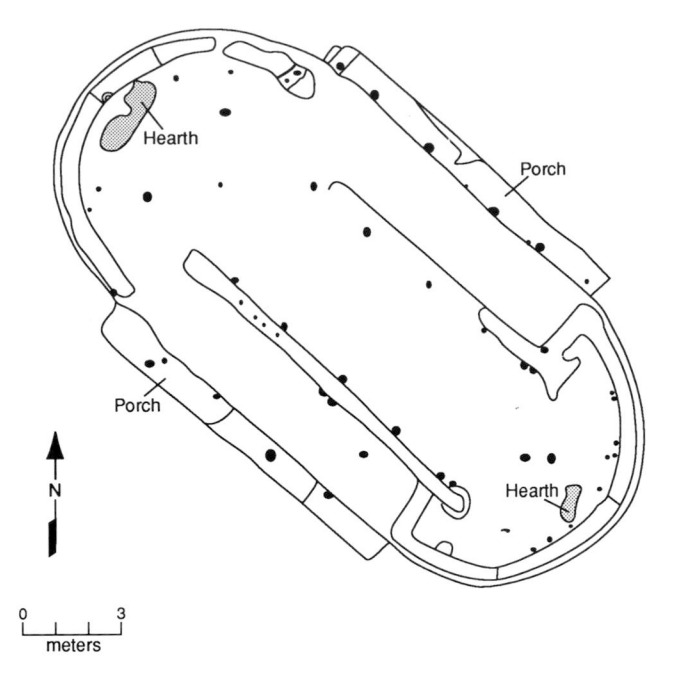

83 Floor 4 of Mound 6 at Paso de la Amada, the base of a possible "initiates' temple" from the Chiapas Coast. Note the double porches.

What was taking place in those more distant regions? Some of them were undergoing evolutionary changes similar to Oaxaca's, while others were not.

The Pacific Coast of Chiapas seems to have been a second region of Mesoamerica where strong community leaders were emerging, attracting followers and competing to erect bigger and bigger "initiates' temples." The Chiapas structures were not, however, similar to the ones at San José Mogote, which presently are unique in their rectangular shape, early use of white stucco, lime-filled pits, and orientation. The Chiapas buildings are so different as to suggest an independent lowland architectural tradition; they are also much larger than their Oaxaca counterparts.

For a glimpse of these buildings we turn to the coastal village of Paso de la Amada, excavated by John Clark and Michael Blake.[34,35] Mound 6, one of the largest earthen mounds on that site, contained a sequence of *at least* seven structures – perhaps more – rebuilt one above the other between 1400 and 1100 BC. All had virtually the same orientation, roughly northwest–southeast.

As can be seen in ills. 83 and 84, these structures were oval wattle-and-daub buildings. The one associated with Floor 4, shown in ill. 83, was 21 m long by 11 m wide and rested on an earthen platform 0.75 m high. It was open on both of its long sides, and each of those doorways was flanked by a porch above an earthen stairway. At opposite ends of the building were a pair of hearths, reminiscent of the twin "sacred fires" of the New Guinea *yolam*.

Like the Tierras Largas phase Men's Houses with which they are contemporary, the Chiapas structures were built one above the other on Mound 6. A later stage, associated with Floor 2, measured 17.5 by 9 m and had an apsidal plan with three large center posts supporting the roof; at least 25 more posts appeared along the walls, which were daubed with clay but not lime-plastered. Blake estimates that it would have taken 25 persons 20 days to build this structure.[36]

While it is not always easy to know whether wattle-and-daub structures are

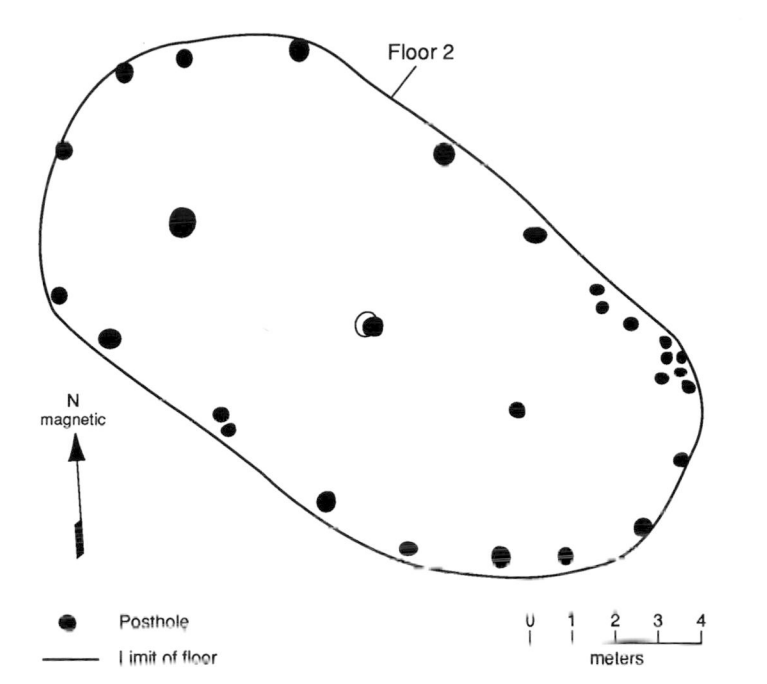

84 Floor 2 of Mound 6 at Paso de la Amada, the base of a possible "initiates' temple" built above Floor 4 and with the same orientation.

residences or public buildings, there are 7 reasons why we interpret these very important Paso de la Amada structures as the latter. (1) They were built on one of the village's highest mounds, a typical location for public buildings. (2) Several of the structures had subfloor dedicatory offerings, a feature common in temples but not in early residences. (3) Each structure involved a labor invest ment well beyond the capabilities of a family; we associate such effort with public construction. (4) While it was not unusual for early Mesoamerican temples to be rebuilt many times on the same spot and to the same plan, we know of no examples of early residences rebuilt seven times in this way. (5) The twin hearths and large twin doorways of Floor 4 look to us like the features of a ritual structure. Like the later temples of Monte Negro (see Chapter 12), they suggest a building where initiates entered through one doorway, participated in ritual, and exited out the opposite doorway. (6) Several buildings in the sequence were burned, possibly intentionally. Temples, as we saw in the case of the Mountain Ok and those we will see later in Oaxaca, were the frequent targets of raids. (7) Several of the buildings had large decorated serving vessels and food refuse asso ciated with them. Ritual meals are one of the frequent activities at buildings where "full initiates" congregate.

We strongly suspect, therefore, that the Valley of Oaxaca was only one of several regions of Mexico where charismatic individuals were able to organize labor for public construction, attract large numbers of followers, organize trade, and stimulate craft production. In none of those areas, however, do we as yet see evidence that leaders controlled more than one village. The Paso de la Amada buildings, like those of the Tierras Largas phase, show no evidence of construc tion materials contributed by other communities. What they do show is a shape and orientation so different from Oaxaca's that the two architectural traditions must have had independent origins. This is an important point, because it sug gests we are dealing with parallel evolution.

Finally, we are struck by our current lack of evidence for similar public buildings on the Gulf Coast of southern Veracruz and Tabasco. Thirty years ago that coastal plain, sometimes referred to as the Olmec region, was labeled "precocious" in its social evolution. The last two decades have shown that view to be partly true, partly hyperbole, and partly the result of our previous ignorance of Chiapas and Oaxaca. There were indeed villages in the Olmec region between 1400 and 1200 BC, but their pottery has recently been described as a "country-cousin version" of the more sophisticated ceramics at contemporary sites on the Chiapas Coast.[37]

The Limitations on Growth: Continuities with the Archaic

One of the most important continuities with the Archaic shown by Tierras Largas society is that leadership was still not hereditary. By accumulating followers, a self-selected Big Man can temporarily overcome the tendency of his village to fission when it reaches a certain size; when he dies, there is no longer a way to hold it together. Through his leadership in raiding, he may inspire the ephemeral alliance of two villages against a common enemy; when he dies, they go their separate ways. Without permanent leadership, it is less likely that villages will become truly large, or that networks of subject hamlets will develop around them.

These limitations on growth were made clear by Douglas Oliver in his study of the *mumis*, or Big Men, on Bougainville in the Solomon Islands.[38] These charismatic leaders' competition for prestige stimulated agricultural production, the building of Men's Houses, the accumulation of shell ornaments, the crafting of goods for rituals, and the taking of captives from other villages. The *mumi's* high level of prestige was tolerated because other men believed that he possessed magic, or was aided by powerful demons; when he died, it was often attributed to witchcraft performed by the sorcerers of a rival village. The death of an unusually powerful *mumi* frequently led to the violent breakup of his realm of influence, often to avoid the black magic that had caused his death. Much of his shell "money" might be burned on his funeral pyre, and his ghost would be invoked long after his death, in the belief that it retained his magic.

While showing us how stimulating a Big Man can be to the productivity of an egalitarian society, Oliver's study also shows the *mumi's* limitations. He could organize scores of followers, but he could not pass the role of leader on to his son. He was seen as having powerful supernatural help, but there was no expectation that his heirs would have it. He could command his own followers to help him, and fine them if they refused; he could also pay members of other villages to help him, but because those villages remained autonomous, he could neither command them to do so nor fine them if they refused.

What further changes must take place in order for these limitations to be overcome? First, a way of ensuring that the village would *always* be under the leadership of someone with powerful supernatural connections; second, a way of inducing smaller hamlets to give up their autonomy and become satellites of larger villages. We believe that both changes were to take place in Oaxaca during the next 300 years.

The Emergence of Rank and the Loss of Autonomy

In the evolution of any civilization there are defining moments, turning points when a new social framework is adopted. We believe that the period between 1200 and 1150 BC may have been such a point in the evolution of Zapotec civilization. It would seem that an important step was taken at that time, one whose effects can be seen during the 300-year period that followed. That period is called the San José phase (1150–850 BC), and we believe it was then that *rank*, or hereditary inequality, emerged in the Valley of Oaxaca. This chapter will be devoted to the question of how ranking began, and how archaeologists can identify it.

Archaeologists differ in their explanations of ranking. To some it is the inevitable outcome of population pressure on resources; to others it is the result of a change in *ideology*, or political philosophy. Ironically, even those who seek the causes of hereditary inequality in population pressure or control of strategic resources are likely to use ideological change as their proof that rank has emerged. That is, they turn to the symbols of hereditary status and the special ways in which highly ranked people are buried.

In this chapter we first consider evidence for hereditary inequality, the hallmark of rank society. We then consider evidence for the loss of village autonomy, Robert Carneiro's hallmark for the chiefdom.

One of the classic studies of ranking is Edmund Leach's study of the Kachin of highland Burma.[1] For centuries these mountain people maintained a *gumlao*, or egalitarian, society which contrasted with that of the Shan kingdoms in the nearby lowlands. But the Kachin region was a source of jade that Shan princes coveted, and the Shan eventually began sending noble women to marry Kachin leaders. These marriages raised the status of Kachin leaders, and gave their Shan fathers-in-law access to jade.

Intermarriage with Shan women overcame the egalitarian philosophy of some Kachin lineages, giving rise to *gumsa*, or rank, society. Now considering themselves a hereditary elite, some Kachin began to dress and act like Shan nobles, even emulating them by adopting Buddhism. The change was not irreversible, however, since this aristocratic behavior was irritating to other Kachin who had not accepted the new ideology. Periodically they would oust their Kachin "nobles" and revert to the old egalitarian system. For decades they oscillated between *gumlao* and *gumsa*.

A Model for the Origins of Ranking

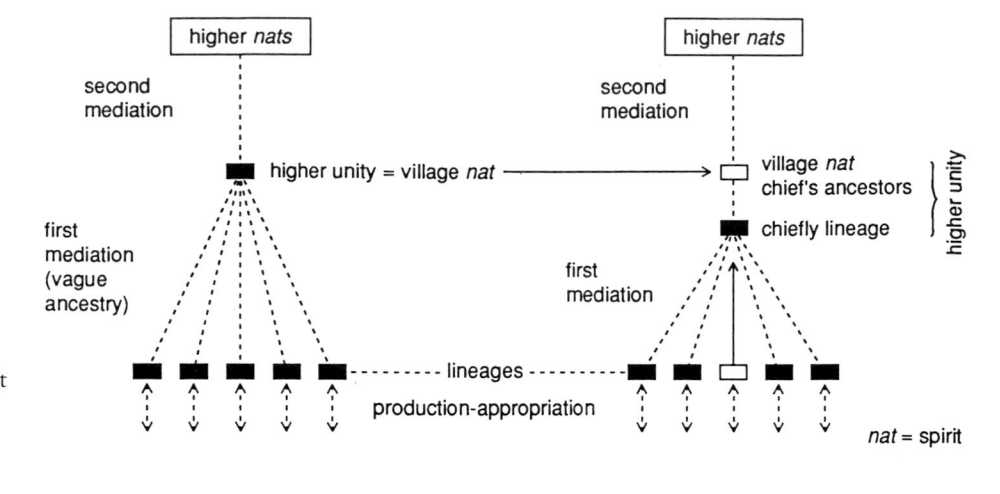

85 Jonathan Friedman's model for the shift from egalitarian to rank society in Southeast Asia.

Leach's study warns us that people cannot be forced to accept ranking if it runs counter to their political philosophy. As we learned from the Big Men of Bougainville, it is one thing to give orders and another to be obeyed.

While the Kachin only periodically accepted rank society, many Southeast Asian peoples accepted it permanently. Jonathan Friedman, drawing on both Leach's work and his own, has modeled the philosophical changes necessary for the evolution of such "Asian social formations."[2] His reconstruction of the ideological shift from egalitarian to rank society is relevant to our study of the Zapotec.

Friedman's model begins with an egalitarian society like those of Burma (ill. 85). Such societies are composed of a series of lineages of equal prestige. Each local lineage has its own set of ancestral spirits, arranged in genealogies of three or four generations. There is also a village spirit, called a *nat*, who represents the local territory and is regarded as its owner. This "village *nat*" is conceived of as a remote ancestor of all local lineages. On a still higher plane lies a series of "celestial *nats*" which, at this egalitarian stage, can be approached by any lineage with the aid of its ancestral spirits.

At the egalitarian level, all lineages take turns sponsoring ritual feasts to which members of neighboring communities are invited. Giving a truly impressive feast is regarded as evidence that the *nats* have smiled on the host lineage, since only with supernatural approval could they amass sufficient resources. It is a little like the Bougainville belief that Big Men achieve their success through supernatural backing.

Each lineage is supposed to take its turn sponsoring communal rituals. In Friedman's model, however, one lineage works extraordinarily hard, gradually accumulating enough resources to begin taking over the job of host on a permanent basis. In many societies this would promote jealousy, but in Friedman's model it is interpreted as evidence for a closer association with the *nats* – evidence, in other words, that the wealthy lineage is actually *descended* from powerful spirits.

The transition to a rank society is achieved when this wealthy lineage's neighbors begin to see it as having descended directly from the village *nat* who owns all lands belonging to the community. Eventually, the celestial *nats* are transformed as well; they are now ranked by age (following earthly rules of succession), and the high-ranking human lineage can be traced back to the highest celestial *nat*.

The head of this elite lineage, since he is genealogically related to the spirits who control the village's well-being, becomes a hereditary leader who serves as the mediator between his community and the supernatural. His favored genealogical status entitles him to special privileges, which are tolerated because the old egalitarian philosophy has now been superseded by a philosophy of hereditary inequality.

In terms of action theory, this transformation is accomplished by taking one of the old theorems of egalitarian life – the belief that one must have supernatural help to amass resources – and converting it into the belief that the most successful lineage must have supernatural ancestors. Now the stage is set for the loss of village autonomy. Since the highest celestial *nat* governs a region far beyond the individual village, the authority of his human descendants should be regional as well. Strategic marriages can then be used to tie the leaders of nearby hamlets to the elite lineage of the largest village.

Friedman's model for the origins of ranking is relevant to the Valley of Oaxaca because of its emphasis on the genealogical relationship between humans and celestial spirits. During the San José phase in the Valley of Oaxaca, we see carved on pottery our first examples of what may be the celestial ancestors of human lineages.

For most speakers of Otomanguean languages, including the Zapotec, Earth and Sky were seen as important supernatural entities. While Earth was generally viewed as benevolent, it had the capacity to show anger. The Earth resented being wounded or burnt, as when postholes were dug in its surface, harvests removed, or land cleared by fire.[3] One way Earth showed its anger to the Zapotec was through *Xòo*, or Earthquake, when its surface rumbled and fissures opened. It was this angry face of Earth that the later Zapotec most often depicted in art, using a glyph for motion or a snarling earth-mask with a cleft in its skull. Plants were often depicted growing out of the cleft in the earth.

Sky was a place of celestial spirits, as well as ancestors who had metamorphosed into clouds. It, too, had its angry side, best exemplified by a bolt of Lightning (*Cociyo*) with its accompanying thunder roll or *Xòo Cociyo*, "Lightning's Earthquake." Early Oaxacans pictured Lightning as a fiery serpent with a bifid tongue and flames rising from its eyebrows.

When Earthquake and Lightning first appeared on the pottery of the Valley of Oaxaca – sometime around 1150 BC – they were highly stylized. Thus they may have been supernatural forces long believed in, and only recently transferred to pottery. Lightning was depicted with deeply-carved bars, inverted U's standing for the gums of the "fire-serpent," and scrolls or curves representing the flames from its eyebrows. Earth could be represented as a map with a center and four quadrants, or as Earthquake – a finely-incised mask with the snarling mouth of a feline with a cleft in its skull.

Earth and Sky appear to have been the ancestors of certain male descent groups in San José phase villages. When found with burials old enough to have their gender determined, the vessels bearing these motifs occur exclusively with males. They also occur with infants too young to have their gender determined

The Emergence of "Earth" and "Sky"

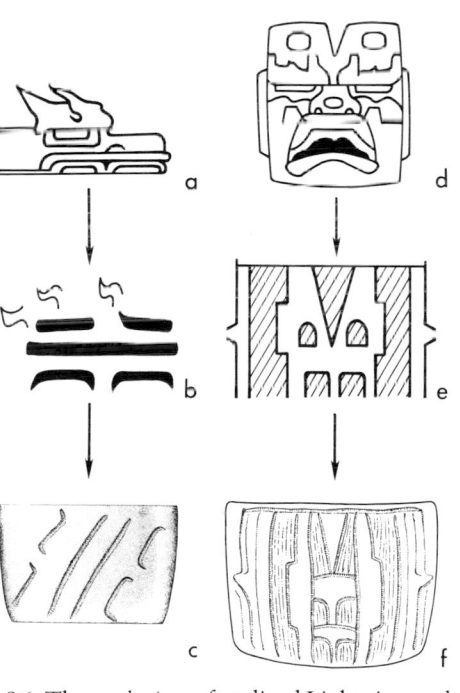

86 The evolution of stylized Lightning and Earthquake motifs on San José phase pottery. (*a*) Lightning as a realistic "fire-serpent"; (*b*) typical stylized version of (*a*); (*c*) carved vessel from Abasolo; (*d*) Earthquake as a realistic "cleft head" mask; (*e*) typical stylized version of (*d*); (*f*) carved and incised vessel from Tierras Largas.

– presumably young males, since we have other infant burials with vessels like those typically found with adult women.

These two motifs were almost mutually exclusive in their distribution. Small villages like Abasolo and Tomaltepec had almost exclusively Sky (Lightning) vessels; Tierras Largas had almost exclusively Earth (Earthquake) vessels. At the large village of San José Mogote there were different residential wards, some occupied by people descended from Earth and others by people descended from Sky. Both the burials and the household refuse reflect this dichotomy of ancestral "celestial spirits."[4]

The Emergence of Status Gradients

Despite our inability to identify the precise moment at which the shift to rank society took place, we can document a far greater range of statuses for San José phase society than for the preceding Tierras Largas phase. One line of evidence involves status differences that could either be inherited, or achieved, or both. A second line involves differences that *must have been inherited*, since they occur with children too young to have achieved high status.

Possible Evidence for Authority and Subordination

87 The "mat" motif, a symbol of authority, carved on San José phase pottery.

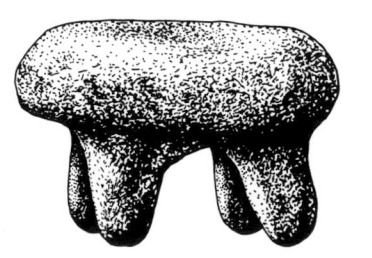

88 A miniature four-legged stool from a San José phase house. Diameter 3 cm.

In later periods of Mesoamerican prehistory, rulers emphasized their nobility by preventing various parts of their bodies from touching the ground. They wore sandals rather than going barefoot; they placed reed or palm mats on the floors of their audience rooms; they sat on stools, benches, or thrones. In time, motifs for mats and stools came to be used by Mesoamerican artists as symbols for authority.[5]

It is in the San José phase that we see our first use of the "mat" motif, carved on pottery at San José Mogote. At this time we also get our first miniature copies of four-legged stools, made from the same clay as the human figurines and to the same scale. In the sixteenth century, many Central American chiefs had special stools carried wherever they traveled, so that they would always be seated higher than their subordinates. We suspect that our miniature versions were made to be used with seated figurines of high-status individuals. We find this likely, because figurines of costumed men seated on four-legged stools have been found in nearby Chiapas at this time.[6]

More evidence for social differentiation comes from the burials and figurines of the San José phase. Both show a dichotomy between: (1) individuals in stereotyped positions of authority; and (2) individuals in stereotyped "obeisance postures" like those described for chiefdoms elsewhere.[7]

Near Tomaltepec, in the piedmont of the Tlacolula subvalley, Michael Whalen discovered a large cemetery on the outskirts of a 1.2-ha San José phase village.[8] There were more than 60 graves, and because some graves held more than one person, the number of individuals was close to 80. For the first time we see paired burials of men and women, meaning that some people were now treated as husband-and-wife rather than as individuals. One such couple consisted of a woman with an iron-ore mirror and a man with a bowl carved to depict Lightning. There are also primary burials accompanied by secondary burials, suggesting that people who died earlier were sometimes exhumed to be reburied with spouses or relatives. The cemetery contains only persons old enough to have gone through initiation at puberty – that is, no infants or young

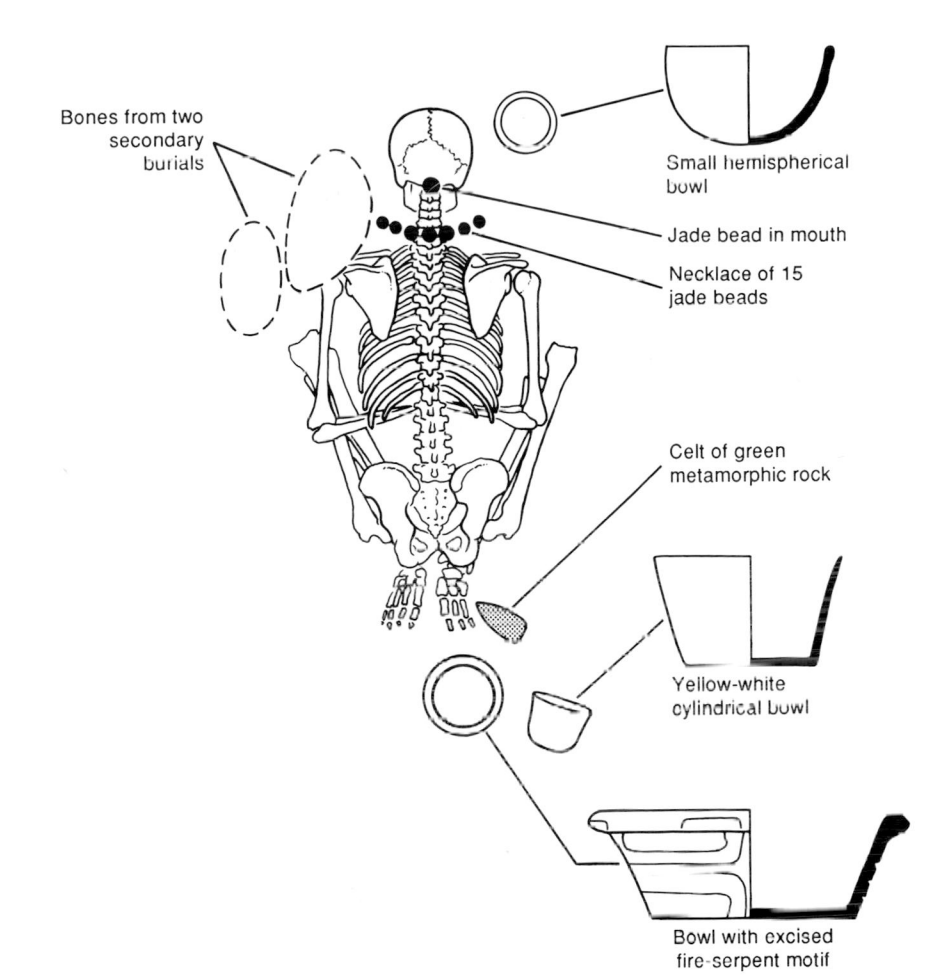

Bones from two
secondary
burials

Small hemispherical
bowl

Jade bead in mouth

Necklace of 15
jade beads

Celt of green
metamorphic rock

Yellow-white
cylindrical bowl

Bowl with excised
fire-serpent motif

89 Burial 11 at Tomaltepec, a tightly
flexed 30–40-year-old high-status male
accompanied by two secondary burials.

children. Almost all primary burials were fully extended, prone, with their arms
at their sides.

A group of six men in the cemetery, however, stood out as different. All were
buried in a kneeling position, so tightly flexed that they must have been tied or
wrapped. Although they constituted only 12.7 percent of the cemetery, these six
males had 50 percent of the vessels with motifs of Lightning, and 88 percent of
the jade beads. Two-thirds of the burials covered by stone slabs belonged to this
small group; most secondary reburials in the cemetery had also been added to
the graves of these six flexed men, suggesting that some may have had more than
one wife. Almost certainly these were the burials of Tomaltepec's community
leaders.

A small neighborhood cemetery at San José Mogote adds more information
on burial position. Unlike the larger village cemetery at Tomaltepec, it contained
infants and children as well as adults. Both sexes were present and most were
buried fully extended, face down. Almost all adults had a single jade bead in the
mouth and one or more pottery vessels; as usual, vessels with depictions of Sky
(Lightning) were found only with men. There were husband-and-wife pairs, such
as the couple in ill. 90. He was prone in a grave outlined and covered with stone
slabs, perhaps a precursor of the later Zapotec tomb; she was buried beside him,

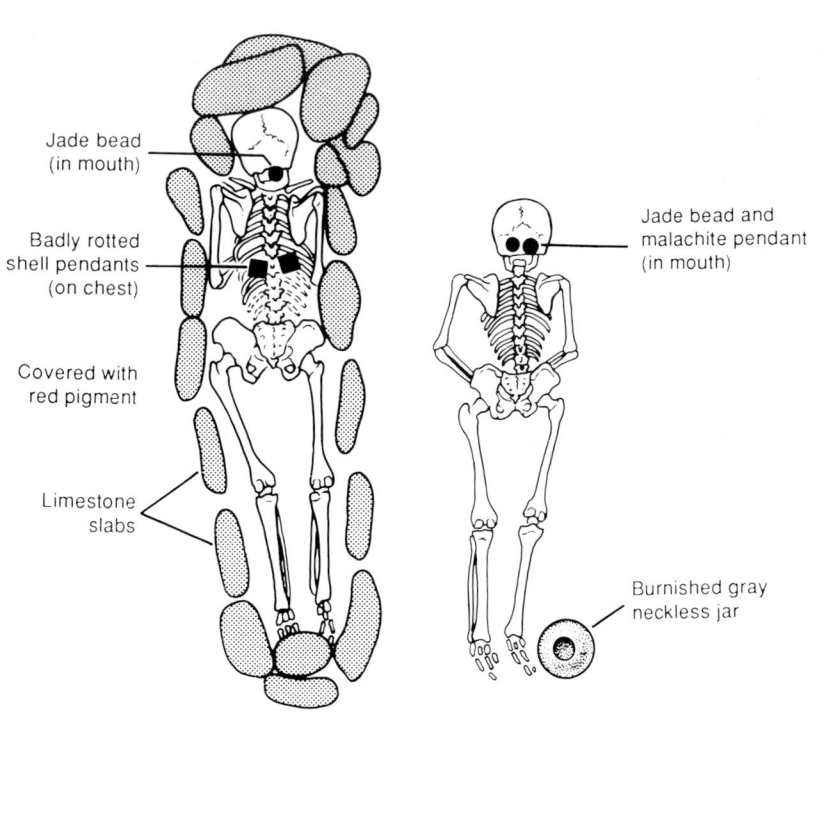

90 A likely husband-and-wife pair buried
at San José Mogote. The man (left) was
35–40 years of age, the woman (right)
20–29 years.

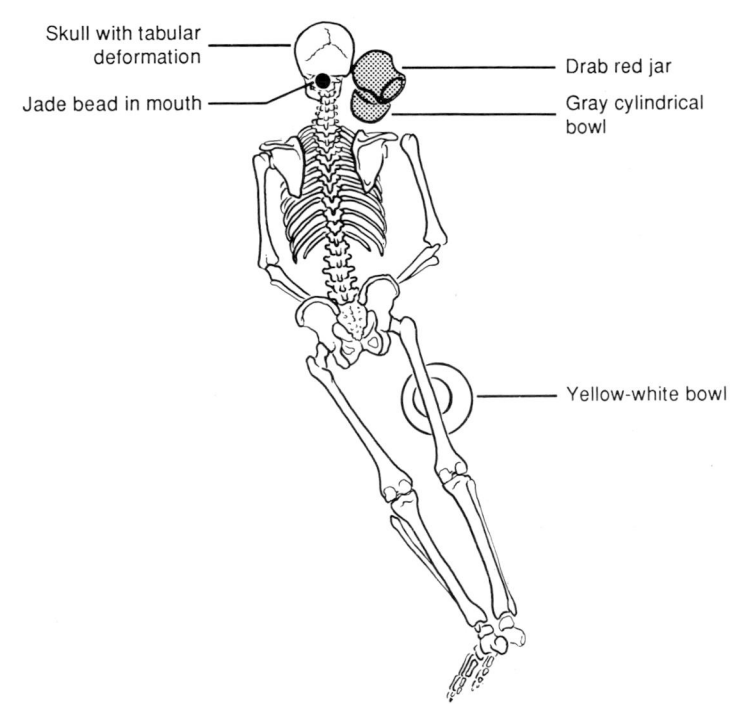

91 Burial 17 at San José Mogote, a woman
over 50 years of age buried in the prone
position.

but without the slabs. All burials in this neighborhood had relatively modest offerings, and there were no men in seated or flexed positions.

We consider the tightly flexed burials of this phase to be persons of importance, whose bodies were bundled and kept for a time before burial. We are particularly intrigued by seated burials. Some appear to have been buried with legs folded, while others have their knees drawn up. Individuals of either group might have been buried seated on wooden stools that later disintegrated.

In contrast, we consider the men and women buried prone and fully extended to be in a more subordinate position. This is the most common burial position of the period, and would seem to apply to the largest group of adults in San José society. Buried in this position, their heads would always have been lower than someone of higher status. At the same time, the offerings with these prone burials form a continuum from meagre (i.e. nothing at all) to relatively rich (e.g. jade earspools, mother-of-pearl pendants, and fine pottery).

As we look at the small, hand-made figurines of the San José phase, we are struck by a dichotomy of positions similar to that of the burials. Some figurines, like those shown in ills. 92 and 93, depict men seated with hands on knees. Others, like that in ill. 94, may represent male corpses tightly wrapped for burial. Still others, like that shown in ill. 95, show men and women standing erect, some with arms at their sides and others with arms folded on their chests. The position with arms folded looks stereotyped, as if the maker of the figurine were trying to depict an "obeisance posture."

Whatever the figurine assemblage of this period was designed to communicate, one of its messages seems to be that there were people of authority and people subordinate to them. We believe that these figurines were made by women and used in rituals invoking their recent ancestors, some of whom may have been persons of authority and some of whom may have been subordinates.

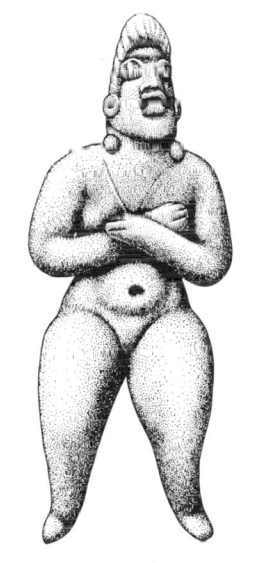

92 Figurine of a seated man with pendant, ear spools, and possible filed teeth, San José Mogote. Height 6.8 cm.

93 Figurine of a seated man, found with a burial in the Tomaltepec cemetery (front and side views). Height 8.1 cm.

94 This figurine from San José Mogote may represent a man prepared for seated burial. Height 8.5 cm.

95 A figurine in possible "obeisance posture," San José Mogote. Height 15 cm.

On occasion, figurines seem to have been arranged to form small ritual scenes. One such scene had been buried beneath the floor of House 16, a lean-to attached to House 17 at San José Mogote. Three human figures lay fully extended supine, with their arms crossed on their chests. Above them was a figure

The Possible Representation of a High-Status Burial

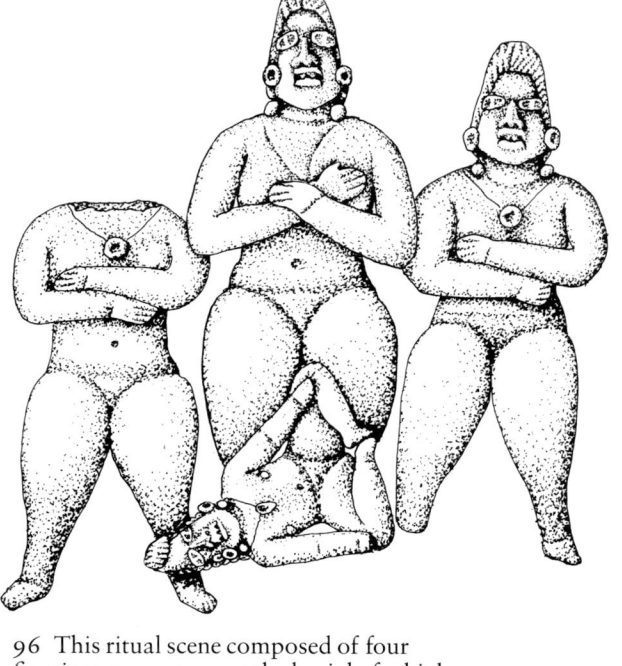

96 This ritual scene composed of four figurines may represent the burial of a high-status individual with three retainers. House 16, San José Mogote. Height of tallest figurine, 15 cm.

97 Grave 26 from Coclé, Panama: the burial of a seated chief (Skeleton 12) with 21 retainers. The date of this grave is thought to be roughly AD 1000.

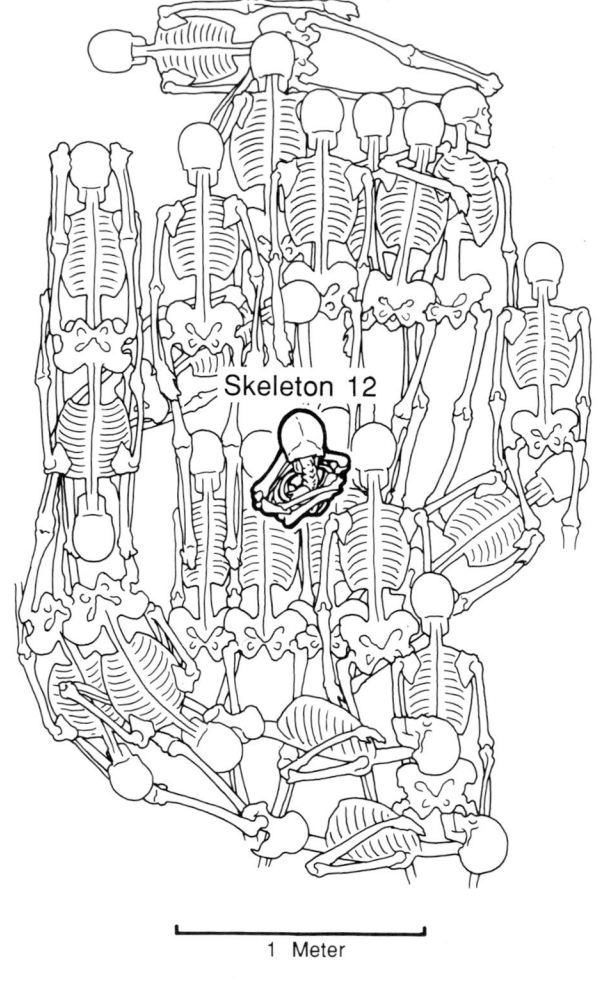

Skeleton 12

1 Meter

in seated position with hands on knees. The latter may originally have been upright, before toppling under the weight of the earth. All the figures wear pendants and earspools.

This scene may represent an individual in one of our positions of authority, buried atop three individuals in positions of subordination. Though different in scale, it calls to mind Grave 26 from the Coclé site in Panama, the burial of a chief with 21 retainers. Those retainers were buried fully extended (18 prone, 1 supine, 2 on their sides). Skeleton 12, the chief, was seated atop them. To be sure, the Coclé burial was more elaborate than anything we have found in the San José phase. But the concept – the seating of an elite individual above his recumbent subordinates – may have been the same.

Ethnohistoric data suggest that Panamanian chiefs were often buried in tight bundles, after having been desiccated in a smokehouse.[9] Some were buried seated on stools. The retainers buried with them could be captives taken from enemy chiefdoms, or even women of their own group who volunteered to be buried with the chief. Retainers buried prone had their arms at their sides or folded on their chests. Some of the face-down burials even had gold with them, suggesting that the prone position itself did not necessarily imply low status. Prostrating oneself in the presence of a chief may only have been a way of showing deference.

In later Mesoamerican societies, elite individuals used a variety of sumptuary goods to distinguish themselves from commoners. The nobility wore cotton mantles; commoners wore agave-fiber mantles. The nobility wore jade spools in their earlobes, jade necklaces, lip plugs of jade or turquoise, and ornaments in the septum of the nose. Their garments were fringed with shell tubes that tinkled as they moved; they wore capes woven of quetzal, hummingbird, trogon, cardinal, or grosbeak feathers. Jade, turquoise, and quetzal plumage were prized because they were blue-green – a color shared with the center of the universe.

Many of these materials appear in the San José phase, and some were undoubtedly associated with status differences. The problem is proving that those status differences were *inherited*, rather than *achieved*. We often cannot show a clear dichotomy between people who could, or could not, use sumptuary goods. For most materials there is a continuum of greater to lesser use; such a continuum is typical of rank societies.

Marine shell, mica, and jade provide examples of this continuum. San José phase villagers evidently decorated themselves with pieces of mica cut from naturally occurring "books," or layers of mica sheets. Some houses had none; some had a few fragments; some had dozens of fragments, plus evidence for the actual working of mica.

It was not uncommon for men and women to have a single jade bead placed in the mouth when they were buried. Not everyone, however, had a jade gorget like Burial 40 at Tierras Largas. And Burial 18 of San José Mogote, a woman of 50, was unusual in having two jade earspools and three jade beads. Although later Mesoamerican societies restricted the use of jades to nobles, in San José phase society there was a continuum from people who had none, to people who had a few, to people who had many.

Variations in access to shell were even more complex, because the craftspeople who made the ornaments may have had different trading partners or elite

Possible Sumptuary Goods

98 Trimmed piece of black mica, San José phase. Length 7 cm.

99 Shell ornaments from San José Mogote. The object at upper left may be a mother-of-pearl holder for a magnetite mirror; to the right is an almost complete valve of pearl oyster.

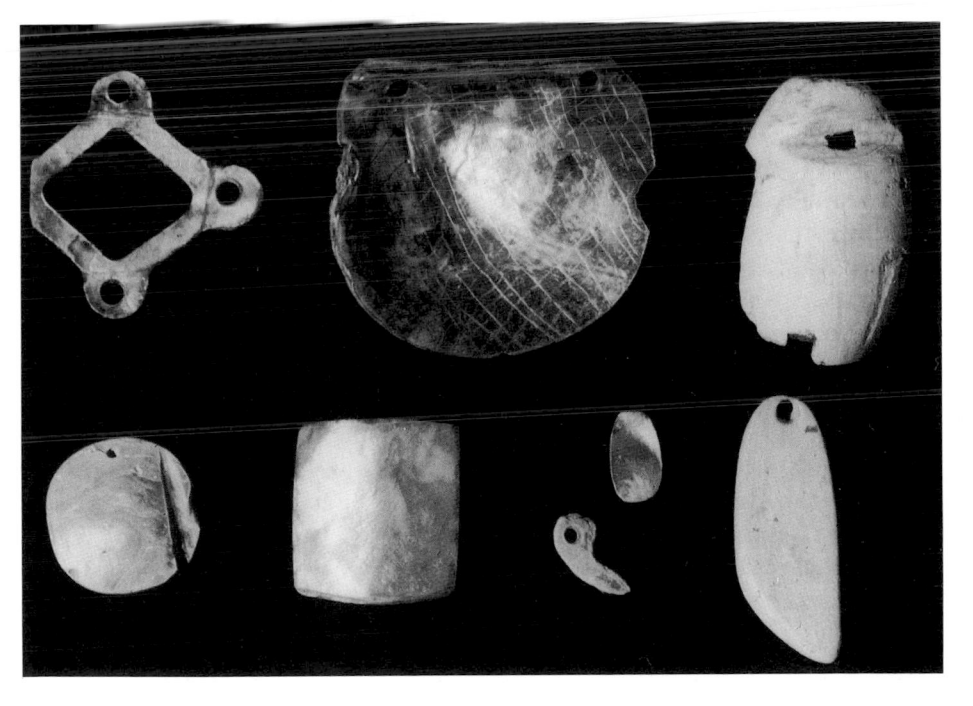

100 Chert perforators were used to make shell ornaments at San José Mogote. Each has one or more small, nipple-like projections on the upper edge. Height of upper left tool, 2.4 cm.

101 Small mirrors of magnetite from San José Mogote.

1 cm

patrons. Near the western limits of San José Mogote, occupants of House 4 worked mainly Pacific shell; those of House 9 worked mainly Atlantic shell. There are even cases where a family seems to have worked one kind of shell, but had access to finished ornaments of another kind. Household C3 near the eastern end of the village had finished Pacific Coast shell ornaments, including a mother-of-pearl holder for an iron-ore mirror; the household's shell waste products, on the other hand, were mostly Atlantic mussel.[10]

Despite our suspicion that ornaments of mother-of-pearl and spiny oyster may have served as sumptuary goods, we cannot show a dichotomy between people who could, and could not, use them. Instead we have households with little or no access to shell; households with a few ornaments, but no evidence of shellworking; and households with very fine ornaments and evidence for shell-working. Complicating our analysis may be the fact that the craftspeople who made the shell ornaments were not always the elites on whose bodies the ornaments would eventually be displayed.

Ironically, it is with locally available iron ores, rather than exotic foreign imports, that we can make our best case for sumptuary goods. Surface survey at San José Mogote revealed a unique 1-ha concentration of 500 iron-ore chunks, including magnetite, hematite, and ilmenite.[11] This amounts to 99 percent of all the archaeological iron ore ever found in the valley. Every household excavated in this part of the village was involved in the grinding and polishing of small mirrors, mostly of magnetite, with hematite powder used as the abrasive.

Magnetite does not show the continuum of access seen in mica, shell, and jade; its use seems to have been much more restricted. One high-status woman at Tomaltepec was buried with a magnetite mirror, but there was no evidence of iron-ore working at the site. One magnetite lump was found at Tierras Largas, but no ornaments. Even the other residential areas at San José Mogote show no evidence of magnetite working, suggesting that mirror-polishing may have been under the strict control of one group of families.

Moreover, some of the mirrors made at San José Mogote were destined for exchange with elite individuals in other regions of Mexico. Two mirrors made of Oaxaca magnetite have been found at San Lorenzo, Veracruz, on the southern Gulf Coast; another has been found at Etlatongo in the Valley of Nochixtlán. A lump of high-quality Oaxaca magnetite reached the site of San Pablo in the state of Morelos.[12] All three villages are ones at which there is reason to suspect an emerging elite.

Clearly, the leaders of San José phase society ornamented themselves with mica, shell, jade, and magnetite. Only for magnetite, however, can we make a case that use may have been restricted by sumptuary rules. For shell, jade, and mica, we see a continuum from people who had very little to people who had quite a lot.

There are two reasons why this pattern should not surprise us. First, chiefdoms tend to have a gradient of statuses, rather than a division into two classes. Second, differences in achievement – such as the ability to accumulate trade goods – remain important even in societies with hereditary rank.

Households in San José society also suggest a gradient in prestige from low to high, without a division into social strata. Near one end of the gradient were modest residences like House 13 at San José Mogote; near the other end were more elaborate residences like Houses 16–17. In addition to their differences in construction, such residences show differential access to deer meat, mica, and marine shell.

House 13 is reconstructed in ill. 102. It was roughly 3 × 5 m in size and relatively poorly made, with slender posts and no coating of whitewash. Its corners were slightly rounded rather than neatly squared. The contents included small bone needles for sewing, but none of the longer basketry-making needles found at better made houses. The occupants of the house were modest producers of

Gradients in the Status of Households

102 Artist's reconstruction of House 13 at San José Mogote, a relatively low-status residence.

103 Artist's reconstruction of House 17 at San José Mogote, a relatively high-status residence with an attached lean-to or roofed work area (House 16). Feature 61 was a fire-pit used for heating chert to make it easier to flake.

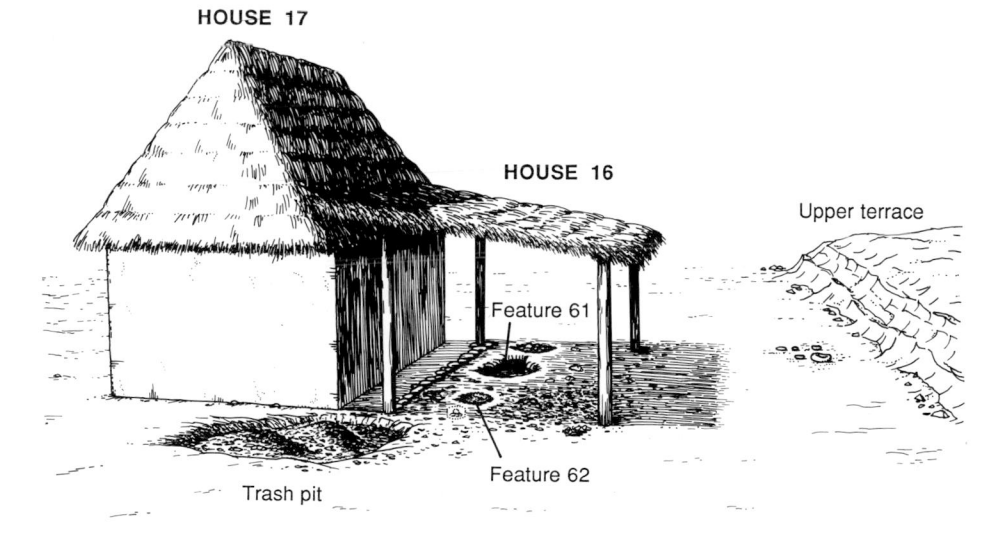

HOUSE 17

HOUSE 16

Upper terrace

Feature 61

Feature 62

Trash pit

104 The residents of House 17 at San José Mogote probably used this stingray spine for ritual bloodletting. Length 9.7 cm.

spiny oyster and freshwater mussel ornaments, and consumers of mother-of-pearl ornaments made elsewhere. Remains of mica were numerous, but there was little evidence for jade. House 13 lay in the part of the village devoted to magnetite mirror working, but it contained only six unworked fragments of ore. It had less chipped stone and deer bone than other houses in that residential area. Pottery imported from other regions was limited to a few sherds.[13]

Houses 16–17 are reconstructed in ill. 103. House 17 was a well-made residence with nicely squared corners and a thick coating of whitewash over its wattle-and-daub walls. House 16 was a lean-to or roofed work area of some kind, probably attached to House 17 in the manner shown in the drawing. This lean-to contained a fire pit for heat-treating chert, and the occupants had been engaged in the manufacture of chert bifaces.[14] Other crafts in evidence were basket making with large bone needles; mother-of-pearl ornament manufacture; and the production of mold-made pottery.[15] Cached beneath the floor of House 17 were two tools that could be for planing and smoothing wood. Houses 16–17 had more evidence of deer bone than House 13. They also had more spiny oyster shell, ceramic masks, stingray spines, and pottery imported from the Basin of Mexico, the Gulf Coast, and the Tehuacán Valley. One occupant of House 17, a middle-aged woman, was buried beneath the floor; she was accompanied by two jade earspools and three jade beads. An even more elegant jade earspool was found on the floor of her nearby lean-to.

These houses, and others of the San José phase, suggest that the higher a family's status in the community, the more likely that family was to be involved in craft activities and have greater access to deer meat, marine shell, jade, and imported pottery.

105 Burial 18, a middle-aged woman, was associated with House 17 at San José Mogote. She had five jade ornaments.

106 (Far right) Two jade earspools (length 14 mm) and three jade beads associated with Burial 18 at San José Mogote.

107 (Below) This elegant jade ear ornament was found in House 16, the lean-to associated with House 17, San José Mogote. Diameter 2.8 cm.

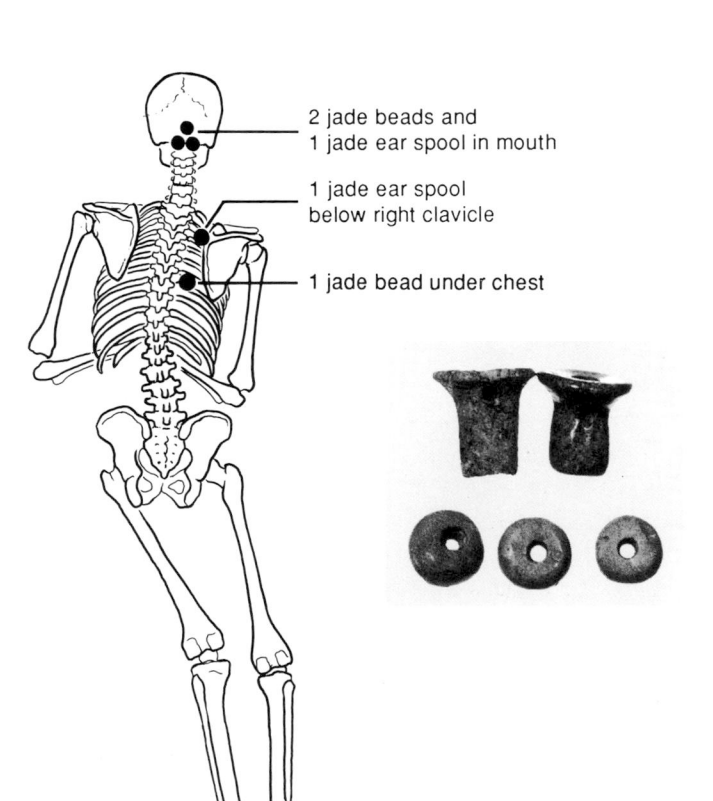

2 jade beads and 1 jade ear spool in mouth

1 jade ear spool below right clavicle

1 jade bead under chest

Thus far we have looked at a series of phenomena – positions of authority and obeisance, possible sumptuary goods, gradients in access to resources – all of which probably reflect status differences in San José society. All, however, share the same problem: we cannot prove that the differences are *inherited*, rather than *achieved*. To demonstrate hereditary inequality we must find *status differences that show up with infants or young children, individuals too young to have achieved prestige during their lifetimes.* There are, in fact, two differences among San José phase individuals that show up in childhood. Let us look at some examples.

As we have seen, the association of certain individuals with Earth or Sky appears to have been present from birth. Even infants could be buried with vessels bearing Lightning or Earthquake motifs, and sometimes their offerings were more impressive than those of the average adult at the same village.

Burials 1, 2, and 4 from Abasolo were all infants, buried close together in a small neighborhood midden. While their gender could not be determined owing to their age, their burial offerings show the same dichotomy seen between adult men and women.

Burial 2 was accompanied by two small neckless jars, one of them a squash effigy. These appear to be child-size versions of the offerings found in many women's graves. Burials 1 and 4 were each accompanied by a nested set of three bowls; two from each set had carved Lightning motifs. These vessels were small versions of the offerings found in some men's graves. Since none of these infants were old enough to have "achieved" anything in their lifetimes, we conclude that descent from Lightning was hereditary through the male line. The question is, did it also confer high rank?

Burials with Earth or Sky motifs did not necessarily have more shell, jade, or magnetite than other burials. It should be remembered, however, that achievement does not become an irrelevant factor simply because inherited rank has emerged. Not everyone born to a chiefly lineage becomes a chief. Descent from Lightning was acknowledged at birth in San José society, but that may only have been the first round of competition. Years of accomplishment, ritual initiation, and the elimination of rivals may have been needed to turn one of "Lightning's children" into a chief.

Now let us turn to another attribute that cannot reflect achievement: deliberate cranial deformation. At the time of the Spanish Conquest it was considered a sign of nobility, like the wearing of quetzal plumes and jade earplugs. Cranial deformation must be done early in life, while the skull is still growing and its bones still separated by cartilage. For the ancient Maya, cranial deformation took place shortly after birth. The sixteenth-century Spaniard Diego de Landa says "four or five days after the infant was born, they placed it stretched out upon a little bed, made of sticks of osier and reeds; and there with its face upwards, they put its head between two small boards one on the back of the head and the other on the forehead, between which they compressed it tightly, and here they kept it suffering until at the end of several days, the head remained flat and molded."[16]

Some sixteenth-century Aztec informants revealed that "When the children are very young, their heads are soft and can be molded in the shape that you see ours to be, by using two pieces of wood hollowed out in the middle. This custom, given to our ancestors by the gods, gives us a noble air."[17]

Possible Hereditary Traits

108. Two small neckless jars found with Burial 2 at Abasolo. The vessel at the top, a squash effigy, is 11 cm in diameter. Such vessels were usually found with women.

109 Two small cylindrical bowls with carved Lightning motifs, found with Burial 4 at Abasolo. Such vessels were usually found with men. Diameter of upper vessel, 8.3 cm.

110 Burial 1 at San José Mogote, a 15–20-year-old woman with deliberate cranial deformation.

Cranial deformation results from actions taken by one's parents, long before one is old enough to have achieved anything; thus, if cranial deformation reflects high rank, it must be *inherited* high rank. Two types of deformation were practiced in early Mesoamerican villages. *Tabular* deformation, the most common, was caused by pressing the skull between a fixed occipital cradleboard and a free board on the forehead. *Annular* deformation was caused by tying a band around the head. Each type of deformation could be *erect* or *oblique*, depending on the angle at which it was applied.[18]

Tabular deformation was the most common type in the San José phase, and could occur with either sex; some of the men buried with Lightning vessels were so deformed. One teenage girl from San José Mogote, however, showed annular deformation, a practice still rare at this time. It is possible that she was a bride from another ethnic region, where annular deformation was more common. The girl's burial position – face up, arms folded on her chest – was also atypical for that residential ward.

We believe that certain children inherited the right to have their skulls deformed, and that certain male children inherited the right to be buried with Earth or Sky motifs. Because such burials were not always accompanied by impressive sumptuary goods, one cannot make a simplistic claim of "chiefly burials" for them. We suspect that these were children born into the descent groups from which future leaders were likely to come. However, not everyone born into such a group automatically became a leader. Almost certainly, to receive truly elegant burial gifts, one had to add *achievement* to one's high-status pedigree.

San José Phase Settlement Patterns

From 1150 to 850 BC, the Valley of Oaxaca witnessed a remarkable and asymmetrical growth in population. The number of communities doubled, to about 40; the estimated population more than tripled, to at least 2000. This growth did nothing to decrease the heterogeneity seen in the Tierras Largas phase, since fully half the communities still occupied the Etla subvalley.

Most settlements – including virtually all the newly-founded ones – are estimated to have been hamlets of 100 persons or fewer. In contrast, perhaps half the population of the valley may have lived at San José Mogote. The Settlement Pattern Project reconstructs it as a cluster of three sites covering 79 ha, with an estimated 791–1976 persons.[19] We reconstruct it as a main village with numerous outlying barrios. The main village covered 20 ha, and if all outlying barrios were truly part of one sprawling community, we estimate its total size at 60–70 ha and its population at 1000. We are left, therefore, with two asymmetries to explain. One is the disproportionate population of the Etla subvalley; the other is the fact that the largest village in the valley was ten times the size of the second largest.

Illustration 111, which superimposes villages on classes of land, implies that rainfall farming on Class I land was still the strategy of choice. At least three-quarters of all settlements were on such land, or on piedmont spurs nearby. Gradually, however, settlement was expanding beyond the zone of *yuh kohp* or permanently humid bottomland. Two irrigation techniques used by today's Zapotec may have facilitated that expansion.[20] One technique is the digging of shallow wells that tap the subsurface water, permitting irrigation by hand with

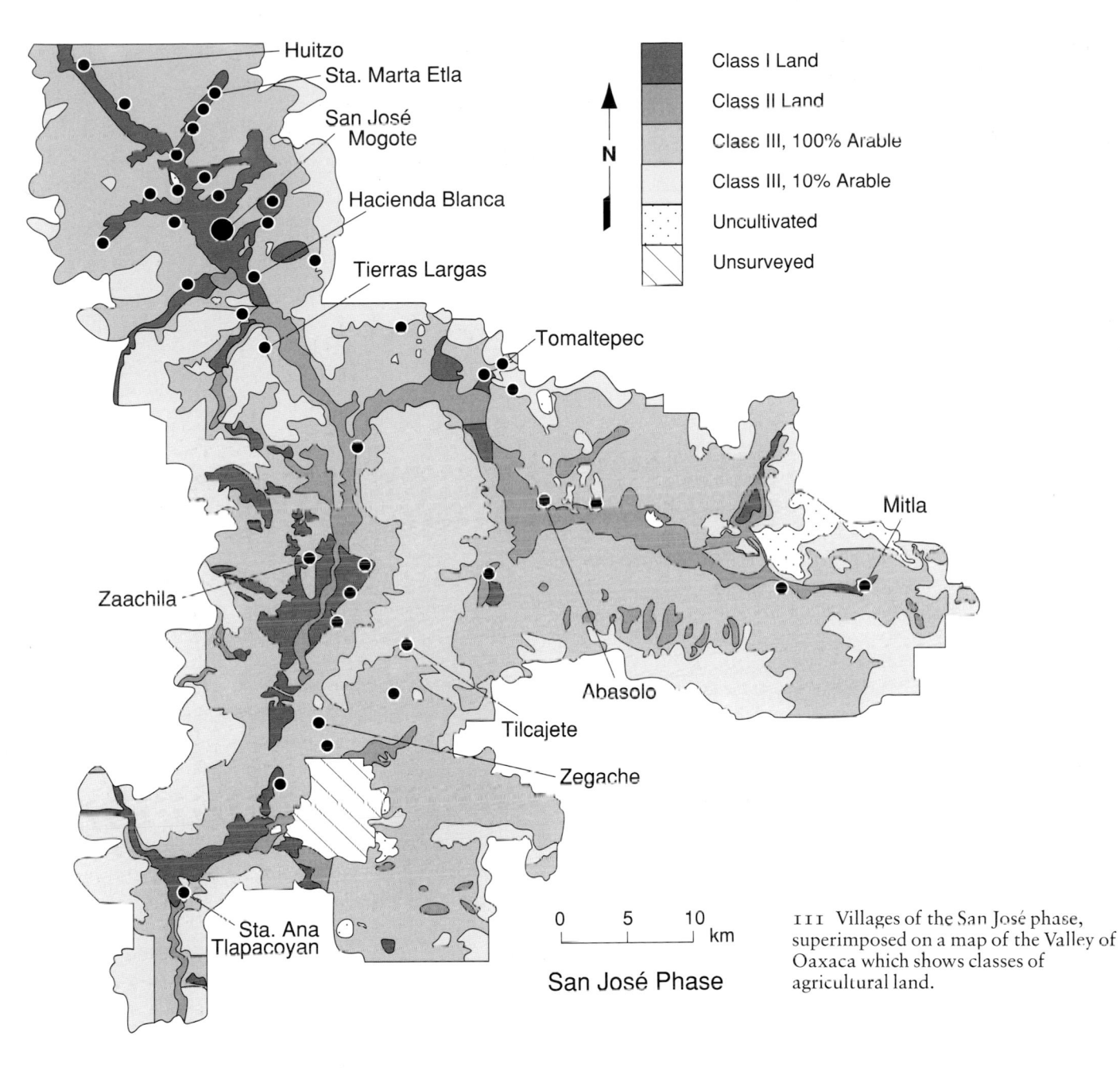

Huitzo
Sta. Marta Etla
San José Mogote
Hacienda Blanca
Tierras Largas
Tomaltepec
Mitla
Zaachila
Abasolo
Tilcajete
Zegache
Sta. Ana Tlapacoyan

Class I Land
Class II Land
Class III, 100% Arable
Class III, 10% Arable
Uncultivated
Unsurveyed

N

0   5   10 km

San José Phase

111 Villages of the San José phase, superimposed on a map of the Valley of Oaxaca which shows classes of agricultural land.

special jars. The other involves the digging of small ditches, either to drain water-logged fields or to divert piedmont streams to the alluvium. San José phase wells have been found at Abasolo in the Tlacolula subvalley; drainage ditches have been found at San José Mogote and Tierras Largas in the Etla subvalley.[21] The fact that such technologies were known may help explain the spread of agriculture beyond the limits of *yuh kohp*. Both techniques are so simple as to be within the labor capacity of a single family.

There are signs, however, that more than gradual agricultural expansion was involved in San José phase settlement. In the 800-km² Valle Grande, large

112 This Zapotec farmer at Abasolo is irrigating his field by hand, using wells which tap into groundwater at a depth of only 3 m.

stretches of Class I land were still unoccupied. In the much smaller Etla subvalley, some 12–14 communities were concentrated within 8 km of San José Mogote. Clearly, the tendency of growing agricultural populations to disperse was being counterbalanced by the advantages of remaining within a two-hour walk of the valley's largest village. It is also clear that even though Class I land was still available, there were already a number of settlements on Class III land.

Finally, we note that there were now villages near the mouths of several major passes into and out of the valley: Huitzo in the extreme northwest, Mazaltepec along a major route to the Mixteca, Tlapacoyan at the extreme south, and Mitla at the extreme east. These locations were not accidental.

We therefore conclude that while access to prime land was still a major consideration, *social relationships* – including attempts by village leaders to concentrate their followers nearby – played a larger role in settlement location than they had in the Tierras Largas phase.

The Loss of Autonomy

One of the most important clues to the emergence of chiefly society is the loss of village autonomy. A Big Man in Bougainville can fine members of his own village for not assisting him in feasting or ritual construction. By neighboring villagers, however, he is not obeyed; he can get help from other communities only by paying for it.[22] Not until a number of separate villages come to obey such a leader does he emerge as the head of a minimal chiefdom.[23]

Our task, therefore, is to document the loss of village autonomy. Our attention is drawn immediately to San José Mogote and the 12–14 smaller communities surrounding it. The latter sites encircle the former like moons orbiting a star – a 70-ha sun with tiny satellites caught in its gravitational pull. Between 1400 and 1150 BC, the leaders of San José Mogote attracted more than 170 people to their village. Between 1150 and 850 BC, it appears that they convinced more than 1000 people to remain within an 8-km radius.

The great disparity between San José Mogote and its satellites gives us a site-

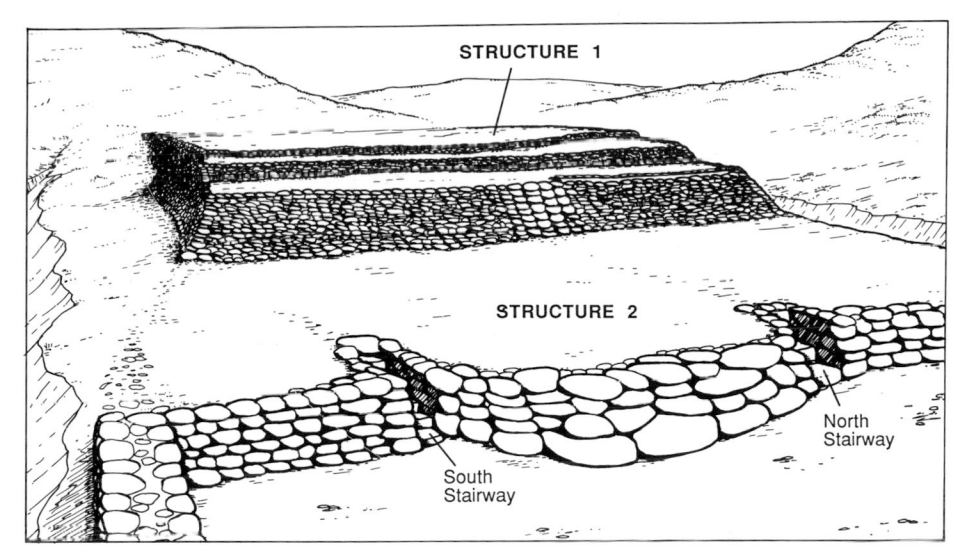

STRUCTURE 1

STRUCTURE 2

North
Stairway

South
Stairway

113 Artist's reconstruction of Structures 1
and 2 at San José Mogote. Many of the
stones used in construction came from the
lands of smaller communities nearby.

size hierarchy with two clear levels – and more than mere size is involved, since
San José Mogote also had a range of public buildings not seen at smaller sites.
During the early San José phase, these structures consisted mainly of lime-plastered Men's Houses; by late San José times, however, unprecedented construction began in the village center.

Structures 1 and 2 were two of the most impressive buildings of the San José
phase. Each appears to be the pyramidal platform for a wattle-and-daub public
building, and their construction involved the first use of an adobe brick so far
known for Oaxaca. Used mainly for small retaining walls within the earthen fill,
these early adobes were circular in plan and plano-convex, or "bun-shaped," in
section.

Structure 2 was 1 m high and at least 18 m wide. Its sloping face had been
built with boulders, some obtained locally and some brought in from at least 5
km away. Some of the latter were of limestone from west of the Atoyac River,
while others were of travertine from east of the river. Two carved stones, one
depicting a feline and one a raptorial bird, had fallen from a collapsed section of

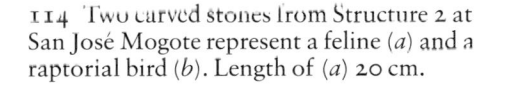

114 Two carved stones from Structure 2 at
San José Mogote represent a feline (a) and a
raptorial bird (b). Length of (a) 20 cm.

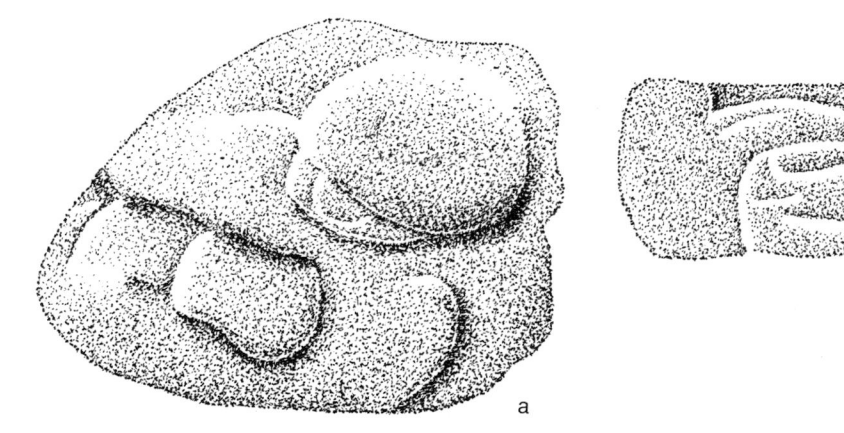

a

b

wall. The east face of the platform included two stone stairways which, although narrow, are the earliest of their kind for the region.

Structure 1, above and to the west, rose in several stages that may have reached 2.5 m in height. Its facing was of smaller stones set in clay, somewhat rough-and-ready, but clearly masonry – the first stage in an architectural tradition brilliantly developed by the later Zapotec.

These two structures reflect a local leader's ability to organize labor on a regional scale not seen previously. The diversity of raw materials used implies that work gangs came from a variety of locales. Some workers had brought volcanic tuff, quarried from outcrops nearby. Others had made round adobes, using the broken-off bases of large jars as molds.[24] Basketloads of earthen fill had been brought from areas of black alluvial soil, red piedmont soil, and gray-green soil from stony ridges. Most significantly, the limestone and travertine came from known quarries on the lands of other communities. It would appear, therefore, that the leaders of San José Mogote could now call on the manpower of other villages for public construction; autonomy had been lost.

It is worth noting that San José Mogote's leaders did not actually *need* the limestone or travertine, since they were sitting on a source of volcanic tuff. Almost certainly it was the *manpower* that they wanted to control. As Edward Schortman and Patricia Urban have recently said, "the goal of all elites is to control the labor and surplus production of as many subordinates as possible."[25]

Proving You Have A Chiefdom

One final point is worth making: in this chapter we have used more than ten lines of evidence to demonstrate that San José phase society had hereditary inequality. We used that many because no single line of evidence, in isolation, would be sufficient.[26]

Some archaeologists seem to believe that finding two burials, one with a jade ornament and one without, is evidence for a "chiefdom." It is not; nor is the mere presence of a public building. Autonomous village societies have all this and more. Only by demonstrating an extensive pattern of asymmetric relations in many aspects of society, including inequalities present from birth, can archaeologists make a convincing case for hereditary rank.

Alliance Building and Elite Competition

Once hereditary ranking has emerged in any region of the world, we can expect the path of social evolution to be even more volatile and disorderly than before. Competing Big Men need only humiliate their rivals with spectacular public works. Competing chiefs may actually have to do away with rivals whose genealogical credentials outrank theirs. The ethnographic record for chiefly societies shows intense raiding, alliance building, abrupt rises to power, and equally abrupt defeats.[1] However, it takes long-term excavation and luck to recover evidence for these processes in the archaeological record.

Some of our most interesting clues to alliance building and chiefly competition come from 850 to 700 BC. This was a period during which some of the processes seen in the preceding San José phase were strongly reinforced, and others were periodically disrupted. On the one hand, the differences between high-status and low-status families were escalating. On the other hand, chiefly centers like San José Mogote may have had trouble retaining control of neighboring hamlets because of emerging competition from rival centers.

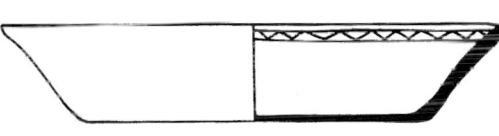

115 The incised motif on this Guadalupe phase bowl from Huitzo shares stylistic features with the pottery of the Valley of Nochixtlán to the north.

One of those rival centers was Huitzo, a village 16 km northwest of San José Mogote. While never as large as San José Mogote, Huitzo put up its own impressive public buildings between 850 and 700 BC, and seems to have done a good deal of "networking" with villages in the Valley of Nochixtlán, some 50 km to the north of the Valley of Oaxaca. Huitzo's pottery shares a number of stylistic features with those of Yucuita, a large settlement in the Valley of Nochixtlán, while maintaining a number of stylistic differences from the ceramics of San José Mogote.

The rise of competing centers, some of which declined to follow the stylistic canons of San José Mogote, has complicated our efforts to define a cultural assemblage for 850 to 700 BC. Such regional variation in pottery becomes a stumbling block for surface survey, because some diagnostic ceramics of the period do not appear to have reached all parts of the Valley of Oaxaca.

In the Etla subvalley we have called the period from 850 to 700 BC the Guadalupe phase, and its diagnostic pottery can be recognized from Huitzo in the north to Tierras Largas in the south. The farther one moves south and east from the Etla region, however, the less one sees these diagnostics; in the southern Valle Grande and the eastern Tlacolula subvalley, the pottery of 850–700 BC is sufficiently different to make the use of the term "Guadalupe phase" a bit inappropriate. On the one hand, this regional diversity tells us that dynamic changes were underway, with competing centers arising in different areas of the valley. On

116 This Guadalupe phase effigy vessel from Tierras Largas shares stylistic features with later Valley of Oaxaca pottery. Height 12.8 cm.

the other hand, it makes it difficult to define a valley-wide ceramic complex, and hence even harder to make population estimates.

Our best guess is that there were 2000–2500 persons in the Valley of Oaxaca at that time, perhaps distributed through some 45 communities. Roughly half those communities were in the Etla subvalley, which still had the lion's share of the population. The Settlement Pattern Project estimates that San José Mogote was now a village of 791–1976 persons distributed over 60–70 ha. San José Mogote was still the largest community in the valley, and it continued to exert a centripetal pull on neighboring hamlets; sixteen smaller settlements were clustered within 8 km of San José Mogote.

Public Buildings of 850–700 BC

If we assume that the construction of public buildings was sponsored by the elite, then we must also conclude that there were elite families at several Guadalupe phase communities. By this time, it had become standard practice to use bun-shaped adobes for the interior retaining walls of earthen platforms. The areas between such walls could then be filled with basketloads of earth, and the platform itself given a facing of stone boulders. Structure 8 at San José Mogote, oriented 8 degrees west of north, had an east wall of undressed field stones 1 m wide, combined with adobe retaining walls up to 70 cm high. Above this was the puddled adobe floor of a massive wattle-and-daub building, unfortunately destroyed by later erosion.

The rival center of Huitzo built comparable structures during the Guadalupe phase. The earliest of these was Structure 4, a pyramidal platform 2 m high and more than 15 m wide, built of earth and faced with stones in the manner of Structure 8 at San José Mogote. Atop this platform, the architects of Huitzo built a series of buildings that may have been one-room temples. The best pre-

117 Structure 8 at San José Mogote, a Guadalupe phase platform for a public building, had retaining walls of bun-shaped adobes and a surface of puddled clay.

118 Artist's reconstruction of Structure 3 at Huitzo, a large wattle-and-daub public building on an adobe platform with an inset stairway.

served of these was Structure 3, a large wattle-and-daub building on an adobe platform with a stairway. Built of bun-shaped adobes and fill, the platform was 1.3 m high and 11.5 m long. There were three steps to its wide stairway, each inset into the platform to strengthen it. The entire structure had been coated with lime plaster. In spite of the small size of the Huitzo community relative to San José Mogote, its public architecture was as impressive as anything built at the latter site during the Guadalupe phase.

An additional line of evidence suggests that San José Mogote and Huitzo were rival centers. In 1976 Stephen Plog compared the repertoire of incised design motifs on pottery from San José Mogote, Huitzo, Fábrica San José, Tierras Largas, and Abasolo.[2] Most of those designs were simplified versions of the Earth motifs discussed in Chapter 8; especially common were incised versions of Earth's cleft head.

While San José Mogote shared many design preferences with Abasolo, Tierras Largas, and Fábrica San José, its design repertoire showed much less similarity to Huitzo's than would have been predicted from the short distance between the two communities. This fact – coupled with Huitzo's sharing of stylistic attributes with the more distant Valley of Nochixtlán – reinforces our notion that the two sites interacted less frequently than expected, probably because their respective elite families were competing for supporters.

Alliance Building Through Hypogamy

We suspect that one method used by the leaders of San José Mogote to build alliances was *hypogamy*. This is the strategy of sending a high-status woman from a chiefly center to marry the leader of a subordinate community. Hypogamy raises the status of the subordinate community leader while obligating him to the donor of the bride. It was a strategy used by many later Mesoamerican civilizations.[3]

Five km east of San José Mogote is the hamlet of Fábrica San José, excavated by Robert D. Drennan.[4] Fábrica San José lies in the eastern piedmont, an area

119 Aerial view of Fábrica San José, an important Guadalupe phase village in the piedmont east of San José Mogote. The low travertine hill in the center of the photograph is a source of saline springs for saltmaking.

suitable for irrigation farming. Its resources include saline springs, which were used as a salt source as early as the Tierras Largas phase, and travertine quarries, which were used as a source of building stone as early as the San José phase.

Drennan estimates that during the Guadalupe phase Fábrica San José covered 2 ha and consisted of eleven households, totaling 50–65 persons. In spite of the community's small size there were significant status differences among its families, as reflected in house type, ceramics, access to craft products, and burial treatment. According to Drennan, the richest Guadalupe phase burials were those of women, suggesting that elite families at San José Mogote may have been practicing hypogamy with the leaders of this nearby salt-producing hamlet.

Burial 39 from Fábrica San José typifies these high-status Guadalupe phase women. Somewhere between 40 and 60 years of age, she was buried prone and fully extended with her arms folded on her chest, accompanied by 53 beads, a jade pendant, and a brown stone bead in her mouth. Beneath her chest was a Delia White beaker (see below). She also had a coarse red jar and two yellow-white bowls. Burial 39 was associated with House LG-1, the most elaborate residence known for the late Guadalupe phase. This house had a partial stone foundation, five superimposed sand floors, several hearths, six human burials, a dog burial, and a jar that had been used to render salt from saline water.

The Delia White beaker is particularly significant, since it served during the Guadalupe phase as a status symbol for elite families. Such vessels typically were

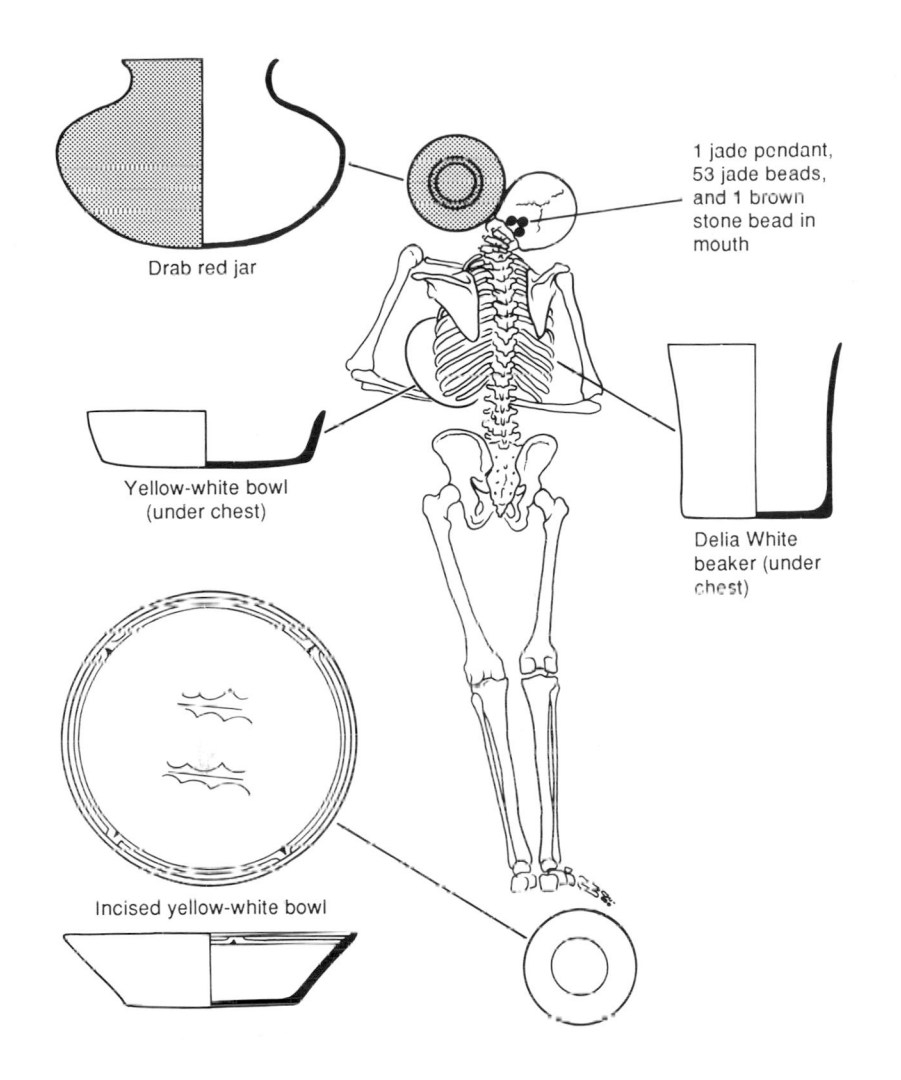

Drab red jar

1 jade pendant, 53 jade beads, and 1 brown stone bead in mouth

Yellow-white bowl (under chest)

Delia White beaker (under chest)

Incised yellow-white bowl

120 Burial 39 at Fábrica San José, a relatively high-status woman.

121 (*Below*) The Delia White beaker, Oaxaca's first clear example of an elite drinking vessel.

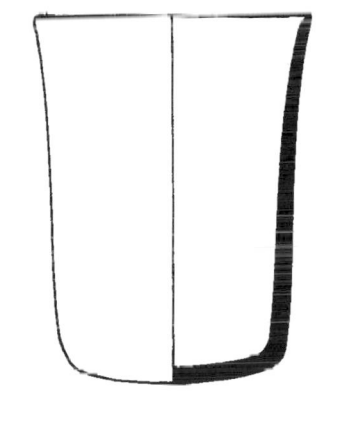

tall beakers with a slightly flaring rim, made of very fine clay, and given a shiny white slip that resembles automobile enamel. Usually holding 600–800 cc of liquid, they were probably used to provide one elite individual with a beverage like chocolate or *pulque* (fermented agave sap). The Delia White beaker is our oldest example of an elite drinking vessel; the tradition would continue in later periods.

Alliance Building Through Feasting

One of the most widespread methods of impressing neighbors and building alliances was the sponsoring of feasts. Feasting, of course, is not diagnostic of any particular evolutionary stage; in an earlier chapter we saw that it is common among autonomous village societies, yet it was also used by Precolumbian states like the Inca.[5]

Evidence of a Guadalupe phase feast comes from Tierras Largas, some 10 km south of San José Mogote. Based on excavations, we estimate Tierras Largas at that time to have been a 3-ha community of 9–10 households, totaling 45–50 persons; based on surface survey, the Settlement Pattern Project estimates its population at 31–157.

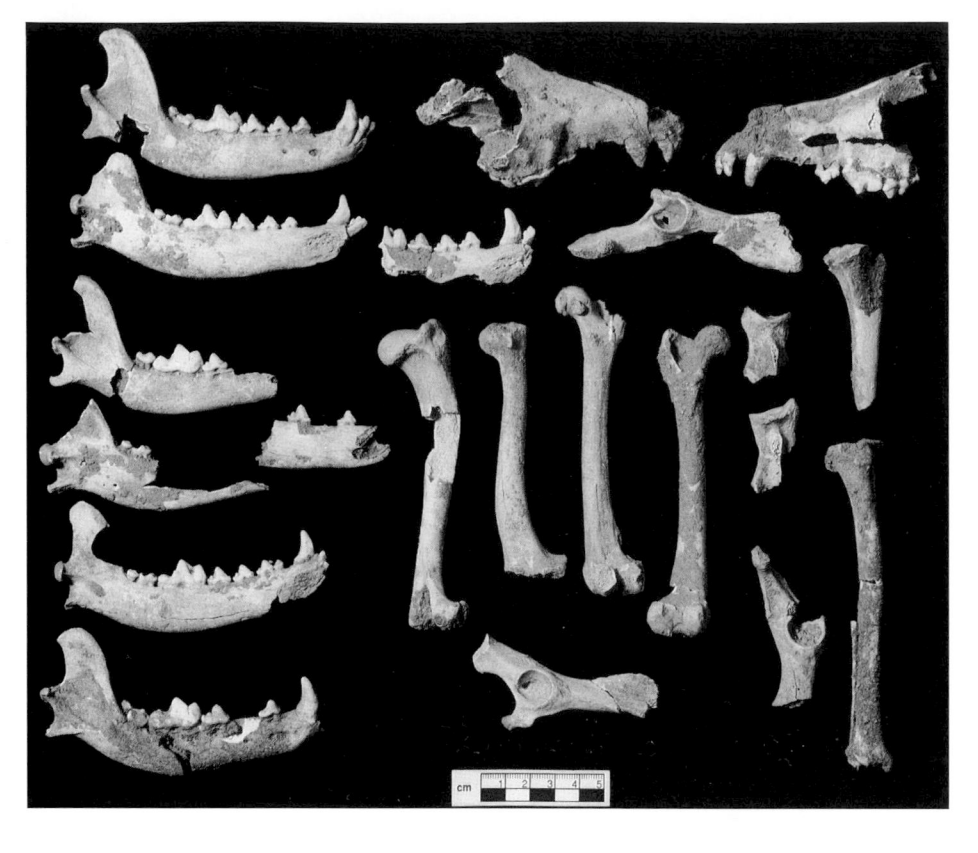

122 A portion of the dog remains from an apparent feast at the village of Tierras Largas. Guadalupe phase.

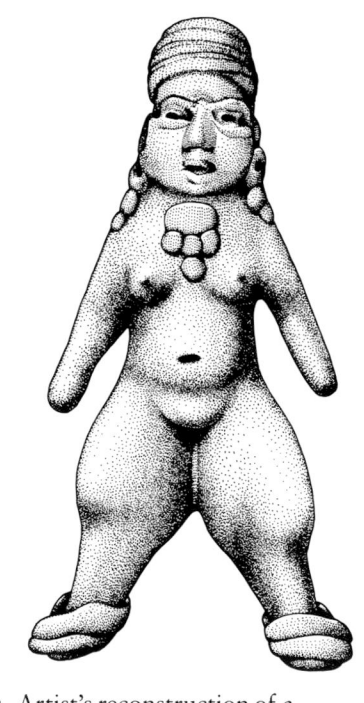

123 Artist's reconstruction of a Guadalupe phase figurine, based on numerous broken specimens. This elite woman wears elaborate ear ornaments, a probable shell pectoral, and elaborate sandals.

At some point in the Guadalupe phase, Tierras Largas was the scene of a feast at which a number of domestic dogs were eaten.[6] Feature 99, a pit used for refuse, contained the remains of at least five dogs (and probably more), all systematically butchered. A number of forelegs were found together, a number of hind legs were found together, and a number of skull elements were found together, as if someone had made a systematic division of the meat in order to provide certain people with specific parts of the animal. All the shoulder blades had been similarly smashed in order to free the humerus and the rest of the forelimb, as if a single chef had done all the butchering.

We do not know whether this feast involved guests from a neighboring community, or only the residents of Tierras Largas itself. Evidence for systematic butchering, cooking, and eating of large quantities of dog meat – at least 50 kg in this case – is rare in the Guadalupe phase, suggesting that Feature 99 records a special event of some kind.

The Appearance of Senior and Cadet Lineages

Robert Drennan's thorough excavation of Fábrica San José reveals another pattern that may be of evolutionary significance. Fábrica San José appears to have been founded during the early Guadalupe phase by a single household, followed soon by a second. By the late Guadalupe phase, when the hamlet had grown to eleven households, the families showing the greatest evidence for high status were those occupying the same locations as the original founders. This phenomenon is consistent with later Zapotec systems of ranking, in which more ancient "senior" or "founder" descent lines were of higher rank than the "junior" or "cadet" lines that branched off them. When people emigrated from growing communities, it was usually the cadet lineages who moved; the senior lineage members stayed behind.

Husband-and-Wife Burials

One of the most interesting developments of the Guadalupe phase was an increase in multiple burials that may include a husband and wife. The pattern is particularly clear at Tierras Largas, where each Guadalupe phase multiple burial included an adult male, presumably a household head. Burial 46 at that site consisted of a 35–40-year-old man, an adult woman, and a child less than a year old. Burial 36 consisted of a seated 25–35-year-old man, a child of 9, and another adult tentatively identified as a woman. Burial 18 consisted of an adult man accompanied by a woman less than 40 years of age.[7]

This trend toward "husband-and-wife" or "family" burials increased with time, supplanting the older pattern of single male burials with Earth or Sky vessels. With increasing frequency it seems to have been important to emphasize one's membership in an elite family rather than in a male line descending from Earth or Sky. Most later Mesoamerican elites reckoned descent bilaterally, emphasizing whichever parent had the most noble pedigree.[8,9] At smaller communities receiving hypogamous brides, little would be gained by emphasizing a father's relationship to Earth, while ignoring an even more highly ranked mother.

Social Information in Guadalupe Phase Figurines

Small solid figurines, presumably still made and used mainly by women, were common in household contexts during the Guadalupe phase. They differed from San José phase figurines, however, in ways that may reflect the escalation of status paraphernalia between 850 and 700 BC. While their facial features remained simple and stereotyped, a great deal of time was spent giving female figurines elaborate turbans, necklaces, and ear ornaments. The makers of figurines also took great pains to depict the details of their sandals, making separate soles and straps and showing just how the latter were interlaced. Almost certainly the makers' intent was to show that high-status women were distinguished by their headgear, their ornaments, and the fact that well-made sandals prevented their feet from touching the ground.

Oaxaca's Relations with Other Regions of Mexico

In Chapters 8 and 9 we have presented evidence for the rise of chiefdoms in the Valley of Oaxaca, rank societies with loss of village autonomy. We do not wish to leave the impression that all this social evolution took place within the boundaries of the Valley of Oaxaca, unaffected by developments elsewhere in Mexico. While we do not believe that the evolution of chiefly society in Oaxaca was caused by events outside the valley, that evolution certainly did not take place in a vacuum. Other societies in Mexico reached the chiefdom level at almost the same time, and those societies were all in contact with each other. Indeed, it is uncanny how similar the process looks in regions as environmentally diverse as the temperate Valley of Oaxaca, the semi-tropical Valley of Morelos, and the tropical coast of Veracruz.

Take, for example, the site of Chalcatzingo in the Valley of Morelos, recently

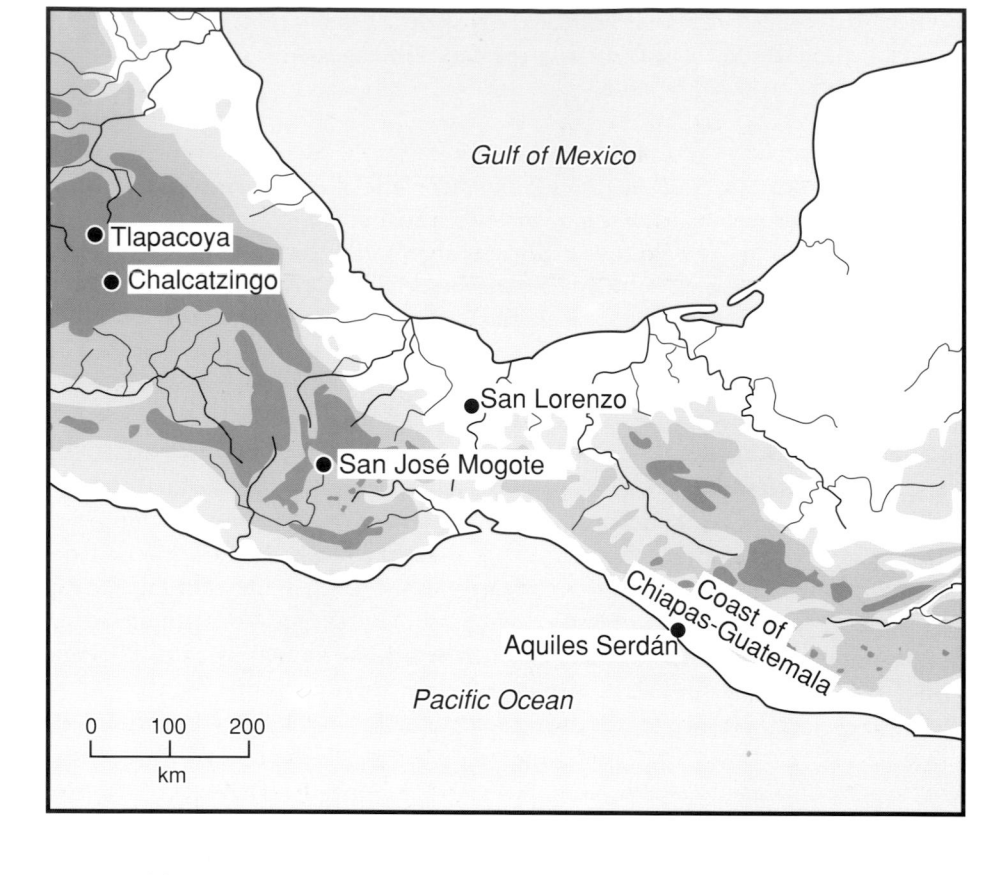

124 A few of the important chiefly centers mentioned in Chapter 9.

excavated by David Grove;[10,11] its hinterland was surveyed by Kenneth Hirth.[12] At 1500 BC Chalcatzingo was a 2-ha hamlet, one of perhaps five local settlements in an area of 800 km². By 1000 BC Chalcatzingo had begun to grow rapidly in surface area, population, and regional importance. Soon it covered 20 ha – one hectare of which was devoted to public buildings – and had dams and terraces constructed on nearby slopes, intensifying agriculture in order to feed its increasingly nucleated population.

By 800 BC, Chalcatzingo had become the dominant civic-ceremonial center for more than 50 settlements. As in the case of San José Mogote, its centripetal pull was such that 50 percent of the region's population clustered within a 6-km radius of Chalcatzingo. Also like San José Mogote, it attracted and held most of the craftspeople of its region and served as a middleman for the movement of local white kaolin clay, Basin of Mexico obsidian, and jade. Between 750 and 500 BC Chalcatzingo had reached 25 ha in extent, with 6 ha devoted to public buildings. Its elite had also commissioned several monumental reliefs, carved into the living rock of the cliffs above the site.

A similiar process can be seen at San Lorenzo in southern Veracruz, excavated in the 1960s by Michael Coe and Richard Diehl[13] and in the 1990s by Ann Cyphers Guillén.[14] In 1350 BC San Lorenzo appears to have been no more than a village, its exact dimensions hidden by later overburden. Between 1350 and 1150 BC there is evidence for the construction of earthen mounds, but as yet no information on whether Men's Houses or "initiates' temples" like those in Oaxaca were built.

During the San Lorenzo phase (1150–850 BC) the site grew enormously; while its exact limits have not yet been ascertained, Coe and Diehl estimate its population at 1000.[15] At this point San Lorenzo had undergone its own ethnogenesis and become a chiefly center of the Olmec culture. Coe and Diehl's work produced no actual buildings of the San Lorenzo phase, no burials, and little in the way of jade. They did, however, produce numbers of magnetite mirrors and considerable evidence for earthen mound construction.

In contrast to the people of San José Mogote, who expended most of their communal labor on architecture, the people of San Lorenzo expended much of their labor on carving and transporting large basalt sculptures. The source of the basalt lay 60 km away and the individual monuments weigh many tons, so the logistics of moving them overland and rafting them up watercourses are impressive. At least one group of carvings, the so-called "colossal heads," are thought to represent paramount chiefs. Other monuments include altars, elite benches or seats, and mythological creatures.

Like Chalcatzingo and San José Mogote, San Lorenzo drew in artisans from a large region, producing shell and iron-ore valuables, fine white pottery, and other materials. This chiefly center may have been the source of many of the conch shell trumpets, stingray spines, and turtle-shell drums traded to the highlands, since San Lorenzo had ready access both to the sea coast and the great rivers of the lowlands.

Between 900 and 700 BC there were periods when this large center, perhaps under attack from rival chiefdoms, suffered loss of population and had many of its monuments defaced or even destroyed. Such acts of destruction were probably the Gulf Coast equivalent of the later burning of Structure 28 at San José Mogote (see Chapter 10). San Lorenzo underwent a brief renaissance between 600 and 400 BC, followed by abandonment.

Unquestionably San José Mogote was in contact with these chiefly societies, as well as others in the Basin of Mexico and Chiapas. Microscopic studies of pottery show that luxury gray ware from the Valley of Oaxaca was traded to San Lorenzo, to Aquiles Serdán on the Pacific Coast of Chiapas, and to Tlapacoya in the Basin of Mexico. Obsidian from the Basin of Mexico, from a source 100 km north of Tehuacán, and from a source in the Guatemalan highlands circulated among all these regions. Oaxaca magnetite reached San Lorenzo and the Valley of Morelos. Pure white pottery, some of it possibly made in Veracruz, was traded to Chalcatzingo, Tehuacán, Oaxaca, and the Chiapas-Guatemala Coast.[16] This means that no rank society of 1150–850 BC arose in isolation; all borrowed ideas on chiefly behavior and symbolism from each other.

It is significant that these early chiefdoms, all featuring carved depictions of Earth and Sky on their pottery, arose at virtually the same time. It is also significant that most show a similar pattern of evolution, whether they arose high in the Oaxaca sierra or at sea level in the Gulf of Mexico lowlands.

In each case a small hamlet, unprepossessing at its founding, underwent a period of rapid and spectacular growth, becoming the demographic center of gravity for a network of smaller sites. Each emerging center – San José Mogote, Chalcatzingo, and San Lorenzo – not only dwarfed the other sites in its region but seems to have exerted a centripetal pull on its entire hinterland. All grew so fast that they must have encouraged immigration, not just normal growth; all emptied the surrounding region of artisans and concentrated them in the paramount chief's village. All were aware of each other and perhaps even competitive; some clearly suffered occasional attacks that left their monuments defaced or their public buildings burned.

What tentative conclusions can we draw from these patterns? First, we do not believe that any one of these early chiefdoms was the "mother culture" from which the others sprang. We see them as "sister cultures" that arose simultaneously through many of the same processes, although we also believe that those processes were accelerated by the fact that all were in contact with each other. This contact meant that an innovation arising in one society could be picked up rapidly by the others; in spite of this, however, not every innovation was picked up. The highlands had suitable raw material, but never adopted the carving of colossal heads from the Gulf Coast. The Gulf Coast, for its part, seems to have been slow in picking up the use of stone masonry, adobe construction, and lime plaster from the highlands.

In spite of their very different environmental settings, all these chiefdoms arose simultaneously, and in such similar ways that ecological functionalism fails to explain them. Some of our colleagues have argued in the past that differences in environmental risk, diversity, and productivity determine the rate and course of social evolution.[17] They single out land and water as two critical variables for which emerging elites competed, commodities whose possession and manipulation determined the course of evolution. Advocates for highland Mesoamerica see irrigation as the key to complex society; advocates for the lowlands see tropical river levee soils as the key. We would argue, on the other hand, that similar *social processes* made the trajectory toward powerful chiefdoms look much the same in the jungles of Veracruz as it did in the thorn forests of Morelos or Oaxaca.

What chiefs in all those regions seem to have desired was the *concentration of manpower*, and it is this process that we see in the hyperdeveloped growth of San José Mogote, Chalcatzingo, and San Lorenzo. One region may have been irrigating with mountain streams, another farming the levees of a tropical river. One region may have been moving 20-ton basalt heads, another moving 20 tons of limestone building blocks. All, however, show the same concentration of population close to the paramount chief's village, the same monopolization of craft production in that community, and the same nucleation of families into one huge chiefly center, regardless of how land and water were distributed.

San José Mogote, Chalcatzingo, and San Lorenzo were not necessarily sitting on the highest concentrations of land and water in their respective regions. They grew large because their chiefs had accomplished what not even the most ambitious Big Man in Bougainville could hope for: they had overcome the autonomy of smaller villages around them, and now controlled the manpower of an entire region.

Chiefly Warfare and Early Writing

> A commonly held view among anthropologists is that chiefdoms
> arose by peaceful means. . . . The Cauca Valley, however, challenges
> this view. . . . It points to the fact that chiefdoms were born out of
> war, were powerfully shaped by war, and continued to be heavily
> involved in war as they evolved.   *Robert Carneiro*[1]

During the period 700–500 BC, known as the Rosario phase, the organization
of the Valley of Oaxaca began to resemble what anthropologists have called a
maximal chiefdom[2] or complex chiefdom.[3] The settlement pattern of such a
society shows a hierarchy of three levels. At the top of the hierarchy we find the
village of a paramount chief, usually the largest and most easily defended community in the region. At the second level of the hierarchy we find several
medium-sized villages, each under the command of a subchief – often a trusted
relative who carries out the orders of the paramount chief. At the third and
lowest level we find small villages or hamlets, whose leaders are under the
command of the subchief at a larger village nearby.

Societies of this type, which once included the Natchez Indians of Mississippi
and the people of Tahiti and Hawaii, show great differences in rank. Often those
differences are reflected in the society's pottery, and the vessels of the Rosario
phase are a case in point. The phase has both: (1) utilitarian pottery, which occurs
in households at every level of the hierarchy; and (2) much more elegant vessels,
which occur mainly in high status residential areas and around important public
buildings.

Even in small villages at the lower two levels of the settlement hierarchy, differences in rank affect pottery distributions. At Fábrica San José, a 3-ha village
in the Etla region, Robert Drennan reports that high-status households had a
higher percentage of bowls, especially decorated bowls of highly burnished gray
ware.[4] Lower-status households had a higher percentage of jars and other drab
storage vessels, especially in coarse brown and buff wares. These differences,
Drennan suspects, result from the fact that high-status families were obliged to
entertain more visitors. Such guests would likely have eaten from bowls of a ware
called Socorro Fine Gray.

Examples of high-status Rosario pottery abound at San José Mogote, the
largest chiefly center in the valley. One of the most obvious elite vessels of this
period was a tall beaker of fine gray ware, decorated with "negative" or "resist"
white motifs. The resist technique was achieved by protecting certain parts of the

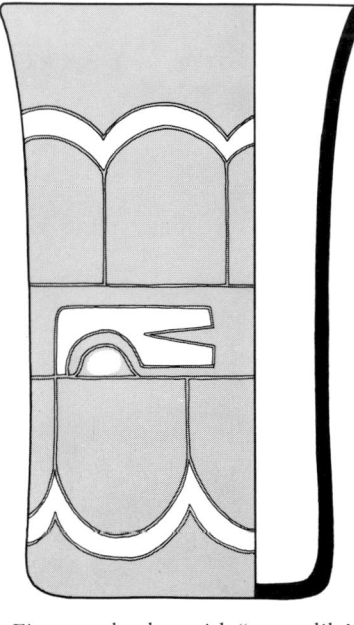

125 Fine gray beaker with "crocodile's foot" motif in resist white. Height 17.4 cm.

126 "Table setting" of miniature fine gray vessels, some with resist white motifs.

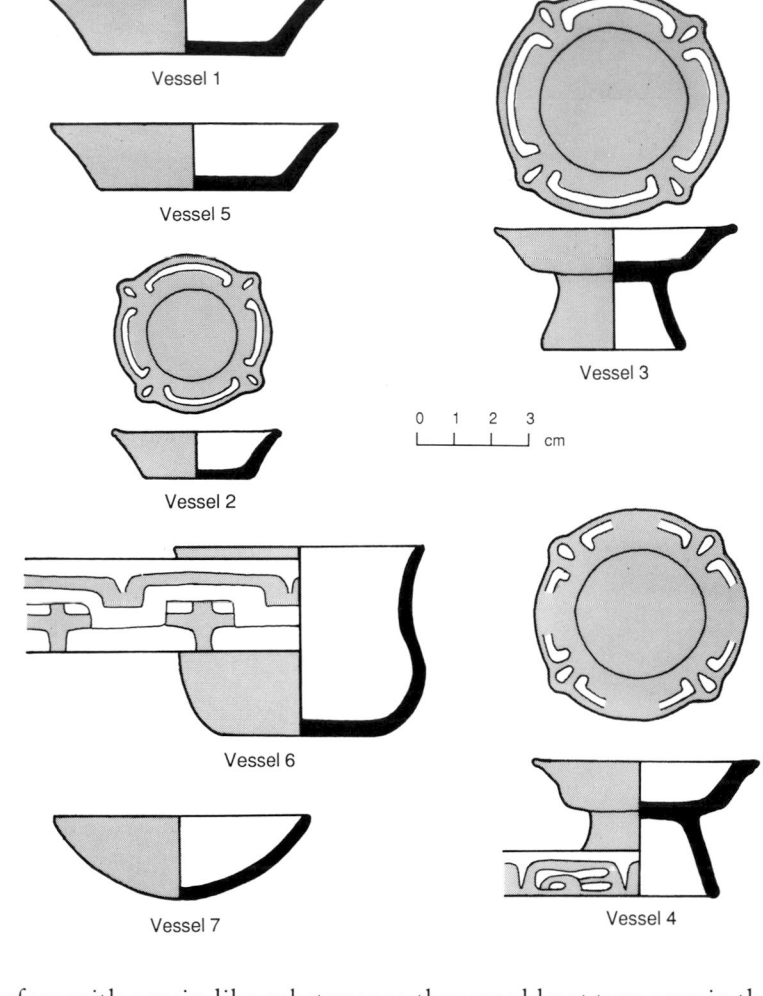

127 Figurine heads of the Rosario phase often featured elaborate hair styles. Height of upper specimen, 6.7 cm.

vessel surface with a resin-like substance so they would not turn gray in the kiln.

Burial 66 at San José Mogote, the remains of two elite youths, featured such a beaker. Like many elegant vessels of its period, it bore an abstract version of the "crocodile's foot" in resist white. This motif was a shorthand reference to Earth, which many ancient Mesoamericans pictured as the back of a giant crocodile.[5] The beaker, shown in ill. 125, was a Rosario phase successor to the Delia White beakers discussed in Chapter 9.

Burial 68, nearby, provides us with a miniature of the "table setting" that elite Rosario hosts might have used. The offering consisted of seven tiny vessels in Socorro Fine Gray, some decorated in resist white. Included were two bowls on pedestals, a decorated jar, and several types of plain bowls. One pedestal bore two references to Earth – the crocodile's foot and several "head clefts" from earth-masks – while a nearby jar was decorated with head clefts and a cross which represents the division of the universe into four quadrants.

While such pottery provides us with information on rank differences among families, it also posed a problem for the Settlement Pattern Project. Simply put, most of the chronological information in Rosario pottery occurs on the elite gray ware. The drab brown and buff wares, so common in low-status residential wards, are difficult to distinguish from the brown and buff wares of the subse-

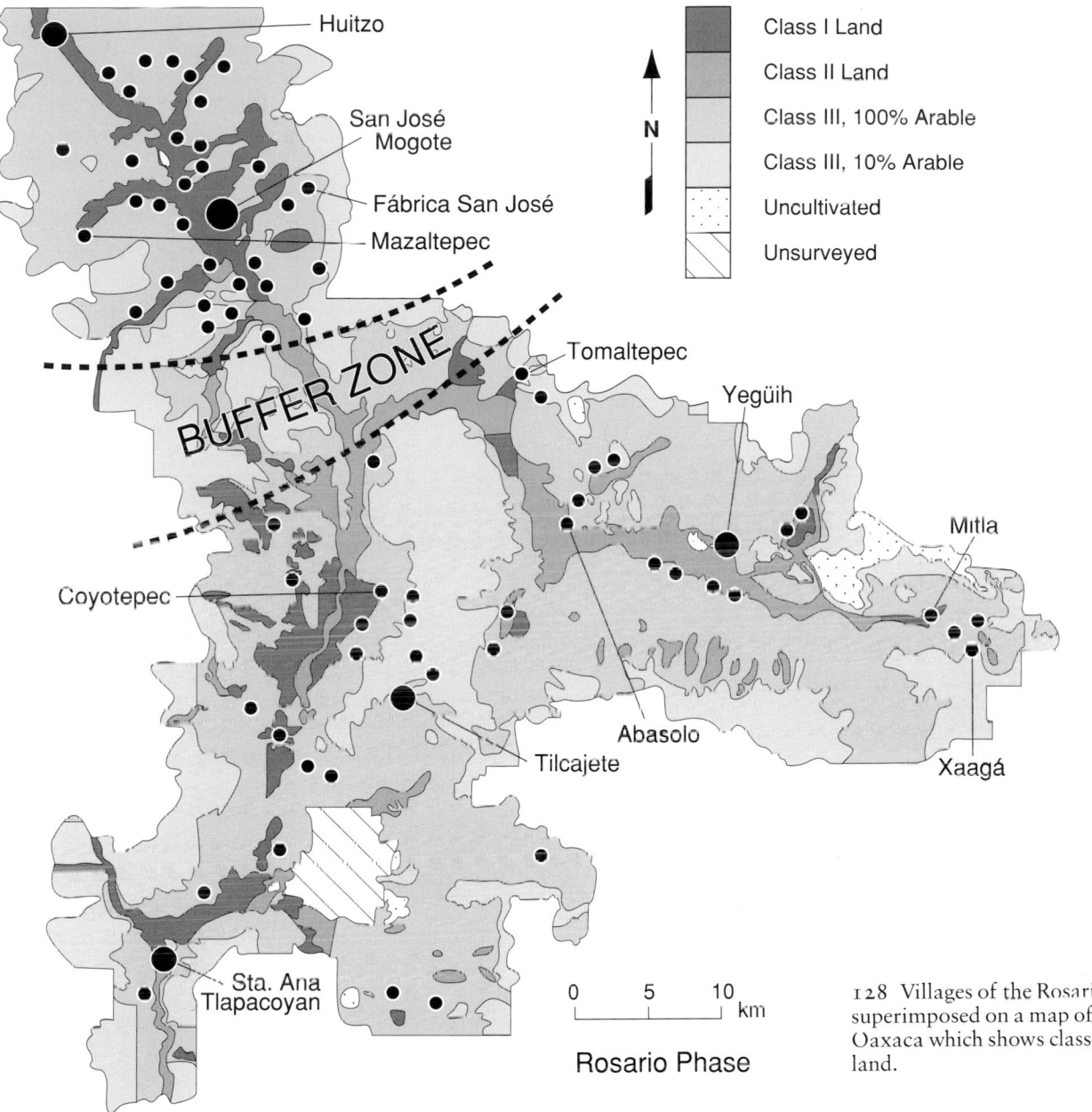

128 Villages of the Rosario phase, superimposed on a map of the Valley of Oaxaca which shows classes of agricultural land.

quent period. Since decorated gray ware is most common on the surface near high-status residences and public buildings, any survey inevitably underestimates the lower-status Rosario population. The estimates we use in this book, therefore, are somewhat higher than those used by our friends on the Settlement Pattern Project.

The Rosario phase saw a substantial increase in the population of the valley, including the occupation of areas never before farmed. There were now between 70 and 85 communities in the valley. Expansion still followed the old settlement

Rosario Phase Settlement Patterns

strategy: a proliferation of small villages that stayed within easy walking distance of the larger villages from which their founders had come.

More than half of all Rosario phase communities were adjacent to Class I land. Perhaps a dozen more were next to Class II land, especially in the central Tlacolula region, where Class I land was scarce. Dozens more, however (including the largest Rosario community in the Valle Grande), lay on Class III land. It seems likely that irrigation made this expansion possible, since 80 percent of all Rosario sites are within 500 m of irrigable land.[6]

We estimate that those 70–85 communities held a *minimum* of 3500 persons, and we would not be surprised if future excavations show the Rosario population to have been 4000 or more. Even the areas where decorated fine gray ware is abundant on the surface had a population estimated at 1800.[7] We consider the latter figure to be an estimate of the Rosario *elite population*, since large areas of low-status Rosario occupation have less decorated gray ware on the surface.

The Effect of Warfare on Settlement Patterns

Warfare, as the lines at the start of this chapter say, can "powerfully shape" chiefdoms. While Carneiro's conclusions were based on Colombia's Cauca Valley, what he says is equally true of the Valley of Oaxaca. Several lines of evidence indicate that warfare had begun to affect Rosario society.

Chiefly warfare usually results from competition between paramounts, or between a paramount and his ambitious subchiefs. Paramounts try to aggrandize themselves by taking followers away from their rivals. Ambitious subchiefs try to replace the paramount at the top of the hierarchy.

Chiefdoms may occasionally clash over resources like good land. Unlike states, however, most chiefdoms do not have the manpower or political structure to conquer and hold on to others' lands. They may therefore content themselves with burning a rival village, destroying its temple or Men's House, killing its chief, then returning home to torture or sacrifice a few prisoners.

This is the kind of raiding the Rosario evidence reflects. Chunks of burnt clay daub appear on the surface of Rosario villages with seven times the frequency seen on typical Valley of Oaxaca sites.[8] Such chunks show up when wattle-and-daub houses or temples are burned, as for example in raids.[9] Later in this chapter we will see an example of a temple deliberately burned, as well as the carved figure of a sacrificed captive.

In chiefdoms with high levels of raiding, villages sometimes were defended with palisades of wooden posts. In later periods in Oaxaca, some villages moved to hilltops and fortified them with stone walls. Indeed, one Rosario village may already have had a defensive wall at this time period.[10] This village, in the piedmont west of San José Mogote, is situated where it could monitor movement into or out of the valley along an old route between the Etla region and the Valley of Nochixtlán.

One way that raiding can affect settlement is by forcing abandonment of regions that cannot be defended. Often a buffer zone, or "no-man's-land," develops between warring chiefdoms. Such a zone seems to have arisen at the juncture of the Valle Grande, Etla, and Tlacolula subvalleys during the Rosario phase.[11]

There was a 9.2-km gap between the southernmost hamlet of the Etla subvalley and its nearest neighbors in the Valle Grande. An even greater gap sepa-

129 A chunk of burnt clay daub from a house, showing the impressions of both the canes in the wall and the cords used to lash them together. Size 7.5 by 8.0 cm.

Site 4-4-14

130 Aerial view of the mounds of Yegüih (Site 4-4-14), on Class II land in the Tlacolula subvalley. Traces of an old floodwater farming channel can be seen in the lower left corner of the photograph.

rated the westernmost hamlet of the Tlacolula subvalley from its nearest neighbors in the Etla region or the Valle Grande. Over 80 km² of this no-man's-land, no Rosario communities have come to light. Despite the fact that it includes plenty of good farm land, this area seems to have been left as a buffer between three competing chiefly societies.

With the wisdom of hindsight, we find it significant that this unoccupied area included the sacred mountain we know today as Monte Albán.

Estimating Rosario Phase Populations

Of the three arms of the valley, it was Etla where society seems to have been the most populous, integrated, and economically well off. Perhaps 2000 people lived in this region, whose paramount center was San José Mogote. This large community was at the top of a hierarchy of 18–23 villages. At the extreme north end of the Etla subvalley was Huitzo, a 3-ha village with its own impressive public buildings. Huitzo may have been wholly or partly autonomous, with a few satellite hamlets of its own.

San José Mogote sprawled over 60–65 ha and had, we believe, about 1000 persons. Within that sprawl were seven areas of elite residence as defined by decorated fine gray ware. These seven areas cover 33.7 ha and had an estimated 564 persons. The "downtown" area of public buildings and elite residences alone covered at least 42 ha. The concentrations of fine gray ware were surrounded by areas of lower-status occupation.

Villages in the hierarchy below San José Mogote included Fábrica San José, with 50–80 persons living in 10–16 households, and Tierras Largas, with 50 persons living in 9–10 households. Fábrica San José, which supplied San José Mogote with salt for seasoning and travertine blocks for construction, still seems to have been linked to the latter community by hypogamous marriages (see below).

The Tlacolula Subvalley

We believe that the Tlacolula subvalley had a population of 700–1000 persons. The main chiefly center for this region was Yegüih, whose total population we estimate at 200–500. There is enough decorated fine gray ware at Yegüih to suggest an elite occupation of 132 persons, and several artificial mounds may have been built during this period. In the hierarchy below Yegüih were villages like Tomaltepec (50–80 persons in 10–15 households), Abasolo (25–50 persons in 5–10 households), and Xaagá near Mitla.

The Valle Grande

We estimate the population of the Valle Grande at 700–1000 persons. In this region there were large Rosario villages in several different environmental settings. We believe that San Martín Tilcajete, occupying a low ridge between two irrigable streams, was the paramount center for this subvalley. At lower levels of the hierarchy were villages like San Bartolo Coyotepec (on Class I land in the broad center of the Valle Grande) and Santa Ana Tlapacoyan (far to the south, in the "Y" between the Atoyac and Mixtepec Rivers).

Cluster, Frontier, and Buffer Zone in the Rosario Phase

Despite their differences in population, the three arms of the valley show similarities. Each arm seems to have had one major population cluster, centered on a large village. Each also had a 3-ha village on its outskirts, as if monitoring the frontier.

In the Etla arm 18–23 villages clustered around San José Mogote, with Huitzo guarding the northern frontier. In Tlacolula, 10–12 villages clustered around Yegüih, with Mitla-Xaagá guarding the eastern frontier. In the Valle Grande, 10–12 villages clustered around Tilcajete, with Tlapacoyan guarding the southern frontier. Finally, in the middle of the valley we find the aforementioned buffer zone, in which it was apparently too risky to settle.

Public Buildings of the Rosario Phase

Public buildings of the Rosario phase reinforce our suspicions of chiefly competition: (1) they include some of the largest and most ostentatious structures seen so far in the valley; and (2) at least some of them were apparently burned by rival villages.

Public Buildings at San José Mogote

The most prominent landmark at San José Mogote is Mound 1, a modified natural hill that towered over the rest of the village. During Rosario times the most important public buildings were placed atop this hill, making them visible from a greater distance but probably reducing their accessibility to lower-status villagers.

Structure 19

Structure 19, built in three stages, was the most centrally placed Rosario building on Mound 1. Its first stage, called 19B, was a rectangular stone platform 17 m on a side and oriented 8 degrees north of east. On top of this building sat Structure 28, a lime-plastered platform of rectangular adobes and earthen fill.

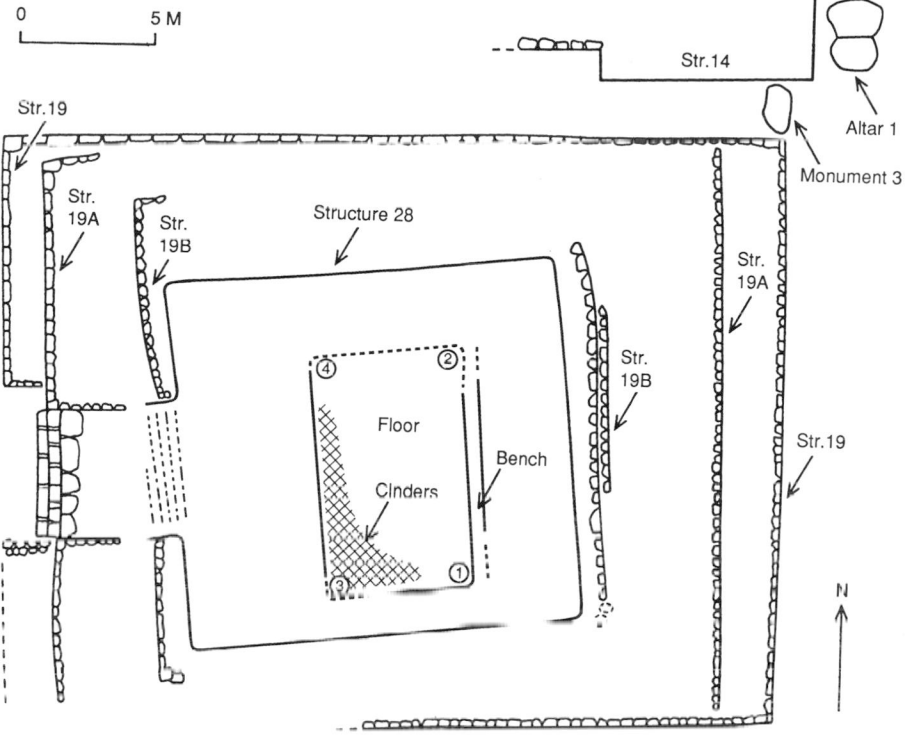

0   5 M

Str.19

Str.
19A

Str.
19B

Structure 28

Str.14

Altar 1

Monument 3

Str.
19A

Str.
19B

Str.19

4 ②

Floor

Bench

Cinders

③ ①

N

131 Plan of Structures 28, 19B, 19A, and 19 at San José Mogote, a series of Rosario phase public structures. The circled numbers indicate places where four offering vessels were buried beneath the floor of the burnt temple on Structure 28. Also shown are Structure 14 and Monument 3.

132 Its point broken off in antiquity, this imitation stingray spine chipped from an obsidian blade was found on the floor of the Structure 28 temple. Length 12 cm.

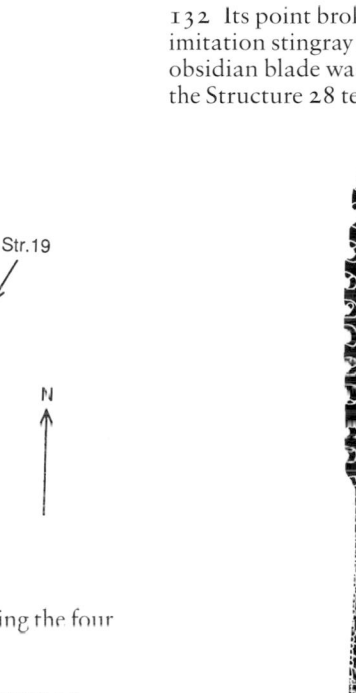

133 (Below) Structure 28 (atop Structure 19) seen from the northwest, showing the four offering vessels found beneath the corners of the temple.

134 (Below, right) The remains of the stone stairway on the west side of Structure 19.

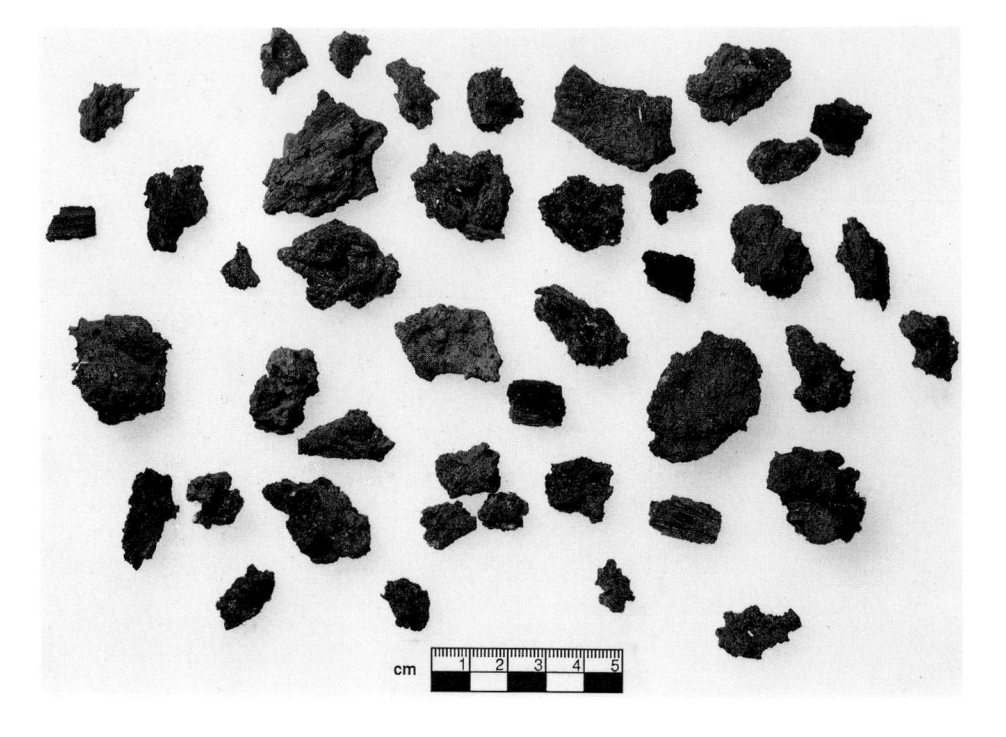

135 A sample of vitrified cinders from the floor of the burnt temple on Structure 28.

Structure 28 evidently supported a massive wattle-and-daub temple whose floor was recessed into the adobe platform. Buried under each corner of that floor was a large serving vessel – burnished brown vessels under the northeast and southwest corners, burnished gray vessels under the northwest and southeast corners. These large bowls, which could have held food for many celebrants during the building's inauguration, were evidently buried as dedicatory offerings. Lying broken on the floor of the temple was an imitation stingray spine for ritual bloodletting, chipped from a large blade of imported obsidian.

Later in the Rosario phase, the village leaders twice enlarged Structure 19. The second stage, called 19A, was 25.5 by 20 m and oriented east–west, with a new stone masonry stairway. The third and final enlargement measured 21.7 by 28.5 m and was done with limestone blocks – some weighing half a ton – hauled from a quarry on the opposite side of the Atoyac River. These limestone blocks had to be brought across 5 km of valley, rafted across the river, and dragged to the top of a 13-m hill.

Evidence for Raiding: Part 1

Now let us turn to the wattle-and-daub temple on Structure 28. Late in its history, this temple had been the scene of an intense fire that destroyed the building and left behind thousands of fragments of burnt daub. So intense was the fire that the clay daub of the temple vitrified, turning to masses of grayish, glassy cinders.

Recent experimental burning of wattle-and-daub buildings shows it to be unlikely that so destructive a fire was accidental. Gary Shaffer, the archaeologist who conducted the experiments, found that to sinter such large quantities of daub, the fire must be set deliberately.[12]

Sixteenth-century documents tell us that when later Mesoamerican societies raided one another, a main objective was to burn their enemies' temple. So common was this practice that a picture of a burning temple became an iconographic convention for raiding among the Aztec.[13] We suspect that the ferocious burning of the Structure 28 temple is evidence for such a raid. It highlights the extent to which warfare had become one of the tactics employed by competing Rosario chiefs.

Structure 14

Late in the Rosario phase, a second building with an east–west orientation was built just to the north of Structure 19. We know much less about this new building, called Structure 14, because it was greatly modified in later periods. Its Rosario stage was a low platform with a monumental stairway on the east, leading down the crest of Mound 1. The stairway was built of limestone blocks weighing up to half a ton; unfortunately, so many of these blocks were "borrowed" in later periods that the original plan of Structure 14 will never be known. We suspect it looked something like Temples X and T-Sur at Monte Negro, a site discussed in Chapter 12.

Evidence for Raiding: Part 2

Separating Structures 14 and 19 at San José Mogote was a narrow corridor. At its eastern entrance, serving as threshold for the corridor, was a horizontal stone slab called Monument 3. Anyone entering the corridor would have stepped on the figure carved on the upper surface of this slab. The carving depicts a naked man sprawled awkwardly on his back, mouth open and eyes closed. A complex scroll motif shows us where his chest had been opened to remove his heart during sacrifice. A ribbon-like stream of blood extends from this scroll to the border of the monument, ending in two motifs that wrap around the edge of the slab.

136 Many Mesoamerican peoples depicted raiding and conquest by drawing a burning temple. This burning temple and unburied corpse are from the Codex Mendoza, an Aztec document.

137 Top and side views of Monument 3 at San José Mogote, an early representation of a sacrificed captive with a hieroglyphic day-name. Length 1.45 m.

These two motifs, each made of a circle and triangle, are stylized drops of blood. In later periods, the same motif would be carved on the stairways of temples where sacrifices were performed.

Carved between the feet of this unfortunate victim are two hieroglyphs – a dot which stands for the number "one" and a glyph for the word *Xòo*, or "Earthquake," the seventeenth day-name in the Zapotec ritual calendar. Based on our knowledge of the historic Zapotec (Chapter 1), we can suggest that this is the victim's personal day-name – "1 Earthquake" – taken from the 260-day calendar.

Monument 3 makes possible the following inferences about the Rosario phase. (1) The 260-day calendar clearly existed by this time. (2) The use of *Xòo*, a known Zapotec day-name, relates the hieroglyphs to an archaic form of the Zapotec language. (3) The carving makes it clear that Rosario phase sacrifice was not limited to drawing one's own blood with stingray spines; it now included human sacrifice by heart removal. (4) Since 1 Earthquake is shown naked, even stripped of whatever ornaments he might have worn, he fits our sixteenth-century descriptions of prisoners taken in battle. This carving of a prisoner, combined with the burning of the temple on Structure 28, suggests that by 600 BC the well-known Zapotec pattern of raiding, temple burning, and capture of enemies for sacrifice had begun. (5) Many later Mesoamerican peoples, including the Maya, set carvings of their defeated enemies where they could be literally and metaphorically "trod upon." The horizontal placement of Monument 3 suggests that it, too, was designed for that visual metaphor.

The Origins of Writing

Finally, we note that it did not satisfy the paramount of San José Mogote to depict his vanquished and sacrificed rival in art: he had to add the victim's calendric name. Like so many patterns of the Rosario phase, this first example of Zapotec writing appears in the context of chiefly competition. It appears that Zapotec writing was born of that competition, and went on in later times to become a weapon in the power struggles of rulers.[14]

Circular Public Structures

During the Rosario phase, for the first time in the Oaxaca sequence, we see public structures with a circular shape. The best known is Structure 31, on Mound 1 at San José Mogote. Evidently a circular platform 6 m in diameter, it

138 The base of a circular adobe platform at San José Mogote. The workman sits on a spoke-like retaining wall as he removes the earthen fill.

had outer adobe walls that may once have been 50–60 cm high. Its interior was earthen fill, strengthened by spoke-like retaining walls of mud brick.

We have no idea how such circular platforms were used. Circular structures are rare in Oaxaca, where even low altars are usually rectangular. We do know that Mesoamerican cultures used circular platforms for acts involving rapid movement. Dancers, for example, were less likely to fall from a circular platform because the distance from center to edge was uniform. Some later Mesoamerican groups also used circular platforms for gladiatorial combat between a skilled warrior and a prisoner taken for sacrifice.

Even villages in the second tier of the settlement hierarchy are known to have had impressive public buildings. Tomaltepec, in the piedmont of the Tlacolula sub-valley, was such a place. Although it probably had only 50–75 persons, Tomaltepec's ritual life centered around an adobe structure more than 3 m high.[15] This platform, which probably supported a modest wattle-and-daub temple, had four dedicatory burials in its fill.

Huitzo, a 3-ha village that may have remained outside San José Mogote's control, had particularly impressive public architecture. Structure 2 at Huitzo was a large temple platform with retaining walls of stone and adobe, and a possible stairway on the west; it was more than 20 m long and oriented 8 degrees north of east. Under one of the retaining walls was the skeleton of a man 35–40 years old, crushed beneath the weight of the adobes. This individual may represent a sacrificial victim incorporated into the platform.

Public Buildings at Second-order Villages

We do not know how many distinctions in rank there were in Rosario society. Certainly the known residences imply a greater range of status than we saw in the San José or Guadalupe phases.

The largest Rosario houses found so far were on Mound 1 at San José Mogote. The best known, consisting of Structures 25, 26, and 30, was built above the ruins of the burned temple already described; it overlooked the rest of the village from a height of 15 m. While badly damaged by later construction, the residence seems to have consisted of a puddled clay patio surrounded by adobe room complexes. Under the floor of the patio was a two-chambered tomb.

The room complex on the west, called Structure 26, was the most complete; its walls were of rectangular adobes over a foundation of stones. Room 1, in its southeast corner, was a 1.7-m² storage unit, sunk more than a meter below the level of the patio. Left behind in this room were five vessels that may have been used for entertaining guests or performing rituals: several large serving bowls, a cooking pot, and an anthropomorphic incense brazier. The brazier is particularly interesting because it represents the first stage in a long Zapotec tradition – the effigy incense burner, used to communicate with departed noble ancestors by sending a column of incense skyward to the clouds where they resided. In later periods we will see more elaborate versions of such braziers.

Room 2 of Structure 26 was only 1 m wide. Flattened beneath one wall of this room was the skeleton of an adult, Burial 55, apparently incorporated into the building at the time of its construction. Farther to the north lay Room 3, under whose floor had been buried a high-ranking woman called Burial 60. She was

Elite Residences from San José Mogote

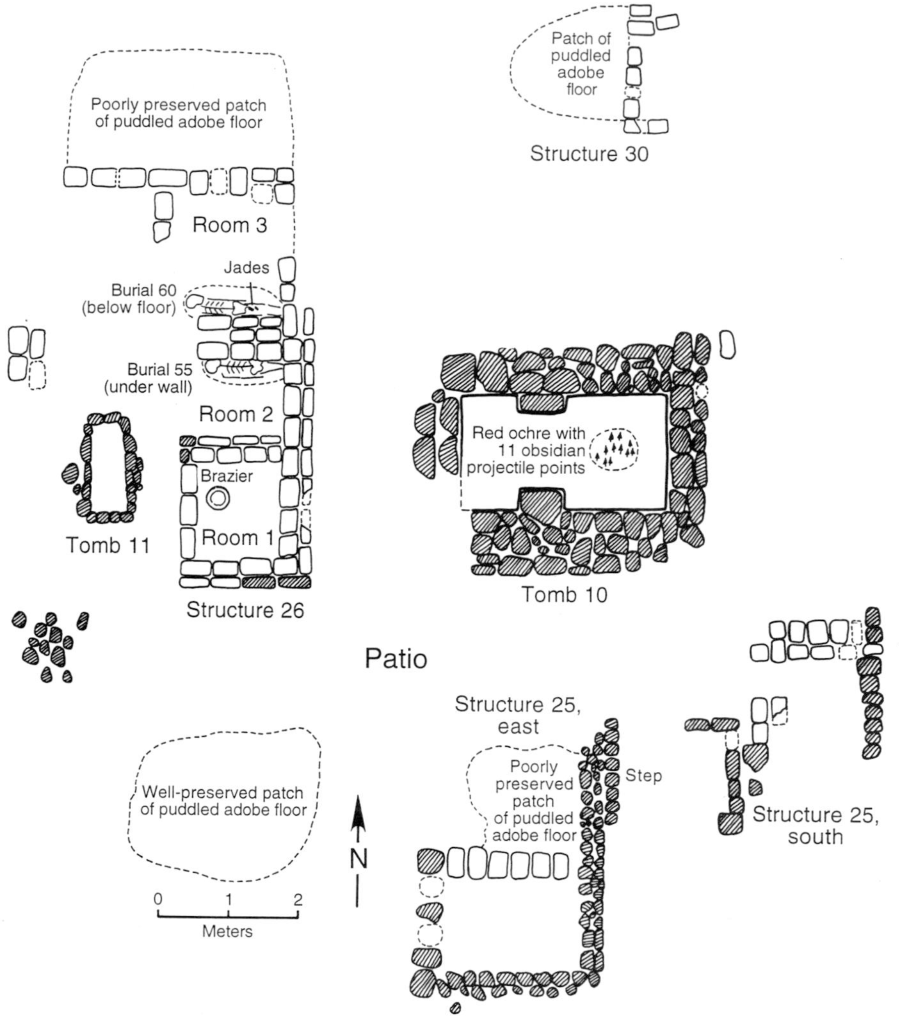

Poorly preserved patch of puddled adobe floor

Room 3

Patch of puddled adobe floor

Structure 30

Jades

Burial 60
(below floor)

Burial 55
(under wall)

Room 2

Red ochre with
11 obsidian
projectile points

Brazier

Tomb 11

Room 1

Structure 26

Tomb 10

Patio

Structure 25,
east

Well-preserved patch
of puddled adobe floor

Poorly
preserved
patch
of puddled
adobe floor

Step

Structure 25,
south

N

0   1   2

Meters

139 (*Above*) Remains of a Rosario phase elite residence at San José Mogote, with interior patio and tomb.

140 (*Top right*) Room 1 of Structure 26 at San José Mogote, an apparent storage unit.

141 (*Center, right*) Anthropomorphic incense brazier from Room 1 of Structure 26. Height *c.* 30 cm.

142 (*Near right*) Burial 60 of San José Mogote, a Rosario phase woman with jade ornaments and tabular erect cranial deformation.

143 (*Far right*) Jade ornaments found with Burial 60 of San José Mogote. Length of largest specimen, 5.3 cm.

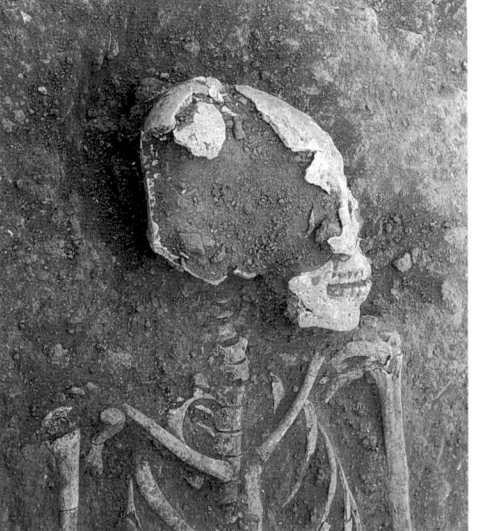

144 Tomb 10 of San José Mogote.

fully extended face up, arms at her sides, accompanied by three jade ornaments; her skull showed the tabular deformation seen in several elite Rosario burials.

Tomb 10, found beneath the patio floor of this residence, was the largest and most complex of its time. Three meters long and almost 2 m wide, it was divided by short walls into a main chamber and an antechamber – our first example of another Zapotec tradition, to be elaborated in later periods. Built of stone masonry, its floor made from flagstones, the tomb had a coating of mud plaster on its interior. It had been emptied late in the Rosario phase, perhaps when the house was abandoned. Evidently the human remains from Tomb 10, along with most of the offerings, had been taken by the departing residents. One knee cap and a few human ribs had been overlooked.

Also left behind in Tomb 10 was an offering of eleven small projectile points, probably missed because they were buried in a large deposit of red ochre. A study by William Parry shows that all eleven points had been made from three large blades of imported greenish-black obsidian.[16] These points may well have been hafted as atlatl darts, and their inclusion in the tomb suggests that some kind of military activity – perhaps raiding, or defense from raiding – might have been expected of the individual buried there.

Chiefly families were usually more involved in village ritual than lower-ranked families, and the objects found near Structures 25, 26, and 30 bear this out. Included was the broken tip of a bloodletting tool, beautifully chipped from imported obsidian. It may be the point of an obsidian "stingray spine" like the one found in the burned temple on Structure 28.

Also included was a pottery whistle in fine gray ware, shaped like the lower leg of a jaguar or puma. This instrument, which makes a high-pitched note like a

145 (*Above, left*) Eleven obsidian projectile points (and one leftover piece of raw material) from Tomb 10, San José Mogote.

146 (*Above, right*) Broken tip of an obsidian bloodletting tool found near Structures 25, 26, and 30, San José Mogote. Length 5.5 cm.

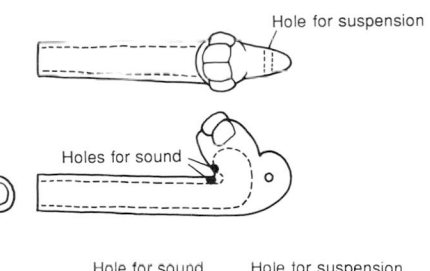

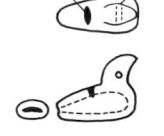

147, 148 Pottery whistles (*above*) in the shape of a jaguar or puma leg, length 6.5 cm, and (*below*) in the shape of a bird, length 2 cm. Rosario phase.

referee's whistle, was perforated for suspension around the owner's neck. Its presence in this high-status house is not unprecedented; a second fine gray whistle appeared in Structure 27, another elite Rosario house found on Mound 1. The second whistle, in the shape of a bird, was also perforated for suspension.

Finding such items in elite context is no surprise. In Mesoamerica the bloodletting of nobles brought supernatural favor to the whole community, the bellow of the conch shell trumpet was used to call people to temples, and the shrill whistles that directed warriors were worn around the necks of a chosen few.

Residences from Tomaltepec, a Second-order Community

As we have seen, Tomaltepec had its own public building during the Rosario phase. It also had families important enough to live in houses of adobe, while their neighbors lived in houses of wattle-and-daub.

Houses 5 and 7 at Tomaltepec formed an L-shaped unit around a patio or work area, each building having roughly 10.5 m² of floor area. Built of adobes over a stone foundation, this two-structure unit may represent the home of an extended family. Associated were a hearth, an earth oven or roasting pit, two infants buried beneath the patio, and a fragment of turtle-shell drum.

Residences from Fábrica San José, a Third-order Community

Fábrica San José, a village linked to San José Mogote through most of its history, is thought by Robert Drennan to have consisted of 10–16 Rosario households.[17] While there is no evidence of high-status residences like those of San José Mogote, Fábrica San José had families who lived in relatively large houses, used sumptuary goods, and displayed cranial deformation.

Household Rosario-1 of Fábrica San José provides an example: the house had a hearth, several middens, two burials, and an apparent earth oven. One of the burials, shown in ill. 149, was a young woman about 15 years of age with an artificially deformed skull. Her offerings included a large hollow human figure in fine gray pottery (perhaps representing an important ancestor); six more fine gray vessels; and offerings of marine shell.[18] This young woman continues the tradition of rich female burials already seen in the Guadalupe phase, suggesting an ongoing pattern of marriages between elite women from San José Mogote and the male leaders of its satellite communities.

Ordinary families at Fábrica San José still lived in houses of wattle-and-daub, some of them quite large. Household Rosario-2, for which a partial plan is available, was more than 11 m long north–south; probably it was divided into smaller rooms by wattle walls. Built on a foundation of stones, Rosario-2 was eventually burned, leaving behind 279 fragments of burnt daub. Associated with this house were six hearths, extensive midden deposits, and two circles of ash that may reflect the use of charcoal braziers.

The artifacts found with Rosario-2 tell us about the activities of a large household of low to medium rank. In addition to subsistence farming, the family was involved in producing salt by boiling the water from a nearby saline spring. They also spun coarse fiber, using sherd discs as spindle whorls. Two bone awls, a gouge, and a bone needle imply sewing and leatherworking. Their gray pottery also shows the "lower than expected frequency of incised decoration" which makes low-status Rosario households so difficult to identify from surface remains.[19]

Opposite

149 Burial 54 at Fábrica San José, a young high-status woman of the Rosario phase.

150 Partial plan of Household Rosario-2 at Fábrica San José, a low- to medium-status household of the Rosario phase.

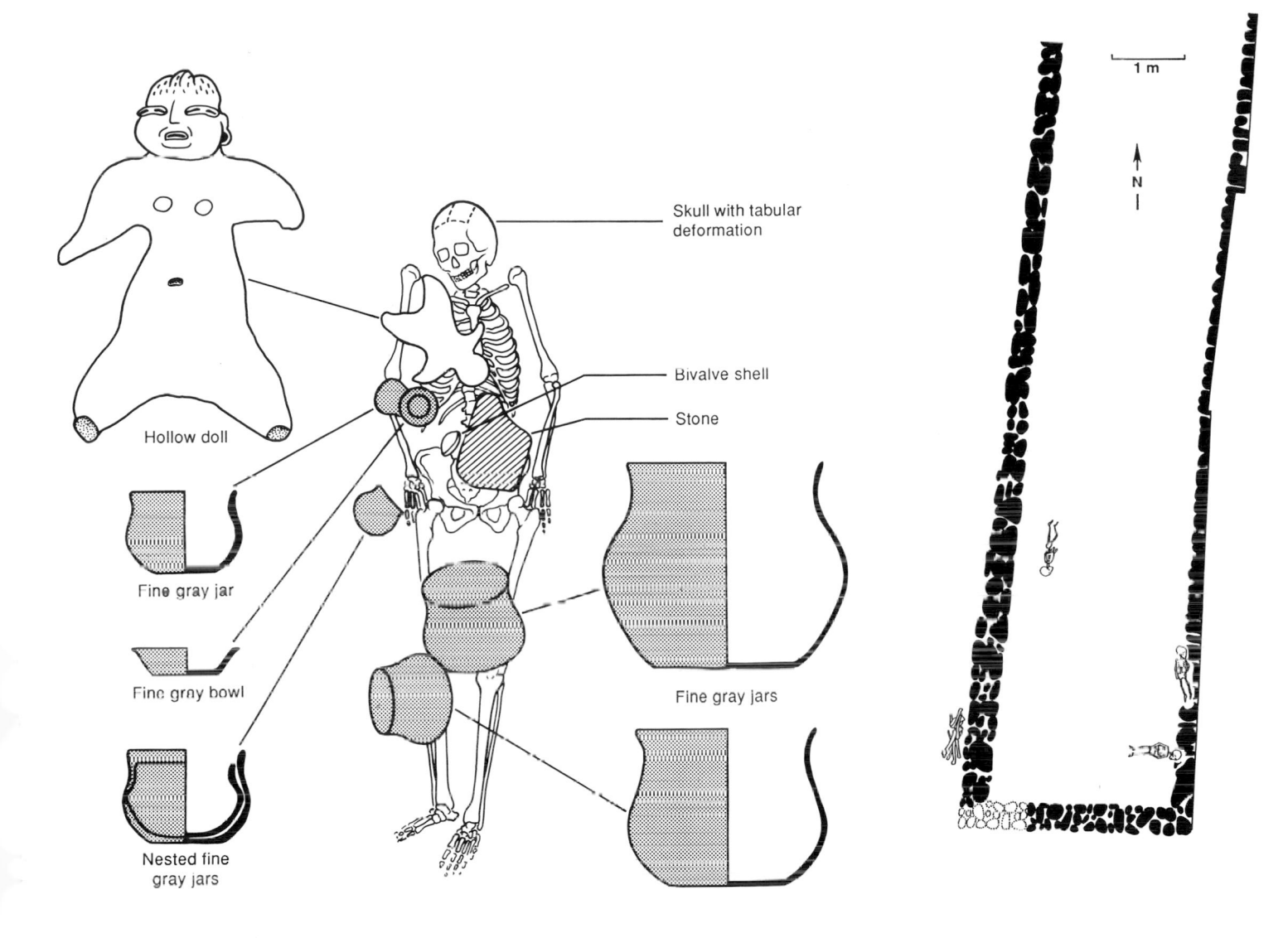

Hollow doll

Fine gray jar

Fine gray bowl

Nested fine
gray jars

Skull with tabular
deformation

Bivalve shell

Stone

Fine gray jars

1 m

N

What picture do all these data give us of the Rosario society? It is a picture not unlike that painted by Robert Carneiro for Colombia's Cauca region. Within a valley occupied by thousands of Indians, paramounts competed with their sub-chiefs for the manpower to grow crops, produce crafts, and build temples. There were raids in which temples were burned and captives taken for later sacrifice. Areas of good farm land were left vacant to serve as buffer zones between the followers of one chief and the followers of another. The Valley of Oaxaca as a whole was not heavily populated, but certain areas had disproportionately high populations, owing to various leaders' attempts to concentrate their supporters.

As we did in Chapter 9, we must now stress that these events were not taking place in a vacuum. They were influenced by, and in turn had influence on, events elsewhere in Mexico.

Developments Elsewhere in Mexico

The Tehuacán Valley

One area where similar events were taking place was the Tehuacán Valley, sepa-rated from the Etla region by 100 km of canyons and mountain passes. The

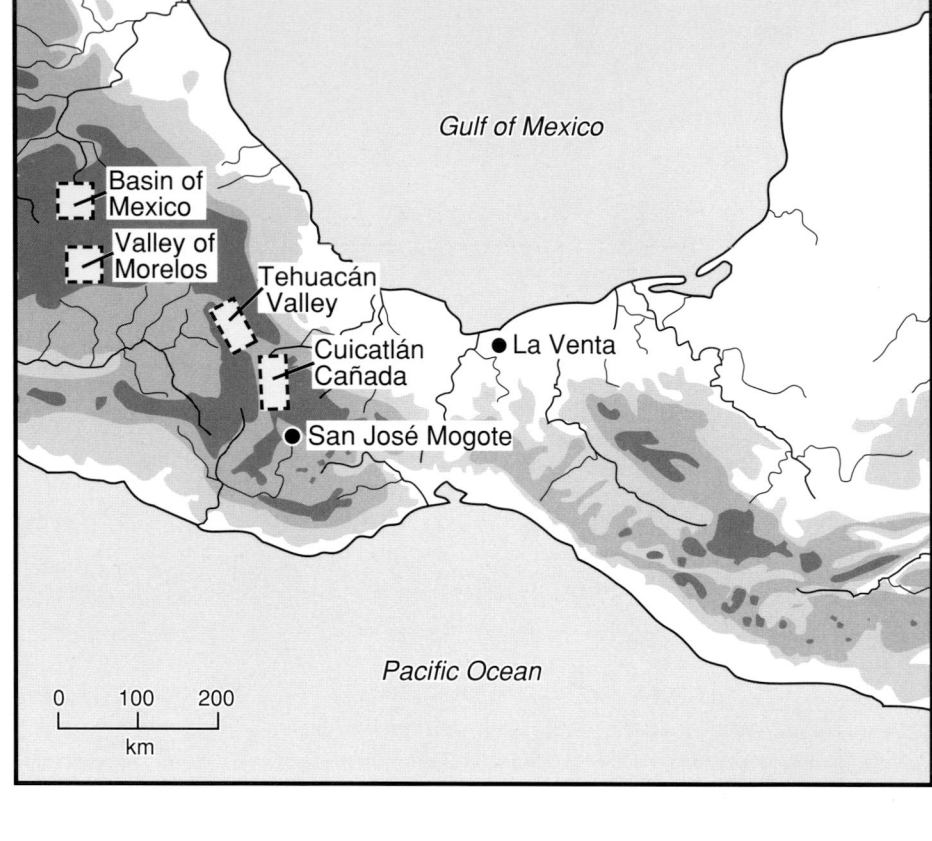

151 Areas to the west and east of the Valley of Oaxaca which underwent similar development between 700 and 500 BC.

southern Tehuacán Valley is a hot, dry area where the probability of insufficient rainfall for most kinds of farming is 80 percent.[20] It does, however, have the potential for irrigation. That potential is perhaps best exemplified by the Arroyo Lencho Diego, a steep-sided canyon investigated by Richard S. MacNeish, Richard Woodbury, James A. Neely, and Charles Spencer.[21-23] Recently, Spencer described the rise of chiefly society in the region.[24]

At a time equivalent to the late Guadalupe or early Rosario phases in the Etla region, one village of 9–12 households appeared in the Arroyo Lencho Diego. Spencer considers the prestige differences in this village to be "modest" and based on achievement. One of the community's most impressive achievements was the construction of a dam in the arroyo, creating a reservoir with an estimated capacity of 37,000 m³.[25] This early dam was 6 m wide, 2.8 m high, and 175 m long. Spencer estimates that it could have been built in a single dry season by a labor force of no more than eight able-bodied persons.

This dam greatly raised the agricultural potential of the Arroyo Lencho Diego. By 600–450 BC the population of the arroyo had risen to 30–34 households living in two villages, one of which had a public building. At roughly the same time that the occupants of San José Mogote were completing Structures 14 and 19, the inhabitants of the Arroyo Lencho Diego greatly enlarged their dam. This second stage gave the dam a width of 100 m, a height of 8 m, and a length of 400 m, creating a reservoir of 1,430,000 m³. Spencer calculates that a labor force of 41–106 persons would have been necessary: (1) to construct a coffer dam and spillway during one dry season; then (2) to build the dam itself over

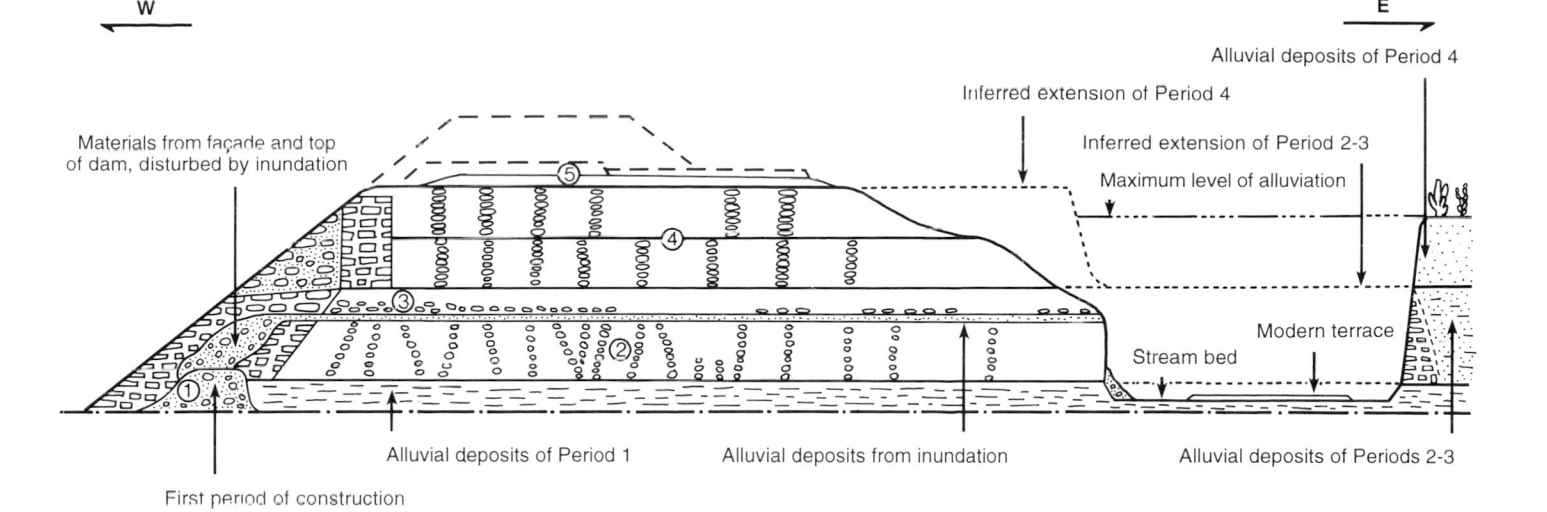

W → E

Alluvial deposits of Period 4

Inferred extension of Period 4

Materials from façade and top of dam, disturbed by inundation

Inferred extension of Period 2-3

Maximum level of alluviation

⑤

④

③

②

①

Modern terrace

Stream bed

Alluvial deposits of Period 1

Alluvial deposits from inundation

Alluvial deposits of Periods 2-3

First period of construction

0　5　10　15　20m

three dry seasons. By this time, village autonomy in the Arroyo Lencho Diego had been overcome, with the labor forces of several villages coming under the control of elite families living upstream from the dam.[26]

Spencer's reconstruction of events, like ours, focuses on the ability of an emerging elite to draw manpower from several communities in the course of large public construction. In both Tehuacán and Oaxaca, elite families lived in houses that were larger and better made than those of other villagers; had higher quantities of goods imported from outside their region; and used greater numbers of fine gray bowls, probably for entertaining.

The pottery styles of Tehuacán and Oaxaca were similar enough at this time to leave no doubt that these two areas were in contact, probably as the result of the obsidian trade moving through the intervening Cuicatlán Cañada. The elite

152 Cross-section of the prehispanic dam in the Arroyo Lencho Diego, showing the deeply buried first and second periods of construction. (Enlargement continued in later periods.)

153 The prehispanic dam in the Arroyo Lencho Diego as it looks today, having since been cut through by the arroyo.

families of the two regions thus knew each other, undoubtedly borrowed ideas from each other, and may even have sought to outdo each other in prestige and public works. Their specific historical trajectories and ecological settings were different, but they now formed part of a larger "system" in which many symbols of prestige were shared.

The Gulf Coast

Farther from the Valley of Oaxaca, in the Olmec region of Mexico's southern Gulf Coast, another maximal chiefdom was reaching its peak. Its paramount center was La Venta in the state of Tabasco, and it is believed to have reached its highest development between 800 and 400 BC. In its later stages, therefore, it overlaps with the Rosario and succeeding Early Monte Albán I phases in the Valley of Oaxaca.

The centerpiece of La Venta was an alignment of artificial mounds and plazas extending for 750 m along an axis 8 degrees west of north.[27] Like their Rosario counterparts, the architects of La Venta made use of rectangular adobes and clay fill; they did not, however, use cut stone or lime plaster. Instead, the builders of La Venta plastered their platforms with red, yellow, or purple clays, and built fences and borders with natural "columns" of columnar basalt. The way in which those columns were used suggests a previous architectural tradition based on logs.

While no elite residences have yet been found at La Venta, one elegant tomb is at least broadly contemporaneous with Tomb 10 at San José Mogote; it had walls and roof of basalt columns and a floor of limestone slabs.[28] While the south end of the tomb was still intact, the north end appeared to have been opened and hastily rebuilt. To the south lay a group of loose columns, and a sandstone sarcophagus with no skeleton inside. As with Tomb 10 at San José Mogote, it appears the La Venta tomb had been reopened, the most important individual removed, and the sarcophagus left behind.

The remaining contents of the tomb were interesting enough. Two bundled juvenile burials, covered with red pigment, had been given jade sumptuary goods: figurines, beads, a pendant in the form of a clam shell, even a jade stingray spine. Thus, while elite Rosario families performed ritual bloodletting with imported obsidian stingray spines, the paramount of La Venta may have used one made from jade.

The elegance of the stone monuments and buried offerings at La Venta would be hard to exaggerate: pavements of serpentine blocks, massive offerings of jade celts, large iron-ore mirrors, carved basalt sculptures weighing 25 tons. What *has* been exaggerated by Olmec enthusiasts, however, is the extent to which this flamboyant chiefdom influenced developments in the more distant Mexican highlands. We now know that the Basin of Mexico, the Valley of Morelos, the Valley of Oaxaca, and the southern Tehuacán Valley had their own chiefdoms and impressive labor forces. They also had their own agendas. Their tastes ran not to colossal heads but to multi-ton stone platforms, bas-relief carvings on cliffs, monuments to chiefs and their sacrificed captives, and large irrigation dams. The chiefdoms of highland Mexico had their own trajectories and were on the verge of doing something the Olmec never did. They were on the verge of becoming urban.

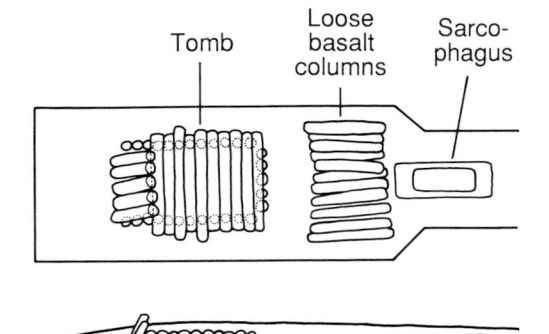

Tomb   Loose basalt columns   Sarcophagus

0 1 2 3
meters

154 Plan and cross-section of a basalt column tomb at La Venta, broadly contemporary with the Rosario phase in Oaxaca.

The Monte Albán Synoikism

By the late sixth century BC the Valley of Oaxaca stood on the threshold of a great transformation. It was about to witness the birth of an urban society, one of the New World's earliest. That society was to appear with startling rapidity and without precedent, having had no earlier urban societies after which to model itself.

The Settlement Pattern Project has provided a skeletal outline of what happened. At the end of the Rosario phase, the population of the valley seems to have been divided into three chiefly societies of unequal size: a larger polity in the Etla subvalley (2000 persons) and two smaller polities in the Valle Grande (700–1000 persons) and Tlacolula subvalley (700–1000 persons). Those polities were separated by an 80-km² no-man's-land whose most prominent landmark was an irregular 6-km² mountain range. The disproportionately large size of each polity's major center – San José Mogote, San Martín Tilcajete, and Yegüih – suggests that each center was making an effort to attract and concentrate as much manpower as it could. Archaeological evidence for burned temples and sacrificed captives indicates that some or all of these polities were in competition with each other.

At the end of the Rosario phase, an unexpected phenomenon occurred: San José Mogote, the largest community in the valley for more than 800 years, suddenly lost most of its population. While scattered barrios of farmers could still be found on adjacent piedmont spurs, the entire 40-ha ceremonial and elite residential core of the village was all but abandoned. Nor was San José Mogote the only Rosario village to lose population; it was soon joined by Tierras Largas, Fábrica San José, and other communities. Surveys reveal that half the Rosario phase villages whose occupation did *not* continue into the next period can be found in the southern portion of the Etla subvalley.[1]

Simultaneous with this widespread abandonment of Etla villages came a rapid and unexpected surge of population into the former no-man's-land in the center of the Valley of Oaxaca. The most striking example of this surge was a sudden and massive settlement atop the irregular 6-km² sacred mountain already mentioned. That mountain, known today as Monte Albán, rises 400 m above the plain of the Atoyac River.

At roughly 600 BC, in the late Rosario phase, Monte Albán appears to have been uninhabited. By roughly 400 BC, in the phase known as Early Monte Albán I, it had an estimated 5280 inhabitants. By roughly 200 BC, during Late Monte Albán I, it had a population estimated at 17,242 persons, making it one of the

155 The mountaintop archaeological site of Monte Albán. Since 1995, work at the ancient city has been under the direction of Arturo Oliveros.

largest cities in the New World at that time. By then 3 km of defensive wall were under construction along the more easily climbed western slopes of the mountain, while an acropolis of public buildings crowned the summit.[2]

What these changes imply is that during the transition from Rosario to Monte Albán I, thousands of Indians from the valley floor left their villages to relocate atop a rocky, previously unoccupied, virtually waterless mountain, forming the largest single community the valley had ever seen. By Late Monte Albán I roughly a third of the valley's population lived at this one fortified city. The term "urban revolution" may be hyperbolic in some prehistoric settings, but in the case of Monte Albán it seems appropriate.

How are we to account for this sudden transformation? Was Monte Albán unique, or are there precedents for it in other parts of the world? Are there other ancient societies that provide analogies for what happened in Oaxaca? As it happens, there are more than a few.

Urban Relocation in Ancient Greece

Documents from archaic and classical Greece reveal that dozens of ancient cities there were founded or relocated, usually as a means of meeting an external threat. Most relevant from the standpoint of this chapter was a process called *synoikism* (from the Greek *oikos*, "home," and *syn*, "together"), during which whole groups of villages left their rural settings and came together to form a city where none had previously existed. These newly created cities, often in defensible or strategic locations, survived because their leaders were able to manage distant landholdings and integrate previously autonomous populations into one *megalopolis* or "agglutinated city."

A recent study by Nancy Demand makes it clear that the underlying causes of such urban relocations were neither environmental, agricultural, nor economic.[3] Communities relocated "only in the face of an overwhelming external threat to their continued existence as autonomous political entities," and villages moved together "to form a large and powerful city that could resist the threat."[4]

The process of synoikism, which was intended to secure the independence of the *polis* by turning it into a megalopolis, "ironically thereby contributed to the demise of the polis itself as the fundamental autonomous political entity of the Greek world."[5] Here is an example of what action theorists would call "unintended consequences." By creating a larger political unit than had ever previously existed, Greek actors changed the "system" and the entire course of Greek history. Let us now look at two examples.

The Peleponnesian Synoikism

Within three years of the Spartan defeat at a place called Leuctra, several new cities were established in the Peleponnesus just to control Sparta.[6] In 369 BC, the town of Messene was moved to Mount Ithome, the strongest natural fortress in the region. New Messene was built on the western slope of the mountain and had an acropolis above it reserved for sanctuaries. Land was allotted to new citizens; the cost of building defensive walls was probably met by booty.

In 368 BC the walled city of Megalopolis was created along the major road from Sparta to Arcadia, giving security to the local population and thwarting Sparta's expansion. As shown by ill. 156, Megalopolis was a true synoikism in which (according to Pausanias and other historians) somewhere between 20 and 39 rural Arcadian communities came together to form one large city. Laid out to take advantage of the hills near an important river, Megalopolis covered 324 ha and had city walls more than 8 km in circumference.

Most of the villages so far identified as *oikists*, or participants in the synoikism of Megalopolis, lay within 10–15 km of the city. Some people, however, were brought in from 30–65 km away. Four communities are known to have resisted incorporation. Many of these resisters were simply brought to Megalopolis by force. In 362 BC there was a later attempt by some occupants to return to their original villages, but they too were forcibly returned. It is believed that these later rebels were from areas 30–65 km distant.

The rulers of Megalopolis made every effort to keep their forcibly integrated populace happy. They brought old cult figures from the abandoned districts of Arcadia and relocated them in the acropolis to prove that theirs was "a synoikism of gods" as well as humans; they established subprecincts in the city so that each group could have its own temples; and they invented a new cult to unite the disparate oikists of Megalopolis.

The Synoikism of Syracuse

Demand's analysis of the synoikism of Syracuse, a Greek city on Sicily, reveals it to be a case of "power building" rather than defense.[7] The story began in 491

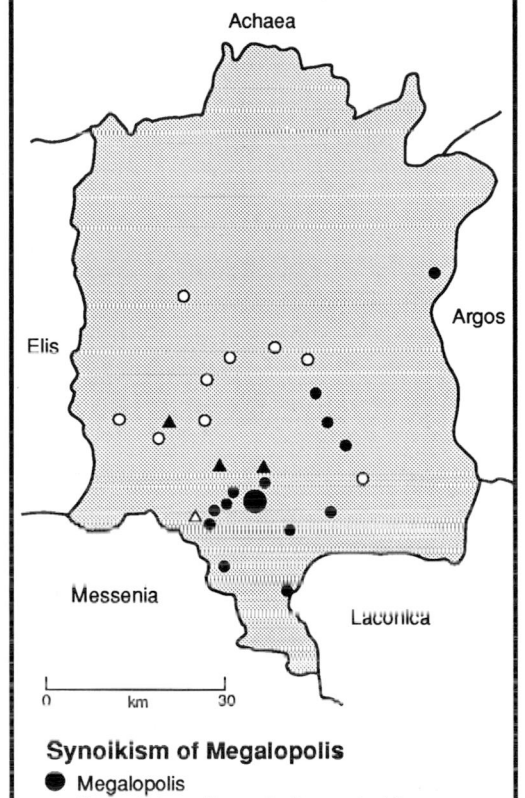

Synoikism of Megalopolis
- ● Megalopolis
- ○ Occupied as villages in Pausanias' time
- ▲ Resisters
- △ Inhabitants remained
- • Other known participants

156 At 368 BC, the ancient Greek city of Megalopolis was created by moving the occupants of many rural communities to a defensible hill.

BC with the death of Hippocrates, a powerful *tyrant* (or hereditary ruler) of Gela. A usurper named Gelon seized power, claiming the right to rule through his hereditary ties to a priesthood in the cult of Demeter and Kore. In 485 BC, Gelon used military alliances to take control of Syracuse; he immediately moved there, making Syracuse his new capital and leaving his brother Hieron in charge of Gela. Half the population of Gela – mostly workers and peasants – was then moved 140 km to Syracuse, to strengthen it by making it bigger.

Like many sixteenth-century Mesoamerican rulers, Gelon hand-picked the administrators of rural towns below Syracuse. When a town named Camarina rebelled, he razed it and moved the population 110 km to Syracuse. When the wealthy elite of Megara Hyblaea rebelled, he forcibly relocated the elite to Syracuse and sold their lower class compatriots into slavery; these slaves were then forced to work to help feed the larger population of Syracuse.

Like the rulers of Megalopolis, Gelon used public works to portray himself as a man intimidating toward humans, yet pious toward the gods. He built an elaborate system of waterworks, raised shrines to Demeter and Kore, and built a temple to Athene on the summit of a pediment. While Demand refers to Gelon's tactics as typical of a Greek tyrant, they are equally typical of the Mesoamerican rulers described in sixteenth-century documents. The latter also seized power by force, resettled peasants, appointed their own family members to control secondary communities, and impressed their subjects with public works while displaying piety toward the gods.

Archaeological Evidence for Synoikism

We have discussed synoikism in some detail because we think it provides the best analogy for the urban revolution in Oaxaca. Monte Albán did not grow slowly from village to city. It went from an unoccupied natural fortress, like Mount Ithome, to a 365-ha city, like Megalopolis, in a very short period of time. Its founding was accompanied by the abandonment of a number of valley-floor villages, many of them within 10–15 km of the city. Early in its history, while the bulk of the population lived on its slopes, Monte Albán's rulers directed the construction of major public buildings on its summit and 3 km of defensive wall along its most easily climbed side.

Before looking at Monte Albán in detail, let us consider some characteristics of synoikism which might be of significance to our Oaxaca case.

First, synoikism was not a rare event. It was something that happened over and over again, becoming one of the most common processes through which ancient Greek cities arose. At the same time, it was a process set in motion by specific human actors. We have seen that a noble named Gelon was behind the relocation of Syracuse; it is believed that a Theban noble named Epaminondas was behind the synoikism of Megalopolis. This should remind us that important leaders – whose names we will unfortunately never know – must have been behind the Monte Albán synoikism.

Second, we are reminded that Demand found no evidence that Greek cities relocated for environmental, agricultural, or economic reasons.[8] There is a great cost involved in moving so many people, and the primary motivation in every case seems to have been political. Rulers engaged in synoikism to "build power," or to create a city strong enough to preserve its autonomy in the face of external threat.

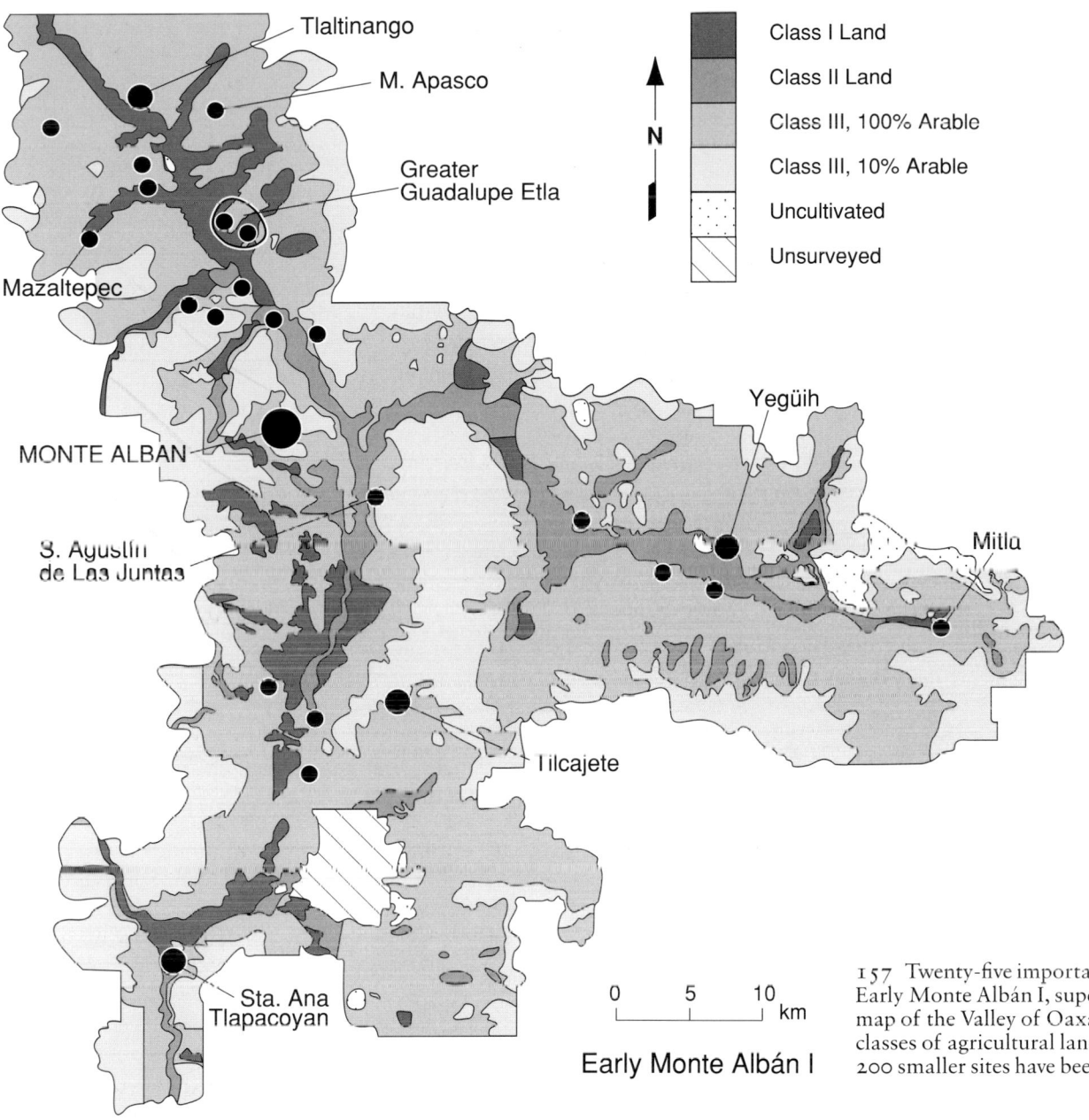

157 Twenty-five important settlements of Early Monte Albán I, superimposed on a map of the Valley of Oaxaca which shows classes of agricultural land. (More than 200 smaller sites have been omitted.)

Third, Demand points out that even though the motives may have been political, there were unintended economic effects. Relocation was expensive. Many relocated people, now far from their original lands, gave up farming forever and became urban laborers. These laborers, as well as the elites for whom they worked, had to be fed. In ancient Greece this was done by intensifying agriculture near the city, importing food from more distant areas, exacting tribute from conquered peoples, and using serf labor. We will present evidence that the rulers of Monte Albán used many of these methods as well.

Settlement Patterns during Monte Albán I

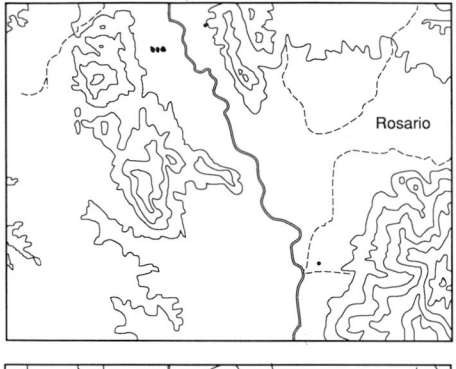

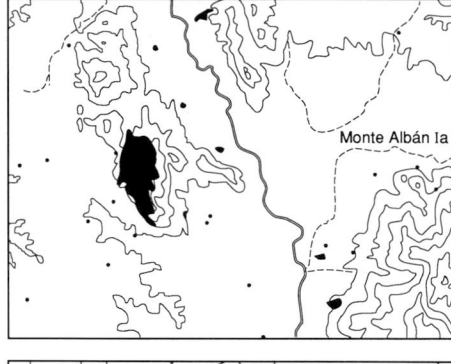

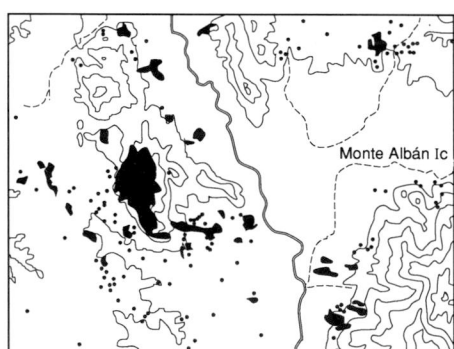

158–160 Communities of the central Valley of Oaxaca. (*Above*) Rosario phase. (*Center*) Monte Albán Ia. (*Below*) Monte Albán Ic.

161 Site 2-6-136 near San Agustín de las Juntas, an important Monte Albán Ic administrative center in the piedmont of the central Valley of Oaxaca.

In his original definition of the Monte Albán I period, the great Mexican archaeologist Ignacio Bernal distinguished three pottery horizons which he called Ia, Ib, and Ic.[9] The Settlement Pattern Project found that only Ia ("Early Monte Albán I") and Ic ("Late Monte Albán I") could be distinguished on the surface of sites. We follow their lead in considering Ia and Ic to be discrete phases, with Ib serving as the transition between them.

During Monte Albán Ia – which probably began by 500 BC and ended by 300 BC – there were 261 sites in the Valley of Oaxaca. Some 192 of these, including Monte Albán itself, were brand new settlements. Despite this unprecedented redistribution of the valley's population, strong continuities in ceramics and architecture from Rosario to Monte Albán Ia indicate that we are dealing with the same ethnic group. Roughly 96 percent of the new sites are considered to be villages of fewer than 100 persons. In contrast, Monte Albán's estimated population exceeded 5000.[10] This was a very high percentage of the valley's population, which we estimate to be between 8000 and 10,000.[11]

Further evidence that Monte Albán was founded through synoikism can be found in the 65 ha of the city where the surface density of Period Ia pottery is highest. Those 65 ha are divided into three discrete clusters of dense occupation, separated by areas where Ia sherds are less frequent. Richard Blanton, who directed the Monte Albán survey, sees this as evidence that Monte Albán was founded by at least three groups of colonists who established separate residential areas.[12]

The founding of Monte Albán also changed the demography of the central Valley of Oaxaca, including the 80-km² area that had been a no-man's-land during the Rosario phase. The central valley had had only five small Rosario villages. By Monte Albán Ia, that figure had risen to 38 villages, and by Monte Albán Ic it had exploded to 155 villages and small towns. In effect, the entire demographic center of gravity of the valley had shifted from Etla to the region surrounding Monte Albán. Satellite communities – undoubtedly producing much of the maize eaten in the city – now clustered around Monte Albán, much as they had clustered around San José Mogote centuries earlier.

During Monte Albán Ic – which probably began by 300 BC and ended by 150–100 BC – the valley's population had increased to the point where the

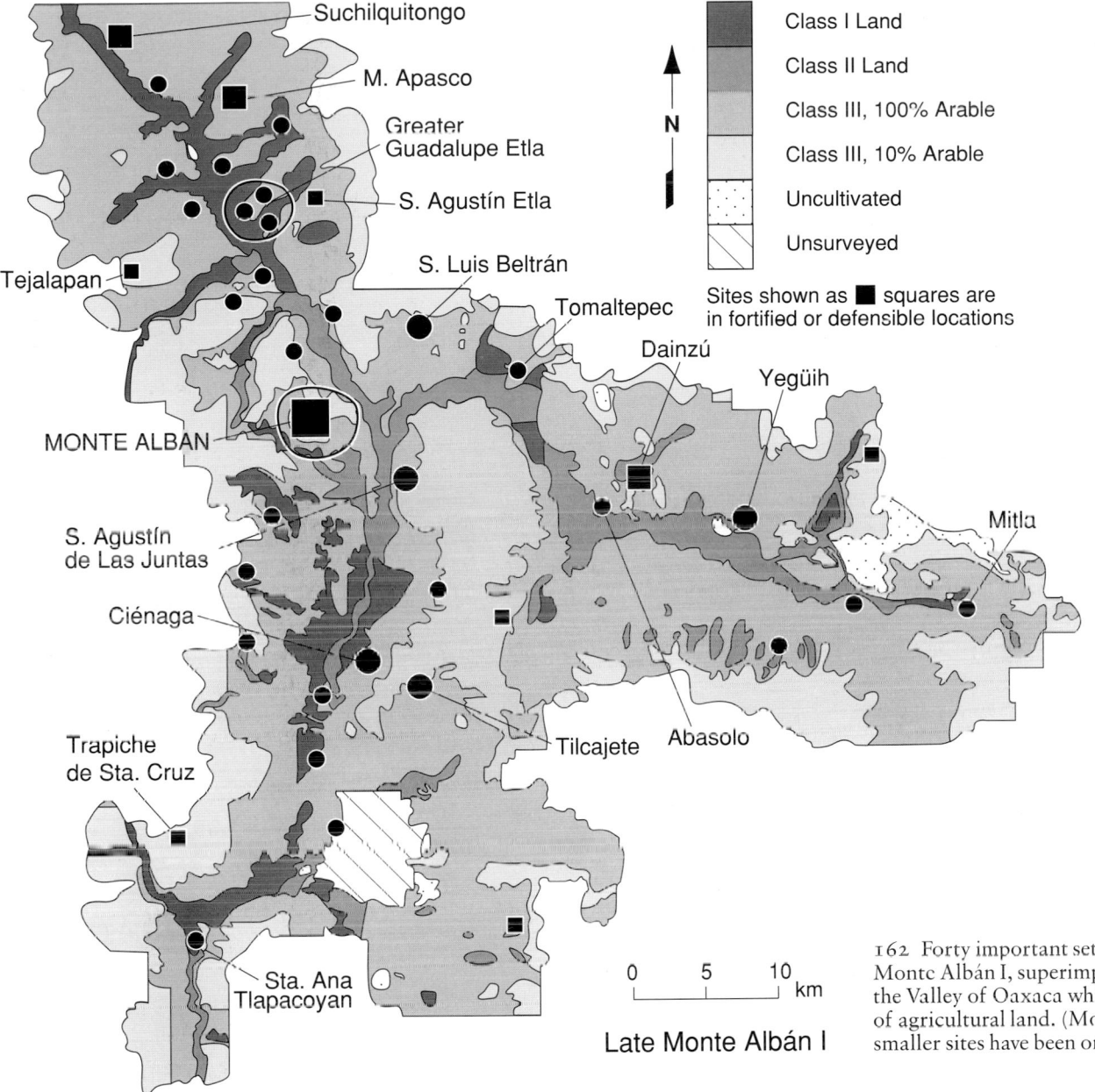

Class I Land

Class II Land

Class III, 100% Arable

Class III, 10% Arable

Uncultivated

Unsurveyed

Sites shown as ■ squares are
in fortified or defensible locations

N

Suchilquitongo

M. Apasco

Greater
Guadalupe Etla

S. Agustín Etla

Tejalapan

S. Luis Beltrán

Tomaltepec

Dainzú

Yegüih

MONTE ALBAN

Mitla

S. Agustín
de Las Juntas

Ciénaga

Tilcajete   Abasolo

Trapiche
de Sta. Cruz

Sta. Ana
Tlapacoyan

0   5   10
├──┴──┴──┤ km

Late Monte Albán I

162 Forty important settlements of Late
Monte Albán I, superimposed on a map of
the Valley of Oaxaca which shows classes
of agricultural land. (More than 700
smaller sites have been omitted.)

Settlement Pattern Project estimates it at 50,000. One-third of that population
(an estimated 17,242) lived at Monte Albán; in addition, three-quarters of the
population increase between Monte Albán Ia and Ic had taken place within 20
km of the city. Below Monte Albán were 744 communities. A few of those were
towns of 1000–2000 persons, but the overwhelming majority were villages with
populations estimated at less than 150.

Three clear trends can be seen in the rural settlement pattern data for Monte
Albán Ia–Ic. One is the already mentioned tendency for new settlements to
cluster around Monte Albán itself. The second is a doubling of settlement in the

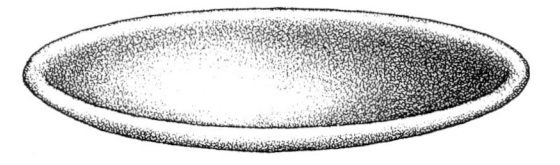

163 The *comal*, or pottery griddle for making tortillas, appeared for the first time in Early Monte Albán I.

Below

164 Simple brush-and-boulder dams are still used to divert streams for irrigation in the Oaxaca piedmont.

165 Water from piedmont streams is still carried to agricultural fields in Oaxaca by hand-dug canals like the one shown here.

Canal Irrigation and the "Piedmont Strategy"

foothill zone of the valley; 30 percent of the Monte Albán Ic sites are up in the piedmont, compared with only 16 percent in Monte Albán Ia. The third trend is a dramatic increase in the number of sites in defensible localities. Some 39 percent of the Monte Albán Ic population lived at thirteen sites which are either on hills, or have defensive walls, or both. This is an increase over Monte Albán Ia, during which there had been only three such sites.[13]

These trends are not unexpected, given our earlier discussion of synoikism. The increasing selection of defensible localities, the building of fortifications at Monte Albán, and other signs of militarism to be discussed below, remind us that synoikism is often designed to meet an external threat. The expansion of settlement into the foothills of the mountains, which the Settlement Pattern Project has called the "piedmont strategy," reminds us that newly created cities must be fed. The piedmont had the nearest vacant land to which Monte Albán could turn in order to intensify agricultural productivity.

One other trend of Monte Albán I is worthy of note. Large pottery griddles, known in Mexico as *comales*, appear for the first time in Period Ia. Such griddles are used to bake tortillas, unleavened cakes of maize that can be mass-produced by the thousands. The sudden appearance and rapid increase of *comales* in Period I could mean that large teams of workers were now being paid for their labor in rations of tortillas.

Canal irrigation has a long history in the Valley of Oaxaca, but its use increased dramatically in Monte Albán Ic. Almost certainly that escalation resulted from the need to provision the city of Monte Albán. It is not so much the Atoyac River that was used for canal irrigation in ancient Oaxaca, but its smaller tributaries in the piedmont.[14,15] Many of those streams can, with a relatively low expenditure of manpower, have part of their water diverted into small canals by the use of brush-and-boulder dams. All such systems are small, usually only serving the lands of one or two communities.

The Valley of Oaxaca is therefore a region of numerous small canal systems, rather than one large system. In contrast to regions like southern Mesopotamia, the north coast of Peru, or even the nearby Tehuacán Valley, central Oaxaca is not an area conducive to models of "despotic control" of downstream polities by upstream polities.[16] The Atoyac River, the largest watercourse in the valley, creates a strip of periodically flooded *yuh kohp* in which canal irrigation is usually unnecessary.

Owing to small stream size, canal irrigation serves only 9 percent of the cultivated land in the Valley of Oaxaca today. Significantly, much of that land is in the Etla subvalley. Twenty-five percent of the Etla region is canal irrigated, as compared to 7 percent of the Valle Grande and 3 percent of the Tlacolula region. This may explain why the Etla subvalley experienced some of the highest population growth during Monte Albán Ic, especially with respect to the founding of new villages in piedmont areas.[17]

Small ditches go back at least to the San José phase, when they were used to divert rain runoff away from houses.[18] This simple technology eventually allowed agriculture to move out of the humid bottomlands and into the piedmont, where small ditches could be used to lead stream water onto otherwise marginal land. We suspect that early piedmont villages like Fábrica San José and Tomaltepec were already doing some canal irrigation. Not until Monte Albán Ic, however, had the practice become so widespread that actual fossil canal systems were left behind.

A Canal System below Monte Albán

A team led by Michael J. O'Brien has discovered a small irrigation system on the southeast flank of the mountain on which Monte Albán lies.[19] The system consists of a dam and a 2-km canal. The dam, approximately 10 m high at its center and 80 m in overall length, spans the width of a natural barranca and consists of boulder fill with an outer casing of limestone blocks. The canal begins at the south end of the dam and follows the contour of the mountain along the south end of the barranca, proceeding down a piedmont spur toward the valley floor. To either side of the canal are agricultural terraces.

This canal system provided water for a settlement that was founded in Monte

166 In the piedmont near Tomaltepec, one can still see the traces of former irrigation canals like the one in the foreground.

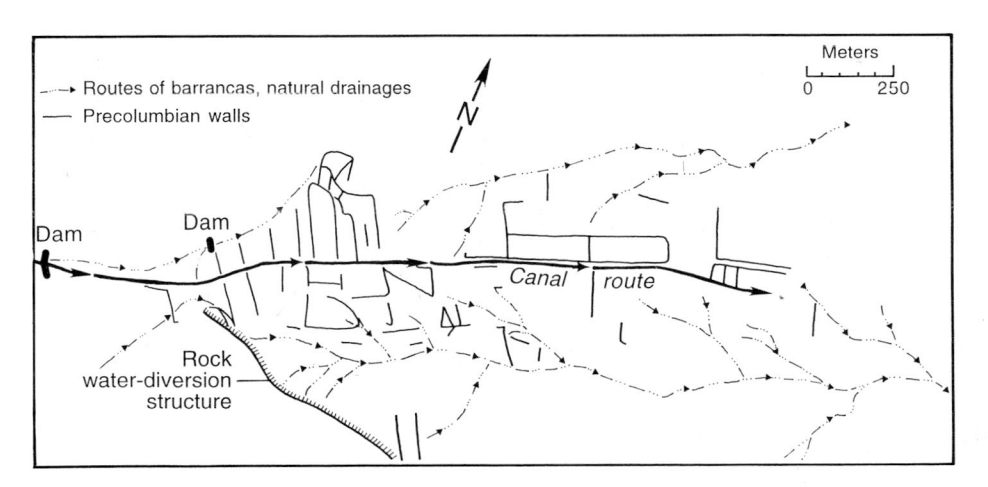

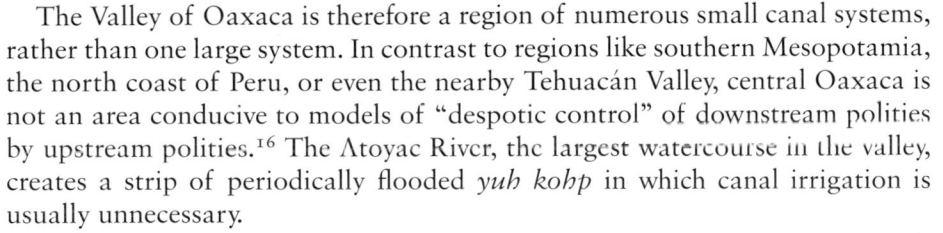

167 This canal and terrace system on the slopes below Monte Albán irrigated some 50 ha during Monte Albán I.

Albán Ia, peaked in Period Ic, and declined during Monte Albán II. The cultivated area is estimated at 50 ha and could probably not have supported more than 250 persons; thus it fell far short of provisioning all of Monte Albán. We have to assume that it was just one of many small canal systems of its period – one of the few preserved.

Other Small Systems

The Settlement Pattern Project discovered at least two other Monte Albán I irrigation systems. One, consisting of a 35-m-long earthen dam, lies in an arroyo near Loma Larga, some 5 km west of Mitla in the eastern Tlacolula subvalley.[20] The other lies in the foothills 10–12 km east of Monte Albán.[21]

Hierve el Agua

Perhaps the most impressive prehispanic water control system in the region lies in the mountains east of Mitla. This is the spring-fed system of Hierve el Agua, recently subjected to a detailed analysis by archaeologist James Neely, hydrochemist Christopher Caran, and diatom specialist Barbara Winsborough.[22]

Hierve el Agua is spectacular because the mineral salts in its artesian springs have literally turned the ancient canals to travertine. Below the springs, remnants of fossilized canals and stone masonry terraces cover more than 1 square km, with the uppermost 2 ha being the most complex. The main canals snake their way down the slopes, periodically giving rise to secondary canals that run along the walls of each terrace. Neely's excavations in the earthen fill of the terraces indicate that their construction had begun by Monte Albán Ic, although the system evidently reached its greatest complexity during later prehispanic times (AD 300–1300).

Because the mineral content of the springs at Hierve el Agua is so high today, Neely originally suspected that the locality was used for saltmaking rather than agriculture.[23] None of the terraces, however, appear to be shallow evaporating pans; most are narrow and deep, and many appear to have had their fertility deliberately increased by the addition of ancient organic refuse. Moreover, computer models designed by Caran show that if the spring water is allowed to evaporate, the first salts to emerge are not those we think of as "comestible" (such as sodium chloride), but a series of very bad-tasting precipitates.

It is possible, of course, that the ancient builders of Hierve el Agua thought of such foul salts as medicinal, believing the water to have healing properties. Indeed, there are ancient structures near the springs that could be pools for bathing. In this respect Hierve el Agua resembles the famous Aztec "Baths of King Nezahualcoyotl" in the Basin of Mexico.[24] There the ruler of Texcoco is thought to have bathed in healthful waters, after which they were allowed to flow downward over a series of irrigation terraces more extensive even than those of Hierve el Agua.

Whether or not Hierve el Agua was a combination spa and irrigation system, its builders seem to have known a great deal about removing harmful salts from mineral water. First, their addition of organic refuse to the terraces would have drawn boron – potentially the most harmful of the water's chemicals – away from any crop plants. Second, the terrace walls seem to have been given "weep

168 Literally turned to stone by the evaporation of carbonate-rich water, the spring-fed canals of Hierve el Agua wriggle down a terraced mountainside.

holes" to maximize drainage and prevent sodium from building up in the soil column. Third, since the terraces lie in a region of 600–700 mm of annual rainfall, canal irrigation may have been no more than a supplement which tided the crops over the periods between rains – some of which may have been hard enough to wash many of the salts out of the terraces. Neely, Caran, and Winsborough note that waters every bit as mineral as those of Hierve el Agua "are routinely used for irrigation in the Pecos River Valley and adjacent areas of New Mexico and Texas."[25]

Major Loci of the "Piedmont Strategy"

Unfortunately, only a few of the canals engineered during Monte Albán I have survived to be studied by archaeologists. We must therefore turn to the Settlement Pattern Project in order to learn which irrigable foothill regions witnessed the highest population growth in Monte Albán Ic – the first phase during which the "piedmont strategy" becomes clear.

Not unexpectedly, one such region is the rolling piedmont just south and southwest of Monte Albán itself. This is mostly Class III land, but its small and intermittent streams could be tapped for irrigation to help feed the growing population of the city.

Perhaps even more important, however, was the Etla subvalley, where a quarter of the cultivable land is suitable for canal irrigation. New settlements grew in the piedmont north and east of Monte Albán, extending as far as San Luis Beltrán in the western Tlacolula subvalley.[26] While much of the piedmont is Class III land, a great deal of it had never been cleared, and would initially have been more fertile than it is today.

As we have seen, all synoikisms create the problem of feeding a large new city. In the case of Monte Albán, it is virtually certain that the piedmont strategy was aimed at this problem. The Settlement Pattern Project has identified nineteen areas whose increase in new piedmont sites during Monte Albán Ic was greater than one standard deviation above the mean for the valley as a whole. Fifteen of those areas are in the Etla or central regions of the valley; ten lie within 15 km of Monte Albán.[27] Fifteen km would be less than a day's trip for a man carrying a load of maize to Monte Albán.

Using crop yield data for various soil classes, Linda Nicholas has calculated that Monte Albán's need for maize could have been met in a normal year by a region comprising the Etla subvalley, the northern Valle Grande, and the central valley near Monte Albán itself.[28] Specifically, her calculations suggest that the Etla region could produce enough for itself, plus another 10,600 persons; the central region could produce enough for itself, plus another 5000 persons; and the northern Valle Grande could produce enough for itself, plus another 9000 persons. Such figures suggest that in a good year, the estimated 17,242 occupants of Monte Albán would hardly have had to do any farming themselves. It would have been difficult for them to do so anyway, since the lands adjacent to Monte Albán were so densely settled during Period Ic. An unresolved question is what would have happened in a drought year, when rain was insufficient and many piedmont streams dried up. In such years, tribute in maize from more distant fields might have been needed.

Was There an "External Threat"?

We have seen historical evidence that Greek synoikism was often a response to external threat. No comparable historical data are available for Monte Albán, but there is evidence of external threat in its carved stone monuments and defensive works.

Winding 3 km along the western and northern boundaries of the early city is a wall of earth and stone some 15–20 m wide. Along a stretch called the Cañada Norte it survives to a height of 4–5 m; south of this point there are places where it still stands 9 m high. Its northern sector is a double wall, the outer structure better preserved and the inner wall heavily eroded, "possibly indicating an older construction that was later joined to the outer wall."[29] It would not surprise us to learn that the older wall was begun at the time the city was founded. Only one

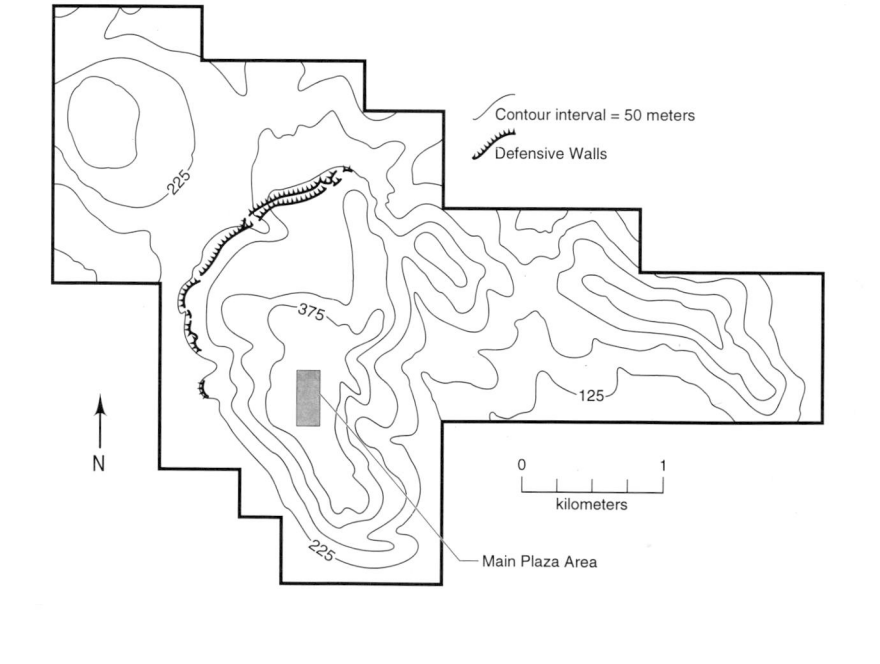

169 The defensive walls of Monte Albán protected 3 km of the more easily climbed north and west slopes.

170 Peña de los Corrales, near Magdalena Apasco in the Etla subvalley, is typical of the defensible hilltop locations chosen by many Monte Albán Ic communities.

small section of the younger wall has been excavated, and it dates to Monte Albán Ic or earliest II.[30]

Nor was Monte Albán the only site in the valley to be defended by walls or natural topography; by the end of Monte Albán I, more than a third of the valley's population lived at such sites. The trend began in Monte Albán Ia with two walled sites in the western piedmont of the Etla subvalley. By Monte Albán Ic the number of sites on defensible hilltops had increased to thirteen, with walls visible on the surface of at least six.[31] The presence of so many communities in fortified or defensible places provides a striking contrast with earlier periods.

The settlement pattern data for Monte Albán I, which suggest that the need for defense had become an important variable influencing site location, are complemented by the carved stone monuments of the period. More than 300 of the earliest monuments at Monte Albán depict slain or sacrificed enemies like the one we saw earlier at San José Mogote. There is reason to believe that during Monte Albán Ia, all of these carved stones were part of one huge display on the front of a public building on the city's acropolis. Unfortunately, over time that building came to be buried under larger constructions; and hundreds of the carved stones were reused in later buildings, sometimes as the risers or treads of steps.

A remnant of the early display, now partly buried under Monte Albán's Building L, preserves four rows of the carved stones in their original position. Each stone bears the figure of a single male victim, stripped naked, eyes closed, mouth usually open, sometimes with a scroll of blood indicating genital mutilation. Most are sprawling in grotesque, undignified positions, as they would

171 The sexually mutilated corpse of an enemy, Monte Albán I. Height 1.17 m.

172 A sexually mutilated enemy, accompanied by hieroglyphic captions. Monte Albán I. Height 1.4 m.

173 Partially buried under Monte Albán's Building L was this remnant of a huge display of hundreds of slain enemies.

174 Carved stones of slain captives, reused as steps in a later stairway of Monte Albán's Building L. Lower carved step, 88 by 35 cm.

look to an observer standing over them as they lay on the ground. Had these carvings been set horizontally, like the sacrificed captive on Monument 3 at San José Mogote, their true meaning would have been clear even to the nineteenth century explorers who first found them.[32] The fact that most were set vertically in a wall led some observers to misinterpret them as "dancers."

The corpses in the lowest row are set vertically, all facing to their left. Since this row would be the easiest to see from close up, it contains the most elaborate figures, including some with necklaces, earspools, complicated hairdos, and what appear to be hieroglyphic personal names. One frequently occurring glyph, which resembles part of a spearthrower or atlatl, may indicate that the man was taken in battle.

The second row of carved stones, all set horizontally, shows simple sprawled figures with their heads facing north. The third row, set vertically, resembles the lowest row except that all corpses are facing to their right; they also lack the hieroglyphic captions of the first row. The fourth row from the bottom, like the second, shows sprawled figures set horizontally. It is likely that such figures once continued for the full north–south length of the building, and that there were still higher rows of carvings. Some of the horizontal figures in Rows 2 and 4 were reused as steps in a later stairway of Building L, where the nude bodies of Monte Albán's slain enemies would have been trod upon by anyone ascending the stairs. This "treading on the bodies of captives" was a powerful metaphor for conquest, one used often by the later Maya.[33]

When all 300-plus carvings of captives were still in place in the original stage of Building L, it must have been one of the most awesome displays of military propaganda in all of Mexico.[34] How motivated were Monte Albán's earliest leaders to intimidate their enemies with this display? Consider that these carvings amount to 80 percent of the monuments known from the entire 1200-year heyday of the city. Add to this the fact that more than a third of the valley's population lived at defensible or fortified localities, and there are grounds for believing that the Monte Albán synoikism was indeed prompted by external threat. But who posed the threat? Was it an emerging polity somewhere else in Mexico, or a rival polity within the Valley of Oaxaca?

Looking outside the Valley of Oaxaca at the end of the Rosario phase, we see no potential threat close at hand. The Valleys of Tamazulapan and Nochixtlán to the northwest, the Cuicatlán Cañada to the north, the Valleys of Ejutla and Miahuatlán to the south, all have been surveyed; none appear to have had the manpower or political clout to challenge the Valley of Oaxaca.[35]

Farther away, there were several important centers in the late sixth century BC – Cuicuilco in the Basin of Mexico, La Venta on the southern Gulf Coast, Chiapa de Corzo in central Chiapas. As impressive as these centers may have been, we find it difficult to believe that they posed a threat to the Valley of Oaxaca. They lay, after all, hundreds of kilometers away over rugged mountain trails, and some of them probably had yet to achieve full control of their own immediate regions. On the other hand, the Valley of Oaxaca lay along the main prehispanic route from the Basin of Mexico through the Cuicatlán Cañada and on to the Pacific Coast, which probably made it a tempting target.

For various reasons, we do not think that the slain enemies on Building L at Monte Albán came from the Basin of Mexico, the Gulf Coast, or the Central Depression of Chiapas. In later periods at Monte Albán (Chapters 14 and 15), we will see that the Zapotec used two conventions to depict conquered foreigners. One was to associate them with the hieroglyphic name of the foreign province involved; in fact, the initial appearance of the Zapotec "place glyph" was to indicate a subdued *foreign* place. Another convention was to depict foreigners with non-Zapotec headdresses or costumes.

Neither of those artistic conventions was used on Building L. Based on our study of Rosario and Monte Albán I figurines, no hairstyle or ornament shown on the slain captives looks foreign to Oaxaca. And the hieroglyphic captions accompanying the lower row carvings refer not to places but to *personal names*, just as was done with "1 Earthquake" on Monument 3 at San José Mogote. We strongly suspect that when a prisoner was identified by his personal name rather than a place glyph, he was a rival from within the same ethnic group.

Thus, while we cannot rule out an external threat from one of the distant regions mentioned above, we find it likely that the threat came from other districts within the Valley of Oaxaca. Indeed, we see two possible scenarios. (1) In the first scenario, the populations of the Tlacolula and Valle Grande regions might have established Monte Albán to block the expansion of San José Mogote. (2) In the second, San José Mogote might have prepared itself for expansion against its Tlacolula and Valle Grande rivals by creating a powerful confederacy of villages in the Etla region and central valley. The capital of this confederacy – along with many other participating villages – would then have been moved to a defensible mountaintop in a former no-man's-land.

We find the second scenario more convincing. It better accounts for the large number of southern Etla villages abandoned at the end of the Rosario phase, as well as the great florescence of canal irrigation in the piedmont of the Etla and central regions. Like any synoikism, the founding of Monte Albán would have created the task of feeding a large urban population. It looks to us as if that task fell to the Etla and central regions, implying a major role for them in the founding of Monte Albán.

The Unification of the Valley of Oaxaca

So great is the competitive advantage conferred by large size that the larger a society becomes through successful warfare, the likelier it is to become even larger.   *Robert L. Carneiro*[1]

Oaxaca's first city was born of deliberate, and relatively rapid, resettlement of rural populations on a defensible hill. Oaxaca's first state emerged from the gradual subjugation of the rest of the valley by Monte Albán.

One problem in the study of pristine, or first generation, states – those evolving in the absence of pre-existing states on which they could model themselves – is that we can rarely point to a key moment in the archaeological record and say, "Now we have a state." Usually, evidence for the various political institutions of the state accumulates over time until the case becomes convincing.

Rosario phase society, described in Chapter 10, shows virtually no evidence of state institutions. Monte Albán II society, described in Chapter 13, has virtually all the evidence for statehood that an archaeologist could want. That makes Monte Albán I the crucial period of time during which the state must have been forming. We believe that the process began with the synoikism described in Chapter 11 and continued until the entire Valley of Oaxaca had been subjugated. Exactly when total subjugation was achieved is not known, but it must have been largely complete by Late Monte Albán I (300–100 BC). By that time, even areas well outside the valley were feeling the effects of Monte Albán's expansion.

In this chapter we look at the archaeology of Monte Albán I society – its demographic profile, its settlement hierarchy, its public buildings, its elite residences, its distinctive styles of art and writing. We then ask whether Monte Albán I society was still organized as a series of chiefdoms, or had already become a state.

We begin, however, by looking at an example of state formation drawn from another part of the world. It is one of the last analogies we will have to borrow from outside Mesoamerica. That is because the iconography and hieroglyphic writing of Monte Albán I suggest that we are dealing with people who spoke an early version of Zapotec and practiced an early form of Zapotec religion. From this point on, therefore, we will be able to draw more heavily on the direct historical approach and less heavily on ethnographic analogy.

How Do States Form?

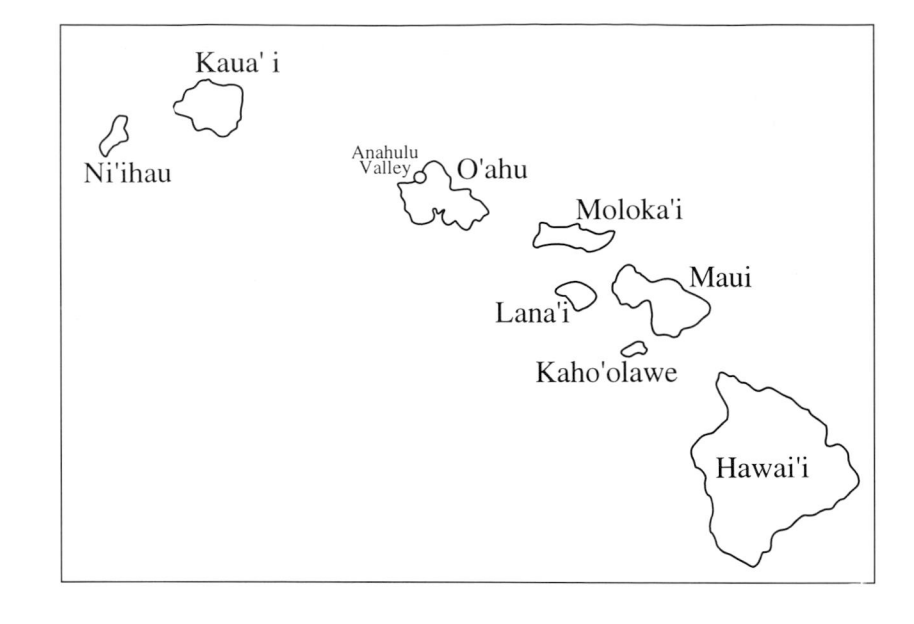

175 The Hawaiian Islands, unified by Kamehameha between 1789 and 1810.

Our model of state formation is drawn from Polynesia, a region far removed from Mesoamerica. We have chosen it because it is one of the few cases where an indigenous state formed while Western observers were on hand to write down what happened.

In the late 1770s, at the time of their discovery by Captain Cook, the Hawaiian Islands were under the control of powerful rival chiefs. Each of the larger islands – Hawai'i, Maui, O'ahu, and Kaua'i – was the central focus of an independent chiefdom. The smaller islands of Lana'i and Moloka'i were frequent battlegrounds for the paramount chiefs of O'ahu and Maui, the larger islands to either side.[2–5]

During Cook's visit in 1778, the paramount chief of Hawai'i was engaged in a battle on Maui, a military campaign that ended with his defeat in 1782. The victorious Maui chief had by then incorporated the formerly independent islands of O'ahu and Moloka'i into his domain.

When the defeated Hawaiian chief died, disputes over the succession to his title split the island of Hawai'i into three rival factions. Under normal rules of succession the title would have passed to the chief's son, but the latter was challenged by his cousin Kamehameha, the principal nephew of the dead chief. Kamehameha, who had made a reputation for himself fighting alongside his uncle in the Maui campaign, was a descendant of the Kona-Kohala chiefs of Hawai'i. That lineage had a history of repeated usurpations by junior collateral relatives of the chief, bypassing the normal route of patrilineal succession.

When three chiefly factions compete for the same title, even a slight selective advantage can determine the outcome. Often it is a demographic advantage; large size, as Carneiro reminds us in the quotation at the beginning of this chapter, is difficult to overcome. Kamehameha's advantage, however, was technological. By trading with European ships that docked at his harbor, he acquired cannons, muskets, and even two European officers who served as his gunners and strategists between 1789 and 1790.

By 1792, Kamehameha had managed to get his chief rival assassinated, allowing him to seize the entire island of Hawai'i. Now with advantages both in technology and manpower, he took O'ahu in 1795. Leaving the latter territory in the hands of his subchiefs, he began to subjugate the other islands of the archipelago. With the aid of European ships and weapons, he conquered every island but Kaua'i; and even its paramount chief capitulated in 1810, because he saw that Kamehameha had an insurmountable advantage.

By 1810, after two decades of warfare, Kamehameha had succeeded in turning a set of rival chiefdoms into a single military kingdom under the rule of one man. Kamehameha died in 1819, after making sure that his son – rather than a usurper like himself! – would inherit the throne.

There are four reasons for presenting this Hawaiian example. First, we suspect that it provides a very general analogy for what was going on during Monte Albán I. One chiefdom – or at the least, one major faction within a chiefdom – seized a defensible hilltop and relocated 5000 people there. They moved still more manpower into the former "no-man's-land" around the base of the hill, and intensified agriculture in the nearby piedmont. Their "piedmont strategy" may be analogous to the intensification of agriculture in O'ahu's Anahulu Valley, which Marshall Sahlins and Patrick Kirch believe was ordered by Kamehameha so he could provision his troops for an assault on Kaua'i.[6,7] The piedmont strategy may have given the polity centered at Monte Albán, which already had a demographic advantage, the necessary resources to begin subjugating the rest of the Valley of Oaxaca. After this period of expansion, which probably lasted through the end of Monte Albán I, we believe that the entire valley had become a single military kingdom. (Of course, Kamehameha did it faster – but he had cannons and muskets.)

Our second reason for presenting the Hawaiian case is to make a point about the evolution from chiefdom to state. We do not believe that a chiefdom simply turns into a state. We believe that states arise *when one member of a group of chiefdoms begins to take over its neighbors*, eventually turning them into subject provinces of a much larger polity. The chiefdom on the island of Hawai'i did not "evolve into a state." What it did was to conquer O'ahu, Maui, Lana'i, Moloka'i, and eventually Kaua'i, reducing the formerly autonomous chiefdoms on those islands to the subordinate districts of a much larger kingdom.

Our third reason for using the Hawaiian example is to make a point about transitional societies. Such societies occur at moments of rapid evolution, between periods of stability or slow evolution. In 1778 the Hawaiian archipelago was a series of chiefdoms; in 1810 it was a militaristic state ruled by a king. But which term would apply during Kamehameha's period of expansion, after O'ahu had fallen but before the capitulation of Kaua'i? More evolved than Kamehameha's former chiefdom, Hawai'i was not yet a state; it was a society in transition between two forms of sociopolitical integration. The anthropological record contains few such societies, probably because most were short-lived. The archaeological record, however, presents us with a number of transitional societies which – like the fossil animals studied by paleontologists – have not survived into the present era. Thus the record of prehistoric societies is more diverse than the record of contemporary societies.

Finally, the fourth reason for using the Hawaiian case is to compare action theory with some of archaeology's more popular approaches. For example, archaeologists committed to ecological functionalism might argue that the

Hawaiian state evolved because population pressure on the farm lands of the big island encouraged expansion to other islands. Those using an approach modeled on natural selection might argue that the big island's possession of cannons, muskets, and European advisors gave it an advantage over rival chiefdoms.

While acknowledging the value of these approaches, action theorists would argue that important human actors had been left out of the equation. They would propose that the Hawaiian kingdom of 1810 was put together by an ambitious chief who had the ruthlessness to assassinate his rivals, the charisma and hereditary authority to attract followers, and the military skill to defeat powerful enemies. Kamehameha was surely a product of his time, his environment, and his culture, but he knew how to manipulate (and eventually transform) the very system that had produced him. That is not how biological evolution works, but it is one of the ways that social evolution works.

Without question there must have been leaders like Kamehameha involved in the Monte Albán synoikism and the creation of the early Zapotec state, but we will never know their names. That is a typical problem in the study of prehistoric societies, which is one reason we are so often limited to selectionist and ecological-functionalist explanations. It is admittedly frustrating not to be able to put the human actors back into social transformations. That is not, however, an excuse to give up on the archaeological record as some recent archaeologists have done.[8]

Ethnogenesis: The Emergence of a "Zapotec Style"

Monte Albán I saw the emergence of hieroglyphic texts tied to an archaic form of the Zapotec language, as well as a body of iconography that can be tied to Zapotec religion. One probable cause for this unitary style was the gradual consolidation of the Valley of Oaxaca. Another may have been a set of agreed-upon elite instructions to craftspeople.

One unintended consequence of bringing together thousands of people in a new city can be an explosion of arts and crafts, especially if many of those people are forced to abandon agriculture. Several urban relocations in archaic Greece "created environments in which intellectual life flourished."[9] Early Monte Albán was such an environment, and its sponsorship of craftspeople penetrated even to the towns in its hinterland. What emerged during Monte Albán I was an art style distinct from that of any other region, a style so closely associated with the Valley of Oaxaca that it is generally referred to as Zapotec.[10]

Pottery

While many utilitarian vessels were cream, buff, or brown, it was burnished gray ware that is considered the hallmark of Monte Albán I pottery. Fired in a reducing atmosphere in covered kilns, it was often incised with geometric motifs or modeled in animal effigy shapes. The burial offerings of Monte Albán Ic make it clear that some elite families owned "place settings" with as many as a dozen different vessel shapes: serving dishes, bowls, ladles, bridgespout jars, even small containers for sauces and condiments.

Some of the most distinctive vessels were effigy bottles like the one shown in ill. 176. Modeled in three dimensions on this vessel, a grotesque face with flame eyebrows and the bifid tongue of a serpent can be seen. It is an anthropomorphic

176 (*Left*) Effigy bottle depicting an anthropomorphized version of *Cociyo* (Lightning), Monte Albán I. Height 17 cm.

177 (*Center*) Effigy bottle from Tomb 33 at Monte Albán, probably depicting a male ancestor in death. Monte Albán I.

178 (*Right*) Effigy bottle from Tomb 43 at Monte Albán, probably depicting a female ancestor in death. Monte Albán I. Height 10 cm.

version of *Cociyo* or Lightning, the most powerful supernatural ever depicted in Zapotec art. His eyebrows and tongue remind us that he evolved from earlier versions of Lightning as a fire-serpent. His human characteristics remind us that later Zapotec nobles claimed a special relationship with Lightning.

Early Zapotec Writing and Calendrics

In Chapter 1 we saw that the sixteenth-century Zapotec had two calendars – a 260-day ritual calendar or *piye*, and a 365-day secular year or *yza*. The day-name "1 Earthquake" on Monument 3 at San José Mogote reveals that the *piye* was in use by 700–500 BC. Our sample of hieroglyphic inscriptions from Monte Albán I is larger, and the 365-day *yza* seems to have been present as well.

At the southern end of the gallery of slain enemies on Building L at Monte Albán (see Chapter 11) were two stone monuments. Called Stelae 12 and 13 by Alfonso Caso, they are associated with the slain enemies and are considered part of the original gallery.[11] These two stelae provide one of Mesoamerica's earliest examples of a "pure text" of eight hieroglyphs in two columns. They also include the first apparent reference to a month in the 365-day calendar (see Box).

179 Stelae 12 and 13 *in situ*, Monte Albán.

In addition to providing us with evidence that both Zapotec calendars were in use during Monte Albán I, Stelae 12 and 13 can be tied to an early form of the Zapotec language. In Chapter 1 we mentioned that the Zapotec ordinal numbers ("first," "second," etc.) were the same as the words used for "first finger," "second finger," and for "first-born," "second-born," and so on. Glyph 2 of Stela 12 shows a hand with prominent thumb, evidently an ordinal number. Since the sixteenth-century Zapotec language uses these same conventions, we can argue that these early glyphs were tied to the Zapotec language. Combined with our evidence for *Cociyo* in pottery sculpture, these stelae leave little doubt that we are dealing with people who were ethnically Zapotec.

Because Stelae 12 and 13 were incorporated into the display of mutilated prisoners on Building L, we might assume that the text was commissioned by the leader taking credit for the defeat of those enemies, and that the date might refer to his alleged victory.

Was Monte Albán I Society a Chiefdom or a State?

Given the size of Monte Albán in Period I, few would hesitate to describe it as a city. But how would we describe the society to which it belonged? Did Monte Albán control the entire valley, or only a part? Were its rulers "kings" or "chiefs"? Was their society "stratified," or only "ranked"?

We have already given our view that Monte Albán I was a society in transition,

Stelae 12 and 13: An Early Zapotec Text

The study of Zapotec writing is still in its infancy, and we cannot pronounce the glyphs on Monte Albán's Stelae 12 and 13 as they were once read. By referring to the illustration accompanying this Box, however, we can go through the text glyph by glyph.

Stela 12

Glyph 1   A Zapotec year sign, with the "year bearer" 4 M inside a cartouche.
Glyph 2   A hand with thumb shown prominently, possibly indicating "first-born."
Glyph 3   Meaning unknown.
Glyph 4   A day, 8 Water, in the 260-day ritual calendar. The glyph for "water" is inside a cartouche; below are the numerals 5 (a bar) plus 3 (3 dots).

Stela 13

Glyph 1   A jaguar or puma, with 2 bars indicating the number 10 (5 + 5). This sign may be the personal name "10 Jaguar" or "10 Puma" (the Zapotec word *peche* is used for both animals).
Glyph 2   A hand grasping an object (there are reasons for reading this as the verb "seized").
Glyph 3   A human head in profile with a finger used as a subfix; the index finger may identify the human figure as a "second son."
Glyph 4   A calendric glyph above 4 dots (the number 4). In other Zapotec texts, this glyph is sometimes associated with numbers larger than 13. Since days in the 260-day calendar could not occur with numbers higher than 13, that makes this glyph an excellent candidate for a month glyph or a glyph that tabulates the number of months in the 365-day calendar. This text may constitute our first evidence for the *yza*, or secular year of 365 days.

Stela 12   Stela 13

1   1

2   2

3   3

4   4

like the archipelago gradually turned into a kingdom by Kamehameha. Clearly more powerful and centralized than any Mesoamerican chiefdom of the sixth century BC, Monte Albán I shows only meagre evidence of state institutions when compared with Period II (Chapter 13).

Monte Albán I society had plenty of elite residences, but thus far no evidence of a palace in which a king might reside. High-status burials were provided with major offerings of pottery, but there was nothing as elegant as the later Zapotec royal tomb, with its offering niches and polychrome murals. There were temples with columns to either side of the doorway, like the Yellow Temple of Dainzú (Plate IX), but as yet no examples of the standardized two-room temple. The significance of these missing institutions will become clearer in Chapter 13 when we show how many of them were present in Monte Albán II.

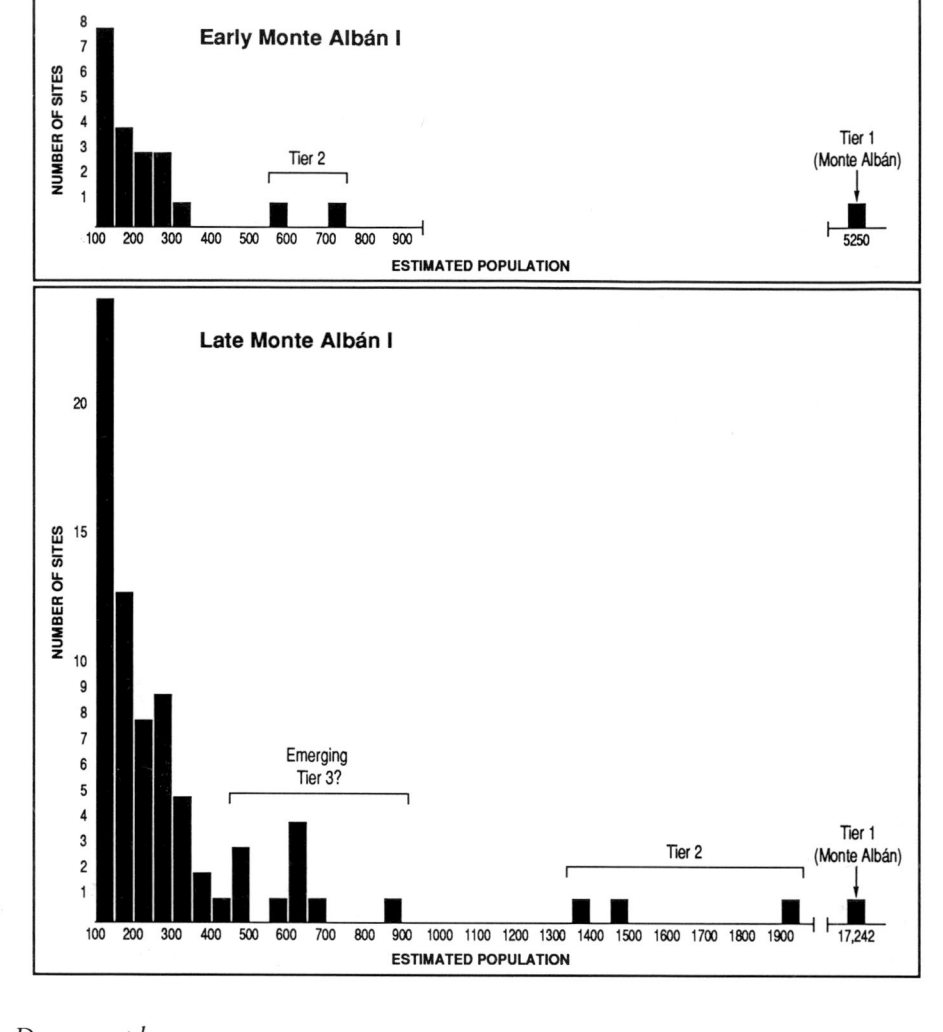

180 Histograms for the largest communities in the Valley of Oaxaca during Early and Late Monte Albán I.

Demography

Let us begin with an analysis of the settlement hierarchy, which has been such a valuable tool in the identification of states since the pioneering work of Henry Wright and Gregory Johnson in the Near East.[12] Wright and Johnson showed that while chiefdoms tend to have a settlement hierarchy with only three levels (or tiers) of communities, states tend to have a hierarchy with four levels: cities, towns, large villages, and small villages.

We are handicapped in our analysis, of course, by not knowing whether or not Monte Albán controlled the entire Valley of Oaxaca during Period I. Clearly there were communities of many sizes in the valley. The question is, how many were actually under Monte Albán's hegemony?

In Monte Albán Ia, there were 261 communities in the valley; 192 of these, like Monte Albán itself, were newly founded. Monte Albán, with 365 ha of Early Period I sherds and an estimated population in excess of 5000, was the only community in Tier 1. Many formerly large communities of the Etla region, including San José Mogote, had been drained of population during the Monte Albán synoikism.[13]

Site 3-2-7

Mixtepec River

Site 3-8-220

Yegüih in the Tlacolula region and Tilcajete in the Valle Grande would probably fall in Tier 2 of the hierarchy. In contrast to San José Mogote, however, they seem to have grown *larger* between the Rosario and Monte Albán Ia phases. This growth suggests that Yegüih and Tilcajete may not have participated in the synoikism; they might still have been the paramount centers of rival polities during Monte Albán Ia. If so, any smaller communities near them would have been under their control, not Monte Albán's.

Illustration 180 shows a histogram for the 22 largest communities in the valley during Early Monte Albán I. One can detect at least three size tiers, leaving the remaining 239 sites (mostly villages of less than 100 persons) as a fourth tier. However, if settlements like Tilcajete and Yegüih were not yet under Monte Albán's control, then the potential second tier of the hierarchy would consist only of large communities in rival polities. Remove Tilcajete and Yegüih, and the hierarchy collapses to three tiers.

When we move to the histogram for Late Monte Albán I sites, a slightly better case can be made for a hierarchy of four tiers. By then there were 745 communities in the valley, the 74 largest of which are shown in the histogram. One-third of the valley's population lived at Monte Albán, and by now many of the com-

181 An aerial view of the southern Valle Grande near Site 3-8-220, Trapiche de Santa Cruz. This Late Monte Albán I site covers 11 ha of defensible hilltop, 200 m above the floodplain of the Mixtepec River. Its defensible locality contrasts with that of the earlier, undefended San José phase site of Santa Ana Tlapacoyan (Site 3-2-7), which lies near the confluence of the Mixtepec and Atoyac Rivers. Site 3-2-7 flourished in an era of minimal raiding; 3-8-220 had to protect itself during a time of extensive warfare. View to the southeast, 1970.

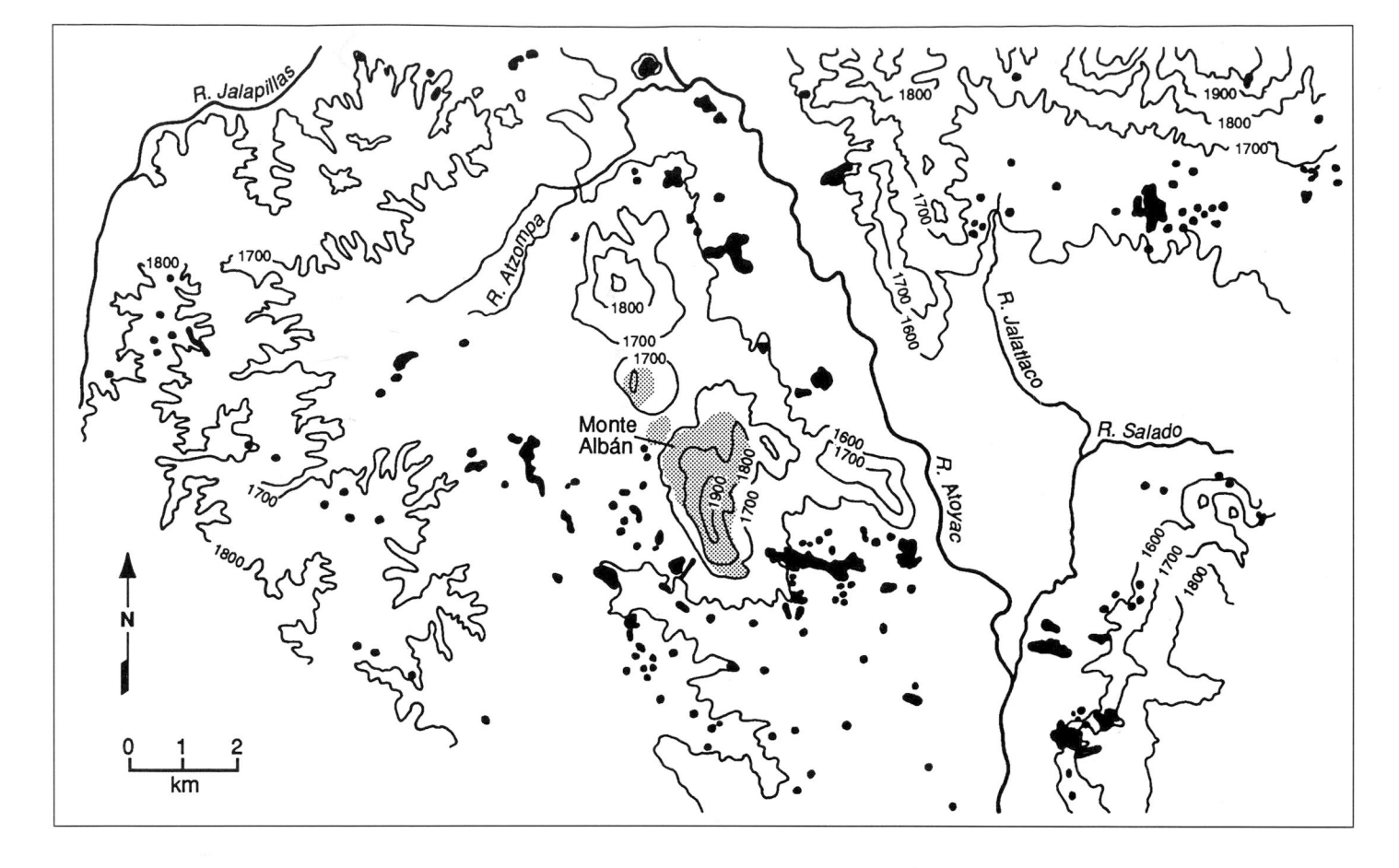

182 During Late Monte Albán I, there was a dense concentration of archaeological sites (black areas) within 10 km of Monte Albán. Gray stipple indicates the extent of the urban occupation at Monte Albán itself.

munities in the second and third tiers surely lay within the area controlled by Monte Albán. Several, like Suchilquitongo and Magdalena Apasco in the Etla region, occupied defensible hilltops; so did more distant sites like Trapiche de Santa Cruz in the southern Valle Grande. Dainzú in the Tlacolula region had a defensible hilltop behind it.

The crucial level of the Late Monte Albán I hierarchy seems to have been Tier 3 – the sites with populations estimated at 500–900 persons. Communities in this size range seem to have been increasing in number, gradually producing a new mode (or "peak") in the histogram that may help to separate Tier 3 from the mass of smaller villages with populations below 500. Many of the communities in this emerging third tier – San Luis Beltrán, San Agustín de las Juntas, and Tomaltepec, among others – lay in foothill regions close to Monte Albán, and probably participated in its "piedmont strategy." At least some Tier 3 sites of this phase are known to have had public buildings, often in groups of three or four.

In short, by comparing the two histograms in ill. 180, one gets the sense that a four-tiered settlement hierarchy was indeed emerging during the course of Monte Albán I. We are still impressed, however, by the concentration of 155 sites within 10 km of Monte Albán. This ring of satellite communities, which according to Linda Nicholas' calculations could have produced enough surplus maize for 5000 people,[14] disappeared in later periods. Its presence during Period I suggests that Monte Albán needed large concentrations of farmers, laborers, and warriors nearby, presumably because it could not yet count on the support of the entire Valley of Oaxaca.

More research is needed before we will fully understand Monte Albán's relationship to its hinterland at this time. We suspect that Monte Albán I was a 400-year period of spectacular demographic and militaristic expansion, beginning with an urban relocation at 500 BC and proceeding to subjugation of the entire Valley of Oaxaca by 100 BC. Outlying areas, both in the valley and in the surrounding mountains, were probably brought under Monte Albán's hegemony by a combination of alliance building, population resettlement, and military force, with those who resisted ending up as corpses on carved stones.

Monte Albán was undoubtedly aided in its expansion by the fact that it was already the largest polity in the valley. As the quotation that opens this chapter puts it, "So great is the competitive advantage conferred by large size that the larger a society becomes through successful warfare, the likelier it is to become even larger."

What Do the Public Buildings and Elite Residences Tell Us?

Although the city of Monte Albán has produced abundant pottery and artifacts from Period I, some of the most important structures of that period lie buried beneath later buildings. For example, Caso, Bernal, and Acosta reported major buildings of Period I under the North Platform, Mound K, and Building L on the Main Plaza.[15] At present these buildings lie safe beneath a heavy layer of stones and cement.

Inability to study these structures deprives us of one important line of evidence: the ground plans of public buildings and elite residences, which tell us a lot about the institutions that produced them. We would like to know, for example, whether the highest-ranking family during Monte Albán I lived in a large adobe house with an interior patio, like the chiefly families of the Rosario phase, or in a huge stone masonry palace like the later Zapotec kings. We would also like to know whether Monte Albán I society had unstandardized, one-room, wattle-and-daub temples like Rosario chiefdoms, or standardized, colonnaded, two-room temples like the later Zapotec state.

Deep inside Mound K at Monte Albán are the buried remains of a Period I structure with a 6-m-high wall of huge stones and a pair of rubble masonry columns; its shape, dimensions, function, and number of rooms are hidden from us by later construction. Far below the surface of the North Platform lies a partly destroyed structure bearing serpentine motifs modeled in stucco; its shape and function are also unknown.[16]

This relative inaccessibility of Monte Albán's earliest buildings forces us to look for other sites of the same period, where the overburden of later structures is not as heavy. Fortunately, such sites are known.

Monte Negro

Fifty kilometers west of Huitzo, separated from the northern Valley of Oaxaca by forested peaks and deep canyons, lies the site of Monte Negro. Like Monte Albán, Monte Negro occupies a ridge towering 400 m above the floor of an

183 Effigy incense brazier from Monte Negro. Height 28 cm.

184 The acropolis of Monte Negro.

intermontane valley. Unlike Monte Albán, it has no overburden of later architecture to hide its early buildings.

Excavated by Alfonso Caso in the late 1930s, Monte Negro appears to be contemporaneous with Late Monte Albán I.[17,18] Its effigy incense braziers are very similar to those of Monte Albán Ic, ill. 183 being an example. Monte Negro might, in fact, be a foothold of Zapotec expansion into the mountains beyond the Etla region – an outpost that was later relinquished.[19]

The acropolis of Monte Negro consists of an L-shaped alignment of buildings oriented to the cardinal points. The longer alignment (140 × 50 m) runs east–west along a narrow street; the shorter alignment (60 × 35 m) runs north–south. While there is one modest patio flanking a temple, the site has no large central plaza. Beyond the public buildings there are numerous low mounds, presumably residential, some on artificial terraces like those of Monte Albán.

At least four public buildings at Monte Negro have been described as "temples." Most are rectangular; some have a "plus-sign" shape. All have foundations of huge limestone blocks enclosing earthen fill, and no building is greater than 20 × 20 m. Exterior walls are of poorly trimmed stones set in irregular courses; their stairways, also made of large blocks, are usually inset into the building. Local red clay was used as mortar, and the buildings above the stone platforms seem to have been of adobe or wattle-and-daub. All temples seem to have columns supporting the roof; we do not know whether this implies a flat roof, as in later Zapotec temples, or a peaked thatched roof, as in the public buildings of earlier times. Most columns were of rubble masonry, although some had a core of drum-like stones stacked one above the other.

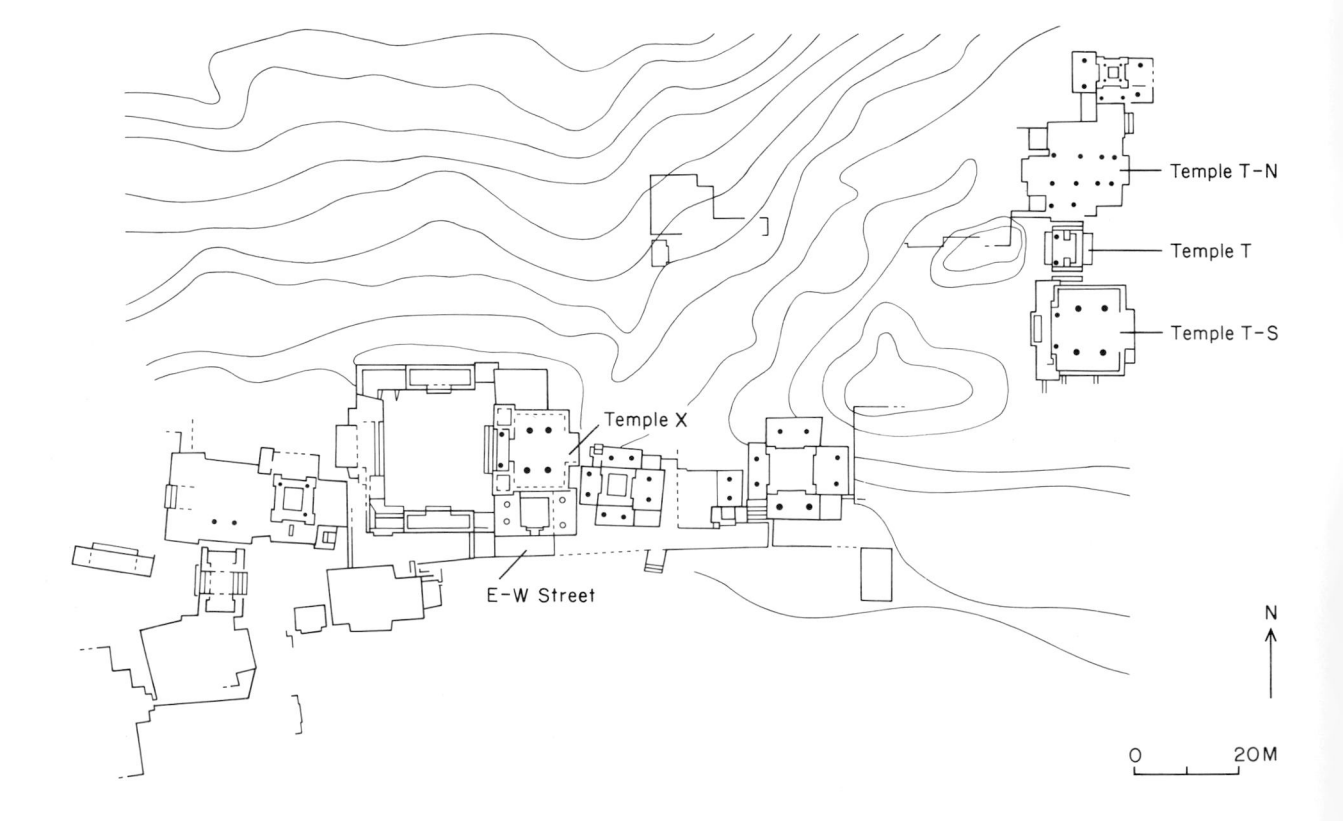

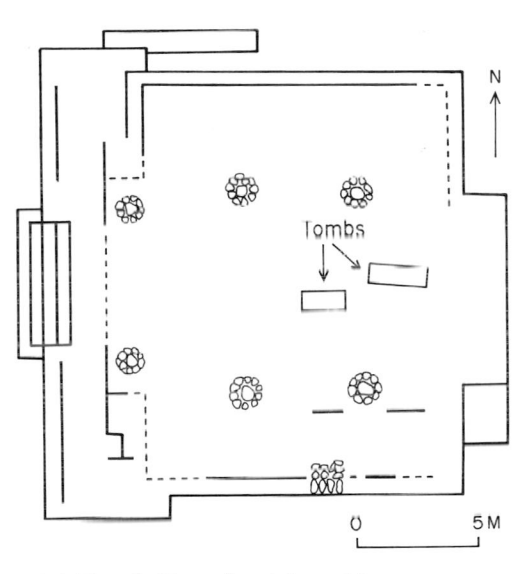

185 Temple T at Monte Negro was open on both its east and west sides; rubble columns flanked the west entrance.

186 Temple T-south at Monte Negro may have been the scene of human sacrifice.

187 Obsidian sacrificial dagger from Temple T-south at Monte Negro. Length 14 cm.

As far as we can tell, the standard two-room temple characteristic of the later Zapotec state was not yet present; it was perhaps most closely approximated by Temple T of Monte Negro. Partly divided into two rooms, Temple T was open on both its east and west sides. Each entrance faced a stairway of large stone blocks; the west entrance was flanked by a pair of columns. Like Floor 4 at Paso de la Amada, Chiapas – the remains of an early building described in Chapter 7 – Temple T might have been designed to allow initiates to enter from the west, perform some ritual, and exit to the east. Alternatively, the west stairway might have been for worshipers and the east stairway for priests.

Its colonnaded entrance and partial division into two rooms make Temple T a logical precursor to the later Zapotec temple, but the fact that it was open on the front and back means that it still lacked the "inner sanctum" of later temples (see Chapter 13). Carved on some of its stairway risers were the same motifs used to represent drops of blood on Monument 3 at San José Mogote (Chapter 10).

Further evidence for blood sacrifice comes from Temple T-south, a larger building adjacent to Temple T. T-south consisted of one large room on a stone masonry platform; its lone entrance was flanked by columns, and four larger columns supported its roof. Two adobe tombs, incorporated into the original foundations of the temple, contained elite burials.

Two bifacially chipped obsidian daggers – the type used in later periods to remove the hearts of human sacrificial victims – were included in Offering 1 of this temple. These daggers were probably once set in wooden handles that had disintegrated over the centuries. Along with the "drop of blood" motif carved on the stairway of Temple T, they indicate that Monte Negro's temples were used for human sacrifice.

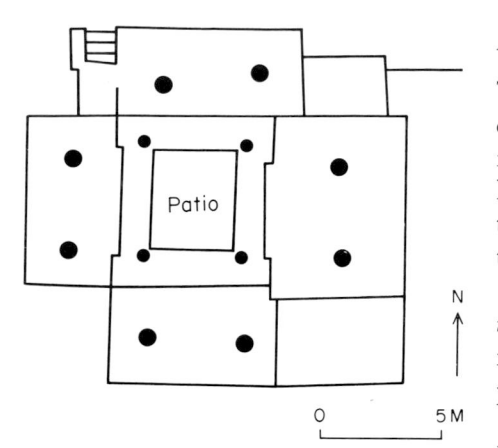

188 This elite residence, just to the east of Temple X at Monte Negro, consisted of four rooms around a central patio, with a small stairway on the northwest. The black circles are column bases.

Elite Residences at Monte Negro

There are several elite houses at Monte Negro. Like the Rosario phase elite residences at San José Mogote (Chapter 10), each consisted of an open patio surrounded by three or four rooms with adobe walls. The Monte Negro houses, however, had stone foundations two courses high, and each room had at least two columns supporting its roof. The courtyards were paved with flagstones, and there were drains below some buildings.

Monte Negro's elite households have been compared to the Roman *impluvium* residence, in which an inner paved court trapped rain runoff and channeled it to subterranean reservoirs.[20] While more elegant than those of the Rosario phase, the Monte Negro houses fall short of the later palaces at Monte Albán (Chapter 13). Like so much in Late Monte Albán I, they seem transitional between the house of a chief and the palace of a king.

While the largest of the elite residences at Monte Negro lies along the east–west street, several others are connected to temples by secret passageways or roofed corridors. These corridors – which made it possible for members of important families to enter and leave the temple without being seen by lower-status persons – appear to be forerunners of the Monte Albán II passageways, tunnels, and roofed stairways of Monte Albán and San José Mogote. The implications of such special entrances for the elite are twofold. First, they indicate that rank differences were still associated with differential access to the supernatural. Second, they suggest an escalation in rank to the point where chiefly individuals did not have to use the same stairways and entrances as more lowly individuals.

Elite Burials

Twenty burials were discovered at Monte Negro, some in adobe tombs and some in simple graves. While some individuals had nothing at all, at least one tomb within Temple T-south had 21 pottery vessels. Evidence of high status took the form of annular skull deformation, jade and shell ear ornaments, and (in the case of one man) glittering inlays of iron pyrite in two upper teeth. Given the pain involved in inserting such inlays, it must have meant a great deal to the elite to have elegantly decorated teeth.

Who Built Monte Negro?

Monte Negro gives us hints of what Monte Albán might have looked like prior to 100 BC. Like Monte Albán, it is perched on a defensible mountaintop several hundred meters above the nearest river. Like early Monte Albán, it has linear arrangements of colonnaded public buildings on stone platforms. Like early Monte Albán, it has evidence of elite families but as yet no true palace. Monte Albán provides evidence of human sacrifice in the form of a prisoner gallery; Monte Negro provides it in the form of obsidian sacrificial knives and the "drop of blood" motif. The two sites share pottery types and vessel shapes, including effigy incense braziers in Zapotec style. Monte Albán was, however, many times larger than Monte Negro.

Archaeological survey by Robert Drennan in the mountains north of the Valley of Oaxaca suggests that Monte Albán I was a period of expansion for the

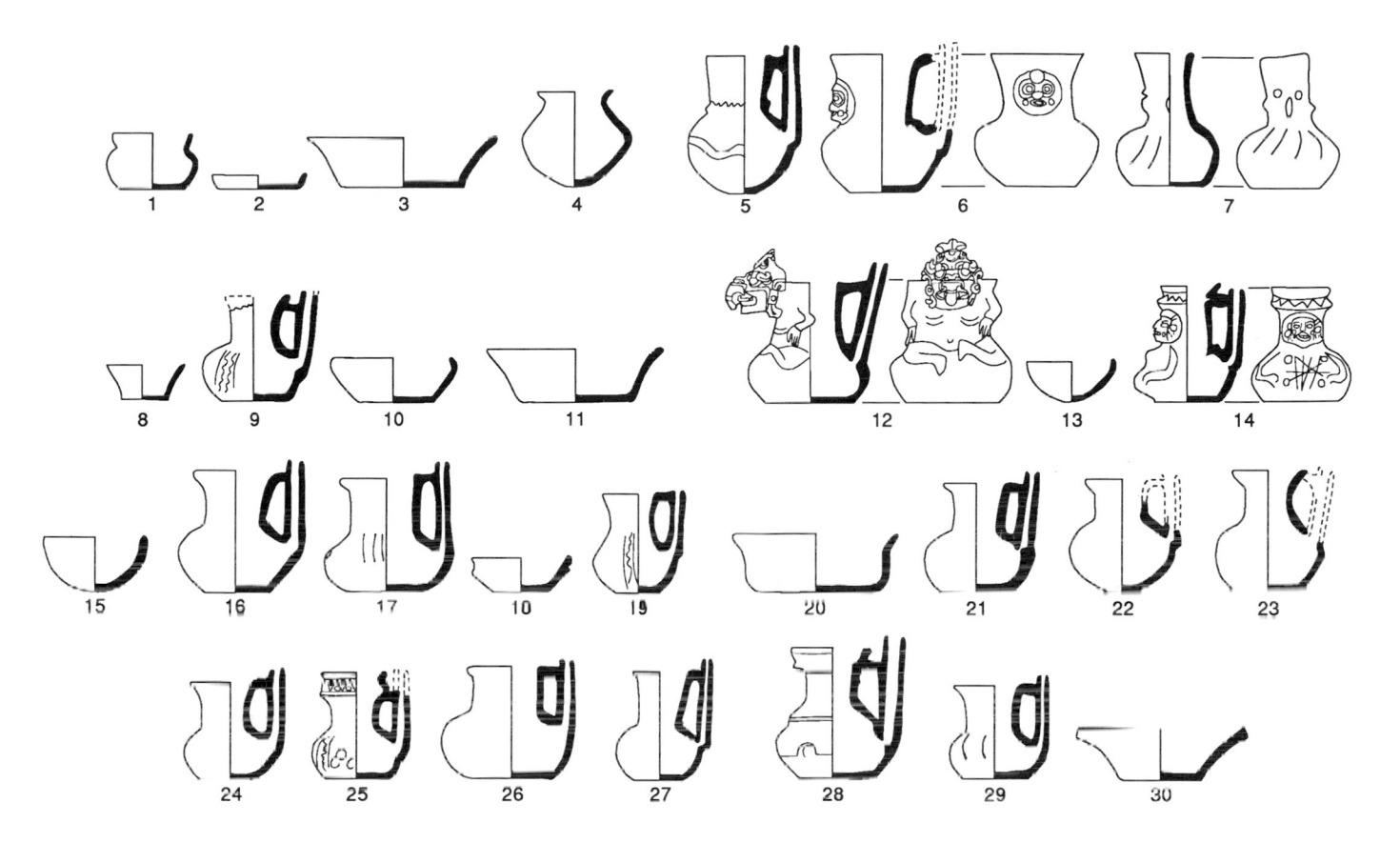

189 Thirty of the vessels from a Late Monte Albán I tomb at Tomaltepec. Tallest vessels, 25–30 cm high.

people of the valley.[21] They founded many new settlements in the mountains during this period, and Monte Negro – only 2–3 days' walk from Huitzo may lie within this zone of expansion. Monte Negro's defensible location hints that it may have been on or near the frontier between the Zapotec and hostile neighbors.

Tomaltepec: A Small Administrative Center in the "Piedmont Strategy" Zone

As we have seen, the early growth of Monte Albán was partly dependent on piedmont irrigation systems. This "piedmont strategy" was not limited to new settlements near previously unused streams; it included the enlargement of pre-existing piedmont communities.

Tomaltepec, only 15 km east of Monte Albán, was a prime candidate for such enlargement because it lay only a half-day's journey from the capital. Tomaltepec overlooks a strip of irrigable Class I land, surrounded by Class III foothills. Already a successful village in the San José phase, it was transformed during Monte Albán Ic into a 5–8-ha community with public buildings, plastered courtyards, and elite households.

Tomaltepec may have been the administrative center for a group of 7–8 villages along two nearby piedmont streams. It occupied Tier 3 of the site hierarchy for Monte Albán Ic, dwarfed not only by Monte Albán itself (400 ha) but by Tier 2 centers like Magdalena Apasco (30–40 ha). Significantly, Tomaltepec had elite burials with offerings nearly as rich as those of Monte Albán itself. This suggests that the piedmont strategy was directed "from the top down," with high-ranking families sent to oversee canal development.

The public buildings at Tomaltepec flank a rectangular plaza 50 m on a side. The largest, Structure 13 on Mound 1, survives only as a patch of stucco floor atop a substantial platform, faced with cut stone and strengthened with adobe blocks. It may have been a temple of some kind.

Not far to the north of Mound 1, excavator Michael Whalen found two rooms that may have been part of an elite residence with an interior courtyard.[22] Each room, roughly 24 m², had a stucco floor, adobe walls over a stone foundation, and cut stone steps. Under the floor of one room was an adobe-walled tomb with the remains of a woman less than 40 years old, an adult of undetermined sex, and a child of about 12 years. This tomb – presumably the resting place of an elite family – had been equipped with 37 pottery vessels, many of them elegant jars whose neck and spout are connected by a bridge. Several jars are human effigies, including one with a seated figure wearing a macaw mask. The prominent position of the woman in this tomb suggests a hypogamous marriage like those seen earlier at Fábrica San José (Chapter 9).

While Tomaltepec's environmental setting makes it a likely center for canal irrigation, it also seems to have specialized in pottery production. Two of the households excavated by Whalen, including the one just described, had in their courtyards what seem to be two-chambered kilns. The majority were pits 60–80 cm in diameter, divided into two chambers by an adobe wall. In such a kiln, very even firing temperatures could be established by placing the vessels in one chamber and the fuel in the other. The subterranean nature of the kiln suggests a reducing atmosphere of the type needed to produce the gray ware of Late Monte Albán I.

The discovery of these kilns at Tomaltepec tells us that although Monte Albán itself provided a venue for urban craft production, it had by no means drawn all the artisans out of its rural hinterland. Craft specialization evidently flourished in some of the valley's large villages, perhaps under the direction of high-status families.

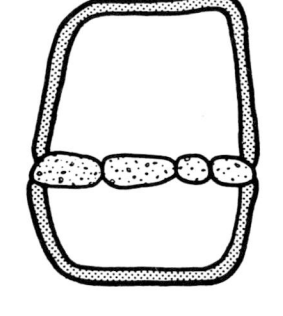

190 Plan and cross-section of a two-chambered pottery kiln from a Late Monte Albán I household at Tomaltepec. A low adobe wall separates the two chambers. Maximum length 90 cm.

An Elite Burial at Abasolo

Even outside the rapidly developing piedmont zone, Tier 3 communities of this period seem to have had elite families. Such was the case at San Sebastián Abasolo, a large village in the central Tlacolula subvalley whose fields were irrigated by shallow wells.[23]

Burials 5a and 5b, possibly a marital pair, were laid to rest side by side. Individual 5a (male) had ten jade beads in his mouth, while 5b (gender indeterminate) had two. This pair of adults was accompanied by 21 vessels typical of Monte Albán Ic – in effect, a complete "table service" for an elite family. Included were effigy bridgespout jars, bowls with combed designs in the bottom, a ladle, miniature "condiment vessels," a small jar with water glyphs, a large flask, and a small sauce vessel in the shape of a turtle.

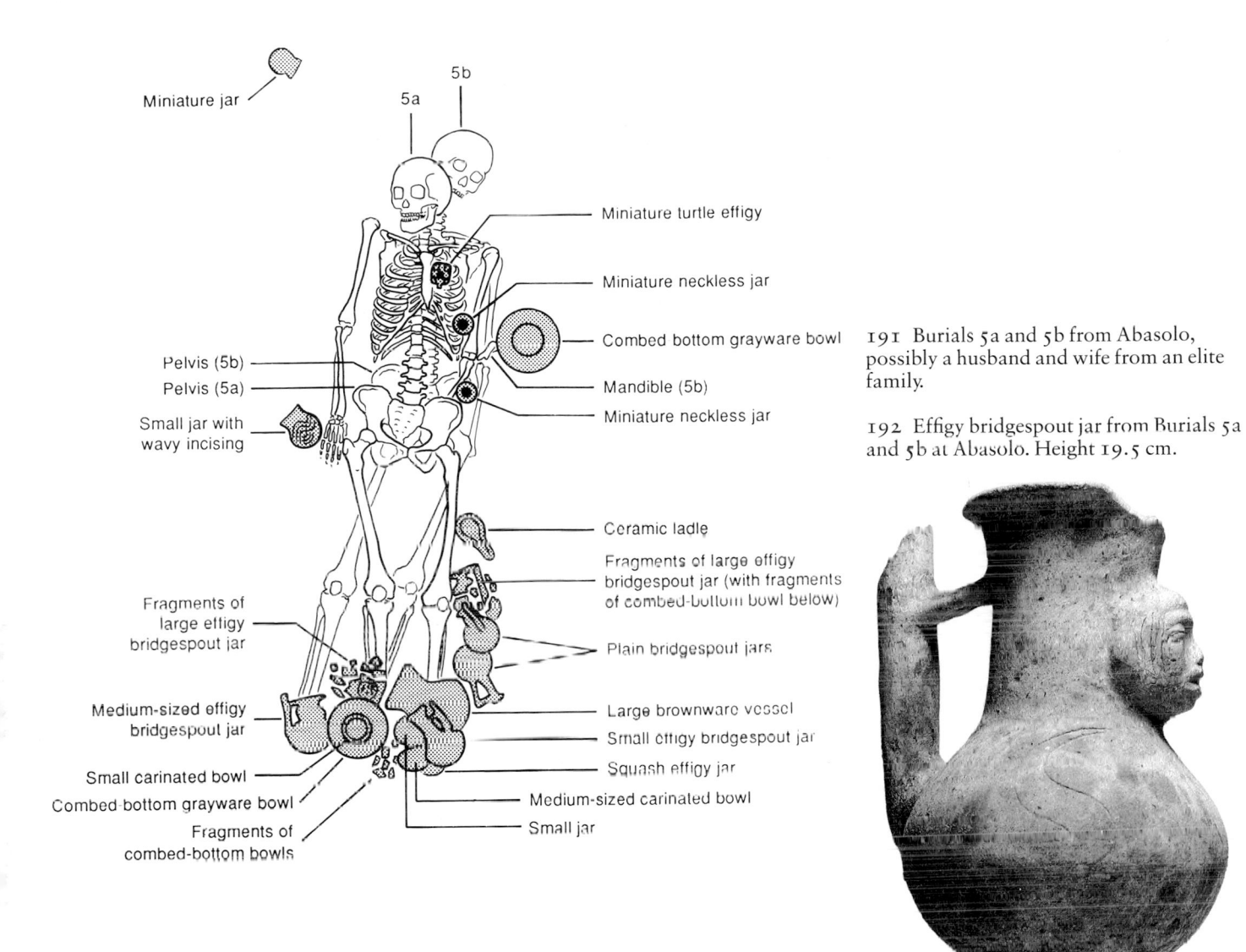

Miniature jar

5a

5b

Miniature turtle effigy

Miniature neckless jar

Combed bottom grayware bowl

Pelvis (5b)

Pelvis (5a)

Mandible (5b)

Small jar with
wavy incising

Miniature neckless jar

Ceramic ladle

Fragments of large effigy
bridgespout jar (with fragments
of combed-bottom bowl below)

Fragments of
large effigy
bridgespout jar

Plain bridgespout jars

Medium-sized effigy
bridgespout jar

Large brownware vessel

Small effigy bridgespout jar

Small carinated bowl

Squash effigy jar

Combed-bottom grayware bowl

Medium-sized carinated bowl

Fragments of
combed-bottom bowls

Small jar

191 Burials 5a and 5b from Abasolo,
possibly a husband and wife from an elite
family.

192 Effigy bridgespout jar from Burials 5a
and 5b at Abasolo. Height 19.5 cm.

Monte Albán I was a society in transition from chiefdom to state, and cannot easily be fitted into one of these two evolutionary stages. Ecological functionalists could argue that Monte Albán's great need for maize to feed its urban population made the subjugation of the entire Valley of Oaxaca necessary. Selectionists could argue that the "competitive advantage" conferred by Monte Albán's large size made it likely that it would eliminate all competitors. Action theorists could argue that a series of aggressive Monte Albán rulers, like Hawaii's Kamehameha, fought relentlessly to subdue the rest of the Valley of Oaxaca – through it all, of course, pursuing goals that were "materially and politically useful within the context of their cultural and historical situation."[24] Whatever the case, by the end of Monte Albán I the entire valley was under Monte Albán's hegemony and Zapotec ethnogenesis was in flower.

Summary

The Emergence of the Zapotec State

One of the most exciting phases of Zapotec prehistory was Period II of Monte Albán. That period began by 100 BC and lasted until AD 200. During Monte Albán II there can no longer be any doubt that Oaxaca society was organized as a state, and an expansionist state at that. Virtually every archaeologically recoverable institution of Period II reflects a state level of sociopolitical organization. Those institutions (many of which have also been detected in early Old World states) will be examined in this chapter; Chapter 14 will document the way the Zapotec expanded through colonization and conquest.

Population Estimates

The Monte Albán II state was very likely supported by a combination of dry farming, irrigation, and tribute. Maize, beans, squash, chile peppers, avocados, agaves, prickly pear, and other wild and domestic plants figured in the diet. There were now so many people in the valley that venison probably had to be restricted to the elite, but there were still plenty of rabbits, mud turtles, pocket gophers, birds, and lizards for commoners. To the domestic dog, still a major meat source, the Zapotec had now added the flesh and eggs of the turkey (*Meleagris gallopavo*). Where and when turkeys were first domesticated is unknown; their wild ancestors can still be found in northern Mexico and the United States.

Monte Albán II also had the most colorful and distinctive pottery seen in Oaxaca since the San José phase. Burnished gray ware remained popular, but it was joined by waxy red, red-on-orange, red-on-cream, black, and white-rimmed black vessels, many of whose shapes and colors reflect an exchange of ideas with neighboring Chiapas. The distinctiveness of this pottery makes it relatively easy to identify on the surface of the ground, and some 518 communities of this period have been identified in the Valley of Oaxaca.

That number is 227 fewer than in Monte Albán Ic, and despite the fact that Monte Albán II sites were larger on average, this decline in number of sites affects the population estimates made by the Settlement Pattern Project. Their estimates for the valley in Monte Albán Ic average 51,000; their estimates for Monte Albán II average 41,000. This decline of about 10,000 is thought to reflect the movement of Zapotecs out of the Valley of Oaxaca as part of a deliberate colonization of neighboring areas.

Many lines of evidence suggest that such a colonization was, in fact, taking place (Chapter 14). However, it should also be remembered that the pottery

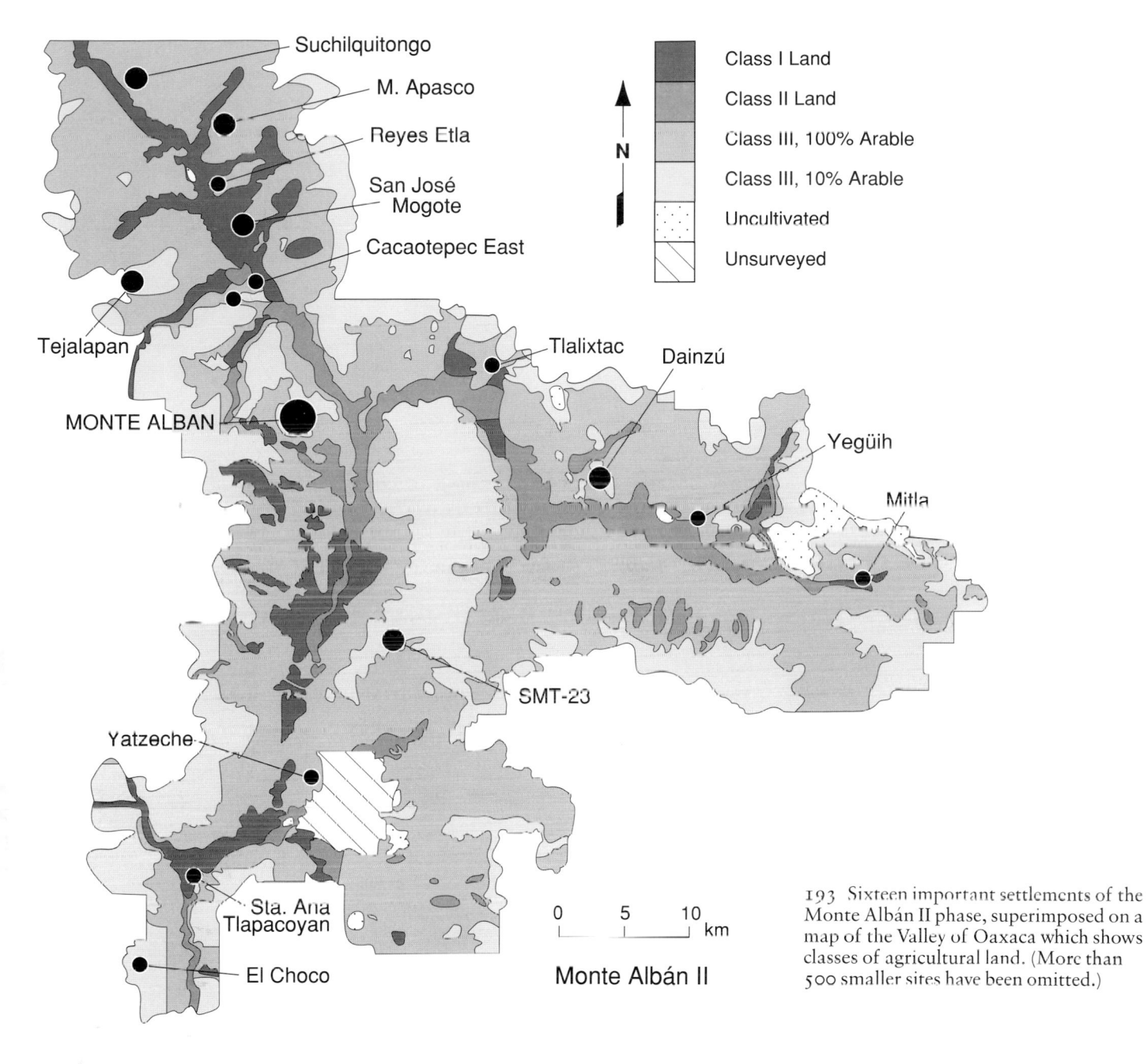

Class I Land
Class II Land
Class III, 100% Arable
Class III, 10% Arable
Uncultivated
Unsurveyed

N

Suchilquitongo
M. Apasco
Reyes Etla
San José Mogote
Cacaotepec East
Tejalapan
MONTE ALBAN
Tlalixtac
Dainzú
Yegüih
Mitla
SMT-23
Yatzeche
Sta. Ana Tlapacoyan
El Choco

0   5   10 km

Monte Albán II

193 Sixteen important settlements of the Monte Albán II phase, superimposed on a map of the Valley of Oaxaca which shows classes of agricultural land. (More than 500 smaller sites have been omitted.)

attributes chosen as diagnostic of a period can affect one's population estimates. In this case, we suspect that part of the population decline in Period II is due to the Settlement Pattern Project's very high population estimate for Period Ic.

Several attributes of the Period II settlement system indicate that the whole valley was now under the control of a single state centered at Monte Albán.

For one thing, the ring of 155 settlements that had surrounded Monte Albán during Late Period I was now gone. The central region of the Valley of Oaxaca, once densely populated, was now reduced to 23 communities. This suggests that

The Emergence of a Central Place Hierarchy

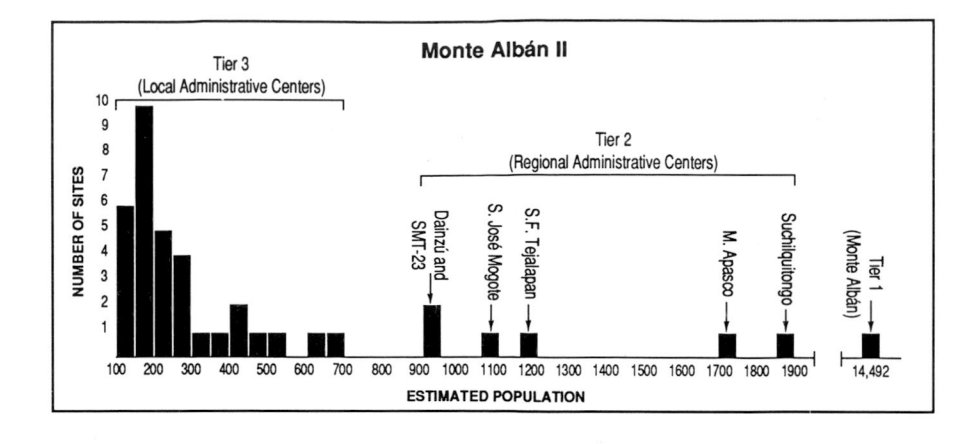

194 Histogram of the 40 largest settlements in the Valley of Oaxaca during Monte Albán II. Only Tiers 1–3 of the settlement hierarchy are thought to have had administrative functions.

Monte Albán no longer needed to concentrate farmers, warriors, and laborers within 15 km of the city, because its rulers could now count on the support of the entire valley.

In addition, there no longer seems to be any ambiguity about a four-tiered hierarchy of communities in the valley. Monte Albán, now covering 416 ha, was the only "city," or occupant of Tier 1; its population is estimated at 14,500.

Six sites with estimated populations of 970–1950 might have been Tier 2 communities, or "towns." All lay between 14 and 28 km of Monte Albán, less than a day's trip. All show surface evidence of having been regional administrative centers. Even the fourth largest of these towns, San José Mogote, covered 60–70 ha.

Tier 3 of the hierarchy consisted of at least 30 "large villages" in the 5–10-ha range, with populations estimated at 200–700 persons. A number of these sites have been excavated, and show evidence of public buildings.

Finally, Tier 4 of the hierarchy consisted of more than 400 "small villages" with estimated populations below 200 people. Almost none of these sites have been excavated, and we lack evidence of administrative functions at any of them.

The strikingly regular distances between some Tier 2 towns and Monte Albán suggest that we are dealing with a "central place hierarchy." This is a term used by cultural geographers for an administrative hierarchy so well integrated that towns encircle the capital city at very regular distances; in turn, large villages encircle towns at regular (and shorter) distances.[1] This makes the settlement

195 Examples of central place lattices from ancient civilizations. (*Left*) The lattice of Tier 2, Tier 3, and Tier 4 sites near the ancient Sumerian city of Eshnunna, Iraq. (*Right*) The lattice of Tier 2 and Tier 3 sites surrounding the ancient Maya city of Calakmul.

Opposite

196 Tentative central place lattice for the Valley of Oaxaca during Monte Albán II. Sites shown as black rectangles are in fortified or defensible settings.

197 Closeup views of the cells of large and small villages that surrounded Tier 2 centers San José Mogote, SMT-23, and Dainzú.

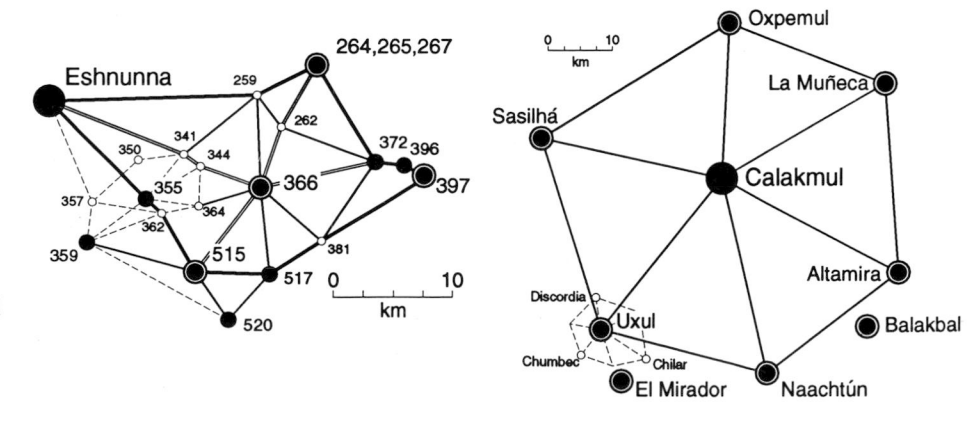

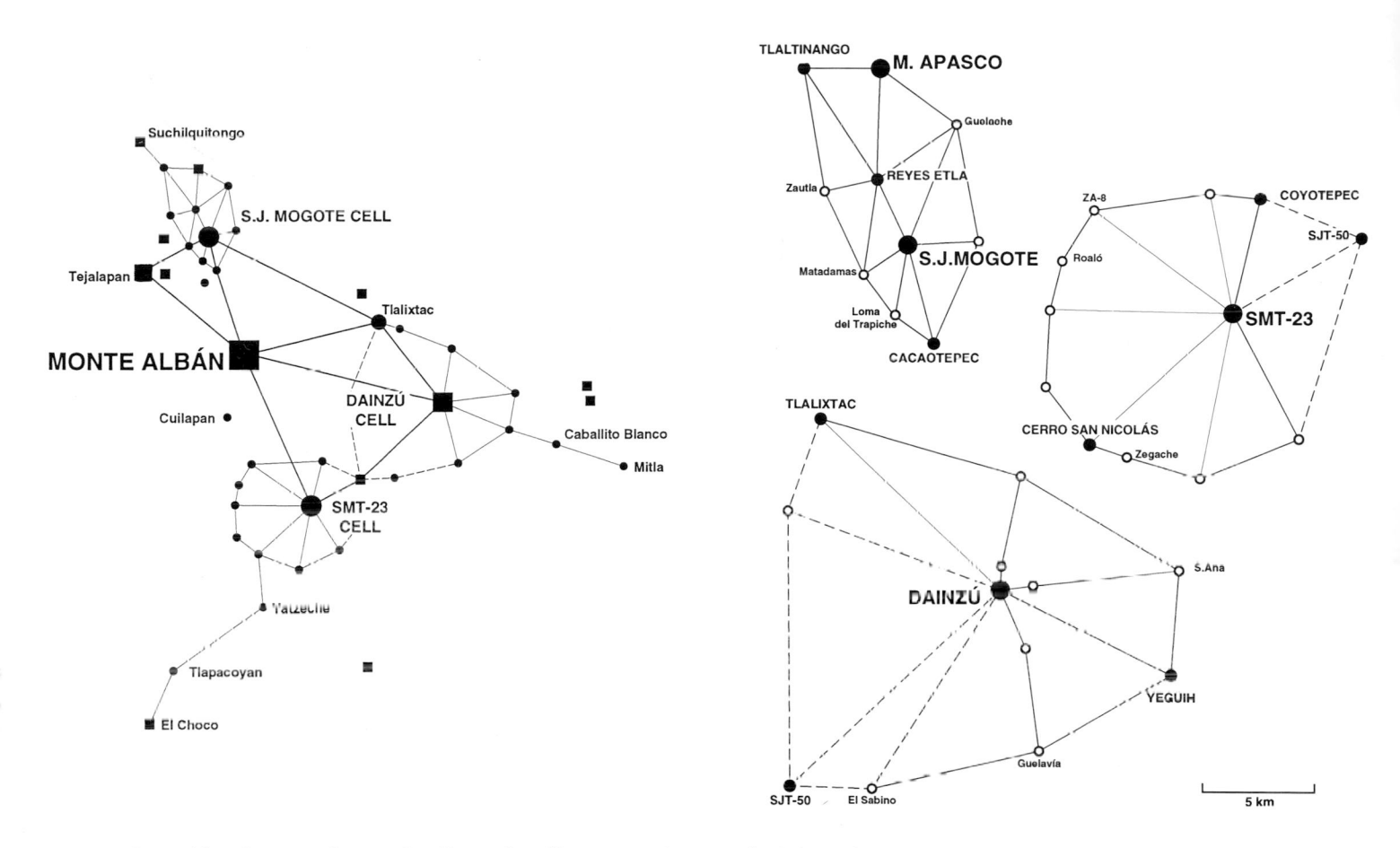

system resemble a lattice of nested cells, each cell representing an administrative unit. Let us now look at some of the more regular Monte Albán II cells.

Four clear Tier 2 administrative centers – San José Mogote, San Felipe Tejalapan, Dainzú, and Site SMT-23 near San Martín Tilcajete – are spaced 15–22 km from Monte Albán. A fifth community, Tlalixtac, although no larger than an average Tier 3 settlement, is in the right location to have served as another Tier 2 center. Tejalapan is in a defensible locality, and Dainzú lies at the base of a defensible hill.

When one focuses on San José Mogote, Dainzú, and SMT-23, each appears to have an irregular cell of large and small villages surrounding it. These cells of subordinate communities suggest that San José Mogote, Dainzú, and SMT-23 were the major regional administrative centers for the Etla, Tlacolula, and Valle Grande regions, respectively. Their dependent large villages are spaced 3–8 km from the nearest town, roughly a 1–2-hour walk.

Two other settlements, classified as Tier 2 centers on the basis of size, do not seem to have been surrounded by comparable cells of large villages. Magdalena Apasco seems to have been a town in the San José Mogote cell. Suchilquitongo, a hilltop center near the upper Atoyac River, may have served to defend the northern entrance to the valley. (A smaller mountaintop center, El Choco, may have defended the pass where the Atoyac River exits the valley on its way south.)

This regular pattern of towns and large villages below the city of Monte Albán reflects a level of valley-wide integration not seen before Period II. Full

198 Huge archaeological mounds rise from a defensible hilltop near Suchilquitongo in the northern Etla subvalley.

North Platform

Sunken Patio

Ballcourt

g

e

d

A

B

K

199 In this artist's reconstruction, Monte Albán's Main Plaza runs for 300 m between the North Platform acropolis and the South Platform pyramid. The major buildings were assigned letters of the alphabet by Alfonso Caso.

understanding of the regional system, however, will require excavation at every tier of the hierarchy. Sheer size is not always a reflection of a site's political importance, and estimates of population from surface remains are tentative.

The Archaeological Ground Plans of Zapotec State Institutions

Many of the institutions of the state are associated with a specific type of public building. Often the ground plan of that building can be recognized in the archaeological record, as can certain types of artifacts associated with the institution. We will now look at a series of buildings from the following four Monte Albán II communities:

1. Monte Albán, the valley capital, our only site in Tier 1.

2. San José Mogote, regional center for the Etla subvalley, a Tier 2 site.

3. Dainzú, regional center for the Tlacolula subvalley, a Tier 2 site.

4. Cuilapan in the Valle Grande, a possible Tier 3 center.

The "Grand Plaza" Design

Monte Albán II saw an enormous increase in types and numbers of public structures. Without doubt, future excavations at Monte Albán will add to our meagre roster of Period I buildings, many of which lie hidden beneath tons of later construction. Even knowing this, we are awed by the explosion of public architecture in Period II.

During this era the rulers of Monte Albán leveled a huge area, 300 m north–south and 200 m east–west, paving it over with white stucco to create the city's Main Plaza. In places where natural outcrops of bedrock were too high to be leveled, the latter served as nuclei for major buildings. One north–south line of structures provided the eastern border of the plaza, another line provided the western border, and a third line covered a series of outcrops in the center of the plaza.

The northern limits of the plaza were set by the North Platform, a huge acropolis 250 m on a side, which swallowed up several Period I buildings and went on to be enlarged and modified by later rulers. We do not know what the southern limits of the plaza looked like at this time, since any Period II constructions are now buried beneath the South Platform, an enormous structure which in later times reached 150 m on a side.

This "grand plaza" design was not limited to Monte Albán; at least a few towns in Tier 2 of the hierarchy had plazas laid out in imitation of the one at the capital. Perhaps the best known of these was San José Mogote, which after many centuries of relative abandonment had undergone a major renaissance in Monte Albán II.

Born anew as the leading Tier 2 center in the Etla subvalley, San José Mogote was given a Main Plaza 300 m north–south and 200 m east–west, very like Monte Albán's. Similarities in layout between the two plazas are remarkable. Mound 8 of San José Mogote, which forms the northern limit of the plaza, seems to have

200 Artist's reconstruction of San José Mogote during Monte Albán II. In the foreground is Mound 1, a modified hill equivalent to the South Platform at Monte Albán. At the far end of the Main Plaza is Mound 8, a smaller version of Monte Albán's North Platform. The Atoyac River delimits the site on the south.

corresponded to Monte Albán's North Platform. Each supported a governmental structure reached by climbing a large stairway and passing through a colonnaded portico; Monte Albán's portico had a double row of six columns, San José Mogote's a single row of six. Monte Albán's governmental structure had a sunken patio 50 m across and 4 m deep; San José Mogote's had a sunken patio 20 m across and shallower. Both structures appear to be places for elite assembly; each, however, had "reception rooms" behind its sunken patio.

To continue the comparison of Monte Albán and San José Mogote, we see that both sites had two-room temples along both sides of the plaza, as well as on natural rises within it. San José Mogote had at least ten such temples in Period

201 (Left) The sunken patio of Monte Albán's North Platform, seen from its northeast corner.

202 (Below) Colonnaded entranceway and sunken patio atop Mound 8 of San José Mogote.

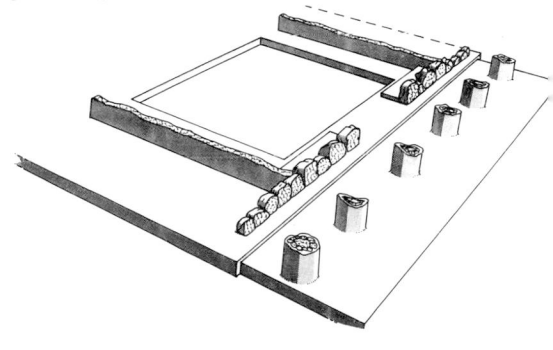

203 One temple on Mound 1 at San José Mogote could be reached by this secret subterranean stairway, originally roofed with stone slabs.

II; Monte Albán may have had twice that many. The vast majority of these temples face east or west. In perhaps five cases at San José Mogote (and at least that many at Monte Albán), pairs of temples face each other along the east–west path of the sun.

As discussed below, some temples at both sites had important offerings beneath their floors. Moreover, a few temples could be reached by secret passageways reminiscent of those seen earlier at Monte Negro. In the case of Monte Albán, there is a tunnel under the eastern half of the Main Plaza that would allow priests to move between buildings without being seen. In the case of San José Mogote there is a subterranean stairway that ascends Mound 1, the temple-crowned promontory at the south end of the Main Plaza, which corresponds to Monte Albán's South Platform.

Finally, the plazas at both Monte Albán and San José Mogote had ballcourts built in the shape of a Roman numeral I. San José Mogote never had more than one of these courts; Monte Albán eventually came to have seven scattered through the city, but many of those were built in later periods.

Palaces and Tombs

Many nobles of this period lived in large palaces, built of adobe brick and lime plaster over a stone masonry foundation. One of our greatest needs is for more complete ground plans of these buildings, such as the one just off the southwest corner of Monte Albán's North Platform. One such residence, built on Mound 9 in the Main Plaza at San José Mogote, was partially excavated by Robert and Judith Zeitlin. Consisting of multiple patios surrounded by 3–4 rooms, it seems to have been modified continuously during its occupation. Many of those modifications involved the dividing up of pre-existing rooms and patios into smaller spaces, possibly in response to an increase in occupants.

The tombs of Zapotec nobles became much more impressive during Period II, suggesting that the simple rectangular tombs of earlier times were no longer elaborate enough for the emergent ruling class. Now tombs might have a vaulted

204 Plan and cross-section of Tomb 118 at Monte Albán.

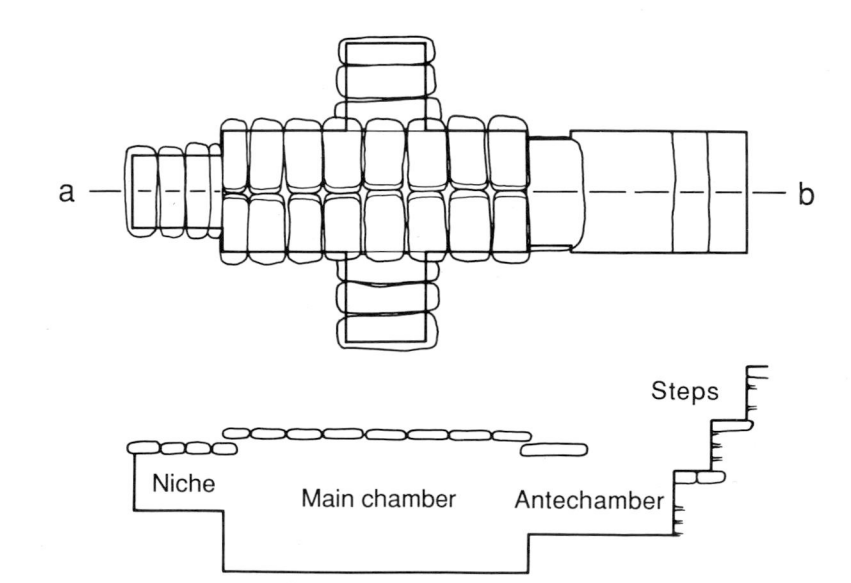

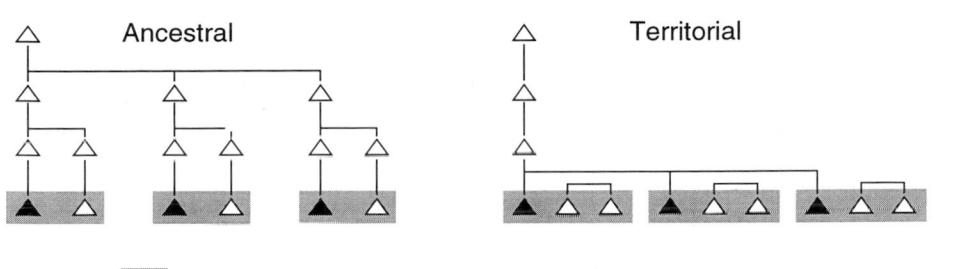

Land Unit ▲ Chief or Land Manager △ Commoner

205 Patrick Kirch's model for the shift from rank society to stratified society in Hawaii. Under the old "ancestral" system, even low-ranking families were still genealogically connected to the chief and his high-ranking close relatives. Under the new "territorial" system, the lowest-ranking families were divorced from the genealogy and became a separate stratum of commoners.

roof, a cruciform plan including several chambers and offering niches, and a doorway reached by descending stairs. It appears that tombs might be reopened on many occasions, as various members of a noble family died and were added to them.

Tomb 118 at Monte Albán was typical. The main chamber, 3.5 m long and 1.6 m high, was extended on the left, right, and rear by 1-m-long niches half the height of the chamber itself. The antechamber was reached by descending a steep, 2-m stairway.[2] We suspect that the monumentality of some Monte Albán II tombs – as well as the growing gulf between them and the graves of ordinary people – signals the rise of a stratified society like that of the sixteenth-century Zapotec (Chapter 1).

In most chiefdoms, there is a continuum of differences in rank from top to bottom. People are ranked in terms of their genealogical distance from the paramount chief, with the lowliest persons being very distantly related indeed. In most archaic states, there was an actual genealogical gap between the stratum of nobles and the stratum of commoners. Lesser nobles knew they were at least distantly related to the king. Commoners were not considered related to him at all. As we have seen, the two strata were kept separate by class endogamy, the practice of marrying within one's class.

There are many possible scenarios for the evolution of stratified society out of chiefly society. An actor-centered explanation might begin with a chief's need to ensure that his offspring would succeed him. The only way he could ensure that goal was by marrying the highest-ranking woman available. The genealogical gap mentioned above could arise through intense competition for the most advantageous marriages. Eventually the more genealogically distant members of society – marriage to whom would only condemn one's offspring to lower rank – might have their kin ties to the elite severed. This apparently happened to low-ranking families in Hawaii just prior to state formation.[3]

Let us hasten to add, however, that the presence of a state cannot be shown simply from elegant tombs. Chiefs also received elegant burials, like that given to Tattooed Serpent, the great chief of the Natchez Indians.[4] It takes *multiple lines of evidence* – central place hierarchies, urbanism, royal palaces, full-time priests, permanent occupation of conquered territories, and more – to make the case for statehood.

The Colonnaded Two-Room Temple

In Chapter 12 we raised the question of exactly when a second room was added to the Zapotec temple, converting it from a generalized religious structure to the *yohopèe* described in sixteenth-century Spanish accounts. This modification, clearly present in Monte Albán II, is significant because it was likely done to accommodate full-time priests who lived in the inner room of the temple.

Such temples fit our sixteenth-century descriptions of the standardized structures of Zapotec state religion. They were built, essentially to the same plan, at every level of the settlement hierarchy down to and including Tier 3.

Full-time priests took a great deal of ritual out of the hands of Zapotec laymen. Men who could have sacrificed their own animals at 1000 BC now had to bring those animals to the less sacred outer room of the temple and hand them to a priest, who would perform the sacrifice in the more sacred inner room. While high priests or *uija-tào* are said to have had comfortable residences, and came and went as they saw fit, the *bigaña* or minor priests are described as "never leaving the temple."[5]

One of the best-known temples of this type was found by Alfonso Caso in 1935 on Building X, just northeast of the Main Plaza at Monte Albán.[6] Built atop a platform, with a stairway on the south side, the temple measured 10 × 8 m. The doorway to the outer room was 4 m wide and flanked by single columns. To reach the inner chamber, one would have to cross the outer room and step up 30 cm through a second doorway flanked by single columns. This second doorway was narrower, and the inner sanctum smaller than the outer room.

Jorge Acosta discovered a still earlier temple below the former one in 1945–46.[7] This Monte Albán II temple is 12.8 × 11.2 m in extent; its inner room has a basin built into the stucco floor, and an offering box in the back of the room at the midline of the temple. These architectural features probably relate to the placement of offerings or incense burners, the washing of sacrificial items, or the collection of blood from sacrificed birds, dogs, infants, or prisoners.

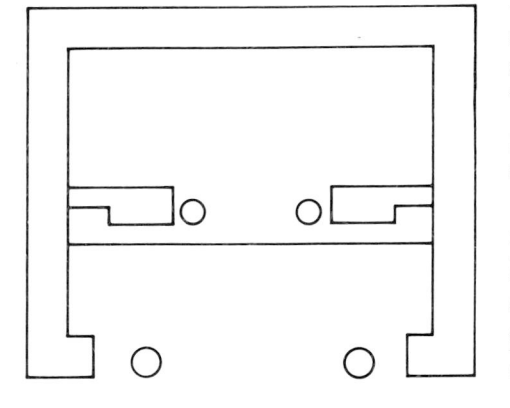

206 (*Above*) Two-room temple discovered by Alfonso Caso on Building X of Monte Albán, 1935. The circles are column bases.

207 (*Right*) Still earlier temple on Building X of Monte Albán, discovered by Jorge Acosta in 1945–46.

208 Pyramidal platform and stairway for Temple g at Monte Albán, where two sacrificed women were buried with offerings of pottery, greenstone, and mother-of-pearl.

Rituals of Sanctification

On the basis of ethnohistoric data, we suspect that specific rulers ordered such temples to be built, and underwrote the cost of construction as an act of royal piety. It appears that before a new temple could be built it was necessary to perform what anthropologist Roy Rappaport has called a "ritual of sanctification."[8,9] This ritual converted secular ground to sacred ground, often requiring the burial of costly or labor-intensive offerings below the temple floor. Once that spot had been converted to sacred ground, future temples could be built above the original one.

Just northeast of the huge sunken patio on Monte Albán's North Platform is a small patio, surrounded by three temples designated e, d, and g. A traffic-flow analysis of Monte Albán, performed by Richard Blanton, has determined this patio to be the least accessible place within the city;[10] it is therefore possible that Temples e, d, and g were used exclusively by the royal family. On the mound of Temple g, Acosta recovered a Monte Albán II dedicatory cache including 6 pottery vessels, 2 necklaces of greenstone and shell, a mother-of-pearl mosaic, and 2 skeletons of women who may have been sacrificed.[11]

At a depth of 9.5 m inside Building I – the platform for a more public temple in the center of Monte Albán's Main Plaza – was a Period II "offering box" typical of Zapotec temples. Inside this stone masonry box was a necklace of marine shell, flower-shaped jade ornaments, two mosaic masks (one of jade and turquoise, the other of iron pyrite and shell), and a carved bone.[12]

One of the most spectacular offerings of Period II, however, came not from a temple but from an "adoratory" or low ritual platform at Monte Albán. This multilevel, altar-like structure lies just to the east of Building H, near the sub-plaza tunnel mentioned above. Here Acosta discovered an important multiple sacrificial burial near the base of the adoratory.[13] At least five skeletons, most of them young adults, had been laid on a flagstone pavement, accompanied by mul-

209 The "adoratory," or low ritual platform, to the east of Building H at Monte Albán. The jade bat mask shown in Plate I was found here, accompanied by a multiple sacrificial burial.

tiple jade necklaces, flower-shaped jade ear ornaments, masks and pectorals of jade, pearls, conchs, and other marine shells. One skeleton wore as its pectoral an incredible mask made of 25 individual pieces of jade, fitted together to form the face of a bat, with eyes and teeth of marine shell. This mask, shown in Plate I, is considered a masterpiece of Zapotec art.

A Temple at Cuilapan

Even temples at Tier 2 and 3 communities could have important dedicatory offerings. For example, one Monte Albán II temple at Cuilapan in the Valle Grande – considered a Tier 3 center at this period – had a sacrificed child beneath its floor. The child was covered with red pigment and accompanied by 17 jade figurines, 400 jade beads, 35 marine shells, 2 pottery ear ornaments, and disintegrated mosaics of shell, obsidian, and hematite.[14]

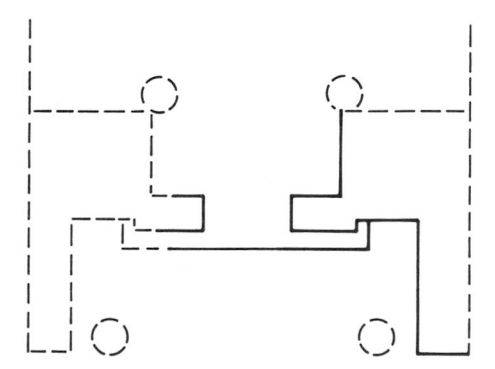

210 Plan of a two-room temple from Cuilapan, whose subfloor offerings included jade, shell, obsidian, hematite, and a sacrificed infant.

"Open" Temples

Not all temples were of the two-room type; some were left open on all sides. An example is Building II of Monte Albán, described by Ignacio Bernal as "a small temple with five pillars in the front and another five in the back. . . . It never had side walls and in fact was open to the four winds."[15] On the south side of this "open" temple, excavators found the entrance to a tunnel which allowed priests to enter and leave the building unseen, crossing beneath the eastern half of the Main Plaza to a building on the plaza's central spine.

Some clues to the possible use of such open temples are provided by a remarkable ceramic sculpture found deep in the North Platform at Monte Albán. Executed in red-on-cream pottery typical of Period II, the sculpture shows a miniature open temple, its roof supported by columns on all sides. Inside, lurking in the shadow of the columns, is a giant macaw caught with its mouth open in mid-cry. Only half the bird's body is visible, as if emerging from some hidden entrance in the floor. One wonders if such open temples, with their secret entrances, could have been a place for spellbinding displays by priests dressed as giant birds, emerging dramatically from tunnels.

A Temple Sequence from San José Mogote

For Monte Albán II, we need not rely as heavily on ethnographic analogy to reconstruct religious rituals as we did for earlier periods. So similar were some rituals of Period II to those of the historic Zapotec that we can turn instead to the direct historical approach.

Three superimposed two-room temples from San José Mogote – Structures 36, 35, and 13 – provide us with information on rituals of sanctification, the burning of incense, the sacrifice of humans and animals, and the metamorphosis of noble ancestors into companions of Lightning. All three temples faced west, and were built of adobe brick with white stuccoed walls and floors.[16]

Structure 36, the oldest temple, dated to early Monte Albán II. It measured 11 × 11 m and was slightly T-shaped, the inner room slightly smaller than the outer. Both columns flanking the inner doorway, and all four columns flanking the outer doorway, were made from the trunks of baldcypress trees (*Taxodium* sp.). So well does cypress wood preserve that identifiable fragments of it were still present in the column bases.

Structure 35, presumably built by a later ruler over the deliberately razed remains of Structure 36, dated to the middle of Period II. It was T-shaped like its predecessor and larger, measuring 12 × 13.5 m. In its columns – one to either side of the inner and outer doorways – tree trunks had now been replaced by large stones, stacked one above the other and surrounded by stony rubble plastered with lime. In the construction debris between Structures 35 and 36 we recovered the remains of quail, a bird favored by the Zapotec as an item for sacrifice.

Yet another ruler had built Structure 13 above the razed remains of Structure 35. This temple, dating to late Monte Albán II, measured 15 × 8 m and was rectangular rather than T-shaped. Its columns – two flanking the inner doorway and four flanking the outer – were of stacked stones, like those of Structure 35. Its inner room had a basin set in the floor, like the temple on Mound X at Monte Albán.

The Offerings of Structure 35

Structure 35 of San José Mogote was of particular interest because its floor, as well as the artifacts left behind on it, had been preserved under a layer of soft adobe debris. The floor itself displayed sooty circles wherever incense burners had been used; particularly favored localities for burning incense were in the centers of the inner and outer rooms, along the back wall of the inner room, and atop the step between the inner and outer rooms. The columns of aromatic smoke from these censers rose until they reached venerated "Cloud Ancestors" in the Zapotec sky.

211 Ceramic sculpture of a giant macaw inside a temple, Monte Albán II. Height 49.5 cm.

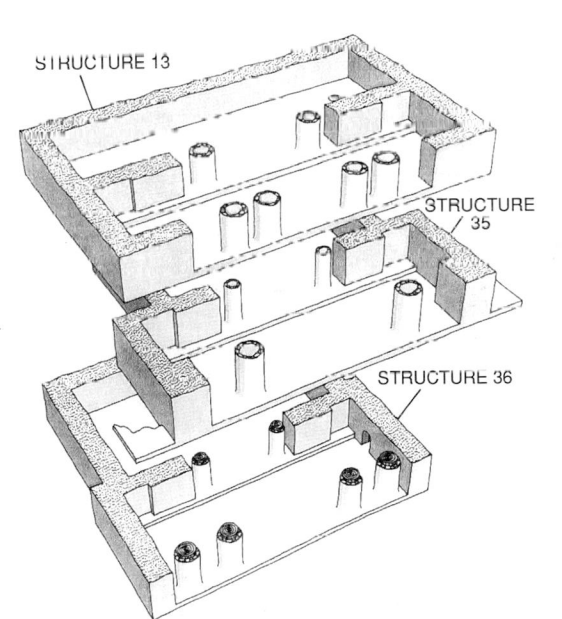

212 Three superimposed Monte Albán II temples at San José Mogote.

213 Structure 35 at San José Mogote. The artist has drawn incense braziers on the ten localities most frequently used for burning incense.

214 Grotesque effigy incense brazier from San José Mogote. Height 55 cm.

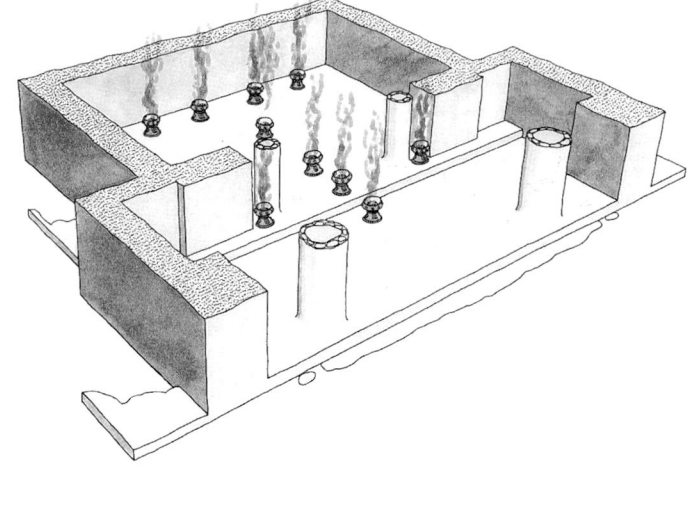

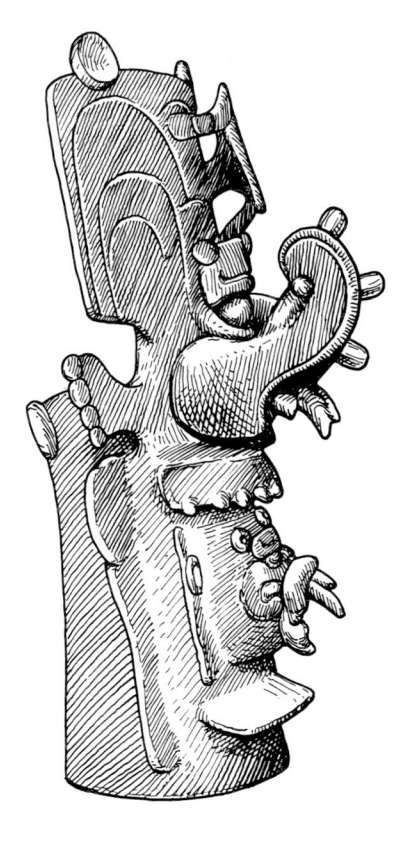

In the southern part of the smoky, windowless inner room, a series of obsidian artifacts had been left on the floor. Included were two broken, leaf-shaped daggers like the one seen earlier from Monte Negro, almost certainly for the removal of human hearts. Scattered around them were 42 prismatic blades of the type used by Zapotec priests to perform ritual bloodletting, or to sacrifice small animals such as quail.

In spite of the fact that Structure 35 was built above an earlier temple, the ruler who commissioned it felt the need to place spectacular dedicatory gifts beneath the floor of the inner room. In an offering box beneath the northern half of the room lay two jade statues, two jade beads, and fragments of jade-working debris in a heap of vermilion pigment. The larger statue is 49 cm tall, standing stiffly erect with arms held rigidly at his sides. His ear lobes have been perforated for ornaments, and the top of his head has a drilled hollow which could have held the base of a perishable headdress; he may represent a sacrificed noble. The piece of jadeite on which he is carved – the largest ever legally excavated in Oaxaca! – shows the characteristic color and venation of a source near the Río Motagua, Guatemala, more than 700 km from San José Mogote (Plate XVI).

Under the south half of the same room was an offering box with seven ceramic pieces arranged in a scene. So complex is the symbolism of this scene that even a knowledge of Zapotec ethnohistory permits only the sketchiest interpretation.

The centerpiece of the scene was a miniature tomb whose walls were made of adobes set on edge, a stone slab serving as its roof. Inside this tomb was a kneeling human figure in an open bowl, flanked by the skeleton of a sacrificed quail. Immediately to the south of the tomb roof was a pair of deer antlers, trimmed as drumsticks for a turtle-shell drum.

The kneeling figure belongs to a type known in Oaxaca as "companions" because of their frequent occurrence in royal tombs. Identified as a member of the nobility by his necklace and large ear ornaments, he kneels with his arms folded across his chest in the "obeisance posture" seen in earlier figurines.

Lying full length on the roof of the miniature tomb was a "Flying Figure" with a long cape flowing behind him. He wore a mask depicting Lightning, carried a stick in his right hand, and held the bifid tongue of a serpent coiled in his left. Since the Zapotec words for "serpent" and "young maize" (*zee* or *ziy*) are

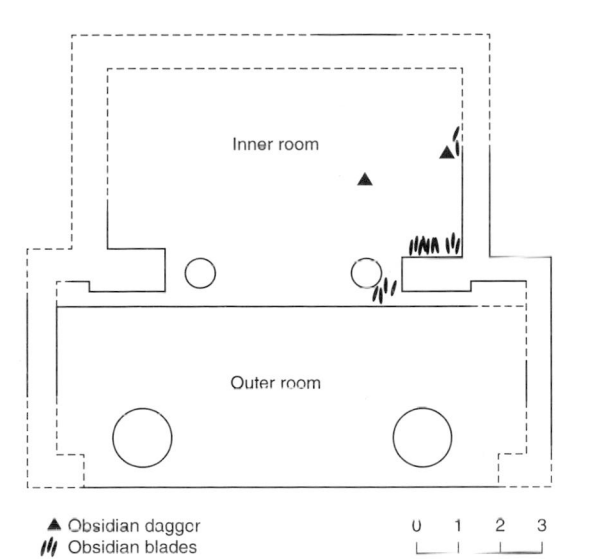

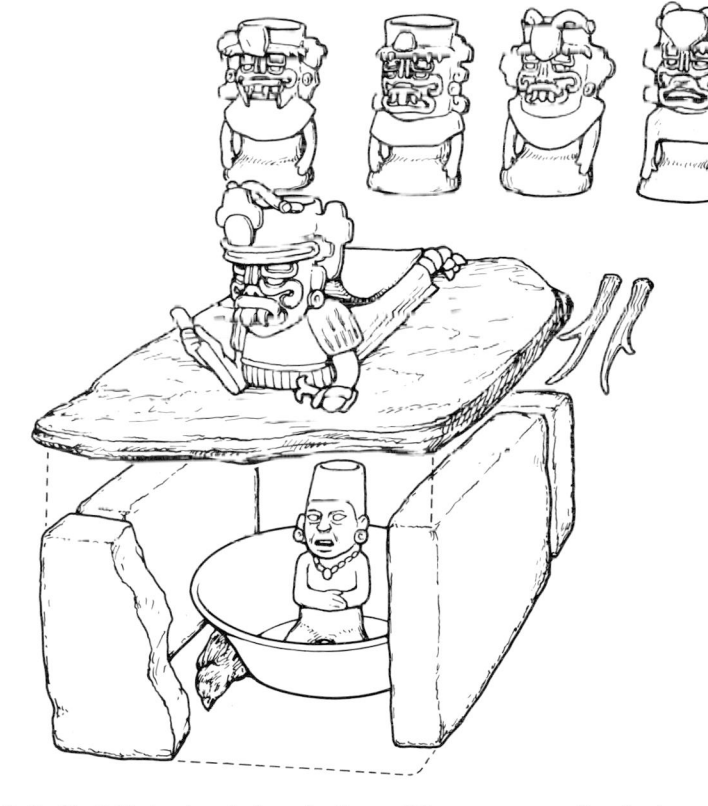

215 (*Above*) Plan of Structure 35 at San José Mogote, showing where obsidian artifacts had been left on the floor.

216 (*Center*) Broken obsidian sacrificial dagger from Structure 35, San José Mogote. Length of fragment 5 cm.

217 (*Right*) Broken obsidian blades from Structure 35, San José Mogote. Longest specimen, 6.8 cm.

218 (*Left*) Offering box below the floor of Structure 35 at San José Mogote, showing two jade statues *in situ*.

219 (*Above*) Beneath the floor of Structure 35 at San José Mogote was this ritual scene. It consisted of a kneeling figure and a sacrificed quail inside a miniature adobe tomb; a metamorphosed "Flying Figure" on the stone lid of the tomb; two deer antler drumsticks; and four grotesque female effigies.

homonyms, we suspect that what we see in the figure's hands are an agricultural dibble stick and a metaphor for newly sprouted maize.

Sitting in a row behind the flying figure were four ceramic effigies, each depicting a kneeling woman with a grotesque *Cociyo* mask. These women, each of whose heads was a hollow receptacle, probably represent Clouds, Rain, Hail, and Wind, the four companions of Lightning (see Chapter 1).

This scene may depict the metamorphosis of a deceased Zapotec lord into a "Cloud Person" (*ben zaa*) or "Flying Figure" who was now in contact with Lightning. He could represent a royal ancestor of the kneeling man in the miniature tomb, or even the partial metamorphosis of that same individual, caught at a stage where his body is still that of a human but his face is *Cociyo's*.

Zapotec Ballcourts

It was apparently during Monte Albán II that "state ballcourts" in the shape of a Roman numeral I first appeared. It is difficult to put these courts in historic perspective, since we have little information on the ballgame itself.

As early as 1000 BC, some small figurines made at Mesomerican villages seem to be wearing gloves, knee guards, and other equipment associated with a prehispanic ball game. This game was played with heavy balls made of latex from the indigenous rubber tree. Three such balls were preserved by waterlogging at El Manatí in southern Veracruz, a site dating to 1000–700 BC.[17]

Actual ballcourts of this age have not yet been identified, perhaps because they were simply rectangular open areas. The oldest ballcourts identified thus far come from the Mexican state of Chiapas and date to 700–500 BC.[18]

At Dainzú, a Tier 2 center in the Tlacolula subvalley, we get our first strong evidence for the Oaxaca version of the ballgame. Dainzú, with a Monte Albán

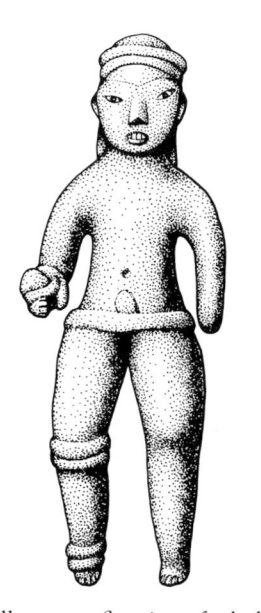

220 Small pottery figurine of a ballplayer, Basin of Mexico. First millennium BC.

221 Aerial view of Complex A at Dainzú, a Tier 2 administrative center in the Tlacolula subvalley. Behind the site is a defensible hill.

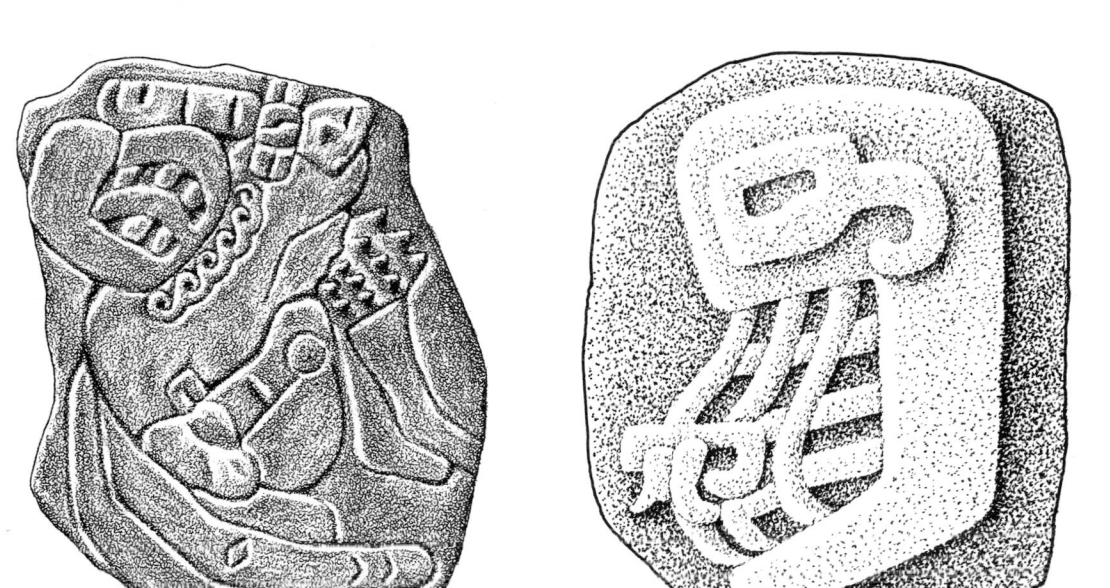

II population estimated at 1000 persons, was built along the base of a defensible hill.

Unlike San José Mogote, Dainzú has no grand plaza laid out in imitation of Monte Albán's. Its architecture does, however, share stylistic principles with the Zapotec capital. Dainzú's major governmental structure, Complex A, measures 50 × 30 m and was built in three stages or terraces, like Building L at Monte Albán. It also includes a roofed passageway like those at Monte Negro, and a narrow roofed stairway like the one at San José Mogote. According to excavators Ignacio Bernal and Arturo Oliveros, Complex A was begun in Monte Albán Ic and reached maximum size in Period II.[19,20]

In the manner of Building L at Monte Albán, the lowest terrace of Complex A had many carved stones in its outer wall. These carved stones, however, do not show slain captives; more than 47 of them depict ballplayers. A typical slab shows a single player, wearing a protective mask like those worn by fencers and holding a small ball in his right hand. The figures also wear long gloves, short pants, and protective padding.

No other display of carved stones in Oaxaca really compares with this series of ballplayers from Dainzú. In his excavations at Monte Albán, however, Alfonso Caso found a carving of a ballplayer's mask, suggesting that such equipment was used at the capital as well.[21,22]

On what type of court was this ballgame played? Evidently not on I-shaped courts like those at Monte Albán and San José Mogote, for Dainzú had no such court during Period II. Bernal and Oliveros suggest that Dainzú's carvings depict an early version of the ballgame, one that was played at Dainzú before Monte Albán had subdued the whole valley. That early game featured a ball about the size of an orange which was held, thrown, or struck with a reinforced glove. It may have been played on rectangular courts that would be difficult to identify archaeologically; Dainzú has several 20-m by 20-m plazas that could have been ballcourts.

222 (*Left*) Carved stone from Dainzú showing a ballplayer with protective mask, gloves, and knee guards, holding a ball in his right hand.

223 (*Right*) Carved stone from Tomb 6 at Monte Albán, showing a ballplayer's protective mask. Height 40 cm.

224 I-shaped ballcourt on the east side of the Main Plaza at Monte Albán. Maximum length 41 m.

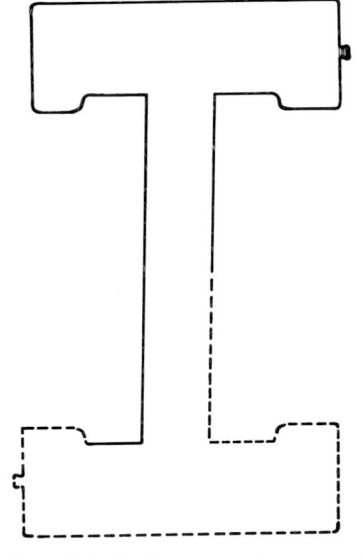

225 Plan of the ballcourt on the west side of the Main Plaza at San José Mogote. Maximum length 41 m.

With the emergence of the state, however, came the formalization of a new ballgame, played on I-shaped courts with high sloping walls to either side of the central playing area. So standardized are our few Monte Albán II-III examples of these courts that we suspect we are dealing with an "official" game. The courts on the Main Plazas at Monte Albán and San José Mogote are virtually identical: 41 m in maximum length and 24 m in maximum width, with a central court 26–27 m long.

This later type of court was called *lachi* by the Zapotec, and the game was called *queye* or *quiye*. While we do not know the rules by which it was played, it probably resembled the Aztec game called *olamaliztli* or *ulama*, in which the ball could not be touched with the hands; it was struck instead with the hips, elbows, and head as in modern soccer.[23]

The Dainzú Ballcourt: A Cautionary Tale

The later version of the ballgame was also played at Dainzú, on an I-shaped court built long after the period we are discussing. The excavation of that ballcourt provides us with a cautionary tale for archaeologists, to wit: no ballcourt can be dated until it has been excavated.

Given the numerous Monte Albán Ic-II depictions of ballplayers at Dainzú, Bernal and Oliveros had every reason to assume that Dainzú's I-shaped ballcourt would date to the same period. In addition, when the members of the Settlement Pattern Project surveyed Dainzú, they found abundant sherds of Monte Albán Ic-II pottery around the ballcourt.[24] When the Dainzú court was finally excavated, however, Bernal and Oliveros found that it had been built very late in the period called Monte Albán IV (perhaps AD 900–1000). Moreover, it did not have the standard dimensions of the Period II ballcourts at Monte Albán and San José Mogote, but was smaller. The reason so many Monte Albán I-II sherds can be found around the court is that thousands of basketloads of earth containing these sherds had been dug up and used in the fill of the structure.

Ballcourts and the Administrative Hierarchy

At what tiers in the Monte Albán II site hierarchy did ballcourts appear, and what was their "official" function? Both questions are hard to answer. The Settlement Pattern Project located almost 40 ballcourts in the Valley of Oaxaca,[25] but most remain unexcavated and therefore undated. If we limit ourselves to *excavated* courts, we would have to say that in Period II they were built only at Tier 1 and Tier 2 settlements.

Why would the early Zapotec state invest in the construction and standardization of I-shaped ballcourts, in effect promoting an "official" game? No one is sure, but some scholars believe that the ballgame played a role in conflict resolution between communities. It has been suggested that when two opposing towns competed in a state-supervised athletic contest, held on a standardized court at their regional administrative center, the outcome of the game might be taken as a sign of supernatural support for the victorious community. This, in turn, might lessen the likelihood that the two towns would actually go to war.

In Chapter 9 we made the point that chiefly societies in Oaxaca did not arise in a vacuum. Despite ethnic and environmental differences between Oaxaca, Morelos, and southern Veracruz, social evolution in all three areas showed strikingly similar patterns.

The archaic Zapotec state did not arise in a vacuum either. In the Central Depression of Chiapas – a region ethnically different, warmer, and wetter – another archaic state arose during a time equivalent to Monte Albán II. Its palaces and royal tombs were comparable to Monte Albán's, and its temples provocatively similar.

The ruins of Chiapa de Corzo extend for more than 1 square km along the right bank of the Grijalva River, some 385 km east of Monte Albán. Here the great river flows at 400 m elevation through a tropical valley receiving 800 mm of rainfall. Unlike Monte Albán, Chiapa de Corzo was not created by synoikism, nor was it in a defensible locality. It grew from a village whose history goes back before 1000 BC.

Parallel Developments Elsewhere in Mesoamerica

The Palace

Many of the buildings around Chiapa de Corzo's main plaza reached maximum size during the period 150 BC–AD 150. Structure H1 of Mound 5, on the east side of the plaza, is the best preserved palace known from the period. Excavated by Gareth Lowe, the building was roughly 26 × 16 m and sat atop an even larger platform with a massive stairway and balustrades.[26]

Like Oaxaca's governmental palaces, Structure H1 would seem to be an administrative building whose residential quarters (if any) were in the rear. The first room entered is described by Lowe as a "grand entranceway, reception room, or gathering place," 8 × 5 m in extent. Its walls were of adobes covered with lime plaster, its roof supported by wooden columns. Behind it lies a complex that could be residential: three small rooms grouped around a sunken courtyard whose doorways were flanked by columns.

To either side of this central complex of rooms are small courts, corridors,

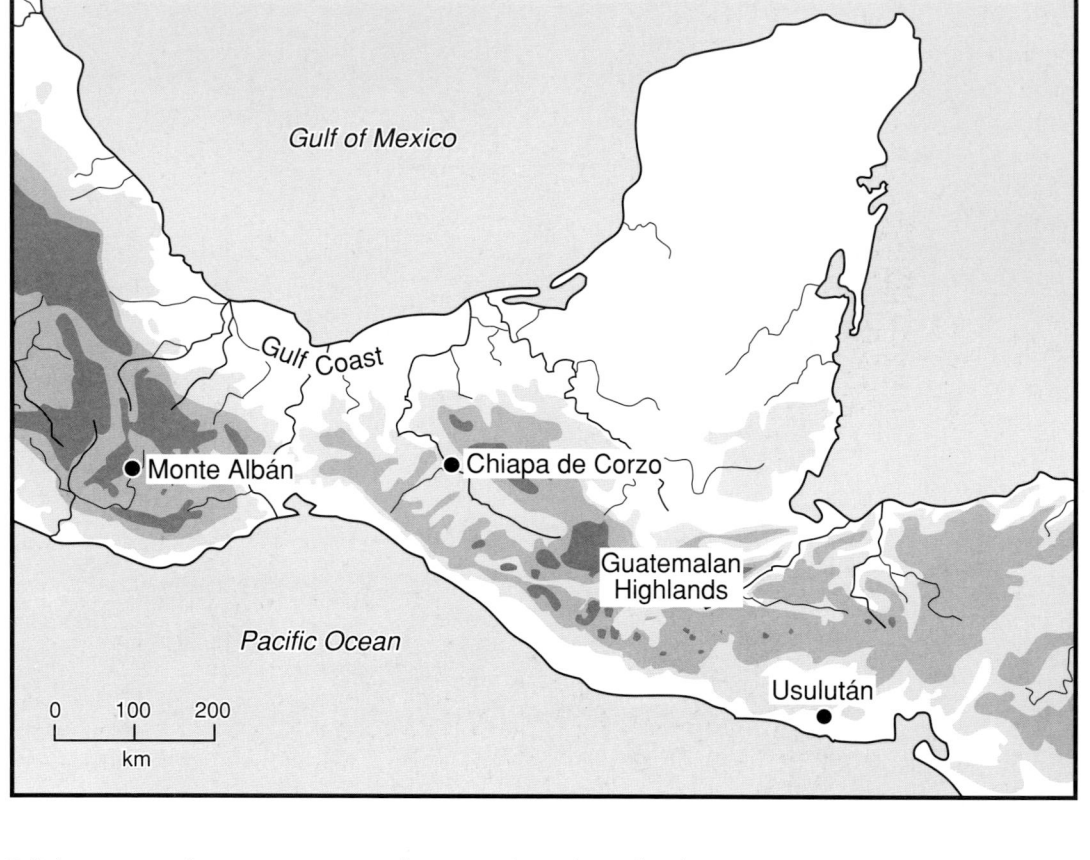

226 Chiapa de Corzo lies in the Grijalva River depression, some 385 km east of Monte Albán.

and accessory units that may have been kitchens, servants' quarters, or store-rooms. At the rear of the palace are two unusual features that may be storage cellars of some kind. Covering only a few square meters, each descended 2.5 m into the underlying platform.

Just as interesting as this palace was the destruction it had suffered. Its occupants had evidently been overthrown, and the palace heavily burned, at roughly AD 100. Accompanying this destruction came "an abrupt change in associated ceramics" denoting "a very definite cultural and probably ethnic shift" at Chiapa de Corzo.[27] This event reminds us that violent competition between elites (already seen in the Rosario phase) continued unabated after the emergence of the state. We do not know where the destroyers of Structure H1 came from. There are hints in the new ceramic styles of AD 100–200 that they may have come from regions to the east.

Here we see, for the first time, an archaeological phenomenon usually associated with conquest or colonization by a foreign power: abrupt replacement of the local pottery style by one from another region. In Chapter 14 we will see how this phenomenon helps us to document conquest and colonization by the Monte Albán II state.

The Royal Tomb

The elite of Chiapa de Corzo, like their Zapotec counterparts, were buried in elaborate tombs. One of the most interesting was Tomb 7, excavated deep in the bedrock below Mound 1. This tomb, dating to the first or second century BC,[28] had walls of adobe brick and a roof of sandstone slabs. Inside lay a young adult on a litter of wooden planks. Adorning the corpse were a jade necklace and composite jade and shell ear ornaments. Two chalcedony spear points and a large obsidian knife had been left in one corner of the tomb.

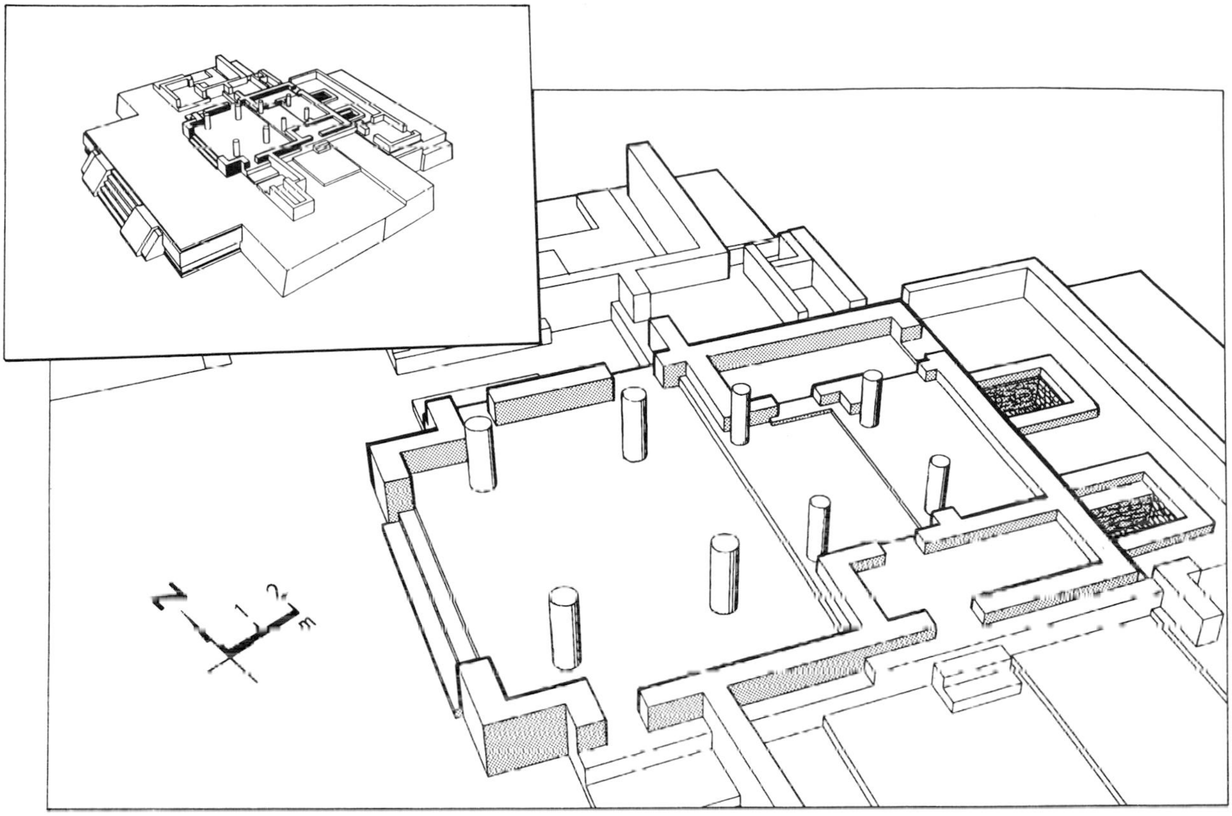

Perhaps most significant was the tomb's offering of 35 pottery vessels, every one of which was imported from elsewhere.[29] Included were stucco-painted vessels from the region of Usulután, El Salvador; white-rim black vessels from the Gulf Coast of Veracruz; fluted red vessels of the Chicanel or Arenal cultures, Guatemala; and effigy bridgespout jars in Oaxaca gray ware, identical to those found at Monte Albán, San José Mogote, and Tomaltepec. It is thus possible that the individual in Tomb 7, in addition to the privilege of being transported in a litter, was given a funeral attended by ambassadors with gifts from many other regions of Mesoamerica.

The Two-Room Temple

Following the death of the noble in Tomb 7, Mound 1 at Chiapa de Corzo underwent several phases of monumental construction. By the first century AD it had been turned into a platform 70 × 40 m in extent, forming the southern border of the site's main plaza. Virtually every structure it supported was a temple of some kind; Structure 1A, excavated by Pierre Agrinier, is particularly interesting because it captures the emergence of the two-room temple.[30]

227 Artist's reconstruction of Structure H1 at Chiapa de Corzo. The small inset (*upper left*) shows the building on its platform.

228 Effigy bridgespout jar of Oaxaca gray ware, found in Tomb 7 at Chiapa de Corzo. This vessel should be compared with those from Burials 5a and 5b at Abasolo (ill. 192). Height 29 cm.

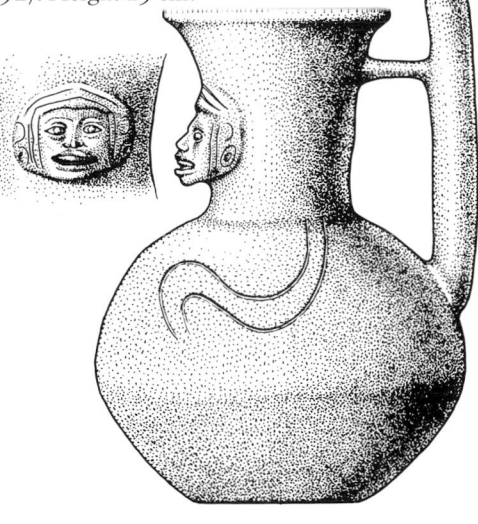

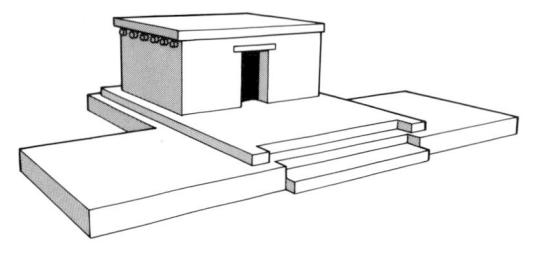

229 Stage G5 of Structure 1A at Chiapa de Corzo, a one-room temple.

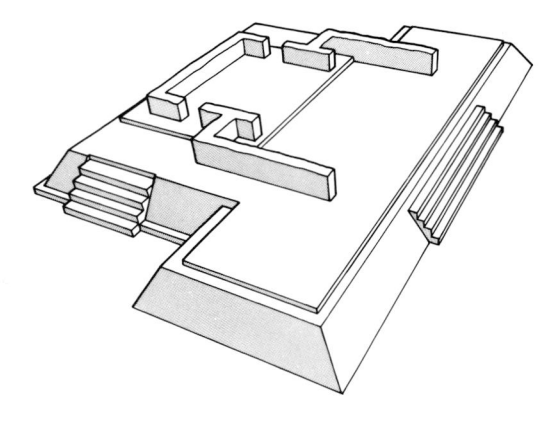

230 Stage G2 of Structure 1A at Chiapa de Corzo, a two-room temple with separate stairways for priests and worshipers.

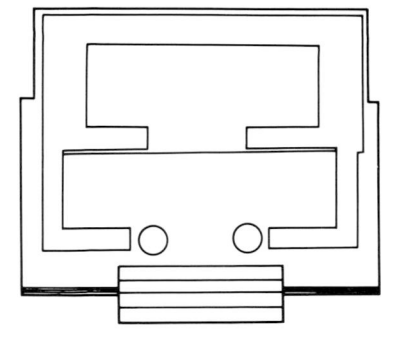

231 Structure 11b, Chiapa de Corzo, a standard two-room temple with columns flanking the outer doorway.

In ill. 229 we see Stage G5 of Structure 1A. At this time, perhaps 250–200 BC, it was a one-room temple 4–5 m on a side, built of adobes and small stones; its walls were covered with clay and its floor with lime plaster.

Between the next two building stages (G4 and G3), a second room was built in front of the previously existing one. The back walls of this outer chamber, which was 27 m² in extent, abutted the sides of the inner room. That inner room was now given two doorways on either side, one of which led to a stairway. By Stage G2 – perhaps 150–100 BC – the floor of the inner room had been raised 15 cm above the floor of the outer room.

The architects of Chiapa de Corzo had now created their own version of the two-room temple. It had a private side entrance for the priests, while ordinary worshipers would have climbed a large stairway to the front entrance. While still lacking the columns of Monte Albán II temples, Structure 1A at Chiapa de Corzo was in all other ways equivalent.

By AD 100–200, following the destruction of the palace on Mound 5, the people of Chiapa de Corzo were building colonnaded temples as well. Structure 11b of Mound 1, shown in ill. 231, was a small two-room temple (48 m²) with columns to either side of the outer doorway. Such temples went on to be popular over the whole of Mesoamerica during the next millennium.

Conclusions

How are we to understand the remarkably similar emergence of the governmental palace, the royal tomb, and the colonnaded two-room temple in Chiapas and Oaxaca between 150 BC and AD 200? Once again we conclude that social evolution does not take place in isolation, and that ecological functionalism explains little of what happened.

Monte Albán, sitting on a walled mountaintop in temperate Oaxaca, arose through rapid urban relocation and supported itself with piedmont irrigation. Chiapa de Corzo grew slowly along the floodplain of a tropical river, farming a region with half again the rainfall of Oaxaca. Each region must be understood in its own environmental setting, yet each produced a state whose political and religious institutions had strikingly similar building plans.

We have suggested that the Zapotec state formed when the polity centered at Monte Albán began to subdue the valley's other polities, reducing them to provinces of a single system. We cannot argue that Chiapa de Corzo took over the Grijalva Valley in the same way. What we *can* argue is that Monte Albán and Chiapa de Corzo were in such close contact that Zapotec bridgespout jars were placed in a Chiapa de Corzo ruler's tomb.

We can also show that competition for positions of leadership was so violent in both regions that Chiapa de Corzo's palace was burned, and Monte Albán built defensive walls. Each region knew the other's political strategies, and neither region's elite would allow themselves to be outdone. Each undoubtedly borrowed ideas from the other, and despite the confident predictions of ecological functionalists, both regions produced similar state institutions at roughly the same period.

Colonization and Conquest

A characteristic of many early states was that their initial appearance was followed by a period of rapid, almost explosive growth, during which they reached their maximum territorial limits.[1] This happened because the earliest, or "pristine," states were usually surrounded by regions still organized on a chiefdom or autonomous village level. The latter, lacking the political and military apparatus of the state, were relatively easy for an expanding kingdom to convert into subject provinces. Only later, when they themselves had learned statecraft, did such outlying provinces become powerful enough to break the grip of imperialism.

Worldwide, there are many cases of rapid expansion in the early stages of archaic states: Uruk in southern Mesopotamia,[2] Wari in the Peruvian highlands,[3] and Tikal in the Maya region[4] are all examples. Teotihuacán in the Basin of Mexico, a contemporary of Monte Albán, established colonies at Matacapan on the Gulf Coast,[5] Los Horcones on the Chiapas Coast,[6] and Kaminaljuyú in the Guatemala highlands.[7] As time passed, all these states began to lose their outlying colonies.

The Zapotec state is yet another example of a kingdom that expanded well past the boundaries of its core physiographic region, the Valley of Oaxaca, reaching its maximum territorial extent during Monte Albán II. That expansion is documented in several ways. First, Monte Albán carved a series of stones with the hieroglyphic names of places it claimed to have colonized or conquered (we say "claimed" because many Mesoamerican rulers exaggerated their conquests). Second, surveys and excavations in several regions outside the Valley of Oaxaca show the same phenomenon we saw at Chiapa de Corzo in AD 100: an abrupt change in pottery from local styles to the canons of the expanding Zapotec state.

The "Conquest Slabs" of Building J

One of the most unusual buildings erected in Monte Albán's Main Plaza during Period II was Building J. It was built in the shape of an arrowhead, and oriented at an oblique angle from most public buildings at the city. During Period II its outer walls displayed more than 40 carved stones, some of which are still *in situ*. Each stone gives the name of a place in Zapotec hieroglyphs; they are believed to be provinces claimed by Monte Albán (see Box).

A typical slab from Building J would be the one accompanying the box overleaf. It features the head of a jackrabbit above the Zapotec "hill glyph"; below is

232 Building J at Monte Albán, seen here from the south, is associated with more than 40 carved stones showing regions claimed by the Period II state.

an upside-down human head with eyes closed, displaying a complex hairdo. Alfonso Caso's interpretation of this slab would be that a place had been subjugated by Monte Albán, with its dead chief's head shown upside down. It is for this reason that the Building J stones have been called "conquest slabs."

While we generally agree with Caso's interpretation, we would point out that some slabs do not have upside-down heads. This could mean that some provinces joined Monte Albán voluntarily, or were colonized rather than conquered.

Identifying the Building J Places

One of the most interesting aspects of the Building J slabs is that they employ a "hill" or "mountain" glyph. These glyphs usually refer to mountains or natural landmarks rather than towns. That is exactly how sixteenth-century Zapotec rulers defined their territories, and it allows us to use the direct historical approach to interpret the Building J slabs.

Around AD 1540, the conquering Spaniards asked for a map of the territory claimed by the Zapotec ruler of a town named Guevea.[9-13] The native Zapotec artists who drew the map put Guevea in the middle. Around it they drew a circle

Reading the "Conquest Slabs" of Building J

At least two, and sometimes four, elements appear on the "conquest slabs" of Monte Albán's Building J. The two constant elements are:

1 A "hill" glyph signifying "the hill of" or "the place of."
2 A glyph (or combination of glyphs) that varies from stone to stone and gives the specific place. Examples would be "Hill of the Jackrabbit" or "Hill of the Chile Plants."

Some slabs include a third element:

3 A human head upside down below the hill glyph. All these inverted heads face the same direction and are carved to the same scale. The majority have a pattern of lines crossing the face which may indicate facial painting or tattoos; they also wear distinctive headdresses. The eyes are usually closed, or lack a pupil. Alfonso Caso concluded that these upside-down heads represented the dead chiefs of the places named on the slabs, with the distinct headdress reinforcing the name of the place or region.[8]

Some slabs contain a fourth element:

4 A hieroglyphic text which, in its most complete form, includes a year, month, and day, probably a reference to the date when certain places supposedly came under Monte Albán's hegemony.

Jackrabbit

"Hill" sign

Inverted human head

of named landmarks – mostly mountains and rivers – which defined the limits of Guevea's territory. Those landmarks had Zapotec names for places like "Burnt Hill," "Hill of the Puma," or "River of the Tadpoles." Natural hills and rivers were used as landmarks because they remained constant, while towns and villages came and went.

To identify the provinces claimed by Monte Albán, we need to identify the mountains to which the "hill signs" referred. This is so difficult a task that fewer than a dozen have been identified.

Four places can be matched to glyphs in a sixteenth-century document which shows areas of Oaxaca from which the Aztec received tribute.[14] One of those places, Tototepec, meant "Hill of the Bird"; it refers to a defensible mountain not far from the Pacific Coast of Oaxaca. That mountain is still known as "Hill of the Bird" in every local language: Tani Piguiñi in Zapotec, Yucusa in Mixtec, Tototepec in Nahuatl, and Cerro de los Pájaros in Spanish.

Three more places in the Aztec tribute document – Cuicatlán, "Place of Song," Miahuapan, "Canal of the Maize Tassels," and Ocelotepec, "Hill of the Ocelot or Jaguar" – also resemble place glyphs on Building J.[15] A few more slabs have glyphs like "Place of the Pierced Face" (Sosola) and "Hill of the Chile Plants" (Chiltepec) which can be matched to places still known by their ancient names.[16] All those places lie outside the Valley of Oaxaca, 85–150 km from Monte Albán. We believe, using the direct historical approach, that they were named for natural landmarks at the limits of Monte Albán's territory.

Unfortunately, it is unlikely that we will be able to match all of the Building J

233 Glyphs from a sixteenth-century Aztec document listing places in the State of Oaxaca. (*a*) Miahuapan, "Canal of the Maize Tassels"; (*b*) Tototepec, "Hill of the Bird"; (*c*) Ocelotepec, " Hill of the Jaguar"; (*d*) Cuicatlán, "Place of Song."

234 Places whose hieroglyphic names were carved on Building J in Monte Albán II include "Hill of the Bird" (a) and "Place of Song" (b). These probably correspond to Tototepec and Cuicatlán.

235 Not all the places carved on Building J were accompanied by inverted heads signifying "conquest." Examples include "Canal of the Maize Tassels" (c) and "Hill of the Jaguar" (d). These places probably correspond to Miahuapan and Ocelotepec, and may have been brought into Monte Albán's sphere by diplomacy.

236 Two places carved on Building J and accompanied by inverted heads are "Place of the Pierced Face" (e) and "Hill of the Chile Plants" (f). These places probably correspond to Sosola and Chiltepec, and may have been subdued militarily by Monte Albán.

glyphs to actual places. For one thing, many old place names have been lost or changed. Another problem is that the Spaniards who mapped Oaxaca brought Aztec guides and interpreters with them; as a result, many places now have names in Nahuatl or Spanish, rather than Zapotec. Only when the Nahuatl (Aztec) name is a direct translation of the Zapotec name, as in the case of Tototepec, are we likely to be able to match it to a Building J slab.

The Building J slabs are Monte Albán's textual claim that it had expanded well beyond the confines of its core physiographic zone, the Valley of Oaxaca. For confirmation, we must now look for neighboring regions whose ceramics show an abrupt change to Monte Albán's style.

Colonization vs. Conquest

Not every province incorporated by an expanding kingdom must be taken by force. When there is great disparity in population between the core of a state and its periphery, it may only be necessary for the former to send colonists to the latter. Small polities, seeing that resistance would be futile, may accept a face-saving offer. Larger polities, unwilling to lose their autonomy, may have to be subdued militarily. During the expansion of the Monte Albán II state, we think we see both colonization and conquest.

We should say at the outset that it can be difficult to distinguish between colonization and conquest, since a battle is one of the hardest events to document with archaeological evidence. Archaeologists excavate sites; many battles, on the other hand, took place in the open areas between sites. For example, although hieroglyphs for "war" and "battle" have long been known from Maya hieroglyphic texts,[17,18] Maya archaeologists have yet to find an actual battlefield.

Without textual evidence, no one walking over the ancient battlefield at

Hastings in England would know that in AD 1066, history was changed by a battle there. Without the occasional lucky find of a burned palace like the one at Chiapa de Corzo, almost all our evidence for warfare is textual, iconographic, or circumstantial.

The "conquest slabs" of Building J are textual evidence for Zapotec warfare. Circumstantial evidence for warfare includes the defensive walls and hilltop localities of many Monte Albán II sites. There are also Monte Albán II ceramic pieces that show warriors with their heads inside the open jaws of coyote, puma, or raptorial bird helmets. Ethnohistoric accounts show that such animal costumes were awarded to warriors who had distinguished themselves in battle.[19]

Perhaps the most frequently used circumstantial evidence for colonization is the aforementioned "abrupt change in ceramic style" that tends to occur when a province is taken over. Even when such abrupt change is present, however, textual evidence may be needed to distinguish between diplomatic and military takeovers.

Two towns in adjacent valleys on the Peruvian coast, both taken over by the Inca around AD 1470, illustrate this problem. At La Centinela in the Chincha Valley, the local ruler made a deal with the Inca and was allowed to retain many of his noble perquisites (which included being carried in a litter and engaging in long-distance trade). At Cerro Azul in the nearby Cañete Valley, the local nobles resisted the Inca and were slaughtered.

Despite ethnohistoric accounts of the Inca conquest, no direct evidence for a battle has been found at Cerro Azul. Circumstantial evidence for the Inca takeover includes a stone building in pure Inca style, but no true Inca ceramics.[20] No Inca stone building has ever been found at La Centinela, but there was an influx of Cuzco-style Inca pottery. No evidence of military coercion has been found at La Centinela.[21] Thus, without textual evidence it would be nearly impossible to distinguish between the diplomatic takeover of La Centinela and the military takover of Cerro Azul.

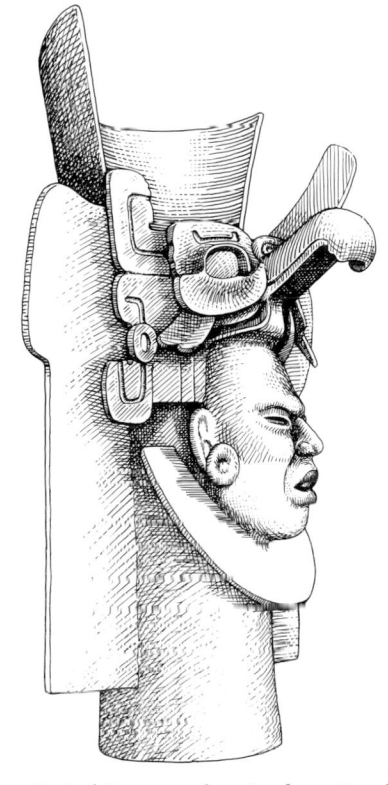

237 Period II incense brazier from Tomb 77 at Monte Albán. The piece depicts a warrior with the lower half of his face painted white, his head enclosed in a helmet depicting a raptorial bird.

The Spread of Monte Albán Ic-II Pottery

The spread of Monte Albán II pottery (or in the case of Monte Negro, even earlier Monte Albán Ic pottery) is one of our best lines of circumstantial evidence for the expansion of the Zapotec. We are not referring here to the occasional Oaxaca bridgespout jar that shows up at places like Chiapa de Corzo. Such isolated vessels, which stand out from the local ceramics, can probably be attributed to trade or elite gift-giving. What we are talking about are those regions whose previously autonomous ceramics are literally swamped or replaced by Monte Albán gray wares.

The Valley of Ejutla

The Valley of Ejutla, some 55 km south of Monte Albán, has been surveyed by Gary Feinman and Linda Nicholas.[22] During Monte Albán Ia the region was a sparsely settled frontier; even in Period Ic, following substantial population growth, settlements were dispersed and had no single dominant chiefly center.

This is the type of weakly-organized periphery that can easily be incorporated by a well-organized state, and Feinman and Nicholas found "a significant settlement shift between Monte Albán I and II." While many of the Period Ic villages

Site 6-7-16

238 The Ejutla Valley was drawn into Monte Albán's sphere during Period II. Site 6-7-16, the major administrative center for the valley, became a "middle man" in the flow of marine shell ornaments to Monte Albán. The southern Valley of Oaxaca lies just beyond the tallest mountain range in the background.

dwindled or were abandoned, a major Period II center with at least a dozen monumental buildings grew up near the Ejutla River. This major town, whose ceramics show strong ties to Monte Albán, became the Ejutla equivalent of a Tier 2 center in the Valley of Oaxaca.

Lying as it does along one of the major routes between Monte Albán and the Pacific Ocean, Ejutla evidently became a "middle man" in the importation of marine shells and their conversion into ornaments. Excavations by Feinman and Nicholas at Ejutla's major Period II center reveal dense concentrations of debris where spiny oyster, mother-of-pearl, conch, and more than 40 other species were turned into artifacts. Many of the beads and pendants match those buried with elite individuals at Monte Albán and San José Mogote.

While it seems clear that Monte Albán colonized (and economically stimulated) Ejutla in Period II, there is as yet no evidence that this process required military force. With its sparse population and vulnerable location – only 2–3 days' travel from Monte Albán – Ejutla would have had little chance to resist. More than likely, its rulers struck a deal that allowed them to remain in power while paying tribute in shell ornaments. If Zapotec hieroglyphic texts from half a millennium later are relevant, such a deal might even have included royal marriage alliances between the two valleys.[23]

The Valley of Miahuatlán

The Valley of Miahuatlán, only 30 km south of Ejutla and on the same route to the Pacific, underwent a similar transformation. Surveys by Donald Brockington and Charles Markman show the region to have been sparsely occupied before

Monte Albán II.[24,25] During Period II a cluster of seven sites arose near the main river, with the largest of these coming to dominate the region. Ceramics in Monte Albán II style were abundant, as were marine shells of many of the same species worked at Ejutla.

In Aztec times Miahuatlán was known as Miahuapan, "Canal of the Maize Tassels," a reasonable translation of its Zapotec name. Its sixteenth-century place glyph featured maize tassels growing out of an irrigation canal, and it matches a glyph on one of the Building J "conquest slabs."[26] We believe that Miahuatlán was colonized by Monte Albán in Period II, but there is as yet no evidence that the takeover required force. Significantly, the Building J slab depicting Miahuatlán is one with no upside-down head below the place glyph, perhaps indicating that military overthrow was unnecessary.

The Valley of Nejapa (Nexapa)

Nejapa, some 50–60 km southeast of Monte Albán, lies along a different route to the Pacific – one leading to the great lagoons of Tehuantepec. Nejapa has not yet been systematically surveyed, but it does have sites dating to the period of Monte Albán II imperialism.

Nejapa is a particularly interesting case because its early village periods – equivalent in time to the San José and Guadalupe phases in the Valley of Oaxaca – had pottery like that of the Tehuantepec Coast. By Monte Albán II, however, Nejapa's pottery reflects its incorporation into the Zapotec state.

The Region of Tututepec (Tototepec)

Tututepec (ancient Tototepec, "Hill of the Bird") is a region of mountains along the Río San Francisco, 25–30 km inland from the Pacific Ocean, and 140 km southwest of Monte Albán. At the time of the Spanish Conquest it was the realm of a Mixtec ruler who paid tribute to the Aztec.[27] A terraced hilltop site of that period, still known as "Hill of the Bird," was discovered by Gabriel DeCicco and Donald Brockington not far from San Pedro Tututepec.[28]

It is the earlier site of San Francisco Arriba, however, that is most germane to this chapter. Lying at the base of a defensible mountain 3 km northeast of Tututepec, San Francisco Arriba has pottery described by DeCicco and Brockington as "closely related" to Monte Albán during Periods I and II. This evidence for Zapotec pottery reinforces Monte Albán's claim that Tututepec was one of the provinces on its periphery. Unfortunately, the "Hill of the Bird" slab from Building J is broken in such a way that one cannot be sure whether or not it had an upside-down head below the hill glyph. Thus we do not know whether Monte Albán was claiming conquest of the Tututepec region, or merely political and diplomatic colonization.

What impact might the expanding Monte Albán II state have had on areas beyond the provinces it claimed? In the case of Tututepec, we have a tentative answer to that question.

Some distance to the southwest of San Francisco Arriba, an area of 200 km² near the mouth of the Río Verde has recently been investigated.[29,30] While this coastal area is too far beyond Tututepec to shed light on the latter's incorporation into the Zapotec state, it too felt the impact of Monte Albán's expansion.

While not yet intensively surveyed, the mouth of the Río Verde was apparently only sparsely populated before 500 BC. The number of communities increased between 400 and 100 BC, and some 278 burnished gray sherds of this period (a relatively large number, given the scale of excavations so far) are "identical in both appearance and mineralogy to [Monte Albán I] pottery from the Valley of Oaxaca."[31] The bulk of these imported gray wares were found in relatively high-status residential areas, suggesting ties between important Río Verde families and the Zapotec.

From 100 BC to AD 100 – the peak of Monte Albán II expansion elsewhere – there was a disruption of previous exchange patterns in the lower Río Verde. Local settlements increased, but they now featured imitations of Monte Albán pottery rather than actual imports. Then – just as significantly – by AD 100, similarities between the ceramics of the Río Verde and the Valley of Oaxaca declined. This comes as no surprise since, as we shall see, many outer provinces of the Zapotec state broke away following Monte Albán II.

The Río Verde data suggest that even areas beyond the frontiers claimed on Building J felt the impact of Monte Albán's expansion. Many of those distant areas, including the Río Verde, were so sparsely populated that the Zapotec would hardly have needed an army to subdue them had they wanted to. Indeed, the large numbers of Monte Albán gray wares found in the lower Río Verde (which exceed the amount expected under conditions of ordinary "trade") might reflect actual movement of Zapotec entrepreneurs into the area.

Ocelotepec

One of the Building J slabs shows a place called "Hill of the Jaguar;" it has no upside-down head. This suggests that no local lord had to be overthrown in order to make Ocelotepec a landmark on the periphery of the Monte Albán II state.

In the sixteenth century, Ocelotepec was a Zapotec-speaking province ruled by a noble named Petela.[32] Spanish accounts describe it as a mountainous region "22 leagues" beyond Miahuatlán. It appears that ancient Ocelotepec is the 300-km² district, 30–40 km southeast of Miahuatlán, which today has a cluster of eight villages known as Ozolotepec. No archaeological survey has yet been done in the region, which lies along an important route from Miahuatlán to the marine shell sources of the Pacific Coast.

Pottery in Monte Albán II style is definitely known from that particular stretch of coast; it was found by DeCicco and Brockington at Sipilote, only a few hundred meters from the sea.[33] We therefore suspect that ancient Ocelotepec was a Zapotec province on the model of Miahuatlán. Sipilote, on the other hand, may be another area which – like the lower Río Verde – lay beyond the frontier, but was visited by Zapotec entrepreneurs.

Sosola

Sosola, a rugged region 30–40 km beyond the northwest limits of the Etla sub-valley, may be another of the provinces mentioned on Building J. It likely corresponds to the slab depicting the "Place of the Pierced Face," accompanied by the upside-down head of a defeated noble.

The region of Sosola has yet to be intensively surveyed. However, it lies just to the west of a mountainous, 650-km² area surveyed by Robert Drennan in 1971.[34] His survey showed expansion into that region, as early as Monte Albán I, by people using Valley of Oaxaca pottery.

Monte Negro

In Chapter 12 we described Monte Negro, a mountaintop site 60 km northwest of Monte Albán. Monte Negro's pottery and architecture have strong ties to the Valley of Oaxaca; they might reflect Zapotec colonization of the Tilantongo Valley during Late Monte Albán I. Unfortunately, we have not yet identified a "conquest slab" on Building J that mentions Tilantongo, "Black Mountain."

Peñoles

The Sierra de Peñoles is a mountainous region west of the Valley of Oaxaca. It lies along one of the main prehispanic routes between the Etla subvalley and the Mixtec-speaking Valley of Nochixtlán. Some 850 km² of this sierra have recently been surveyed by Stephen Kowalewski and Laura Finsten.[35] Sparsely settled prior to Monte Albán I, Peñoles saw its first significant population increase at a time corresponding to Monte Albán I-II. Many sites of this period are on defensible mountaintops, and have pottery described as "imports or local imitations" of Monte Albán wares.

It would appear that Peñoles was yet another province colonized during Monte Albán II. No landmark in the Peñoles region has so far been linked to a place glyph on Building J.

The Cuicatlán Cañada

The Cuicatlán Cañada is a long, north–south river canyon, strategically located between the Valleys of Tehuacán and Oaxaca. In contrast to the temperate Valley of Oaxaca, whose floor averages 1500–1700 m above sea level, the Cañada is a tropical region whose floor averages 500–700 m elevation. It is thus an area where cotton, coyol palm (*Acrocomia mexicana*), and tropical fruits not found in the Valley of Oaxaca can be grown. Their growth requires irrigation, however, since the canyon lies in a rain shadow between two mountain ranges.

At the time of the Spanish Conquest this province was known as Cuicatlán, "Place of Song." Its sixteenth-century place glyph, a human head with a feathered "song scroll" emerging from its mouth, is similar to one on a Building J conquest slab. That slab has an upside-down head, suggesting conquest.

The Cuicatlán Cañada has been surveyed by Elsa Redmond and Charles Spencer, whose excavations brought to light a community either overthrown by the Zapotec or punished for later rebellion.[36-38] It provides us with our best fit between excavation data and Monte Albán's hieroglyphic claims of conquest.

Cuicatlán is another region whose pre-Monte Albán I pottery shows stylistic canons different from those of the Valley of Oaxaca. By 100 BC, however, its communities had "abundant pottery showing close stylistic affinity to that of Monte Albán II."[39]

239 The stone masonry walls of the Fortress of Quiotepec, in the northern Cuicatlán Cañada, rise out of a forest of thorny legume trees and columnar cacti.

This stylistic change was accompanied by the building of an actual fortress at a place called Quiotepec. The fort is located at a natural pass through the mountain ridge that seals off the Cuicatlán Cañada from the Tehuacán Valley. Quiotepec, whose pottery and noble tombs are in Zapotec style, also has defensive walls, large public buildings, and a plaza through which travelers fording the river would have to pass.

To the north of the fort, Redmond and Spencer found a 7-km-long no-man's-land of the period 200 BC–AD 200. The first major site to the north of this unoccupied buffer zone had pottery in the style of Tehuacán, not Monte Albán.

The fortress of Quiotepec would therefore seem to mark the northernmost expansion of the Monte Albán II state. Its location could not be more strategic, since one of the major routes between Oaxaca and Central Mexico passes through the Cuicatlán Cañada. By sealing off the pass, Monte Albán not only took control of the Cañada but also prevented expansion southward by rival kingdoms in Tehuacán, Puebla, Tlaxcala, and the Basin of Mexico.

To the south of the fortress, Spencer and Redmond excavated La Coyotera, a community that may have been punished for resisting Zapotec subjugation. Between 700 and 300 BC La Coyotera had been a 2.5-ha village on an alluvial terrace of the river. With the arrival of the Zapotec in Monte Albán Ic or II, however, this settlement became one of many local communities that were moved from alluvial terraces to the nearby piedmont. This move was apparently part of a Zapotec strategy to irrigate the Cañada more intensively, and was accompanied by the building of large aqueducts and canals.

240 The Fortress of Quiotepec guarded this natural pass in the mountains between the Tehuacán Valley and the Cuicatlán Cañada. All travelers fording the river in the foreground would have to pass through the plaza below the fortress.

241 (*Below*) Artist's reconstruction of the *yàgabetoo*, or skull rack, left by the Zapotec conquerors of La Coyotera in the Cuicatlán Cañada.

Carbonized plant remains of this period show a much higher density of tropical crops, suggesting to Redmond and Spencer that "extra land was brought under cultivation during Late Period I-Period II for the primary purpose of increasing the production of tropical fruits and nuts. This increase, in turn, may have been in response to demands by the Zapotec state for tribute in the form of [tropical] agricultural produce."[40]

One unexpected discovery shows that Zapotec colonization of the "Place of Song" might have required force. After La Coyotera had been moved to a piedmont ridge during Monte Albán Ic-II, it became a 3-ha community with public buildings. In front of the largest pyramidal mound, Spencer and Redmond discovered what appears to have been a skull rack – 61 human skulls aligned in rows, as if left by the collapse of the gruesome display known to the Zapotec as *yàgabetoo* and to the later Aztec as *tzompantli*. Such displays of severed heads served to discourage those who might consider refusing to pay their tribute.

Was There a Zapotec "Empire"?

Beginning in Late Monte Albán I and continuing through Monte Albán II, Zapotec rulers began bringing provinces outside the Valley of Oaxaca under their control. More than 40 such places, listed on Building J at Monte Albán, probably specify the limits of the territory claimed by the Monte Albán II rulers. We will never know where all those places were. Nor will we know how many of the places claimed were actually subdued; for example, the later Aztec claimed dominion over provinces that repeatedly broke away and had to be reconquered.[41,42]

Zapotec expansion is confirmed by the large number of neighboring regions whose pottery sequences show an abrupt change to the Monte Albán style. What we do not know is which regions were so strong as to require conquest, and which were so weak as to require only colonization. Miahuatlán, whose place glyph is not accompanied by an inverted head, so far has produced no evidence of battle. Cuicatlán, whose slab does have an inverted head, has produced both a fortress and a skull rack.

We remind the reader, however, that even in regions subdued by force it might require incredible luck to find archaeological evidence for a battle. Had Redmond and Spencer not excavated in front of the main pyramid at La Coyotera, we would have no skull rack from Cuicatlán. Even the fortress of Quiotepec was probably built not so much to conquer the Cañada as to discourage expansion by rival states to the north.

When one plots on a map all those provinces where Zapotec expansion is indicated, either by pottery changes or textual claims, it appears that Monte Albán was trying to establish a north–south "corridor of influence" between Tehuacán – the gateway to Central Mexico – and the Pacific Coast, the gateway to the tropics.[43] At its peak in late Monte Albán II, that corridor may have included 20,000 km² of subject territory.

The Zapotec were able to expand during Monte Albán Ic and II because none of the provinces they subdued were as powerful politically and militarily as the Valley of Oaxaca. By AD 500, however, during the period known as Monte Albán IIIa (Chapter 15), many of those provinces had become strong enough to break away. Ironically, even while the city of Monte Albán was growing to its maximum size, the boundaries of its tribute territory had begun to shrink.

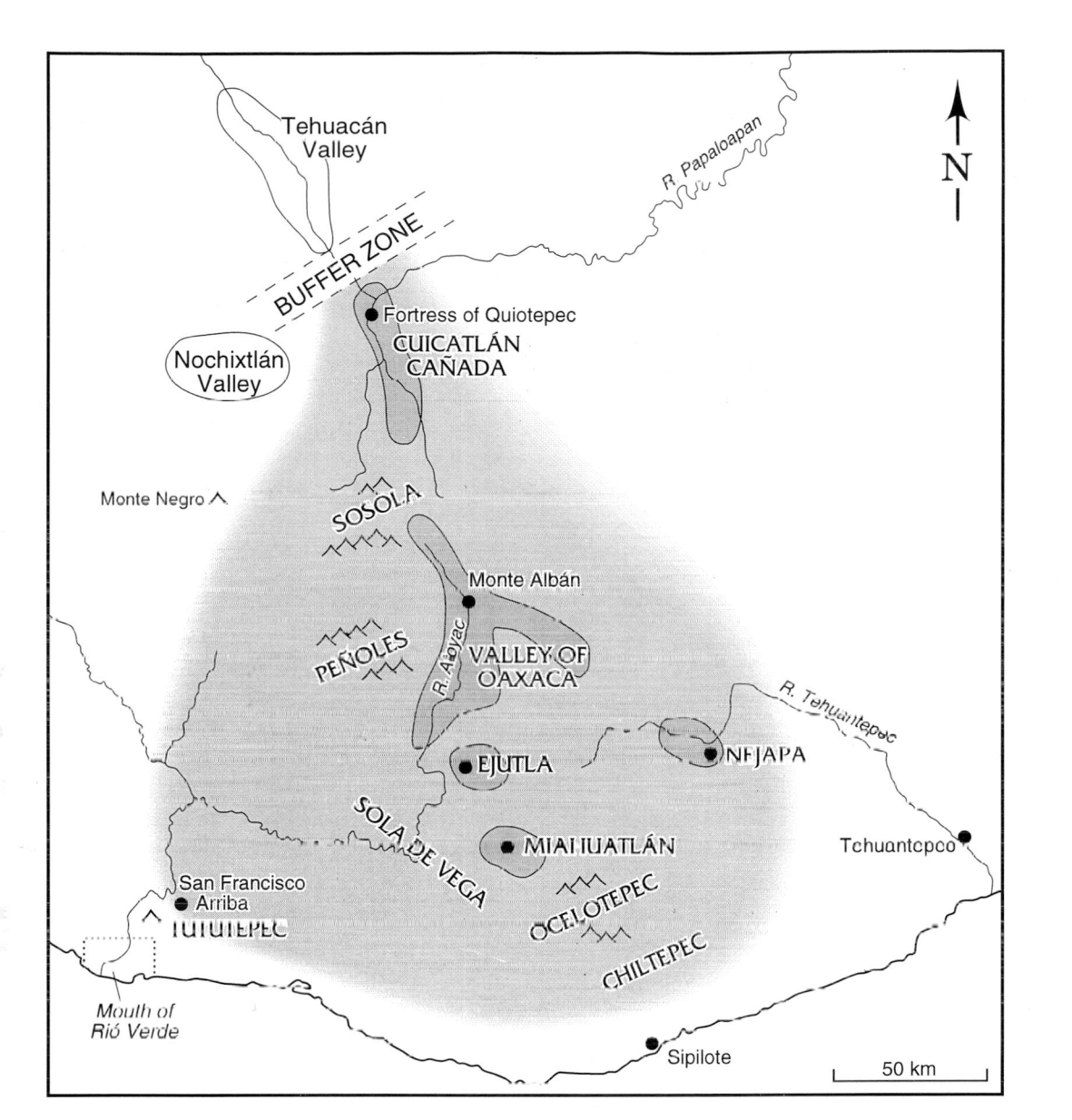

242 Zapotec expansion during Monte Albán Ic-II is indicated, either by pottery style changes or hieroglyphic inscriptions, in all the provinces within the shaded area. This is as close as the Zapotec came to having an "empire."

Is it accurate to use the expression "Zapotec empire"? To answer, we must first look at the way the term has been defined. *For a state to become an empire, most anthropologists would argue, it must incorporate people of other languages and ethnic groups.* By this criterion the Monte Albán II expansion did, for a time, create a kind of empire. It is very likely that the regions Monte Albán called the "Place of Song," the "Hill of the Bird," and the "Hill of the Chile Plants" spoke languages other than Zapotec. The empire produced by their subjugation, however, was modest compared to those attributed to later Mesoamerican states like the Aztec.

The Golden Age of Zapotec Civilization

By AD 200 the Zapotec had extended their influence from Quiotepec in the north to Ocelotepec and Chiltepec in the south. Their noble ambassadors had presented gifts to the rulers of Chiapa de Corzo and established a Zapotec enclave at Teotihuacán in the Basin of Mexico. Monte Albán had become the largest city in the southern Mexican highlands and would remain so for the next 500 years. That half millennium, from AD 200 to 700, has been called "the golden age of Zapotec civilization."

For this "classic" phase of Zapotec civilization, known as Monte Albán III, it is usually unnecessary to use ethnographic analogy to interpret the archaeological record. So many of the institutions known from Zapotec ethnohistory are present that it is possible to rely mainly on the direct historical approach.

The Zapotec *coquì*, or hereditary lord, and his *xonàxi*, or royal wife, lived in residential palaces fitting the historic description of the *yòho quèhui*, or "royal house." Many of these were residences 20–25 m on a side, divided into 10–12 rooms arranged around an interior patio. Typical features were L-shaped corner rooms, some with apparent sleeping benches. Privacy was provided by a "curtain

243 Panorama of the Main Plaza at Monte Albán, showing many of the buildings discovered by Alfonso Caso, Ignacio Bernal, and Jorge Acosta.

wall" just inside the main doorway, which screened the interior of the palace from view. Doors were probably closed with elegant weavings, or even brightly colored feather curtains. In some Zapotec palaces, no two rooms have their floors at exactly the same level. This might have been a way of ensuring that the *coqui's* head was higher than anyone else's, even when he was asleep.

As for the rulers themselves, they are often depicted in ceramic sculpture – seated on thrones or crosslegged on royal mats, weighed down with jewelry and immense feather headdresses. Rulers evidently had a variety of masks, so many that one wonders if their faces were ever seen by commoners. Rulers in many cultures have disguised themselves to maintain the myth that they were not mere mortals, and Zapotec kings seem to have had numerous costumes depending on the occasion. Their ties to Lightning were reinforced by jade or wooden masks depicting the powerful face of *Cociyo*; their roles as warriors were reinforced by wearing a mask made from the facial skin of a flayed captive.

A magnificent example of the latter can be seen in the funerary urn from Tomb 103, a royal burial beneath a palace at Monte Albán. The Zapotec ruler sits on his throne in the guise of a warrior, holding a staff or war club in his right hand. In his left he grasps the hair of an enemy's severed head, as he peers through the dried skin of a flayed enemy's face. His headdress, featuring the plumes of birds from distant cloud forests, covers not only his head but also the back of his throne. Jade spools in his earlobes, a massive jade necklace, and a kilt covered with tubular sea shells add to his elegance. Note that, in the tradition of the figurines of 850–700 BC, the sculptor has paid great attention to every detail of the lord's sandals, right down to the tying of the laces (ill. 245).

A second urn, this time from Tomb 104 at Monte Albán, shows a different persona for the Zapotec lord. Here he sits crosslegged, wearing a mask with the fangs and curled-up nose of a crocodilian monster. On his chest he wears a human mask with three tubular shells dangling from it, reminiscent of the three

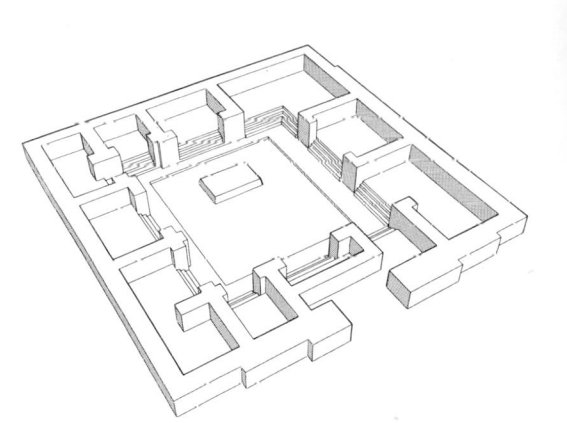

244 The Building S palace at Monte Albán.

245 (*Above*) Funerary urn from Tomb 103 at Monte Albán: the ruler as warrior. Height 51 cm.

246 (*Center*) Funerary urn from Tomb 104 at Monte Albán: the ruler with ritual mask. Height 40 cm.

247 (*Right*) Funerary urn of the royal woman 13 Crocodile, Monte Albán.

pendants on the bat mask seen in Plate I. The ruler wears a short cape decorated with braid, and his hair is tied in a topknot that projects from his forehead.

An earlier generation of scholars assumed that these spectacular urns, usually found in royal tombs, depicted "gods." Today we believe that most of them represent venerated ancestors of the main individuals in the tomb.[1] Like the royal woman shown in ill. 247, some urns bear glyphs with names taken from the 260-day calendar. Supernaturals like Lightning, being immortal, were not named for days in the Zapotec calendar. It is also the case that the figures on most urns, even when grotesquely masked, are undeniably human behind their disguises.

In cosmology it is always crucial to distinguish between actual supernatural beings – depicted in Mesoamerica by combining parts of different animals, so as to create something obviously "unnatural" – and real humans who had metamorphosed into the heroes and heroines of legend. The latter were humans who had acquired, through death and heredity, some of the attributes of the supernatural. We suspect that Zapotec funerary urns – many of which are one-of-a-kind masterpieces made to accompany rulers in their tombs – provided a venue to which the *pèe*, or animate spirit, of these heroes and royal ancestors could return. This would allow the deceased ruler to continue to consult with his or her important ancestors, much as we think the women of the early village period invoked their ancestors through figurines.

It is significant that as funerary urns increased in number, the small solid figurines of earlier times disappeared. Largely gone by Monte Albán II, the small solid figurines had no role to play in Zapotec state religion. From Monte Albán II onward, the ancestors of commoners were no longer important. Only the ancestors of royalty, who were allied with Lightning and would become "Cloud People" after death, had the power to intercede on behalf of Zapotec society.

So important was the afterlife to a Zapotec ruler that the construction of his tomb was as crucial as the construction of his palace. In many cases, the area for the tomb had to be excavated even before the palace could be built above it.

Many of the best-known Zapotec tombs occur below palaces north of the Main Plaza at Monte Albán.[2] These palaces appear to be largely residential, lacking the colonnaded portico and huge sunken patio of the governmental palace. At times, however, someone – perhaps the lord's descendants – continued to place additional offerings in the antechamber of the tomb in later periods. This indicates that some palaces served a commemorative role after the death of the *coquì*.

The palace associated with Tomb 105 shows that the architects first excavated into bedrock, laying out a large cruciform tomb chamber, a smaller antechamber, and a flight of stone masonry stairs. Only then was the palace built, with the tomb stairway descending from the patio, and the chamber itself located beneath a back room of the palace. The walls of the tomb were painted with polychrome murals, one of which depicts royal Zapotec couples exiting the tomb in single file. These couples, perhaps relatives or ancestors of the deceased, have names

Royal Tombs

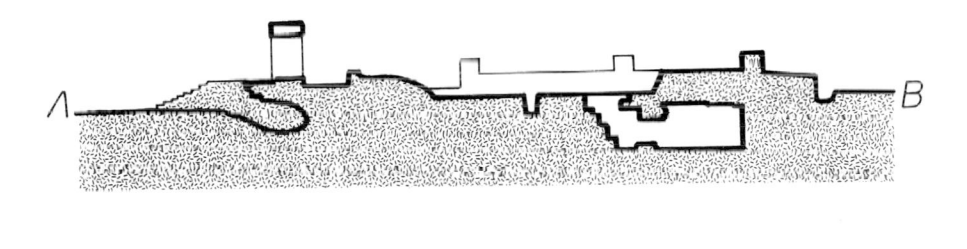

248 Cross-section of the palace associated with Tomb 105, Monte Albán (A is the front, B the rear). Note the size of the tomb and the stairway descending to it.

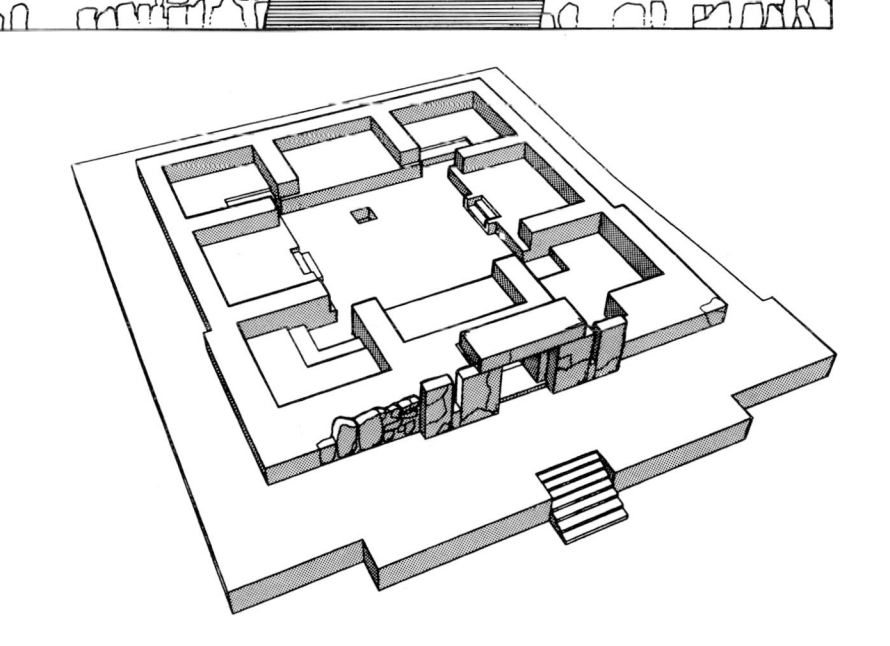

249 Artist's reconstruction of the façade (*left*) and ground plan (*below*) of the palace associated with Tomb 105, Monte Albán. The square opening in the patio leads to the tomb.

250 Mural from the wall of Tomb 105, Monte Albán.

taken from the ritual calendar. The men wear sandals and carry staffs or spears, while the women walk barefoot and wear elaborate skirts. Above this scene we see the "Jaws of the Sky," a motif indicating royal descent.

While some tombs contain a single individual, others held marital pairs; still others were veritable ossuaries to which a dozen bodies had been added over time.

Tomb 104

251 (*Opposite*) Funerary sculpture in a niche on the façade of Tomb 104, Monte Albán. Height 91 cm.

One of the most famous Zapotec royal burials is Monte Albán's Tomb 104, believed to date to the middle of Period III.[3] Its elaborate façade includes a niche with a large funerary sculpture. The latter has a headdress containing two jaguar or puma heads, huge ear ornaments, a large pectoral with marine shells, and a bag of incense in one hand.

Inside the main chamber of the tomb was a single skeleton, fully extended face up. At its feet was the funerary urn shown in ill. 246, flanked by four *acompañantes* or "companion figures." The chamber had been equipped with five wall niches, many of which were filled with pottery; dozens of additional vessels were

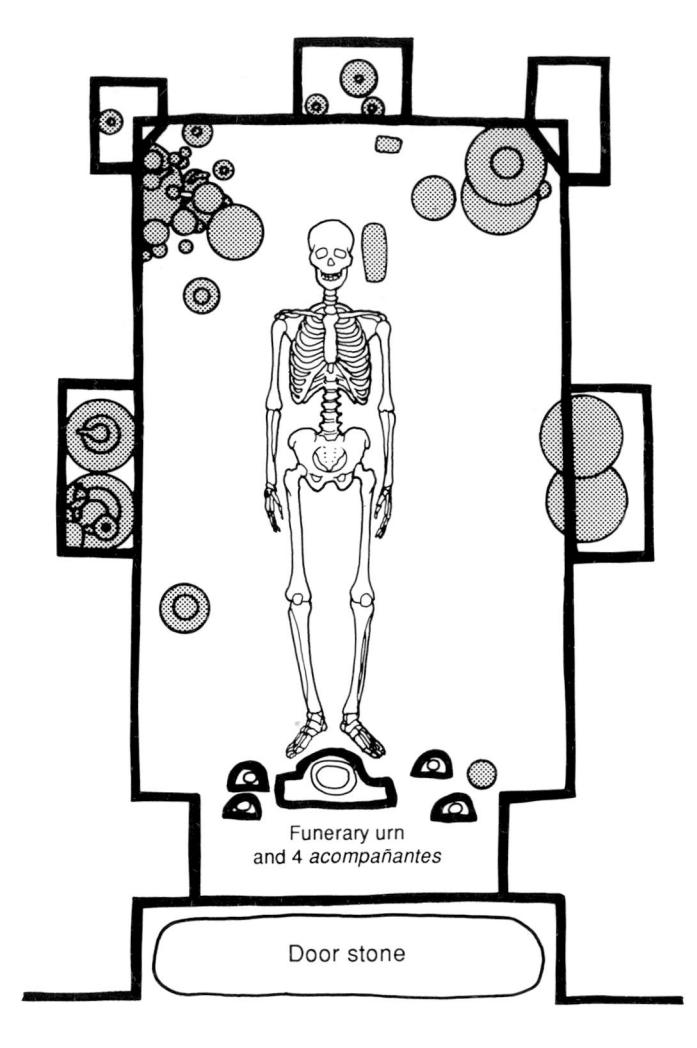

252 The plan of Tomb 104 at Monte Albán showing the door stone, the funerary urns, wall niches, and pottery vessels (stippled).

253 The variety of pottery vessels left as offerings in Tomb 104, Monte Albán.

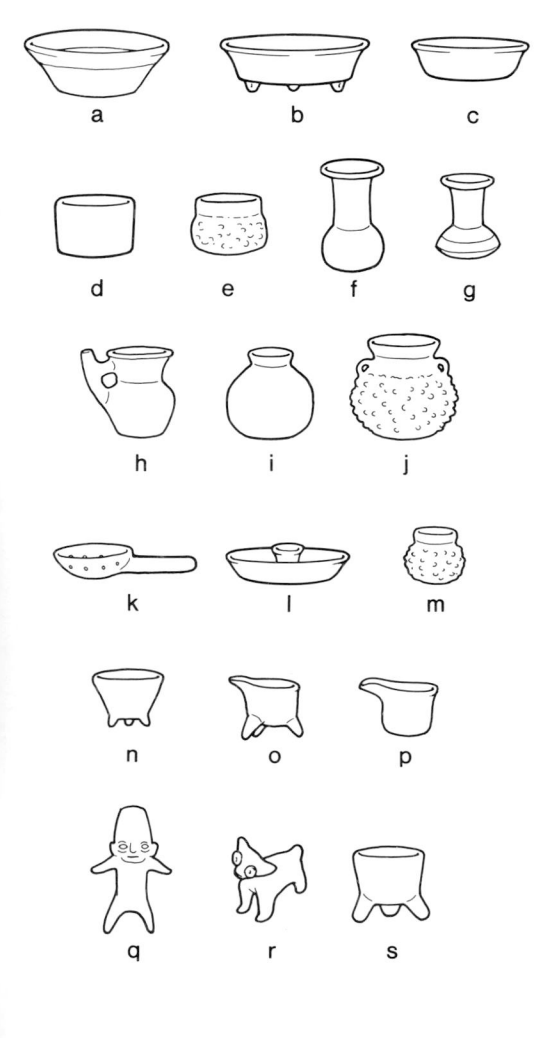

Funerary urn
and 4 *acompañantes*

Door stone

stacked on the floor. As can be seen from ill. 253, the pottery was extremely varied in form and function – in effect, a complete "table setting" for a Zapotec lord or lady. Included were bowls and vases (a–g), bridgespout jars (h), ladles (k), "sauce boats" (o, p), and a stone mortar of the type now used for making guacamole or chile sauce (s). There were also figures of humans and animals (q, r).

Running around the wall of the chamber was the mural shown in ill. 254. At the left (the south wall of the chamber) we see a male figure holding an incense bag in one hand. Next comes a niche in the wall with an "offering box" and a parrot painted above it. Then come two hieroglyphic compounds, 2 Serpent(?) and 5 Serpent; below them is another "offering box." On the back wall of the tomb (the west side) are three niches and a complex painting that features a human face (probably an ancestor) below the "Jaws of the Sky." The date (or day-name) 5 Turquoise appears to the left of the jaws.

At the far right (the north wall of the tomb) we see another male figure with an incense bag. Above a niche in this wall we see the "heart as sacrifice" and above that the glyphs for 1 Lightning, and to the left we see the dates or day-names 5 Owl(?) and 5(?) Lightning. A feathered speech scroll is associated with

254 Painted murals on the left, rear, and right walls of Tomb 104, Monte Albán. The stippled areas are offering niches.

5 Owl(?). All these names probably refer to important royal ancestors of the individual in the tomb.

Finally, the door of the main chamber was closed by a large stone, carved on both sides.⁴ In ill. 255 we see the hieroglyphic inscription on the inner surface of the door. The inscription shares several day-names with the mural inside the chamber. On the right side appear the glyphs 6 Turquoise, a glyph designated "Glyph I" by Alfonso Caso, and a human figurine showing the same stiff posture seen in the jade statues beneath an earlier temple at San José Mogote (Chapter 13). On the left side appears the large glyph 7 Deer, flanked by smaller glyphs for 6 Serpent, 7 "Glyph I," and four small cartouches accompanied by the number 15. In the center of the stone we have an abbreviated "Jaws of the Sky" and the glyph 5 Turquoise. Below this we find a buccal mask in profile, and the same glyph for 1 Lightning seen on the north-wall mural of the tomb chamber.

The repetition of the names 5 Turquoise and 1 Lightning on the mural and door stone suggests that these individuals were very important. Together with the funerary urns, the scores of ceramic offerings, and the elaborate construc-

255 Carved inner surface of the door stone, Tomb 104.

tion of the tomb, these references to ancestors were an integral part of royal burial ritual.

A Late Classic Tomb from Reyes Etla

256 (*Above*) Carved jambs from a tomb at Reyes Etla, showing Zapotec lords in jaguar or puma costumes.

In the second half of Monte Albán III, referred to as Period IIIb (AD 500–700), Reyes Etla was an important Tier 2 or 3 center in the Etla region. One tomb there had its doorway flanked by two remarkable carved stone jambs. Each shows a Zapotec lord in jaguar or puma warrior costume, holding a lance in his hand. Their names are given as 5 Flower and 8 Flower. Each stands below the "Jaws of the Sky" and has a "hill sign" beneath his feet. These jamb figures may represent relatives or ancestors who guarded the tomb, suggesting that even the nobles of Tier 2–3 centers were persons of great importance.

The Inauguration of 12 Jaguar

For many ancient Mesoamerican states, the inauguration of a new ruler was a time for elaborate ritual and royal propaganda.[5] Inauguration rituals sent the

257 The South Platform at Monte Albán, its giant balustrades now overgrown with vegetation.

ideological message that kingship and the state would continue in a just, orderly, predictable manner under a deserving new ruler.

Mesoamerican groups such as the Aztec, Mixtec, and Maya tried to designate the old ruler's successor in advance of the former's death. Between the time of that designation and his or her actual assumption of the throne, the future ruler was expected to engage in a series of important activities. He or she might travel to consult the leaders of other ethnic groups; raid enemy communities to get captives for sacrifice; mark off the boundaries of the polity to reinforce them; and perform some act of piety, like building a new temple or visiting a shrine.[6]

The classic Zapotec were no exception to this pattern. Sometime during Early Period III, a ruler named 12 Jaguar was inaugurated at Monte Albán. Part of his inauguration ritual included the dedication of a massive pyramidal structure, the South Platform of the Main Plaza, for whose construction (or enlargement) he sought to take credit. In preparation for his inauguration, he commissioned a carved stone monument which shows him seated on his throne. He also had taken a number of captives for sacrifice, six of whom are depicted on other stone monuments. He seems to have documented his right to rule by using a monument that refers to a previous Zapotec ruler, perhaps claiming him as an ancestor. Finally, he commissioned carved scenes of eight visitors from Teotihuacán, a city in the Basin of Mexico which was a powerful contemporary of Monte Albán. These scenes show Teotihuacanos visiting Monte Albán in what may be a demonstration of support for the new ruler. Dedicatory caches were placed beneath three corner stones bearing these scenes.

The Inaugural Scene

Stela 1, a large stone in the northeast corner of the platform, shows the new ruler seated on a jaguar-pelt cushion. Below the cushion is an immense throne, displaying two heads of Lightning back-to-back. The ruler wears a regal jaguar or puma costume and an elaborate headdress; in his left hand he holds a lance or staff of office. His Zapotec name, 12 *Peche* (Jaguar or Puma) appears as the fourth glyph in the second of two vertical columns of glyphs. The associated text includes glyphs referring to his divine descent, pilgrimages, divination, and offerings that were part of his pre-inaugural and inaugural rites.

258 Stela 1 at Monte Albán, showing a seated ruler apparently named 12 Jaguar. Height 2.08 m.

Like many important monuments at Monte Albán, Stela 1 can be measured in multiples of the Zapotec *yaguén*, a unit discussed in Chapter 1. It was cut to 8 × 8 *yaguén*, roughly 2.08 × 2.08 m in the metric system.

Military Captives

Also set in the walls of the South Platform are six stelae showing prisoners with arms tied behind their backs. While some are dressed in little more than a breech-clout, others wear the kind of full animal costume given to warriors who had distinguished themselves in battle. Each captive stands on a place glyph naming the region from which he came; unfortunately, the regions have not as yet been securely identified. If the density of Early Period III sites on defensible hilltops can be used as a guide, we suspect that regions south and east of the Valley of Oaxaca were the scene of considerable warfare during Early Period III (see below).

A Noble Ancestor

Stela 4 of the South Platform shows a noble warrior conquering a region by driving a spear into its place sign. The curious object in his right hand may be a cord of the type used by warriors to tie their prisoners' arms behind their backs. The glyphs near this noble's knees identify him as 8 Deer, perhaps a distinguished ancestor claimed by 12 Jaguar.

Foreign Visitors

It was not uncommon for ruler-designates to spend part of their pre-inaugural period lining up the support of neighboring states. This may help to explain the fact that noble visitors from Teotihuacán are carved on four stelae set in the South Platform.[7-9] These visitors, however, are not shown on the faces of the four monuments, but on the *edges*. While the public faces of the stones display such themes as 12 Jaguar on his throne, the visitors from Teotihuacán are carved on edges that would be hidden from view once the stones had been set in place.

In ill. 261 we see the scene carved on the lower edge of the Estela Lisa, a monument set in the northwest corner of the platform. From left to right we follow four Teotihuacanos whose hieroglyphic names are given as 13 Knot, 9 Monkey, 1 Owl, and "Sacrificed Heart." Each wears an elegant headdress and carries a pouch of incense, considered an ambassadorial gift. A path marked by human footprints shows that the visitor named 9 Monkey had left a temple whose roof was decorated in typical Teotihuacán style. All four visitors are being met by a Zapotec lord wearing a Lightning headdress and holding a staff in his hand. Between this Zapotec lord and the Teotihuacanos is the place sign "Hill of 1 Jaguar" – perhaps an ancient name for Monte Albán, a name derived from an earlier ruler or "founder."

A second scene of Teotihuacán visitors, also shown in ill. 261, comes from the lower edge of Stela 1 in the northeast corner of the platform. This is the very stela whose public face shows 12 Jaguar on his throne. The scene consists of four

259 (*Above, left*) Stela 8 at Monte Albán, showing a military captive with his arms bound behind his back. Height 2.27 m.

260 (*Above, right*) Stela 4 at Monte Albán, showing the noble warrior 8 Deer driving his spear into a conquered place. Height 1.86 m.

ESTELA LISA

261 "Hidden" scenes of noble visitors from Teotihuacán, carved on the edges of stelae in Monte Albán's South Platform.

STELA I

compartments, each with an abbreviated reference to some of the same Teotihuacán ambassadors seen on the Estela Lisa. Moving from left to right, the names are: 13 Knot; 3 Serpent + a glyph designated "Glyph C" by Alfonso Caso; and 9 Monkey. The fourth compartment is damaged. Once again, the individual named 9 Monkey is shown leaving a temple decorated in Teotihuacán style.

Dedicatory Caches

The hidden scenes of Teotihuacán visitors were placed at the four corners of the South Platform. Under three of those corners, the builders of the platform placed offering boxes with standardized dedicatory caches.[10] These caches show that the carved stones were part of the Early Monte Albán III platform, since the boxes contain offerings of that period. No offering was placed under the south-east corner, apparently because bedrock was deeper there and more construction fill was required.

262 The northeast corner of the South Platform at Monte Albán, showing the location of the subterranean offering box.

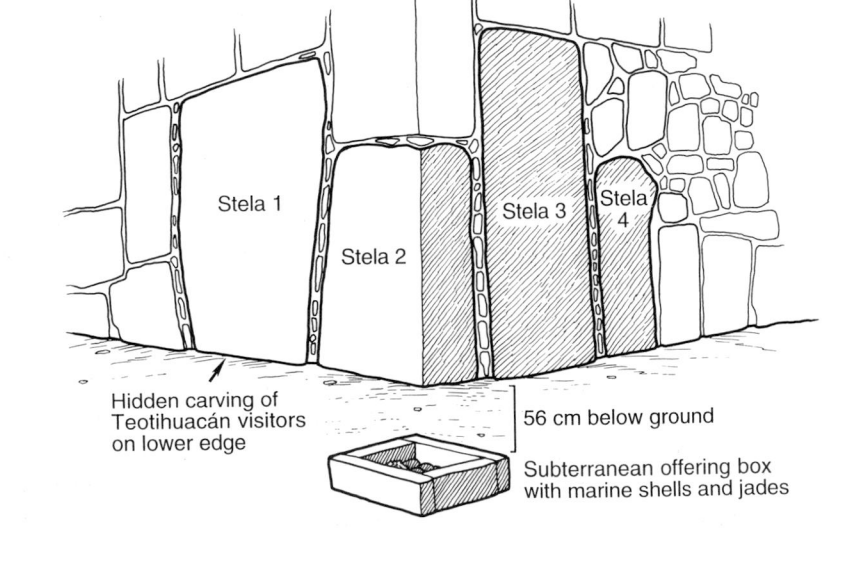

Stela 1

Stela 2

Stela 3

Stela 4

Hidden carving of Teotihuacán visitors on lower edge

56 cm below ground

Subterranean offering box with marine shells and jades

Illustration 262 shows the location of the offering box beneath the northeast corner of the platform, the corner featuring the scene of 12 Jaguar's inauguration. Note that Stela 2, one of the stones depicting a captive, was placed so that both its carved front face and north side would have been visible; the carved underside of Stela 1, on the other hand, would have been hidden.

The offering box below Stela 1 contained 10 spiny oyster shells, 10 tent olive shells, and 7 jade beads.[11] Offerings under the northwest and southwest corners had identical sets of shells and jade, as well as typical Early Monte Albán III vessels. The spiny oyster shells are particularly interesting because they were frequently used as receptacles for offerings of royal blood.[12] Similar offerings of jade and *Spondylus* shells have been found at Teotihuacán,[13] strengthening the association of the South Platform offerings with the scenes of Teotihuacán visitors.

Why Leave "Hidden Scenes"?

At first glance, it might seem strange that scenes carved in stone would be hidden from view. There are, however, numerous examples of such "hidden scenes" elsewhere in Mesoamerica. For example, the Aztec often carved elaborate depictions on the underside of multi-ton stone sculptures.[14,15] These "hidden" depictions could be seen only by those who witnessed their dedication and initial placement. But the Earth itself was the permanent witness, and both the items in the cache and the "hidden" carvings were regarded as offerings to the Earth.

Royal Propaganda

There must have been many rulers of Monte Albán during Period III. None seem to have expended as much energy legitimizing their right to rule as did 12 Jaguar. He seems to have taken credit for building (or adding to) the South Platform; commissioned eight monuments showing his inauguration, his captives, and a venerated ancestor; and made sure his fellow nobles knew that he had the support of Teotihuacán. Why was so much royal propaganda necessary? Was it because of a dispute over his accession to the throne? Had 12 Jaguar – as competing lords sometimes do – wrested the throne of Monte Albán from the true heir, perhaps with the tacit approval of Teotihuacán?

Whatever the reason, the stelae commissioned by 12 Jaguar display two types of royal propaganda: vertical and horizontal.[16] The message on the public faces of his monuments – showing his inaugural scene, his captives, and his heroic predecessor – traveled "vertically" from the ruler down to the commoners. The message of support from Teotihuacán, carved on the hidden edges of the same stelae, traveled "horizontally" from the ruler to his fellow nobles, and did not need to be seen by commoners.

How Commoners Lived

Obviously, not all of Zapotec society lived in elaborate palaces. Richard Blanton, who directed the urban survey of Monte Albán, estimates that during Late Period III the city had 57 "elaborate residences" and 2899 "non-elaborate residences."[17] If we accept Blanton's estimates of 5–10 persons per non-elaborate residence (*yòho*) and 10–20 persons per elaborate household (*quèhui*), it means

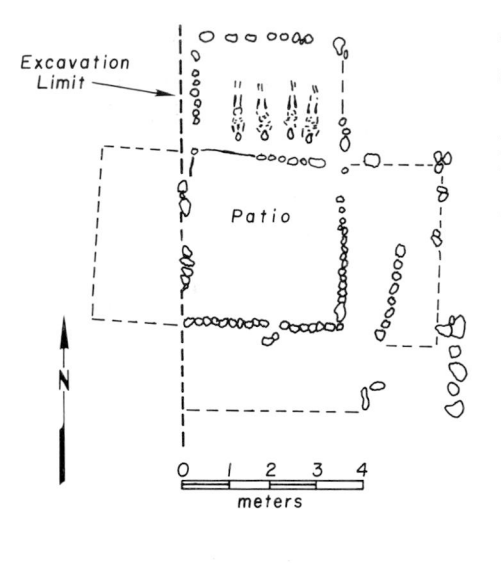

that less than 5 percent of the city's residents were members of the ruling stratum.

Ordinary residences have rarely been studied. Excavations on one set of occupational terraces, 1 km northwest of Monte Albán's Main Plaza, have exposed three Late Period III households spaced 25 m apart.[18] One house consisted of four rooms, each 3–4 m on a side, surrounding a central patio. Under the floor of one room, on the north side of the patio, four occupants had been buried in slab-lined graves.

The ordinary residences on this set of terraces were built of adobe brick over a cobble or boulder foundation. At least some households had been involved in pottery production, using domed semisubterranean kilns to produce two of the most common utility wares of Late Monte Albán III.[19] The presence of these kilns, coupled with a lack of storage facilities for agricultural products, indicates that some of Monte Albán's commoners were more heavily involved in craft production than farming.

Temples

263 (*Above*) Ordinary residence at Monte Albán, consisting of four adobe rooms around a central patio. There were four burials beneath the north room.

The temples of classic Zapotec civilization, like their Monte Albán II prototypes, had inner and outer rooms and stood on pyramidal platforms. Through a new line of evidence, not available in earlier periods, we can see that Period III temples were far from uniform. Various of them may have been dedicated to royal ancestors, legendary dynastic heroes, or supernatural forces.

This new line of evidence consists of small temple models, probably made to serve as guides for the architects and masons who built the temples. Most of these models were found in general debris, having been discarded when no longer needed. All show temples with flat roofs, sometimes decorated in the style called "double scapulary" architecture. That style, especially common at Monte Albán

264 Ruins of a two-room temple at Monte Albán.

265 Small stone model of a Zapotec temple with "double scapulary" decoration.

266 The balustrade of this temple platform at Monte Albán shows three "double scapularies." (The photograph, taken in 1946, shows carved stelae which have since been moved to storerooms.)

267 Small stone model of a Zapotec temple whose doorway is closed by a feather curtain.

268 Model of a Zapotec temple dedicated to Lord 3 Turquoise.

during Period III, consists of two superimposed stone masonry panels that overhang the building like epaulets.

One model of a temple from the Tlacolula subvalley is particularly interesting, as its doorway is shown as having been closed with a feather curtain.[20] Such curtains were luxurious furnishings made by sewing together thousands upon thousands of feathers from brightly colored birds; they may also have been used to close the doors of palaces.

As in the case of other archaic states, it was undoubtedly the rulers who commissioned the temples, provided the building materials, and fed the workmen. This underwriting of temple construction was supposedly an act of royal piety, but its hidden agenda was often to outdo rival lords and impress the commoners. Any ruler building a temple was inevitably associated with it, and some may even have dedicated temples to ancestors who could intercede with Lightning on their behalf.

Several lines of evidence support the latter possibility. One temple model from Monte Albán has the glyph 3 Turquoise framed in its doorway, possibly the calendric name of a royal ancestor to whom it was dedicated.[21] The model clearly indicates that the temple was to be reached by ascending a tall stairway, set in a platform with double scapularies.

Temples were also a place for gifts bearing the calendric names of past rulers, some of them perhaps considered the founders of royal dynasties. Those offerings took the form of beakers in burnished gray ware, perhaps Monte Albán III analogues to the "resist" white-on-gray beakers used by Rosario phase elites (Chapter 10). Carved on the sides of these beakers were hieroglyphic names such as 5 Eagle or 13 Monkey. Such personalized drinking cups – perhaps filled with prestigious liquids like chocolate or *pulque* – have been found as offerings on temple floors, in the rubble of abandoned temples, or even near important residences.

269 Drinking vessels carved with the calendric names 5 Eagle (*left*) and 13 Monkey (*right*).

270 Carved drinking vessel with the name of Lord 1 Jaguar; it was left as an offering in the rubble of an abandoned temple at San José Mogote. Height 10.5 cm.

One particularly important royal couple, Lord 1 Jaguar and Lady 2 Flower, repeatedly show up on pairs of beakers found together. They may have been the legendary founders of one of Monte Albán's royal dynasties – the Zapotec equivalent of the legendary Mixtec royal couple, Lord 1 Deer and Lady 1 Deer.[22] Often depicted on funerary urns at Monte Albán,[23] 1 Jaguar and 2 Flower were commemorated on beakers at Tier 2 centers as widely separated as Ejutla[24] and San José Mogote.

Settlement Patterns

The golden age of Zapotec civilization can be divided into two phases, called Monte Albán IIIa and IIIb. While far too few radiocarbon samples from either phase have been run, the available dates (and traded pottery from other regions) suggest that IIIa falls roughly between AD 200 and 500, while IIIb falls roughly between 500 and 700.

Period IIIa, because of its distinctively decorated pottery, shows up strongly on surface survey. This is fortunate, since it makes it easier to show the significant changes in settlement pattern that took place between Monte Albán II and IIIa. Those changes included substantial increases in population, great shifts in the demographic center of gravity of the Valley of Oaxaca, and increased use of defensible localities. We will look at Period IIIa settlement patterns in detail below.

Period IIIb, in contrast, had relatively drab pottery which is difficult to distinguish from that of the subsequent phase, Monte Albán IV (roughly AD 700–1000). When large Period IIIb sites are excavated, they often contain pottery types traded from the Maya region, types whose ages are well established. On surface survey, however, Periods IIIb and IV are difficult to separate unless one has a very large sample of pottery.

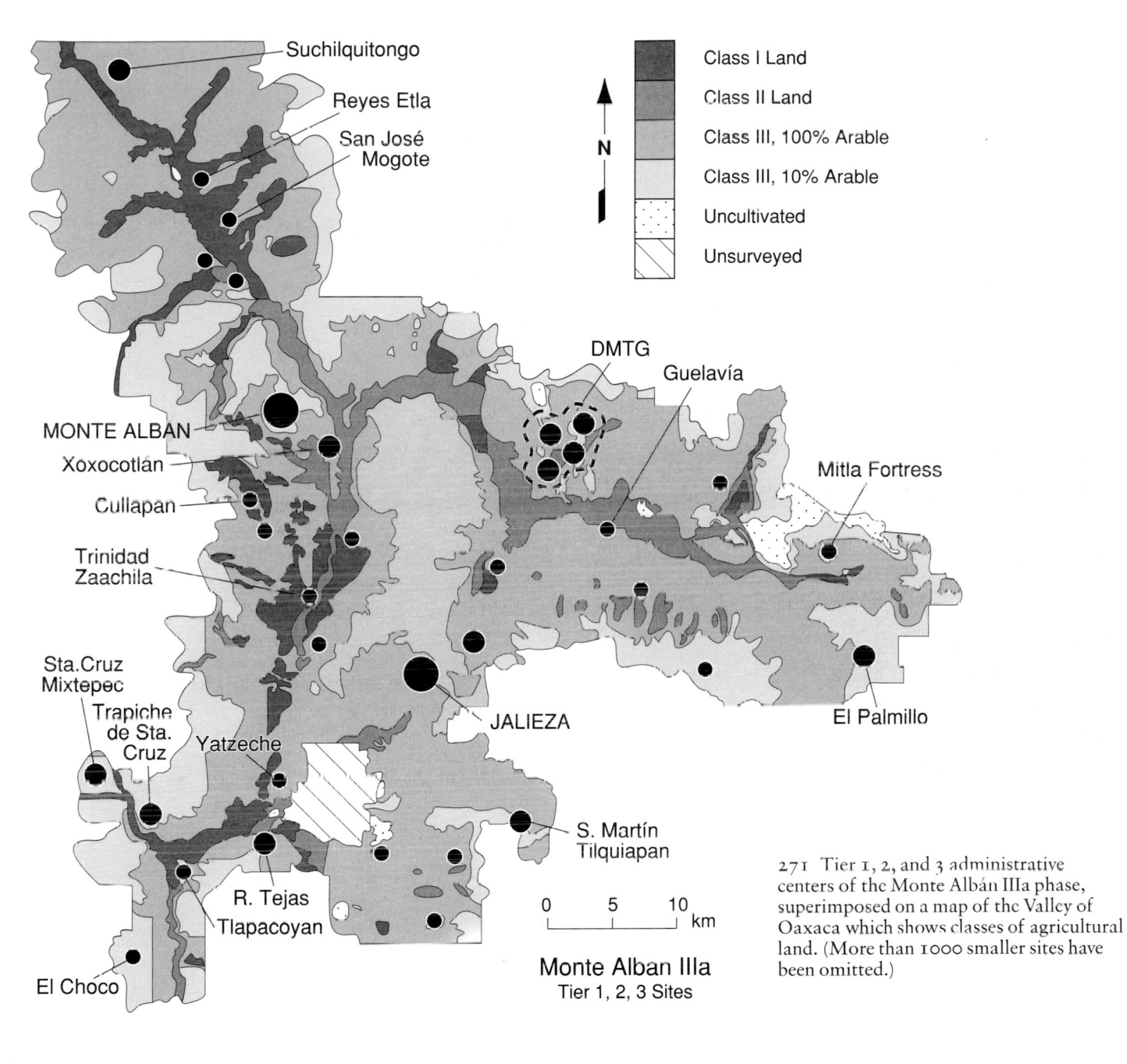

Class I Land
Class II Land
Class III, 100% Arable
Class III, 10% Arable
Uncultivated
Unsurveyed

N

Suchilquitongo
Reyes Etla
San José Mogote
DMTG
Guelavía
MONTE ALBAN
Xoxocotlán
Mitla Fortress
Cullapan
Trinidad Zaachila
Sta.Cruz Mixtepec
Trapiche de Sta. Cruz
Yatzeche
JALIEZA
El Palmillo
S. Martín Tilquiapan
R. Tejas
Tlapacoyan
El Choco

0   5   10
km

Monte Alban IIIa
Tier 1, 2, 3 Sites

271 Tier 1, 2, and 3 administrative centers of the Monte Albán IIIa phase, superimposed on a map of the Valley of Oaxaca which shows classes of agricultural land. (More than 1000 smaller sites have been omitted.)

Fortunately, the problems of distinguishing Periods IIIb and IV on survey need not concern us here; our story is almost told. After reaching its maximum population during Period IIIb, the city of Monte Albán declined precipitously in size and importance, and the heyday of Zapotec civilization was over.

The population of the Valley of Oaxaca rose to an estimated 115,000 persons during Monte Albán IIIa.[25] This growth was accompanied by tumultuous changes in the distribution of population throughout the valley. Of the 1075 known communities, 510 (or nearly half) were now in the Tlacolula subvalley.

The Monte Albán IIIa Pattern

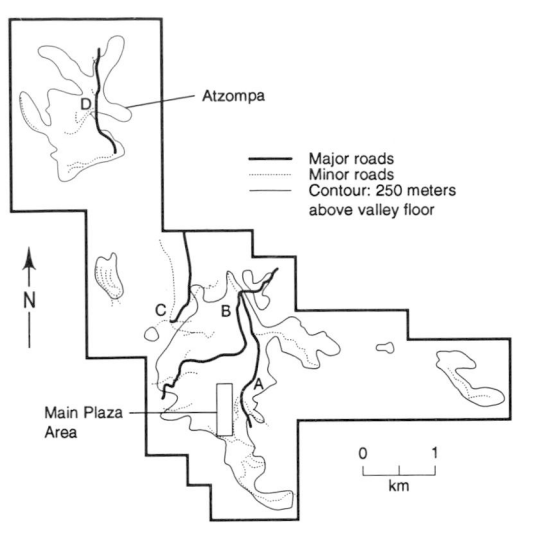

272 During Period III, the city of Monte Albán expanded to cover the nearby hill of Atzompa. Many parts of the city were connected by major or minor roads.

273 Aerial view of unexcavated terraces and public buildings on the hill of Atzompa, Monte Albán's northernmost sector.

Another 455 appeared in the Valle Grande, with 137 of those found in the once sparsely occupied Ocotlán district. Occupation of the Etla and central regions, once the demographic center of gravity of the valley, was limited to 110 communities.

The city of Monte Albán now had an estimated 16,500 persons, living on 1196 occupational terraces. A magnificent hilltop center with palaces, temples, ballcourts, and hieroglyphic inscriptions, it was still the largest concentration of population in the valley – but not by as wide a margin as before. Two other population centers, one in the Valle Grande and one in the Tlacolula region, were now approaching it in size.

The most impressive of those new cities was Jalieza, a site covering 408 ha on a mountain ridge in the southern Valle Grande. Jalieza overlooks the valley from 1600 m elevation, some 250 m above the alluvium. Naturally protected by its steep hilltop setting, Jalieza has no clear defensive walls. Its Period IIIa population, estimated at 12,835 persons, was spread over 676 artificial terraces and served by more than twenty public buildings. From its vantage point, Jalieza could monitor traffic through a major pass between the Valle Grande and Tlacolula regions.

No single community dominated the Tlacolula subvalley. In the center of that region, however, was a tight cluster of four towns whose combined population reached an estimated 12,292 persons. The staff of the Settlement Pattern Project believes that those four neighboring communities – Tlacochahuaya (4925 persons), Guadalupe (2218 persons), and the twin centers of Dainzú and Macuilxochitl (5149 persons) – could have been parts of a dispersed Tier 1 com-

Jalieza

Contour interval, 50 m

⊠ Artificial mound

◖ Architectural terrace

▨ Area of site

N

250 meters

274 Jalieza, covering 408 ha of a mountain ridge in the southern Valle Grande, became a city second in size only to Monte Albán during Period IIIa.

munity which they refer to as DMTG.[26] If that scenario is accepted, it would give each arm of the valley a Tier 1 central place with 12,200–16,500 persons, spaced 33 km (a day's travel) from the other two central places.

Below Tier 1 of the settlement hierarchy came at least 8–9 Tier 2 centers, with populations estimated at 2000–4500. Many of those sites were on the frontier of the Valley of Oaxaca, often in defensible localities. Suchilquitongo occupied a mountaintop at the northern end of the Etla region; El Palmillo commanded the heights near Matatlán, at the eastern end of the Tlacolula subvalley; Santa Cruz Mixtepec, Rancho Tejas, and San Martín Tilquiapan lay along the southern rim of the Valle Grande. A series of smaller hilltop sites, such as the Fortress of Mitla and the site of El Choco, add to our overall impression that defense was a priority.

275 The Fortress of Mitla, a defensible hilltop site in the Tlacolula subvalley.

276 Aerial view of El Choco, a defensible hilltop site in the southern Valle Grande.

That impression is reinforced when one considers ill. 277, a map showing only those Monte Albán IIIa sites with fortification walls or defensible settings. There were 38 such sites in Period IIIa, more than in any previous period, and almost two-thirds of the valley's population lived at them.[27] When one plots those defensible sites on a land class map of the valley, as we have done, it is clear that defense was far more of a priority – and access to Class I farm land much less a priority – than in previous periods.

To be sure, our maps do not show the hundreds of small hamlets at the bottom of the settlement hierarchy. Many of those hamlets were located on good alluvium, growing maize for the nobles who lived on hilltops nearby. Nevertheless,

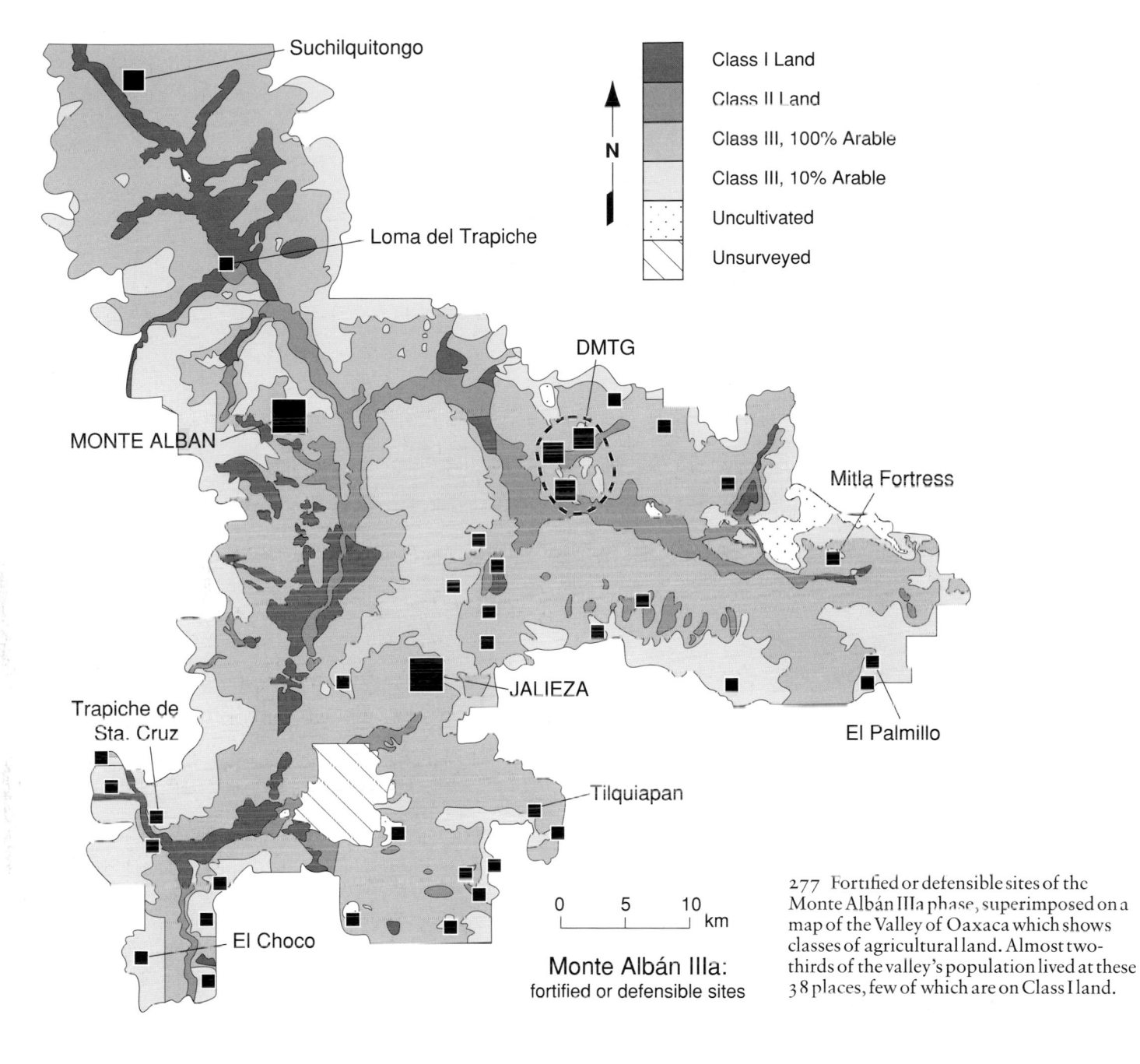

Suchilquitongo

Loma del Trapiche

N

Class I Land

Class II Land

Class III, 100% Arable

Class III, 10% Arable

Uncultivated

Unsurveyed

DMTG

MONTE ALBAN

Mitla Fortress

JALIEZA

El Palmillo

Trapiche de
Sta. Cruz

Tilquiapan

El Choco

0   5   10
km

Monte Albán IIIa:
fortified or defensible sites

277 Fortified or defensible sites of the
Monte Albán IIIa phase, superimposed on a
map of the Valley of Oaxaca which shows
classes of agricultural land. Almost two-
thirds of the valley's population lived at these
38 places, few of which are on Class I land.

it is clear that many formerly great towns near Class I land, like Magdalena
Apasco and San José Mogote, were gradually undergoing abandonment. At the
same time, major new towns like El Palmillo were rising to prominence in defensible localities on Class III land.

Why was defense such a priority during this period? For one thing, the Zapotec
were beginning to lose many of the outer provinces they had colonized or conquered during Monte Albán II. The mountaintop site of Monte Negro was by
now largely abandoned, and the Quiotepec fortress in the Cuicatlán Cañada

The Need for Defense

278 Fine gray Monte Albán IIIa vessels from Tomb 4, San José Mogote. The carvings are known as "pseudo-glyphs."

279 Obsidian lance head which snapped off and remained in the chest of Individual 1, Tomb 4, San José Mogote. Surviving length 10 cm.

would eventually be given up as well. Powerful neighbors to the north and west – the Mixtec – were building their own major centers at places like Yucuñudahui.[28] The Mixtec probably had designs on the Valley of Oaxaca, and would in future periods establish a foothold there.[29] If vulnerability to attack was one reason for the decline of settlement in the Etla region, the Mixtec would seem to constitute the most clear and present danger. As survey proceeds through the mountains north and west of Etla, it will be interesting to see whether a line of defensible sites appears there, equivalent to those guarding the eastern and southern valley.

Insight into the intensity of Period IIIa warfare is provided by Tomb 4 at San José Mogote. While it had declined in size during this period, San José Mogote was still important enough to be occupied by members of the hereditary nobility. Several nobles were buried in Tomb 4, accompanied by elegant Period IIIa vessels. Individual 1, a male older than 40 years, was found with a large obsidian lance buried in his chest. Such was the force of the blow that his left clavicle and several ribs had been broken, while the lance head had snapped off and remained in the victim.

All signs indicate that the Zapotec of Period IIIa had stopped expanding outward, and were content to solidify their control of the Valley of Oaxaca. Hieroglyphic monuments of the period suggest that this was done by two means, diplomacy and warfare (see below). The Settlement Pattern Project also detected a noticeable increase in commercial activity during Period IIIa. Both the Valle

Grande and Tlacolula subvalley had become centers for mass production of pottery, especially gray ware. Gary Feinman has found Period IIIa "kiln wasters" – vessels rejected by the potter for manufacturing flaws – at Tlacochahuaya and Guelavía in the Tlacolula region and Cuilapan, Yatzeche, and Trinidad de Zaachila in the Valle Grande.[30,31] Still other Period IIIa sites, especially in the Tlacolula subvalley, were involved in the production of cores and flake tools from local chert sources.[32] We do not know whether this craft activity was a response to increased demand, a necessary supplement to agriculture, or both.

Just as in earlier periods of Oaxaca prehistory, the events of Monte Albán III did not take place in a vacuum. With upstart polities nipping away at their outer provinces, the Zapotec rulers crafted diplomatic relations with the other super-powers of their world.

Chief among those superpowers was Teotihuacán, a 20-km² city in the Basin of Mexico. Many times larger than Monte Albán, Teotihuacán had its own expansionist ambitions. Still small at 100 BC, it underwent a period of spectac-ular growth during the second century AD.[33,34] Between AD 350 and 550 – a period roughly contemporaneous with Monte Albán IIIa – Teotihuacán estab-lished a military colony at Matacapan on the Veracruz Coast;[35] sent noble traders to Kaminaljuyú in highland Guatemala;[36] and extended its influence as far as the Maya lowlands.[37] To reach some of those areas, Teotihuacán's ambas-sadors almost certainly had to travel through Zapotec territory. It may even have been Teotihuacán that prevented the Zapotec from expanding north of the Cuicatlán Cañada.

Monte Albán's Relations with Other Great Cities

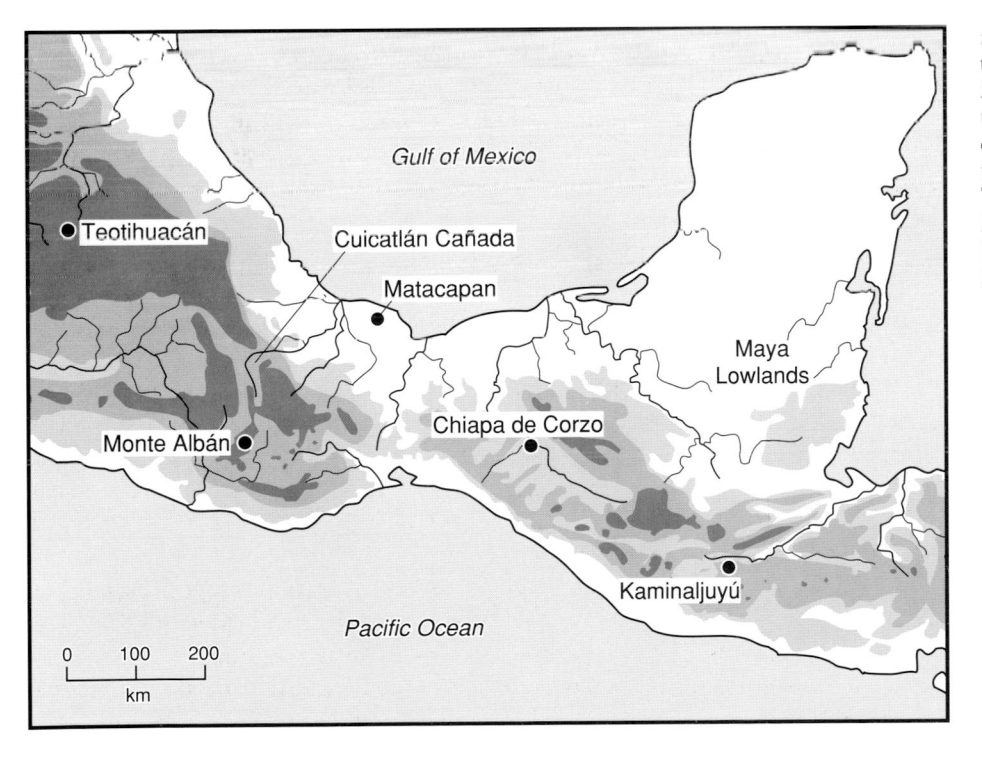

280 Teotihuacán and Monte Albán were two of ancient Mexico's greatest cities. Monte Albán colonized areas as far away as the Cuicatlán Cañada; established an enclave at Teotihuacán; and presented gifts to the rulers of Chiapa de Corzo. Teotihuacán colonized areas as far away as Matacapan; established an enclave at Kaminaljuyú; and sent ambassadors to visit both Monte Albán and the Lowland Maya.

281 The Lápida de Bazán shows an ambassador from Teotihuacán (left) meeting with a Zapotec lord in jaguar or puma costume (right). Height 47 cm.

Through it all, there is no evidence that Monte Albán and Teotihuacán ever went to war with each other. A carved stone monument, known today as the Lápida de Bazán, indicates that this was because of skilled diplomacy.

The Lápida de Bazán is a slab of almost marble-like travertine, found broken in the fill of a temple mound at Monte Albán. Carved on it are two human figures and two vertical columns of hieroglyphic text. On the left we see an ambassador from Teotihuacán, holding an incense pouch and standing on the name-glyph 8 Turquoise. On the right is a Zapotec lord dressed as a jaguar or puma, wearing an elegant headdress and standing on the name-glyph 3 Turquoise. The hieroglyphic text, while it cannot as yet be fully translated, suggests that these two persons traveled, met, spoke, consulted diviners, and burned incense to establish the sacred nature of their agreement.[38] We interpret the Lápida de Bazán as the record of a "summit meeting" between representatives of two great cities 350 km apart. It was presumably through diplomatic agreements like this that Monte Albán and Teotihuacán remained at peace with each other, while both expanded against weaker ethnic groups.

The "Oaxaca Barrio" at Teotihuacán

One byproduct of good diplomatic relations between Monte Albán and Teotihuacán was the establishment of a Zapotec residential ward at the latter city. This "Oaxaca barrio" covered 1–2 ha on the western outskirts of Teotihuacán, roughly 3 km from the political center of the city.[39–41] The Zapotec were not the only foreigners to take up residence at Teotihuacán; excavators René Millon, George Cowgill, and Evelyn Rattray have reported possible enclaves from the Gulf Coast and Maya region as well.[42]

The Zapotec immigrants seem to have lived in standard Teotihuacán apartment compounds, 20 × 50 m in size, using pottery vessels made from local clays but in typical Monte Albán styles. Some of the occupants were evidently of noble birth; excavations in the barrio have produced two Zapotec funerary urns and a tomb jamb inscribed with the Zapotec day-name 9 Earthquake. The tomb held four adults, a child, and an infant – all genetically related, based on 21 qualitative skeletal traits. The study of their bones, done by Michael Spence, suggests that there was only limited intermarriage between this Zapotec enclave and the Teotihuacanos who surrounded them.[43]

While there is no general agreement on how long this Oaxaca barrio persisted at Teotihuacán, the urns and pottery types are mostly in Monte Albán II-IIIa styles. To René Millon the evidence suggests that there was "a kind of 'special relationship' between Teotihuacán and Monte Albán," one that was "closer and of a different kind" than relations between Teotihuacán and other foreign cities.[44]

Most archaeologists assume that the people of the Oaxaca barrio were middlemen in some kind of trade between the two regions. Clear evidence of the commodities traded, however, has not yet been found. It is possible that obsidian blades – produced by the millions at Teotihuacán, which lies near large obsidian sources – were funneled to Oaxaca through the Zapotec barrio. In return, Oaxaca may have funneled mica to Teotihuacán.

No comparable barrio of Teotihuacanos has ever been found at Monte Albán. Occasional vessels in Teotihuacán style, such as the cylindrical tripod vessel and

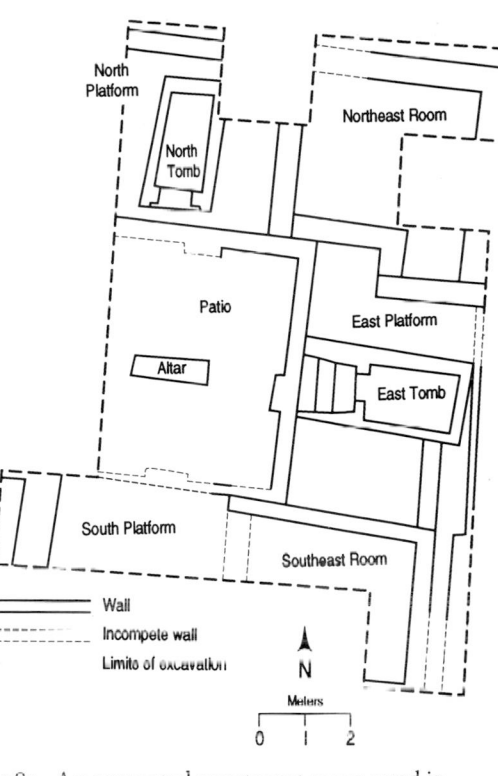

282 An excavated apartment compound in the Oaxaca barrio at Teotihuacán.

283 (*Left*) Zapotec funerary urn from the Oaxaca barrio at Teotihuacán. Height 34 cm.

284 (*Right*) Tomb jamb inscribed with the Zapotec calendric name 9 Earthquake, found in the Oaxaca barrio at Teotihuacán.

233

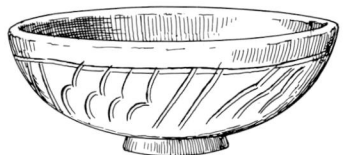

ring-based bowl shown in ill. 285, have been found at Monte Albán in Period III context. Such Teotihuacán imports, however, are largely restricted to elite areas such as Monte Albán's North Platform. This suggests that they were gifts from one city's nobles to the other's, rather than items widely traded.[45]

Trade vs. Takeover

Not only are Teotihuacán vessels relatively rare at Monte Albán; locally made Oaxaca-style pottery is rare at Teotihuacán outside the Zapotec enclave. This fact underscores our position – laid out more fully in Chapter 14 – that when an outlying province's pottery shows abrupt change to the style of a nearby expansionist state, that province has probably been colonized or conquered. When there is no such takeover – as in the case of Oaxaca and Teotihuacán – each region's style will often continue unchanged, even when there are enclaves of foreign traders in its very midst.

Epilogue

285 (*Above*) Teotihuacán-style vessels found at Monte Albán. Cylindrical tripod bowl with hollow slab feet, and ring-based hemispherical bowl in orange ware.

286 (*Opposite*) This carved stone "genealogical register" from the Valle Grande shows a series of life-crisis rites in the early life of a Zapotec ruler named 2 Vessel. In the middle register we see the newborn 2 Vessel with his mother, 2 Water (left); then, on the right, he is presented to his father. In the uppermost register, we see a priest tying a band around his head while his parents watch. A flying turtle or "Cloud Ancestor" hovers above the scene. Such carved stones, placed in the antechambers of tombs, established one's ancestral rights to a particular throne. Height 1 m.

The golden age of Zapotec civilization lasted for half a millennium. Monte Albán may have reached its peak of urban development during Period IIIb, with a population estimated at 24,000.[46] It had grown well beyond its earlier defensive walls, annexing the nearby hill of Atzompa and expanding to 6 km². The population of the Valley of Oaxaca – difficult to estimate in light of the similarity of Monte Albán IIIb and IV ceramics – was undoubtedly above 100,000.

Then, like so many early cities in ancient Mesoamerica, Monte Albán went into decline. Its Main Plaza was deserted; most of its great temples ceased to be maintained; the bulk of its urban population drifted away. The city was never completely abandoned, but by AD 900 it was no longer a Tier 1 administrative center. Jalieza, though never as impressive architecturally as Monte Albán, became the largest city in the Valley of Oaxaca during Monte Albán IV.

Freed from the burden of helping to support Monte Albán, many large towns on the valley floor invested their maize and manpower in their own development. Areas south and east of Monte Albán seem to have been the first to break away, while Etla stayed loyal to the old capital for a while.[47] Towns like Cuilapan and Zaachila in the Valle Grande and Lambityeco and Mitla in the Tlacolula region became prominent in their respective subvalleys.

Despite their emerging importance, the lords of those towns still wrapped themselves in Monte Albán's aura by preserving many of its traditions. One of the most frequently encountered monuments of Monte Albán IIIb-IV was the "genealogical register," a carved stone placed in a tomb antechamber to inform other nobles about the deceased's ancestors.[48,49] We have no doubt that, were a large enough sample of these registers available, we would find some Period IV nobles trying to trace their ancestry back to the dynasties of Monte Albán.

The fall of Monte Albán and the subsequent history of the Valley of Oaxaca cannot be told here, as they would fill a book of equal length. Nor would the story end with the arrival of Cortés, for there are still more than 300,000 speakers of Zapotec in the Mexican state of Oaxaca. Having battled the Aztec to a standoff, having survived the Spanish Conquest and centuries of labor on the great haciendas, they carry on the legacy of a remarkable people who brought civilization to the southern Mexican highlands.

Evolution Without Stages

Ten thousand years of evolution separate the earliest Oaxaca societies from Zapotec civilization. Having surveyed those 10,000 years in high gear, we are now ready to alight from our battered field vehicle. We will end our survey, as archaeological tradition demands, at a charming establishment called "Odd Job's" in the northern Valle Grande. Sit down, reach out for a shot of mezcal and a plate of *carnitas*, and get ready for a surprise. We are about to describe the results of our survey without referring to evolutionary stages.

Don't get us wrong; we think stages are heuristically useful. Band, autonomous village, and rank society do for the archaeologist what fish, reptile, and mammal do for the paleontologist. They provide shorthand references to widely-agreed-upon categories of societies, each characterized by an interrelated set of social and political institutions. We can recognize those categories both in the anthropological present and in the archaeological past.

Action theory, however, provides us with a way to analyze long historical sequences in terms of changing relations between the actors and the system. In such an analysis it is *the social and political institutions, not the stages*, that provide the milestones along the way. Transitional periods – those brief phases of rapid evolution during which the system changed, or the actors deliberately changed it – become more crucial to our analysis than the long, stable periods which gave rise to our typology of stages.

The "Original" System

When we first see humans in Oaxaca, they had already been shaped by a system made up of: (1) their previous cultural background; and (2) the Chihuahuan environment of the late Ice Age. Their previous cultural background evidently included sexual division of labor, and an egalitarian ethic with a strong emphasis on sharing. They had chosen to deal with risk at the group level, escaping drought through a strategy of high mobility. At the end of migrations up to 400 km long, they came together for large communal hunts. Such was their need to share the food from those hunts that deviations from their egalitarian ethic must have been discouraged.

The Environment Changes

By 8000 BC the environment had changed from a cooler Chihuahuan steppe to a warmer and more forested Holocene environment with the dry winter/rainy summer pattern we see today. The system had presented the actors with a problem to solve: surviving in an environment with a greater variety of edible plants, a smaller number of species suitable for communal hunting, and lots of unpredictable variation in annual rainfall.

There were many strategies open to the actors. The one they chose was to cope with risk at the local level. Abandoning the longer migrations of the Ice Age, they settled into a seasonal round of shorter moves between oak-covered uplands, piedmont thorn forest, and valley-floor thickets of mesquite. During the leanest times of the year they accepted risk at the family level, dispersed through the wilderness. During times of abundance they came together at larger camps where risk was shared by the group. Many social and ritual activities seem to have been deferred to the seasons of those larger camps.

We suspect that there were several unintended consequences of this strategy. First, the time spent scattered through the wilderness established a pattern in which the family was the basic unit of harvest and storage. This pattern persisted into the era of village life, which may explain why our actors chose to live in nuclear family houses with separate storage facilities, rather than "long houses" with communal storage. Second, we note that large camps had an area set aside as ritual space. We believe that this pattern also persisted into the village era, where space was set aside for more permanent ritual buildings.

The Strategy of Foraging

While dispersal and coalescence helped the actors cope with the short-term pattern of wet and dry seasons, it did little to buffer the longer term, unpredictable succession of years with above-average or below-average rainfall. For the latter, the Indians developed several strategies. One was to use a wider variety of plant foods, including species that could only be made edible by grinding, roasting, leaching, popping, soaking in water, or baking in earth ovens. Plants needing roasting included the seeds of wild gourds and squashes; those needing soaking in water included the seeds of wild beans; those needing grinding or popping were the seeds of teosinte, the wild ancestor of maize.

A second strategy was to increase the availability of certain useful plants by deliberately planting them near the camp. This might have required the removal of other wild species, such as mesquite, which grow on the best alluvial soil. This was labor-intensive, but had a payoff: squash, beans, and teosinte all do better on disturbed patches of humid alluvium than they do in their native piedmont. The reason they do not normally grow on such soils is that they are shaded out by mesquite and driven out by competing species. The Indians changed the rules of the system by removing that competition.

The Strategy of Collecting

Sometime around 3000 BC our actors made another decision they did not necessarily have to, one which also had unintended consequences for the future. They began to spend a greater part of the year in large encampments, and less in dispersed family groups. Instead of moving to where the plants and animals were, they sent out small "task groups" of men or women to bring the plants and animals to them.

This decision to shift away from "foraging" and toward "collecting" laid the groundwork for future villages. It encouraged the group to spend more effort on planting, weeding, tending, and harvesting domestic plants. And it probably led to population increase through two documented consequences of sedentary life: lowered infant mortality and shortened intervals between births.

Redefining the Environment

The result was a whole new environment, divided into unmodified wilderness (which the Zapotec called *quijxi*) and agricultural fields (which they called *quèela*). The former required no maintenance, continuing to provide venison and wild plants if one chose to travel to it. The latter needed maintenance, but required no travel if one chose to live next to it. Our actors chose not only to live next to it, but to defend it against persons not belonging to the group who cleared it and maintained it. This was perhaps their first modification of an ethic based on widespread sharing.

Increased sedentism, population growth, and favorable genetic changes in their crops led at least a few families to build permanent houses on piedmont spurs overlooking Class I land. In these first hamlets the nuclear family was still the basic unit of production and storage, and the main division of labor was still along gender lines. By 1300 BC some villages had 50–150 inhabitants, many times the population of any previous settlement. One could argue that such large communities had a great competitive advantage over neighbors living in smaller settlements.

Population Growth

Population growth – the unintended consequence of sedentism and agriculture – created a whole new set of problems for our actors to solve. Ecological-functionalist approaches cannot help us much here, for in ecological terms, population growth is a sign of success. Problems? What problems? Weren't these people increasing in numbers? Yes, and they had no social mechanism for integrating so large a group. Before sedentism and agriculture, all tensions and disputes could be solved simply by fissioning. Now they could not fission, because to leave the village was to lose one's investment in housing, storage facilities, and land.

While the specific solutions chosen by Oaxaca's early villagers can be found in other societies, we cannot see how any ecological functionalist could predict them. We believe they were crafted, to borrow Sahlins' phrase, by "changing the meaning of existing relations."

Three of those existing relations have been alluded to in Chapter 4. First, from 8000 to 2000 BC, people tended to live and work with their blood relatives and in-laws. Second, although some men were better providers than others, they found ways to downplay their success. Third, men and women divided the labor required to survive.

Descent Groups and Fraternal Orders

Let us now look at the way the actors of 2000–1000 BC changed those relations. (1) They created larger groups of "blood relatives" by asserting that many seemingly unrelated men had, in fact, descended from a common mythological ancestor. Two such ancestors – carved in pottery as early as 1150 BC – were Earth and Sky, dual divisions of the Zapotec cosmos. (2) They ceased to downplay the fact that some men were better providers than others. Skilled and respected men, drawn from all descent groups, were now to be initiated into fraternal orders from which less respected men were excluded. (3) Village ritual was divided along gender lines. Women's ritual was performed in the home, where immediate ancestors were invoked. Men's ritual was performed in the Men's House, a ritual structure built by the initiates of a fraternal order, where remote ancestors like Earth and Sky were invoked.

While such solutions made possible the integration of large communities, they also had unintended long-term consequences. In particular, the exclusionary nature of men's ritual (some men were initiated, some were not) strained the old egalitarian ethic. Now there were asymmetrical relations, like those between Made People and Dry Food People in the Tewa pueblos.

Achieved Asymmetry

To be sure, differences in prestige were still based on achievement. But now the ambitious man could work harder than his neighbor, grow more maize than he needed, and invest it in the construction of a new Men's House. He could support more than one wife. He could give finer gifts to the fathers of his brides. His own daughter could have more mother-of pearl in her dowry. Because he had worked his way up through an exclusionary ritual system, such a man could behave in ways that would have gotten an Archaic hunter chased out of his camp.

When a village society is without hereditary authority, much of the burden of integration falls on its ritual system. We see this clearly in the villages of 1500–1000 BC, since their rituals were of the type that consume lots of paraphernalia: marine shell, mica, macaw feathers, stingray spines, conch shell trumpets, turtleshell drums. The fact that many of these materials were traded from other regions of Mesoamerica put the early villagers of Oaxaca in touch with many ethnic groups. Now the "system" in which they were embedded was far more global. They were keenly aware of the self-interested goals and solutions of neighboring actors, and could use them as models for their own behavior.

Inherited Asymmetry

Oaxaca society entered the late twelfth century BC with unprecedented population growth. Stable villages integrated by ritual, fraternal orders, and large descent groups had spread throughout the valley, displacing other settlement types. Some villages grew larger than others because self-selected leaders who worked hard, accumulated valuables, led raids, and built Men's Houses were able to attract a lot of followers. Their leadership, however, was not transferrable to their offspring; it died with them.

We should stress that this society was not necessarily on a trajectory toward civilization. It could have remained stable, in its late twelfth-century BC form, until the Spanish Conquest.

Changes in the Ideology of Descent

At this point, however, our actors once again "changed the meaning of existing relations." For centuries, the success of ambitious village leaders had been attributed to the support of supernatural forces. That was the only plausible explanation for unequal success in egalitarian society. Gradually, however, a different explanation was crafted: successful leaders had actually *descended* from those supernatural forces. Through intervening generations of distinguished ancestors, they had monopolized access to the very celestial spirits on whom the life of the village depended. Only the immediate offspring of these elite individuals were qualified to lead; their more distant relatives were born to follow.

Two of the supernatural forces implicated were the aforementioned Earth and Sky. In their angriest forms, Earthquake and Lightning, they were carved on vessels buried with less than 20 percent of all villagers.

For centuries, the women in Oaxaca's villages had invoked their recent ancestors by making small figurines to which the latter's spirits could return. Now some of those figurines appeared in postures of authority, and others in postures of obeisance. Some families' ancestors were simply more powerful than others,' and that ideological principle supported leadership based on inherited rank.

We argue that this change was "interest-related," not "strain-related." It was not forced on the villagers by population growth, shrinking farmland, or an external threat. It happened in an atmosphere of intense competition among ambitious leaders, who had previously possessed no way of bequeathing their achieved power to their offspring.

In turn, this change set the stage for loss of autonomy by smaller villages. Through hypogamous marriages to the sisters and daughters of highly ranked men at large villages, the leaders of small villages could raise the status of their own offspring. The rewards for such alliance included access to the sumptuary goods being imported into the valley by their in-laws. The price they paid was becoming part of a larger system, one in which their small village could be ordered to provide tons of boulders when a big village wanted to build a new temple.

The New System

By 700 BC, it is clear that Oaxaca societies were being shaped by a system in which the culturally defined goals of a leader were to have as many farmers, craftspeople, and warriors under his control as possible. The two main strategies for reaching those goals were: (1) alliance building – through feasting, gift-giving, and bride exchange; and (2) warfare, mostly at the level of raiding and burning rival villages. The rich archaeological record now featured burials of high-ranking women at subordinate villages; status symbols like cranial deformation and the wearing of jade; pits with the refuse of large feasts; public structures built with substantial manpower; temples burned in raids; and carvings of sacrificed enemies, whose personal names were given in hieroglyphic captions.

Competition and Defense

One unintended consequence of our actors' strategies was the creation of a system featuring relentless competition and periodic violence. The highest-ranking family at each large village wanted nothing more than to incorporate the lands and manpower of rival villages into its sphere. Since some of those villages controlled populations of 700–1000 persons or more, the threat of serious conflict was high. In response to this systemic change, a no-man's-land developed in the center of the valley. The need for defense had now become as crucial a variable as the need for Class I land.

Urbanism and Disruptive Change

What happened next was the least predictable event in the history of the Valley of Oaxaca. Were we writing about paleontology rather than archaeology, it would be appropriate to use the biological term "emergent novelty." So dramatic was the urban relocation of 500 BC that it must have had both strain-related and interest-related causes. Somehow the leaders of several thousand people, many of them living in the Etla region of the valley, convinced them to leave their villages and found a city on a 400-m mountaintop.

When prehistorians study such urban relocations in ancient Greece, they assign them either to: (1) the need for defense from an external threat (a strain-related motive); or (2) power building (an interest-related motive). In the case of Oaxaca, we assign the founding of Monte Albán to both. Perhaps it is in such historic settings, when the power-building goals of leaders are rationalized by an external threat to their followers, that great evolutionary transitions are possible.

The great emergent novelty of 500–200 BC was an urban society, something without precedent in Mesoamerica. As we have seen, however, the path taken by the founders of Monte Albán was not the only possible path to urbanism; it was the result of decisions made in the context of a specific cultural-historical setting. Other great population centers, like Chiapa de Corzo, arose as the result of different decisions, made in different cultural-historical settings. What fascinates us is how similar the *institutions* of these early regional capitals turned out to be. Perhaps part of their similarity can be explained through contact, through those societies' participation in a shared Mesoamerican system. Not all of it can be explained that way, however, because some of the similarities are shared with ancient Greece, Egypt, and Mesopotamia – regions far outside the Mesoamerican system.

The Piedmont Strategy

One of our clearest examples of a "problem posed by the system" was the difficulty of provisioning Monte Albán between 500 and 100 BC. It was, of course, a problem of the actors' own doing: their deliberate urban relocation had turned the central valley, a former no-man's-land, into the most densely populated region of Oaxaca.

Their solution to the problem was to develop the piedmont within 15 km of Monte Albán by means of canal irrigation. Rich tombs at small sites in the piedmont show that this strategy was implemented from the top down, with elite administrators living even at large villages. Maize produced at piedmont villages supported the warriors and diplomats needed to subjugate the entire Valley of Oaxaca, and perhaps even to begin expansion into the surrounding mountains.

Interestingly enough, once Monte Albán's hold on the entire valley had been consolidated, this intense occupation of the central valley and its piedmont began to dissipate. By the first century BC the major areas of population growth lay farther from Monte Albán, perhaps in regions newly allied to the capital.

From Ranking to Stratification

At some point in their consolidation of the valley, the elites of the Valley of Oaxaca made another "change in the meaning of existing relations": they figured out how to further solidify their privileged status by preventing vast numbers of their own countrymen and women from marrying them. The result was a society in which a gulf of class endogamy yawned between two strata. This change was clearly interest-related, intended to ensure that future rulers and their mates would likely come from the families already in power. Like conquest and political alliance, it was a strategy of consolidation seen among many ancient civilizations.

This new division into ruling and commoner classes, like the earlier emergence of hereditary rank, had to be rationalized plausibly or it would not be accepted. The solution was a new ideology in which nobles and commoners were seen as having separate genealogical origins. Nobles were descended from Lightning, the angry form of Sky, now iconographically depicted as *Cociyo*. They wore images of Lightning in their headdresses, and when they died they metamorphosed into flying figures who joined their supernatural ancestors in the clouds. Commoners, on the other hand, were only descended from previous commoners.

As part of this new ideology there developed a complex symbolic system in which jaguars or pumas became associated with rulers, and bats and owls with various members of the nobility. The attributes of predatory animals were also used to encourage warriors to fight fiercely; those who distinguished themselves were given costumes with eagle or coyote headdresses.

Accompanying the two-class system was a dichotomy of noble speech and commoner speech. Noble speech was not only true but elegant, depicted iconographically by an elaborate speech scroll; commoner speech was full of lies and confusion. The visual form of noble speech was hieroglyphic writing, carved on stone monuments at places like Monte Albán. This writing, first used to record the names of rival chiefs slain or sacrificed, went on to become a tool of Oaxaca's ruling class. It was used in their endless competition for positions of leadership, prestige, territory, tribute, and politically advantageous marriages. It was also used to advance royal propaganda, either vertically (between noble and commoner) or horizontally (among nobles).

Somewhere in this process, the people of the Valley of Oaxaca had become identifiably Zapotec. Their iconography now depicted supernatural forces and beings which they, alone in Mesoamerica, worshiped. Their writing system, in its structure and especially in its use of fingers as ordinal numbers, seems to reflect an archaic form of the Zapotec language.

Creating a Larger System

The self-interest of Zapotec noble actors provided enormous energy for the changes of 100 BC–AD 200. Their need to control thousands of farmers, laborers, and warriors required that many tasks be delegated to administrative, religious, scribal, architectural, craft, and military specialists. One result was a multi-tiered hierarchy in which 5–8-ha large villages oversaw dozens of small villages that lay within a 1–2-hour walk. In turn, 50–70-ha towns oversaw the large villages of their district. Finally, some important towns were spaced only a day's travel from Monte Albán, making it possible for the capital to oversee the actions of hereditary lords at secondary administrative centers. In spite of gifts, marriage alliances, and other rewards designed to keep the lords of those secondary centers loyal, the rulers of Monte Albán must have known that the greatest threats of revolt and usurpation would come from the lords of those large towns.

One way to keep potential rivals busy, of course, is to send them out to distinguish themselves by conquering still more distant provinces. For perhaps 300–400 years, generation after generation of Monte Albán's rulers did just that; but they were also shrewd enough to avoid confrontation with the mightiest kingdoms in other regions.

Their expansion seems to have relied on three strategies. (1) When a neighboring region was underpopulated, and in no position to resist, the Zapotec simply sent in colonists. (2) When a region resisted – as in the case of the Cuicatlán Cañada – they sent in soldiers, burned a few villages, and set up a few racks of severed heads. (3) When their expansion came up against that of a rival civilization the size of Teotihuacán's, they used skilled diplomacy. Such diplomacy could include "summit meetings" between ambassadors, the carving of mutually agreed-upon hieroglyphic texts, or even the establishment of a Zapotec barrio at the foreign capital. Through this tripartite strategy of colonization, conquest, and diplomacy, the Zapotec of Monte Albán may have come to dominate some 20,000 km² of Mesoamerica by AD 300–400.

The Problem of Hostile Neighbors

Classic Zapotec civilization existed in a larger system beyond the dreams of the most ambitious actors of earlier periods. The enormous demographic advantage of Monte Albán had led to a reshaping of Mesoamerica by the fourth century AD. Their "greater system" now stretched beyond the Valley of Oaxaca to include neighbors like Teotihuacán, the Mixtec, and the people of Chiapas. Buffering them from those rival states were a series of outer provinces, which were rapidly learning statecraft from their Zapotec colonizers.

What happened next was a change in the system, one widespread among early civilizations. Taking advantage of its higher population, military strength, and greater degree of political centralization, Monte Albán had turned dozens of outlying regions into tribute-paying provinces. Ironically, however, Monte Albán's self-interested development of these provinces (for example, the canal and aqueduct systems installed in the Cuicatlán Cañada) had given those subjugated regions the very skills they needed to get stronger. By AD 400 these regions were more centralized, more skilled at alliance building, more highly populated, and eager for autonomy. Gradually they began to break away from the grip of Monte Albán. The frontiers of Zapotec civilization were being rolled back to a point closer to the Valley of Oaxaca.

Eventually surrounded by hostile neighbors, the Zapotec were forced into yet another "strain-related" solution. Defense became a critical variable in settlement location. By AD 500, roughly 64 percent of the estimated 115,000 citizens of the Valley of Oaxaca lived at 38 defensible sites. Caught between the need to be near Class I land and the need to defend themselves, they chose to give up some of their more distant provinces in order to consolidate their grip on their core physiographic region.

This decision led to large concentrations of population in the more easily defended portions of the Valley of Oaxaca. The urban concentrations at Jalieza in the Valle Grande and at Dainzú-Macuilxochitl-Tlacochahuaya-Guadalupe in the Tlacolula region almost rivaled Monte Albán's. So spectacular was Jalieza's growth that it may even provide us with a second example of synoikism, or urban relocation.

Given our evidence for regional warfare, it would be easy to see Jalieza's growth as a response to external threat. Once large, however, Jalieza was in a position to do its own "power building." That power building may have hastened the decline of Monte Albán. In effect, there were now three different concentrations of 12,200–16,500 persons in the Valley of Oaxaca, spaced roughly a day's walk from each other. Never again would one of those concentrations dominate the valley as Monte Albán had for 500 years.

From this point on, the story of Zapotec civilization was to become much more complicated. Instead of one historic trajectory for the Valley of Oaxaca, each of the population concentrations mentioned above had its own. One trajectory led to marriage alliances with the Mixtec, bringing foreign nobles into the western valley. Another led to the sacred city of Mitla in the eastern valley. Still a third, begun at Zaachila in the southern valley, saw the Zapotec battling an Aztec army on the Pacific Coast. So complex is the later history of Oaxaca that this is a good point to end our discussion.

Action Theory and Social Evolution

In these final pages we have tried to construct an "evolution without stages." By describing the rise of Zapotec civilization in terms of action theory, we present it as a long sequence of historic changes. Some of these changes began in the larger cultural and historical system in which the actors were shaped. Others came about when the actors, determined to have what was materially and politically useful for them, changed the meaning of relations within the system.

In such a historic sequence, periods of transition, or rapid evolution, are more important than periods of stability. Evolutionary theory has often been criticized for focusing too heavily on stable periods of slow evolution, which form the basis for stages like autonomous village, chiefdom, and so on. Action theory, by concentrating instead on transitions, may help to rejuvenate an exhausted paradigm. By putting the actors back into the scheme, action theory also responds to complaints that most evolutionary theory makes humans little more than cogs in a machine.

We must not forget, however, that the Zapotec are only one case of prehistoric social evolution. Dozens of "first generation" civilizations arose in other parts of Mesoamerica, in the Andes, in Mesopotamia, in Egypt, in India, and in China.

Action theory is appropriate for studying the evolutionary history of a single group like the Zapotec; it forces us to investigate the specific cultural and historical contexts in which the actors were shaped and their decisions were made.

However, once we begin to compare the Zapotec to other civilizations – Tikal in the Maya jungle, Wari in the Peruvian sierra, Uruk on the levees of the Euphrates — we discover that those societies were shaped by different cultural and historical systems, and by different actors' decisions.

Action theory is less useful for comparing all civilizations, for when we do so we find that their transitions, or periods of rapid change, are not necessarily similar. More often than not, it is the periods of stability, or slow evolution, that look similar.

That is where concepts like band, autonomous village, rank society, and archaic state become useful. These abstractions from societies of the recent past allow us to compare the stable periods in different evolutionary sequences. There are stages in the rise of all archaic states that look provocatively similar. One of our goals should be to find out why this is so.

In a recent paper, theoretician Charles Spencer has argued for a dual approach to the study of social evolution.[1] The first approach, the one we have taken in this book, emphasizes the contribution of history in creating a specific civilization. The second approach seeks common principles in the evolution of all civilizations. Like all broadly generalizing approaches, the second has drawn fire, especially when it seems to reduce the actors to pawns. Perhaps by giving social evolution a more human face, we can send both approaches into the debate stronger than before.

Notes to the Text

Chapter 1 (pp. 9–22)

1. West, Robert C., 1964, "Surface Configuration and Associated Geology of Middle America," in *Handbook of Middle American Indians* (vol. 1), Robert Wauchope and Robert C. West (eds.), p. 63. 2. Longacre, Robert, 1967, "Systematic Comparison and Reconstruction," in *Handbook of Middle American Indians* (vol. 5), Robert Wauchope and Norman A. McQuown (eds.), pp. 117–159. 3. Kirkby, Anne V. T., 1974, "Individual and Community Responses to Rainfall Variability in Oaxaca, Mexico," in *Natural Hazards: Local, Regional, and Global*, Gilbert F. White (ed.), p. 119. 4. Marcus, Joyce, "The Reconstructed Chronology of the Later Zapotec Rulers, AD 1415–1563," in Flannery and Marcus (eds.) 1983:301–308. 5. del Paso y Troncoso, Francisco, 1905–1906, *Papeles de Nueva España: Segunda Serie, Geografía y Estadística* (7 vols.). 6. Whitecotton 1977. 7. Kowalewski et al. 1989:513. 8. Whitecotton 1977:138, 306. 9. Córdova, Juan de, 1578, *Vocabulario en Lengua Zapoteca*. 10. Whitecotton 1977:149. 11. Marcus, Joyce, "Royal Families, Royal Texts: Examples from the Zapotec and Maya," in *Mesoamerican Elites: An Archaeological Assessment*, Diane Z. Chase and Arlen F. Chase (eds.) 1992:225–226. 12. Asensio, Gaspar, 1580, "El Pueblo Teutitlán," in *Papeles de Nueva España: Segunda Serie, Geografía y Estadística* (vol. 4), Francisco del Paso y Troncoso (ed.) 1905, pp. 104–108. 13. Asensio, Gaspar, 1580, "Relación de Macuilsúchil y su Partido," in *Papeles de Nueva España: Segunda Serie, Geografía y Estadística* (vol. 4), Francisco del Paso y Troncoso (ed.) 1905, pp. 100–104. 14. Pérez de Zamora, Pedro, 1580, "Relación de Teticpac," in *Papeles de Nueva España: Segunda Serie, Geografía y Estadística* (vol. 4), Francisco del Paso y Troncoso (ed.) 1905, pp. 109–114. 15. Canseco, Alonso de, 1580, "Relación de Tlacolula y Mitla hecha en los días 12 y 23 de agosto respectivamente," in *Papeles de Nueva España: Segunda Serie, Geografía y Estadística* (vol. 4), Francisco del Paso y Troncoso (ed.) 1905, pp. 144–154. 16. Whitecotton 1977:148, 310. 17. Kirkby 1973. 18. Lees, Susan, 1973, *Sociopolitical Aspects of Canal Irrigation in the Valley of Oaxaca, Mexico*. 19. Flannery, Kent V., "Precolumbian Farming in the Valleys of Oaxaca, Nochixtlán, Tehuacán, and Cuicatlán: A Comparative Study," in Flannery and Marcus (eds.) 1983:323–339. 20. Ximénez Ortiz, Juan, 1579, "Relación de Iztepexi," in *Papeles de Nueva España: Segunda Serie, Geografía y Estadística* (vol. 4), Francisco del Paso y Troncoso (ed.) 1905, pp. 9–23. 21. Marcus, Joyce, "Aztec Military Campaigns against the Zapotecs: The Documentary Evidence," in Flannery and Marcus (eds.) 1983:314–318. 22. Renfrew, Colin and Ezra B. W. Zubrow, 1994, *The Ancient Mind: Elements of Cognitive Archaeology*. 23. Flannery, Kent V. and Joyce Marcus, 1993, "Cognitive Archaeology," *Cambridge Archaeological Journal* 3:260–270. 24. Marcus, Joyce, Kent V. Flannery, and Ronald Spores, "The Cultural Legacy of the Oaxacan Preceramic," in Flannery and Marcus (eds.) 1983:36–39. 25. Marcus, Joyce, "The Origins of Mesoamerican Writing," *Annual Review of Anthropology* 5:35–67. 26. Marcus 1992a:206–210. 27. Marcus 1992a:278–287. 28. Espíndola, Nicolás, 1580, "Relación de Chichicapa y Su Partido," in *Papeles de Nueva España: Segunda Serie, Geografía y Estadística* (vol. 4), Francisco del Paso y Troncoso (ed.) 1905, pp. 115–143. 29. Marcus, Joyce and Kent V. Flannery, 1978, "Ethnoscience of the Sixteenth-Century Valley Zapotec," in *The Nature and Status of Ethnobotany*, Richard I. Ford (ed.), pp. 51–79. 30. Marcus, Joyce, 1972, "Report on Zapotec Writing: a Ford Foundation Research Project." 31. Marcus, Joyce, "The First Appearance of Zapotec Writing and Calendrics," in Flannery and Marcus (eds.) 1983:93.

Chapter 2 (pp. 23–32)

1. Carneiro, Robert L., 1981, "The Chiefdom: Precursor of the State," in *The Transition to Statehood in the New World*, Grant D. Jones and Robert R. Kautz (eds.), pp. 37–79. 2. Carneiro, Robert L., 1991, "The Nature of the Chiefdom as Revealed by Evidence from the Cauca Valley of Colombia," in *Profiles in Cultural Evolution*, A. Terry Rambo and Kathleen Gillogly (eds.), pp. 167–190. 3. Ibid., pp. 168–169. 4. Marcus 1992a:274–276. 5. Caso, Alfonso, 1928, *Las Estelas Zapotecas*. 6. Marcus 1980. 7. Marcus 1992a. 8. Caso, Bernal, and Acosta 1967. 9. Paddock (ed.) 1966. 10. Blanton 1978. 11. Kowalewski et al. 1989. 12. Feinman and Nicholas 1990. 13. Feinman and Nicholas 1993. 14. Brockington, Donald J., 1973, *Archaeological Investigations at Miahuatlán, Oaxaca*. 15. Markman, Charles W., 1981, *Prehispanic Settlement Dynamics in Central Oaxaca, Mexico*. 16. Marcus 1980. 17. See several articles in Flannery and Marcus (eds.) 1983. 18. Ortner 1984. 19. Sahlins, Marshall D. and Elman R. Service (eds.), 1960, *Evolution and Culture*. 20. Service, Elman R., 1962, *Primitive Social Organization: An Evolutionary Perspective*. 21. Fried, Morton A., 1967, *The Evolution of Political Society*. 22. Carneiro, Robert L., 1970, "A Theory of the Origin of the State," *Science* 169:733–738. 23. Spencer 1990. 24. Ortner 1984:148. 25. Sahlins, Marshall D., 1981, *Historical Metaphors and Mythical Realities: Structure in the Early History of the Sandwich Islands Kingdom*. 26. Geertz, Clifford, 1973, "Ideology as a Cultural System," in *The Interpretation of Cultures*, C. Geertz (ed.). 27. Ritchie, William A., 1932, "The Algonkin Sequence in New York," *American Anthropologist* 34:406–414. 28. Ritchie, William A., 1938, "A Perspective of Northeastern Archaeology," *American Antiquity* 4:94–112. 29. Strong, William Duncan, 1933, "The Plains Culture Area in the Light of Archaeology," *American Anthropologist* 35:271–287. 30. Wedel, Waldo R., 1938, "The Direct-Historical Approach in Pawnee Archaeology," *Smithsonian Miscellaneous Collections* 97(7).

Chapter 3 (pp. 41–48)

1. Shafer, Harry J., 1986, *Ancient Texans: Rock Art and Lifeways along the Lower Pecos*, pp. 40–41. 2. Watts, W. A. and John P. Bradbury, 1982, "Paleoecological Studies at Lake Patzcuaro on the West-Central Mexican Plateau and at Chalco Bog in the Basin of Mexico," *Quaternary Research* 17:56–70. 3. Flannery, Kent V., "Vertebrate Fauna and Hunting Patterns," in Byers (ed.) 1967, p. 132–177. 4. Spaulding, W. Geoffrey, 1989, "Environment of the Last 18,000 Years in Extreme Southwestern North America," paper presented at the Texas A&M Conference on the Archaic of Southern Texas and Northern Mexico. 5. Flannery, Kent V., 1966, "The Postglacial 'Readaptation' as Viewed from Mesoamerica," *American Antiquity* 31:800–805. 6. Flannery, Kent V., "Pleistocene Fauna of Early Ajuereado Type from Cueva Blanca, Oaxaca," in Flannery and Marcus (eds.) 1983:18–20. 7. Ibid. 8. Aveleyra Arroyo de Anda, Luis and Manuel Maldonado-Koerdell, 1953, "Association of Artifacts with Mammoth in the Valley of Mexico," *American Antiquity* 18:332–340. 9. Aveleyra Arroyo de Anda, Luis, 1956, "The Second Mammoth and Associated Artifacts at Santa Isabel Iztapan, Mexico," *American Antiquity* 22:12–28. 10. Ibid. 11. Wilmsen, Edwin N., 1974, *Lindenmeier: A Pleistocene Hunting Society*. 12. MacNeish, Richard S., 1964, "Ancient Mesoamerican Civilization," *Science* 143:531–537. 13. MacNeish, Richard S., Melvin L. Fowler, Angel García Cook, Frederick A. Peterson, Antoinette Nelken-Terner, and James A. Neely, 1972, *The Prehistory of the Tehuacán Valley*, vol. 5: *Excavations and Reconnaissance*. 14. Flannery, Kent V., "Vertebrate Fauna and Hunting Patterns," in Byers (ed.) 1967:132–177. 15. Flannery, Kent V., 1966, "The Postglacial 'Readaptation' as Viewed from Mesoamerica," *American Antiquity* 31:800–805. 16. Flannery, Kent V., "Vertebrate Fauna and Hunting Patterns," in Byers (ed.) 1967:132–177. 17. Finsten, Laura, Kent V. Flannery, and Barbara Macnider, "Preceramic and Cave Occupations," in Kowalewski et al. 1989:39–53. 18. Personal communication, James Schoenwetter, 1980. 19. MacNeish, Richard S., Antoinette Nelken-Terner, and Irmgard W. Johnson, 1967, *The Prehistory of the Tehuacán Valley*, Vol. 2: *Non-Ceramic Artifacts*: Table 32. 20. Gould, Richard A., 1989, "The Archaeology of Arid-Land Foraging: A Critical Review of Theories and Assumptions," paper presented at the Texas A&M Conference on the Archaic of Southern Texas and Northern Mexico. 21. Reports of the Associated Press, published in *The Ann Arbor News*, December 1981.

Chapter 4 (pp. 49–63)

1. Flannery, Kent V., "Vertebrate Fauna and Hunting Patterns," in Byers (ed.) 1967:132–177. 2. Smith, C. Earle, Jr., 1978, *The Vegetational History of the Valley of Oaxaca*. 3. Flannery, Kent V., 1966, "The Postglacial 'Readaptation' as Viewed from Mesoamerica," *American Antiquity* 31:800–805. 4. Kirkby 1973. 5. Kirkby, Anne V. T., 1974, "Individual and Community Responses to Rainfall Variability in Oaxaca, Mexico," in *Natural Hazards: Local, Regional, and Global*, Gilbert F. White (ed.), pp. 119–128. 6. Binford, Lewis R., 1980, "Willow Smoke and Dogs' Tails: Hunter-gatherer Settlement Systems and Archaeological Site Formation," *American Antiquity* 45:4–20. 7. Wiessner, Pauline, 1982, "Beyond Willow Smoke and Dogs' Tails: A Comment on Binford's Analysis of Hunter-gatherer Settlement Systems," *American Antiquity* 47:171–178. 8. MacNeish, Richard S., 1964, "Ancient Mesoamerican Civilization," *Science* 143:531–537. 9. Steward, Julian H., 1938, *Basin-Plateau Aboriginal Sociopolitical Groups*. 10. Flannery (ed.) 1986:39. 11. Finsten, Laura, Kent V. Flannery, and Barbara Macnider, "Preceramic and Cave Occupations," in Kowalewski et al. 1989:39–53. 12. Flannery (ed.) 1986. 13. Flannery, Kent V. and Ronald Spores, "Excavated Sites of the Oaxaca Preceramic," in Flannery and Marcus (eds.) 1983:23–25. 14. Robert G. Reynolds, 1993, unpublished ms. 15. Binford, Lewis R., 1983, *In Pursuit of the Past*, Fig. 89. 16. Lee, Richard B., 1979, *The !Kung San: Men, Women, and Work in a Foraging Society*, p. 247. 17.

Reynolds, Robert G., "An Adaptive Computer Model for the Evolution of Plant Collecting and Early Agriculture in the Eastern Valley of Oaxaca," in Flannery (ed.) 1986: 439–500.

Chapter 5 (pp. 64–70)

1. Robson, J.R.K. and J.N. Elias, "Nutritional Significance of the Guilá Naquitz Food Remains," in Flannery (ed.) 1986:297–301. 2. Whitaker, Thomas W. and Hugh C. Cutler, "Cucurbits from Preceramic Levels at Guilá Naquitz," in Flannery (ed.) 1986:277. 3. Robson, J.R.K. and J.N. Elias, "Nutritional Significance of the Guilá Naquitz Food Remains," in Flannery (ed.) 1986:Fig. 23.1. 4. Messer, Ellen, 1978, Zapotec Plant Knowledge: Classification, Uses, and Communication about Plants in Mitla, Oaxaca, Mexico, pp. 58–59. 5. Cutler, Hugh C. and Thomas W. Whitaker, "Cucurbits from the Tehuacán Caves," in Byers (ed.) 1967:212–219. 6. Kaplan, Lawrence, "Preceramic Phaseolus from Guilá Naquitz," in Flannery (ed.) 1986:281–284. 7. Flannery (ed.) 1986:303. 8. Niederberger, Christine, 1979, "Early Sedentary Economy in the Basin of Mexico," Science 203:131–142. 9. Byers (ed.) 1967. 10. Beadle, George W., 1971, letter to Kent V. Flannery. 11. Galinat, Walton C., 1983, "The Origin of Maize as Shown by Key Morphological Traits of its Ancestor, Teosinte," Maydica 28:121 138. 12. Galinat, Walton C., 1985, "The Missing Links between Teosinte and Maize; A Review," Maydica 30:137–160. 13. Wilkes, H. Garrison, 1967, Teosinte: The Closest Relative of Maize. 14. Doebley, John, 1992, "Mapping the Genes that Made Maize," Trends in Genetics 8:302–307. 15. Niederberger, Christine, 1979, "Early Sedentary Economy in the Basin of Mexico," Science 203:131–142. 16. Personal communication, James Schoenwetter, 1980. 17. Dorweiler, Jane, Adrian Stec, Jerry Kermicle, and John Doebley, 1993, "Teosinte Glume Architecture 1: A Genetic Locus Controlling a Key Step in Maize Evolution," Science 262:233–235. 18. Mangelsdorf, Paul C., Richard S. MacNeish, and Walton C. Galinat, "Prehistoric Wild and Cultivated Maize," in Byers (ed.) 1967:178–200. 19. Kirkby 1973:Fig. 48. 20. Long, Austin, B.F. Benz, D.J. Donohue, A.J.T. Jull, and L.J. Toolin, 1989, "First Direct AMS Dates on Early Maize from Tehuacán, Mexico," Radiocarbon 31:1035–1040.

Chapter 6 (pp. 71–75)

1. Kirkby 1973:35. 2. Kirkby 1973. 3. Kirkby, Anne V. T., 1974, "Individual and Community Responses to Rainfall Variability in Oaxaca, Mexico," in Natural Hazards: Local, Regional, and Global, Gilbert F. White (ed.), pp. 119–128. 4. Flannery, Kent V., 1973, "The Origins of Agriculture," Annual Review of Anthropology 2:298–299. 5. Binford, Lewis R. and W.J. Chasko, Jr., 1976, "Nunamiut Demographic History: A Provocative Case," in Demographic

Anthropology: Quantitative Approaches, Ezra B.W. Zubrow (ed.), pp. 63–143. 6. Niederberger, Christine, 1979, "Early Sedentary Economy in the Basin of Mexico," Science 203:137. 7. MacNeish, Richard S., Frederick A. Peterson, and Kent V. Flannery, 1970, The Prehistory of the Valley of Tehuacán, Vol. 3: Ceramics, pp. 3–6. 8. Flannery and Marcus 1994:45–54.

Chapter 7 (pp. 76–92)

1. Fried, Morton A., 1967, The Evolution of Political Society. 2. Steward, Julian H., 1938, Basin-Plateau Aboriginal Sociopolitical Groups. 3. Brown, Paula, 1972, The Chimbu: A Study of Change in the New Guinea Highlands. 4. Ortiz, Alfonso, 1969, The Tewa World: Space, Time, Being and Becoming in a Pueblo Society. 5. Rappaport, Roy A., 1968, Pigs for the Ancestors: Ritual in the Ecology of a New Guinea People. 6. Brown, Paula, 1972, The Chimbu: A Study of Change in the New Guinea Highlands. 7. Barth, Fredrik, 1987, Cosmologies in the Making: A Generative Approach to Cultural Variation in Inner New Guinea. 8. Knauft, Bruce M., 1993, South Coast New Guinea Cultures: History, Comparison, Dialectic. 9. Kelly, Raymond C., 1993, Constructing Inequality: The Fabrication of a Hierarchy of Virtue among the Etoro. 10. Brown, Paula, 1972, The Chimbu: A Study of Change in the New Guinea Highlands. 11. Brown, Paula, 1972, The Chimbu: A Study of Change in the New Guinea Highlands, p. 53. 12. Barth, Fredrik, 1987, Cosmologies in the Making: A Generative Approach to Cultural Variation in Inner New Guinea. 13. Kowalewski et al. 1989:56. 14. Sanders, William T., 1965, The Cultural Ecology of the Teotihuacán Valley, p. 50. 15. Winter, Marcus C., 1972, unpublished doctoral dissertation. 16. Nicholas 1989:460. 17. Flannery (ed.) 1976:104–105. 18. Nicholas 1989:463. 19. Lowe, Gareth W., 1959, Archaeological Exploration of the Upper Grijalva River, Chiapas, Mexico, p. 7. 20. Winter, Marcus C., 1972, unpublished doctoral dissertation. 21. Wolf, Eric R., 1966, Peasants, p. 21. 22. Ford, Richard I., 1968, unpublished doctoral dissertation. 23. Drennan, Robert D., "Ritual and Ceremonial Development at the Early Village Level," in Flannery and Marcus (eds.) 1983:46–50. 24. Tobacco, mixed with powdered lime, was used for divining by the Zapotec. See Alcina Franch, José, 1993, Calendario y Religión entre los Zapotecos, pp. 84–85. 25. The Mixtec also used pulverized tobacco for rituals. See Furst, Jill L., 1978, Codex Vindobonensis Mexicanus I: A Commentary, pp. 9, 18. 26. The Maya chewed pulverized tobacco. See Cruz, Pacheco, 1960, Usos, Costumbres, Religión: Supersticiones de los Mayas, p. 111. 27. Whitecotton 1977:137. 28. Redmond 1994. 29. Wiessner, Pauline, 1982, "Beyond Willow Smoke and Dogs' Tails: A Comment on Binford's Analysis of Hunter-gatherer Settlement Systems," American Antiquity 47:171–178. 30. Clark, John E., "The Beginnings of Mesoamerica: Apologia for the Soconusco Early Formative," in The Formation of

Complex Society in Southeastern Mesoamerica, William R. Fowler, Jr. (ed.) 1991:Fig. 8. 31. Pires-Ferreira, Jane W., "Obsidian Exchange in Formative Mesoamerica," in Flannery (ed.) 1976:292–306. 32. The concept of down-the-line exchange was first proposed by Renfrew, C.A., J.E. Dixon, and J.R. Cann, 1968, "Further Analysis of Near Eastern Obsidians," Proceedings of the Prehistoric Society 34:329. 33. Winter, Marcus C. and Jane W. Pires-Ferreira, "Distribution of Obsidian Among Households in two Oaxacan Villages," in Flannery (ed.) 1976:306 311. 34. Clark, John E. and Michael Blake, 1990, "Investigaciones del Formativo Temprano del Litoral Chiapaneco, Temporada 1990," multilithed report to Mexican National Institute of Anthropology and History. 35. Blake, Michael, "An Emerging Early Formative Chiefdom at Paso de la Amada, Chiapas, Mexico," in The Formation of Complex Society in Southeastern Mesoamerica, William R. Fowler, Jr. (ed.) 1991:27–46. 36. Ibid. 37. Coe, Michael D. and Richard A. Diehl, 1980, In the Land of the Olmec, Vol. 1: The Archaeology of San Lorenzo Tenochtitlán, p. 137. 38. Oliver, Douglas L., 1955, A Solomon Island Society: Kinship and Leadership among the Siuai of Bougainville.

Chapter 8 (pp. 93–110)

1. Leach, Edmund R., 1954, Political Systems of Highland Burma: A Study of Kachin Social Structure. 2. Friedman, Jonathan, 1979, System, Structure, and Contradiction: The Evolution of "Asiatic" Social Formations. 3. de la Fuente, Julio, 1949, Yalalag: Una Villa Zapoteca Serrana, p. 265. 4. Flannery and Marcus 1994:136–149. 5. Marcus 1992a:195, 198, 304–305, 334. 6. Clark, John E., "The Beginnings of Mesoamerica: Apologia for the Soconusco Early Formative," in The Formation of Complex Society in Southeastern Mesoamerica, William R. Fowler, Jr. (ed.) 1991:Fig. 5 c, d. 7. Sahlins, Marshall D., 1958, Social Stratification in Polynesia. 8. Whalen 1981. 9. Lothrop, Samuel K., 1937, Coclé: An Archaeological Study of Central Panama. 10. Pires-Ferreira 1975:78. 11. Pires-Ferreira 1975:58. 12. Pires-Ferreira 1975:60. 13. Flannery and Marcus 1994:329–341. 14. Parry, William J., 1987, Chipped Stone Tools in Formative Oaxaca, Mexico: Their Procurement, Production, and Use, pp. 98–106. 15. Flannery and Marcus 1994:333. 16. Cited in Tozzer, Alfred M., 1941, Landa's Relación de las Cosas, p. 125. 17. Torquemada is cited in Tozzer, Alfred M., 1941, Landa's Relación de las Cosas, p. 88. 18. Romero, Javier, 1970, "Dental Mutilation, Trephination, and Cranial Deformation," in Handbook of Middle American Indians (vol. 9), Robert Wauchope and T. Dale Stewart (eds.), pp. 50–67. 19. Kowalewski et al. 1989:61. 20. Kirkby 1973. 21. Flannery, Kent V., "Precolumbian Farming in the Valleys of Oaxaca, Nochixtlán, Tehuacán, and Cuicatlán: A Comparative Study," in Flannery and Marcus (eds.) 1983:323–339. 22. Oliver, Douglas L., 1955, A Solomon Island Society: Kinship

and Leadership among the Siuai of Bougainville. 23. Carneiro, Robert L., 1991, "The Nature of the Chiefdom as Revealed by Evidence from the Cauca Valley of Colombia," in Profiles in Cultural Evolution, A. Terry Rambo and Kathleen Gillogly (eds.), pp. 167–190. 24. Flannery and Marcus 1994:367–371. 25. Schortman, Edward, Patricia Urban, M. Ausec, E. Bell, S. Connell, D. Schafer, and S. Smith, 1992, Sociopolitical Hierarchy and Craft Production: The Economic Bases of Elite Power in a Southeast Mesoamerican Polity, Part II, p. 3. 26. Feinman and Neitzel 1984.

Chapter 9 (pp. 111–120)

1. Redmond 1994. 2. Plog, Stephen, 1976, "Measurement of Prehistoric Interaction Between Communities," in Flannery (ed.) 1976:255–272. 3. Marcus 1992a:227–228, 250–254. 4. Drennan 1976. 5. Morris, Craig and Donald Thompson, 1985, Huánuco Pampa, pp. 90–91. 6. Flannery, K. V., "The Faunal Remains from Tierras Largas," unpublished manuscript. 7. Winter, Marcus C., 1972, unpublished doctoral dissertation. 8. Marcus, Joyce, 1976, Emblem and State in the Classic Maya Lowlands, pp. 137 177. 9. Marcus 1992a:15, 435–436, 443. 10. Grove, David C., Kenneth G. Hirth, David Bugé, and Ann Cyphers, 1976, "Settlement and Cultural Development at Chalcatzingo," Science 192:1203–1210. 11. Grove, David C. (ed.), 1987, Ancient Chalcatzingo. 12. Hirth, Kenneth G., 1987, "Formative Period Settlement Patterns in the Río Amatzinac Valley," in Ancient Chalcatzingo, David C. Grove (ed.), pp. 343–367. 13. Coe, Michael D. and Richard A. Diehl, 1980, In The Land of the Olmec, Vol. 1: The Archaeology of San Lorenzo Tenochtitlán. 14. Cyphers Guillén, Ann, 1993, "From Stone to Symbols: Olmec Art in Social Context at San Lorenzo Tenochtitlán," paper presented at Dumbarton Oaks, Washington, D.C. 15. Coe, Michael D. and Richard A. Diehl, 1980, In The Land of the Olmec, Vol. 1: The Archaeology of San Lorenzo Tenochtitlán. 16. Flannery and Marcus 1994:254–259. 17. Sanders, William T. and David Webster, 1978, "Unilinealism, Multilinealism, and the Evolution of Complex Societies," in Redman, Charles L., Mary Jane Berman, Edward V. Curtin, William T. Langhorne, Jr., Nina M. Versaggi, and Jeffery C. Wanser (eds.), pp. 249–302.

Chapter 10 (pp. 121–138)

1. Carneiro, Robert L., 1991, "The Nature of the Chiefdom as Revealed by Evidence from the Cauca Valley of Colombia," in Profiles in Cultural Evolution, A. Terry Rambo and Kathleen Gillogly (eds.), pp. 180–181. 2. Carneiro, Robert L., 1981, "The Chiefdom: Precursor of the State", in The Transition to Statehood in the New World, Grant D. Jones and Robert R. Kautz (eds.), pp. 37–79. 3. Wright, Henry T., 1984, "Prestate Political Formulations," in On The Evolution of Complex Societies:

Essays in Honor of Harry Hoijer, 1982, Timothy K. Earle (ed.), pp. 41–77. **4.** Drennan 1976:111–113. **5.** Marcus, Joyce, 1993, "Men's and Women's Ritual in Formative Oaxaca," paper presented at Dumbarton Oaks, Washington, D.C. **6.** Kowalewski et al. 1989. **7.** Kowalewski et al. 1989. **8.** Kowalewski et al. 1989:70. **9.** Spencer 1982:216–218. **10.** Elam, J. Michael, "Defensible and Fortified Sites," in Kowalewski et al. 1989:385–407. **11.** Kowalewski et al. 1989:75. **12.** Shaffer, Gary D., 1993, "An Archaeomagnetic Study of a Wattle-and-Daub Building Collapse," *Journal of Field Archaeology* 20:59–75. **13.** Marcus 1992a:369. **14.** Marcus 1992a:32–37, 435. **15.** Whalen 1981:64–67. **16.** Parry, William J., 1987, *Chipped Stone Tools in Formative Oaxaca, Mexico: Their Procurement, Production, and Use*, Fig. 47. **17.** Drennan 1976:133. **18.** Drennan 1976:Fig. 89. **19.** Drennan 1976:121. **20.** Byers (ed.) 1967:54. **21.** MacNeish, Richard S., Melvin L. Fowler, Angel García Cook, Frederick Peterson, Antoinette Nelken-Terner, and James A. Neely, 1972, *The Prehistory of the Tehuacán Valley*, vol. 5: *Excavations and Reconnaissance*. **22.** Woodbury, Richard B. and James A. Neely, 1972, "Water Control Systems of the Tehuacán Valley," in *The Prehistory of the Tehuacán Valley*, vol. 4: *Chronology and Irrigation*, Frederick Johnson (ed.), pp. 81–153. **23.** Spencer, Charles S., 1979, "Irrigation, Administration, and Society in Formative Tehuacán," in *Prehistoric Social, Political, and Economic Development in the Area of the Tehuacán Valley*, Robert D. Drennan (ed.), pp. 13–109. **24.** Spencer 1993:41–74. **25.** Woodbury, Richard B. and James A. Neely, 1972, "Water Control Systems of the Tehuacán Valley," in *The Prehistory of the Tehuacán Valley*, vol. 4: *Chronology and Irrigation*, Frederick Johnson (ed). **26.** Spencer 1993:52. **27.** Drucker, Philip, Robert F. Heizer, and Robert J. Squier, 1959, *Excavations at La Venta, Tabasco, 1955*. **28.** Drucker, Philip, 1952, *La Venta, Tabasco: A Study of Olmec Ceramics and Art*.

Chapter 11 (pp. 139–154)

1. Kowalewski et al. 1989:91. **2.** Blanton 1978. **3.** Demand 1990. **4.** Demand 1990:5–6. **5.** Demand 1990:4. **6.** Demand 1990:107–115. **7.** Demand 1990:47–50. **8.** Demand 1990:166–167. **9.** Bernal, Ignacio, 1946, unpublished master's thesis. **10.** Kowalewski et al. 1989:98. **11.** Our estimates of the Early Monte Albán I population of the valley are somewhat lower than those of the Settlement Pattern Project. We believe that the specific pottery attributes used to distinguish Rosario occupations from Early Monte Albán I occupations tend to underestimate the former and overestimate the latter. **12.** Blanton 1978. **13.** Elam, J. Michael, "Defensible and Fortified Sites," in Kowalewski et al. 1989:385–407. **14.** Kirkby 1973. **15.** Lees, Susan, 1973, *Sociopolitical Aspects of Canal Irrigation in the Valley of Oaxaca, Mexico*. **16.** Wittfogel, Karl A., 1957, *Oriental Despotism: A Comparative Study of Total Power*. **17.** Kowalewski et al. 1989:Fig. 6.3. **18.** Flannery, Kent V., "Precolumbian Farming in the Valleys of Oaxaca, Nochixtlán, Tehuacán, and Cuicatlán: A Comparative Study," in Flannery and Marcus (eds.) 1983:326. **19.** O'Brien, Michael J., Roger D. Mason, Dennis E. Lewarch, and James A. Neely, 1982, *A Late Formative Irrigation Settlement below Monte Albán: Survey and Excavation on the Xoxocotlán Piedmont, Oaxaca, Mexico*. **20.** Kowalewski et al. 1989:126. **21.** Kowalewski, Stephen A., 1976, unpublished doctoral dissertation. **22.** Neely, James A., S. Christopher Caran, and Barbara M. Winsborough, 1990, "Irrigated Agriculture at Hierve el Agua, Oaxaca, Mexico," in *Debating Oaxaca Archaeology*, Joyce Marcus (ed.), pp. 115–189. **23.** Neely, James A., 1967, "Organización Hidráulica y Sistemas de Irrigación Prehistóricos en el Valle de Oaxaca," *Boletín del Instituto Nacional de Antropología e Historia* 27:15–17. There are still some scholars who consider the water of Hierve el Agua too brackish for agriculture (see for example William P. Hewitt, 1994, "Hierve el Agua, Mexico: Its Water and Its Corn-Growing Potential," *Latin American Antiquity* 5:177–181). It should be remembered, however, that the region receives 600–700 mm of annual rainfall, so the spring water would never have been the exclusive source of moisture for crops. **24.** Parsons, Jeffrey R., 1971, "*Prehistoric Settlement Patterns in the Texcoco Region, Mexico*," pp. 122–125. **25.** Neely, James A., S. Christopher Caran, and Barbara M. Winsborough, 1990, "Irrigated Agriculture at Hierve el Agua, Oaxaca, Mexico," in *Debating Oaxaca Archaeology*, Joyce Marcus (ed.), p. 181. **26.** Kowalewski et al. 1989:Fig. 6.3. **27.** Kowalewski et al. 1989:123–126. **28.** Nicholas 1989:479. **29.** Elam, J. Michael, "Defensible and Fortified Sites," in Kowalewski et al. 1989:396. **30.** Blanton 1978:52. **31.** Elam, J. Michael, "Defensible and Fortified Sites," in Kowalewski et al. 1989:Fig. 12.2. **32.** Dupaix, Guillermo, 1969, *Expediciones Acerca de los Antiguos Monumentos de la Nueva España, 1805–1808*, 2 vols., José Alcina Franch (ed.). **33.** Marcus, Joyce, 1974, "The Iconography of Power among the Classic Maya," *World Archaeology* 6:83–94. **34.** Marcus 1992a:393. **35.** The Valley of Tamazulapan has been surveyed by Bruce Byland; the Valley of Nochixtlán by Ronald Spores; the Cuicatlán Cañada by Elsa Redmond and Charles Spencer; the Valley of Ejutla by Gary Feinman and Linda Nicholas: and the Valley of Miahuatlán by Donald Brockington and Charles Markman.

Chapter 12 (pp. 155–171)

1. Carneiro, Robert L., 1992, "The Role of Natural Selection in the Evolution of Culture," *Cultural Dynamics* 5:131. **2.** Service, Elman R., 1975, *Origins of the State and Civilization: The Process of Cultural Evolution*, pp. 154–158. **3.** Kirch, Patrick V., 1984, *The Evolution of the Polynesian Chiefdoms*, pp. 243–263. **4.** Sahlins, Marshall D., 1992, *Anahulu*, vol 1: *Historical Ethnography*. **5.** Kirch, Patrick V., 1992, *Anahulu*, vol. 2: *The Archaeology of History*. **6.** Sahlins, Marshall D., 1992, *Anahulu*, vol 1: *Historical Ethnography*. **7.** Kirch, Patrick V., 1992, *Anahulu*, vol. 2: *The Archaeology of History*. **8.** Bell, James. A., 1994, *Reconstructing Prehistory: Scientific Method in Archaeology*, pp. 241–261. **9.** Demand 1990:3. **10.** Caso 1965a. **11.** Caso, Alfonso, 1928, *Las Estelas Zapotecas*. **12.** Wright, Henry T. and Gregory A. Johnson, 1975, "Population, Exchange, and Early State Formation in Southwestern Iran," *American Anthropologist* 77:267–289. **13.** For example, the Settlement Pattern Project found only six gray ware sherds "diagnostic of Early [Monte Albán] I" on the surface of San José Mogote (Kowalewski et al. 1989:Table 5.3). This tiny number of diagnostics reinforces our notion, based on excavation, that there was hardly anyone left at San José Mogote during Early Period I. **14.** Nicholas 1989. **15.** The buried Period I buildings at Monte Albán are summarized in Flannery, Kent V. and Joyce Marcus, "The Earliest Public Buildings, Tombs, and Monuments at Monte Albán, with Notes on the Internal Chronology of Period I," in Flannery and Marcus (eds.) 1983:87–91. **16.** Acosta 1965. **17.** Caso, Alfonso, 1942, "Resumen del Informe de las Exploraciones en Oaxaca durante la 7ª y la 8ª Temporadas, 1937–1938 y 1938–1939," *Actas del XXVII Congreso Internacional de Americanistas* 2:159–187. **18.** Acosta, Jorge R. and Javier Romero, 1992, *Exploraciones en Monte Negro, Oaxaca: 1937–38, 1938–39, y 1939–40*. **19.** Flannery, Kent V., "Monte Negro: A Reinterpretation," in Flannery and Marcus (eds.) 1983:99–102. **20.** Acosta, Jorge R. and Javier Romero, 1992, *Exploraciones en Monte Negro, Oaxaca: 1937–38, 1938–39, y 1939–40*. **21.** Drennan, Robert D., "The Mountains North of the Valley," in Kowalewski et al. 1989:367–384. **22.** Whalen 1981:88–105. **23.** Flannery and Marcus (eds.) 1983:67. **24.** Ortner 1984:151.

Chapter 13 (pp. 172–194)

1. Haggett, Peter, 1972, *Geography: A Modern Synthesis*, pp. 286–297. **2.** Marquina, Ignacio, 1964, *Arquitectura Prehispánica*, p. 336. **3.** Kirch, Patrick V., 1984, *The Evolution of the Polynesian Chiefdoms*, Fig. 85. **4.** Hudson, Charles, 1976, *The Southeastern Indians*, pp. 328–334. **5.** Espíndola, Nicolás, 1580, "Relación de Chichicapa y Su Partido," in *Papeles de Nueva España: Segunda Serie, Geografía y Estadística* (vol. 4), Francisco del Paso y Troncoso (ed.) 1905, p. 139. **6.** Caso, Alfonso, 1935, "Las Exploraciones en Monte Albán, Temporada 1934–35," *Instituto Panamericano de Geografía e Historia* Publicación 18. **7.** Acosta, Jorge R. "Informes de la XIII, XIV, XV, XVI y XVII Temporadas de Exploraciones Arqueológicas de Monte Albán de los Años 1944 a 1949, manuscript in archives of the Mexican National Institute of Anthropology and History. **8.** Rappaport, Roy A., 1971, "Ritual, Sanctity, and Cybernetics," *American Anthropologist* 73:59–76. **9.** Rappaport, Roy A., 1979, *Ecology, Meaning, and Religion*. **10.** Blanton 1978:61–63. **11.** Acosta, Jorge R., "Informes de la XIII, XIV, XV, XVI y XVII Temporadas de Exploraciones Arqueológicas de Monte Albán de los Años 1944 a 1949, manuscript in archives of the Mexican National Institute of Anthropology and History. **12.** Ibid. **13.** Ibid. **14.** Bernal, Ignacio, 1958, *Exploraciones en Cuilapan de Guerrero, 1902–1954*, p. 25. **15.** Bernal, Ignacio, 1985, *Official Guide to the Oaxaca Valley*, p. 54. **16.** Marcus, Joyce and Kent V. Flannery, 1994, "Ancient Zapotec Ritual and Religion: An Application of the Direct Historical Approach," in *The Ancient Mind: Elements of Cognitive Archaeology*, Colin Renfrew and Ezra B.W. Zubrow (eds.), pp. 55–74. **17.** Ortiz Ceballos, Ponciano and María del Carmen Rodríquez M., "Manatí Project, Veracruz, Mexico, 1989 Field Season: A Report to the National Geographic Society, 1991," manuscript. **18.** Agrinier, Pierre, 1991, "The Ballcourts of Southern Chiapas, Mexico," in *The Mexican Ballgame*, Vernon L. Scarborough and David R. Wilcox (eds.), p. 175. **19.** Bernal, Ignacio, 1968, "The Ball Players of Dainzú," *Archaeology* 21:246–251. **20.** Bernal, Ignacio and Arturo Oliveros, 1988, *Exploraciones Arqueológicas en Dainzú, Oaxaca*. **21.** Caso, Alfonso, 1932, "Monte Albán, Richest Archaeological Find in America," *National Geographic Magazine* 62:499. **22.** Caso, Alfonso, 1969, *El Tesoro de Monte Albán*, p. 24. **23.** Bernal, Ignacio and Arturo Oliveros, 1988, *Exploraciones Arqueológicas en Dainzú, Oaxaca*. **24.** Kowalewski, Stephen A., Gary M. Feinman, Laura Finsten, and Richard E. Blanton, 1991, "Pre-Hispanic Ballcourts from the Valley of Oaxaca, Mexico," in *The Mesoamerican Ballgame*, Vernon L. Scarborough and David R. Wilcox (eds.), pp. 25–44. **25.** Kowalewski, Stephen A., Gary M. Feinman, Laura Finsten, and Richard E. Blanton, 1991, "Pre-Hispanic Ballcourts from the Valley of Oaxaca, Mexico," in *The Mesoamerican Ballgame*, Vernon L. Scarborough and David R. Wilcox (eds.). The statement of Kowalewski et al. (1989:193) that Monte Albán II ballcourts "are not restricted to any particular rank in the civic-ceremonial hierarchy, nor to large sites as measured by population" must be taken with a grain of salt, as it is based on an attempt to date *still-unexcavated ballcourts* via sherds on the surface. The Dainzú ballcourt (built late in Monte Albán IV, using fill containing Period I and II sherds) shows us that one cannot date public buildings without excavating them. **26.** Lowe, Gareth W., 1962, "Mound 5 and Minor Excavations, Chiapa de Corzo, Chiapas, Mexico," *Papers of the New World Archaeological Foundation* 12. **27.** Lowe, Gareth W., 1962, "Mound 5 and Minor Excavations, Chiapa de Corzo, Chiapas, Mexico," *Papers of the New World Archaeological Foundation* 12, p. 18. **28.** Letter from Gareth W. Lowe to Kent V. Flannery, 1992. **29.** Agrinier, Pierre and Gareth W. Lowe, 1960, "Mound 1, Chiapa de Corzo, Chiapas, Mexico," *Papers of the New World Archaeological Foundation* 8:47–52. **30.** Agrinier, Pierre, 1975, "Mound 1A, Chiapa de Corzo, Chiapas, Mexico: A Late Preclassic Architectural Complex," *Papers of the New World Archaeological Foundation* 37.

Chapter 14 (pp. 195–207)

1. Marcus 1992b:392. 2. Algaze, Guillermo, 1989, "The Uruk Expansion: Cross-Cultural Exchange in Early Mesopotamian Civilization," *Current Anthropology* 30:571–608. 3. Schreiber, Katharina J., 1992, *Wari Imperialism in Middle Horizon Peru*. 4. Marcus 1992b:406–407. 5. Santley, Robert S., 1989, "Obsidian Working, Long-Distance Exchange, and the Teotihuacán Presence on the South Gulf Coast," in *Mesoamerica After the Decline of Teotihuacán, AD 700–900*, Richard A. Diehl and Janet C. Berlo (eds.), pp. 131–151. 6. Agrinier, Pierre, 1991, "The Ballcourts of Southern Chiapas, Mexico," in *The Mexican Ballgame*, Vernon L. Scarborough and David R. Wilcox (eds.), pp. 178–179. 7. Sanders, William T. and Joseph W. Michels (eds.), 1977, *Teotihuacán and Kaminaljuyú*. 8. Caso, Alfonso, 1947, "Calendario y Escritura de las Antiguas Culturas de Monte Albán," *Obras Completas de Miguel Othón de Mendizábal*, vol. 1, pp. 115–143. 9. Seler, Eduard, 1908, "Das Dorfbuch von Santiago Guevea," *Gesammelte Abhandlungen* 3:157–193. 10. Marcus 1980:50–51. 11. Marcus, Joyce, "The Reconstructed Chronology of the Later Zapotec Rulers, AD 1415–1563," in Flannery and Marcus (eds.) 1983:301–308. 12. Marcus, Joyce, 1984, "Mesoamerican Territorial Boundaries: Reconstructions from Archaeology and Hieroglyphic Writing," *Archaeological Review from Cambridge* 3:48–62. 13. Paddock, John, "Comments on the Lienzos of Huilotepec and Guevea," in Flannery and Marcus (eds.) 1983:308–313. 14. Barlow, Robert H. and Byron MacAfee (eds.) 1949, *Diccionario de elementos fonéticos en escritura jeroglífica (Códice Mendocino)*. Universidad Nacional Autónoma de México, Publicaciones del Instituto de Historia, Primera Serie 9. 15. Marcus, Joyce, 1976, "The Iconography of Militarism at Monte Albán and Neighboring Sites in the Valley of Oaxaca," in *The Origins of Religious Art and Iconography in Preclassic Mesoamerica*, Henry B. Nicholson (ed.), pp. 123–139. 16. Marcus 1992b:400. 17. Marcus, Joyce, 1976, *Emblem and State in the Classic Maya Lowlands*, pp. 130–149. 18. Fash, William L., 1991, *Scribes, Warriors, and Kings: The City of Copán and the Ancient Maya*, pp. 150–151. 19. Marcus 1992a:357. 20. Marcus, Joyce, 1987, *Late Intermediate Occupation at Cerro Azul, Peru*. 21. Morris, Craig, 1988, "Mas Allá de Las Fronteras de Chincha," in *La Frontera del Estado Inca*, Tom Dillehay and Patricia Netherly (eds.), pp. 131–140. 22. Feinman and Nicholas 1990. 23. Marcus 1992a:245–246. 24. Brockington, Donald L., 1973, *Archaeological Investigations at Miahuatlán, Oaxaca*. 25. Markman, Charles W., 1981, *Prehispanic Settlement Dynamics in Central Oaxaca, Mexico*. 26. Marcus 1980:59. 27. Barlow, Robert H., 1949, *The Extent of the Empire of the Culhua Mexica*. 28. DeCicco, Gabriel and Donald L. Brockington, 1956, *Reconocimiento arqueológico en el suroeste de Oaxaca*. 29. Joyce, Arthur A., 1991, "Formative Period Social Change in the Lower Río Verde Valley, Oaxaca, Mexico," *Latin American Antiquity* 2:126–150. 30. Joyce, Arthur A., 1993, "Interregional Interaction and Social Development on the Oaxaca Coast," *Ancient Mesoamerica* 4:67–84. 31. Joyce, Arthur A., 1991, "Formative Period Social Change in the Lower Río Verde Valley, Oaxaca, Mexico," *Latin American Antiquity* 2:139. 32. Espíndola, Nicolás, 1580, "Relación de Chichicapa y Su Partido," in *Papeles de Nueva España. Segunda Serie, Geografía y Estadística* (vol. 4), Francisco del Paso y Troncoso (ed.) 1905, pp. 115–143. 33. DeCicco, Gabriel and Donald L. Brockington, 1956, *Reconocimiento arqueológico en el suroeste de Oaxaca*, pp. 89–90. 34. Drennan, Robert D., "The Mountains North of the Valley," in Kowalewski et al. 1989:367–384. 35. Kowalewski, Stephen A., 1991, "Peñoles: Archaeological Survey in the Mixtec Sierra, Mexico," report submitted to National Geographic Society. 36. Spencer 1982. 37. Redmond 1983. 38. Redmond, Elsa M. and Charles S. Spencer, "The Cuicatlán Cañada and the Period II Frontier of the Zapotec State," in Flannery and Marcus (eds.) 1983:117–120. 39. Ibid., p. 119. 40. Ibid. 41. Davies, C. Nigel, 1987, *The Aztec Empire*, University of Oklahoma Press, Norman. 42. Hassig, Ross, 1988, *Aztec Warfare: Imperial Expansion and Political Control*, University of Oklahoma Press, Norman. 43. Marcus 1992b:400–401.

Chapter 15 (pp. 208–235)

1. Marcus, Joyce, "Rethinking the Zapotec Urn," in Flannery and Marcus (eds.) 1983:144–148. 2. Caso, Alfonso, 1938, "Las Exploraciones en Monte Albán, Quinta y Sexta Temporadas 1936–37," *Instituto Panamericano de Geografía e Historia Publicación* 34. 3. Caso, Bernal, and Acosta 1967:Table XV. 4. Caso, Alfonso, 1938, "Las Exploraciones en Monte Albán, Quinta y Sexta Temporadas 1936–37," *Instituto Panamericano de Geografía e Historia Publicación* 34, p. 76. 5. Marcus 1992a:303–306. 6. Marcus, Joyce, "A Zapotec Inauguration in Comparative Perspective," in Marcus and Zeitlin (eds.) 1994, *Caciques and their People*. Anthropological Paper 89, Museum of Anthropology, University of Michigan, Ann Arbor, pp. 245–250. 7. Marcus 1980:60–61. 8. Marcus, Joyce, "Teotihuacán Visitors on Monte Albán Monuments and Murals," in Flannery and Marcus (eds.) 1983:175–181. 9. Marcus 1992a:325–328. 10. Acosta, Jorge R., 1958–59, "Exploraciones Arqueológicas en Monte Albán, XVIII Temporada," *Revista Mexicana de Estudios Antropológicos* 15:7–50. 11. Ibid., p. 27. 12. Fash, William L., 1991, *Scribes, Warriors, and Kings: The City of Copán and the Ancient Maya*, pp. 148–149. 13. Séjourné, Laurette, 1966, *El Lenguaje de las Formas en Teotihuacán*, Lámina 47. 14. Townsend, Richard F., 1979, *State and Cosmos in the Art of Tenochtitlán*. 15. Nicholson, Henry B. and Eloise Quiñones Keber, 1983, *Art of Aztec Mexico: Treasures of Tenochtitlán*. 16. Marcus 1992a:11–12, 437–440. 17. Blanton, Richard E., "Urban Monte Albán During Period III," in Flannery and Marcus (eds.) 1983:128–131. 18. Winter, Marcus C., 1974, "Residential Patterns at Monte Albán, Oaxaca, Mexico," *Science* 186:981–987. 19. Winter, Marcus and William O. Payne, 1976, "Hornos para Cerámica Hallados en Monte Albán," *Boletín del Instituto Nacional de Antropología e Historia* 16:37. 20. Caso, Alfonso, 1969, *El Tesoro de Monte Albán*, Fig. 26c. 21. Ibid., Fig. 26b. 22. Furst, Jill L., 1978, *Codex Vindobonensis Mexicanus I: A Commentary*, Fig. 16. 23. Caso, Alfonso and Ignacio Bernal, 1952, *Urnas de Oaxaca*. 24. Gary Feinman and Linda Nicholas, personal communication. 25. Nicholas 1989:Table 14.3. 26. Kowalewski et al. 1989:229. 27. Elam, J. Michael, "Defensible and Fortified Sites," in Kowalewski et al. 1989:405. 28. Spores, Ronald, "Yucuñudahui," in Flannery and Marcus (eds.) 1983:155–158. 29. The Mixtec impact on the Valley of Oaxaca during the late prehispanic period is discussed by a variety of authors in Flannery and Marcus (eds.) 1983:227–290. 30. Feinman, Gary M., 1980, unpublished doctoral dissertation. 31. Feinman, Gary M., "Ceramic Production Sites," in Blanton et al. 1982:389–396. 32. Kowalewski et al. 1989:223. 33. Millon, René, 1973, *Urbanization at Teotihuacán*, Vol. 1. 34. Millon, René, 1981, "Teotihuacán: City, State, and Civilization," in *Supplement to the Handbook of Mesoamerican Indians*, vol. 1, Victoria R. Bricker and Jeremy A. Sabloff (eds.), pp. 198–243. 35. Santley, Robert S., 1989, "Obsidian Working, Long-Distance Exchange, and the Teotihuacán Presence on the South Gulf Coast," in *Mesoamerica After the Decline of Teotihuacán, AD 700–900*, Richard A. Diehl and Janet C. Berlo (eds.), pp. 131–151. 36. Sanders, William T. and Joseph Michels (eds.), 1977, *Teotihuacán and Kaminaljuyú*. 37. Coggins, Clemency C., 1979, "Teotihuacán at Tikal in the Early Classic Period," *Actes du XLII Congrès International des Américanistes, Paris* 8:251–269. 38. Marcus, Joyce, "Teotihuacán Visitors on Monte Albán Monuments and Murals," in Flannery and Marcus (eds.) 1983:179–181. 39. Millon, René, 1973, *Urbanization at Teotihuacán*, Vol. 1. 40. Paddock, John, "The Oaxaca Barrio at Teotihuacán," in Flannery and Marcus (eds.) 1983:170–175. 41. Spence, Michael W., "Tlailotlacan, a Zapotec Enclave in Teotihuacán," in *Art, Ideology, and the City of Teotihuacán*, Janet C. Berlo (ed.) 1993:59–88. 42. Rattray, Evelyn, 1992, *The Teotihuacán Burials and Offerings. A Commentary and Inventory*. Rattray, Evelyn, 1993, "The Oaxaca Barrio at Teotihuacán," *Monografías Mesoamericanas, No.1*. Puebla, Mexico. 43. Spence, Michael W., 1976, "Human Skeletal Material from the Oaxaca Barrio in Teotihuacán, Mexico," in *Archaeological Frontiers: Papers on New World High Cultures in Honor of J. Charles Kelley*, Robert B. Pickering (ed.), pp. 129–148. 44. Millon, René, 1973, *Urbanization at Teotihuacán*, Vol. 1:42. 45. Kowalewski et al. 1989:249. 46. Kowalewski et al. 1989:Table 9.2. 47. Kowalewski et al. 1989:251. 48. Marcus 1980:63–64. 49. Marcus, Joyce, "Changing Patterns of Stone Monuments after the Fall of Monte Albán, AD 600–900," in Flannery and Marcus (eds.) 1983:191–197.

Chapter 16 (pp. 236–245)

1. Spencer 1990:23.

Further Reading

Acosta, Jorge R. 1965 Preclassic and Classic Architecture of Oaxaca. In *The Handbook of Middle American Indians,* vol. 3, edited by Robert Wauchope and Gordon R. Willey, University of Texas Press, Austin.

Bernal, Ignacio. 1965 Archaeological Synthesis of Oaxaca. In *The Handbook of Middle American Indians,* vol. 3, edited by Robert Wauchope and Gordon R. Willey, University of Texas Press, Austin.

Blanton, Richard E. 1978 *Monte Albán: Settlement Patterns at the Ancient Zapotec Capital.* Academic Press, New York and London.

Blanton, Richard, Stephen A. Kowalewski, Gary Feinman, and Jill Appel. 1982 *Monte Albán's Hinterland, Part I: Prehispanic Settlement Patterns of the Central and Southern Parts of the Valley of Oaxaca, Mexico.* Memoir 15, Museum of Anthropology, University of Michigan, Ann Arbor.

Byers, Douglas S. (ed.) 1967 *The Prehistory of the Tehuacán Valley, vol. 1: Environment and Subsistence.* University of Texas Press, Austin and London.

Caso, Alfonso. 1965a Sculpture and Mural Painting of Oaxaca. In *The Handbook of Middle American Indians,* vol. 3, edited by Robert Wauchope and Gordon R. Willey, University of Texas Press, Austin.
———1965b Zapotec Writing and Calendar. In *The Handbook of Middle American Indians,* vol. 3, edited by Robert Wauchope and Gordon R. Willey, University of Texas Press, Austin.

Caso, Alfonso, Ignacio Bernal, and Jorge R. Acosta. 1967 *La Cerámica de Monte Albán.* Memorias del Instituto de Antropología e Historia No. 13, Mexico.

Demand, Nancy H. 1990 *Urban Relocation in Archaic and Classical Greece: Flight and Consolidation.* University of Oklahoma Press, Norman.

Drennan, Robert D. 1976 *Fábrica San José and Middle Formative Society in the Valley of Oaxaca.* Memoir 8, Museum of Anthropology, University of Michigan, Ann Arbor.

Feinman, Gary and Jill Neitzel. 1984 Too Many Types: An Overview of Sedentary Prestate Societies in the Americas. In *Advances in Archaeological Method and Theory,* vol. 7, edited by M. B. Schiffer, pp. 39–102.

Feinman, Gary M. and Linda M. Nicholas. 1990 At the Margins of the Monte Albán State: Settlement Patterns in the Ejutla Valley, Oaxaca, Mexico. *Latin American Antiquity* 1:216–246.
———1993 Shell-Ornament Production in Ejutla: Implications for Highland-Coastal Interaction in Ancient Oaxaca. *Ancient Mesoamerica* 4:103–119.

Flannery, Kent V. (ed.) 1976 *The Early Mesoamerican Village.* Academic Press, New York and London.
———1986 *Guilá Naquitz.* Academic Press, New York.

Flannery, Kent V. and Joyce Marcus. 1994 *Early Formative Pottery of the Valley of Oaxaca.* Memoir 27, Museum of Anthropology, University of Michigan, Ann Arbor.

Flannery, Kent V. and Joyce Marcus. 1983 (eds.) *The Cloud People: Divergent Evolution of the Zapotec and Mixtec Civilizations.* Academic Press, New York and London.

Kirkby, Anne V. T. 1973 *The Use of Land and Water Resources in the Past and Present Valley of Oaxaca, Mexico.* Memoir 5, Museum of Anthropology, University of Michigan, Ann Arbor.

Kowalewski, Stephen A., G. M. Feinman, L. Finsten, R. E. Blanton, and L. M. Nicholas. 1989 *Monte Albán's Hinterland, Part II: The Prehispanic Settlement Patterns in Tlacolula, Etla and Ocotlán, the Valley of Oaxaca, Mexico.* (2 vols.) Memoir 23, Museum of Anthropology, University of Michigan, Ann Arbor.

Marcus, Joyce. 1980 Zapotec Writing. *Scientific American* 242:50–64.
———1992a *Mesoamerican Writing Systems: Propaganda, Myth, and History in Four Ancient Civilizations.* Princeton, Princeton University Press.
———1992b Dynamic Cycles of Mesoamerican States. *National Geographic Research & Exploration* 8:392–411.

Nicholas, Linda M. 1989 Land Use in Prehispanic Oaxaca. in *Monte Albán's Hinterland, Part II: The Prehispanic Settlement Patterns in Tlacolula, Etla, and Ocotlán, the Valley of Oaxaca, Mexico,* by Stephen Kowalewski et al., Vol. 1, pp. 449–505. Memoir 23, Museum of Anthropology, University of Michigan, Ann Arbor.

Ortner, Sherry B. 1984 Theory in Anthropology since the Sixties. *Comparative Studies in Society and History* 26:126–166.

Paddock, John. (ed.) 1966 *Ancient Oaxaca.* Stanford University Press, Stanford.

Pires-Ferreira, Jane W. 1975 *Formative Mesoamerican Exchange Networks, with Special Reference to the Valley of Oaxaca.* Memoir 7, Museum of Anthropology, University of Michigan, Ann Arbor.

Redmond, Elsa M. 1983 *A Fuego y Sangre: Early Zapotec Imperialism in the Cuicatlán Cañada.* Memoir 16, Museum of Anthropology, University of Michigan, Ann Arbor.
———1994 *Tribal and Chiefly Warfare in South America.* Memoir 28, Museum of Anthropology, University of Michigan, Ann Arbor.

Spencer, Charles S. 1982 *The Cuicatlán Cañada and Monte Albán: A Study of Primary State Formation.* Academic Press, New York and London.
———1990 On the Tempo and Mode of State Formation: Neoevolutionism Reconsidered. *Journal of Anthropological Archaeology* 9:1–30.
———1993 Human Agency, Biased Transmission, and the Cultural Evolution of Chiefly Authority. *Journal of Anthropological Archaeology* 12:41–74.

Whalen, Michael E. 1981 *Excavations at Tomaltepec: Evolution of a Formative Community in the Valley of Oaxaca, Mexico.* Memoir 12, Museum of Anthropology, University of Michigan, Ann Arbor.

Whitecotton, Joseph W. 1977 *The Zapotecs: Princes, Priests, and Peasants.* University of Oklahoma Press, Norman.

Acknowledgments and Sources of Illustrations

There is a large community of generous scholars who work in Oaxaca. The research described here could not have been done, nor this book written, without their help.

Two pioneers of Oaxaca archaeology – the late Alfonso Caso and Ignacio Bernal – encouraged us over the years, and John Paddock provided the Human Ecology Project with laboratories and living space during the early years of our research. The Mexican National Institute of Anthropology and History (INAH) gave us the necessary permits to work in Oaxaca, and the National Science Foundation, National Endowment for the Humanities, Ford Foundation, and National Geographic Society supported the bulk of our study.

The combined staffs of the Human Ecology Project and the Settlement Pattern Project have worked together in friendship and cooperation for more than 25 years. We are indebted to all of them, and especially to Richard Blanton, Robert Drennan, Michael Elam, Gary Feinman, Laura Finsten, Suzanne Fish, Richard Ford, Frank Hole, Joseph Hopkins, Michael and Anne Kirkby, Steve Kowalewski, Susan Lees, Ellen Messer, Chris Moser, James Neely, Linda Nicholas, Richard Orlandini, William Parry, William Payne, Steve Plog, Nan Pyne, Elsa Redmond, Robert Reynolds, John Rick, C. Earle Smith, Charles Spencer, Ronald Spores, Kathryn Vaughn, Dudley Varner, Michael Whalen, Henry Wright, and Robert and Judith Zeitlin for sharing their data and good times with us. Over the years, a number of scholars including Robert McC. Adams, Richard E. W. Adams, E. Wyllys Andrews V, Robert Carneiro, Susan Gillespie, David Grove, John Henderson, Frank Hole, Linda Manzanilla, Patricia McAnany, John Monaghan, Craig Morris, Robert Sharer, Mary Elizabeth Smith, and John Yellen encouraged us to write this book. We thank them all.

The editors of this series, Colin Renfrew and Jeremy Sabloff, showed exceptional patience and offered valuable advice. We also thank the editorial, design, and production staff of Thames and Hudson for making the book look even better than we expected.

It has been a pleasure to collaborate over the years with the staff of INAH's Centro Regional de Oaxaca, especially archaeologists Nelly Robles, Roberto Zárate, and Raul Matadamas. Above all, we want to single out the two scholars to whom this book is dedicated. As Director of the Centro Regional, Manuel Esparza opened many doors for us, guided us through rough bureaucratic seas, and guaranteed the success of our research. María de los Angeles Romero Frizzi, another of the Center's outstanding researchers, became our indispensable advocate within the academic community of Mexico. Without their support, neither the Human Ecology Project nor the Settlement Pattern Project could have achieved its goals.

Sources of Photographs

Most photographs were taken by members of the Human Ecology Project or the Settlement Pattern Project. These include all aerial photographs except for ill. 14, which is by Compañia Mexicana Acrofoto. Special thanks go to Chris Moser, the Human Ecology Project's staff photographer, and to Charles Spencer, Elsa Redmond, Gary Feinman, Linda Nicholas, and James Neely, who supplied us with special photographs. Illustrations 17, 24, 246, 266, and 269 are from the archives of the Museum of Anthropology, University of Michigan.

Sources of Line Drawings

Many artists contributed line drawings. They include John Klausmeyer (ills. 1, 11, 18, 20–3, 27–8, 30–3, 40, 92, 94–5, 123, 125–6, 131, 133, 147–8, 163, 176–8, 199, 211, 214, 219, 237, 245, 262), Kay Clahassey (ills. 2, 70, 111, 124, 128, 151, 157–160, 162, 180, 193–4, 196–7, 226, 242, 271, 277, 280), David W. Reynolds (ills. 4, 16, 73, 79, 102–3, 113, 200, 212–3, 244, 249), and Margaret Van Bolt (ills. 13, 171, 250, 254), all of the University of Michigan. Other drawings are by Mark Orsen (ills. 137, 255, 258–260, 281, 286), Lois Martin (ills. 96, 114, 223, 256), Nancy Hansen (ills. 44–8, 118), and William J. Parry (ills. 145–6, 215–7).

Sources of Color Plates

All color photographs are by the authors, except plates II–IV which were supplied by Dr Colin McEwan. The color paintings (Plates I, VI, IX, X, XIV–XVI, and the back cover of the book) are by John Klausmeyer, University of Michigan. Cover photograph © Macduff Everton

Illustrations Redrawn from Other Sources

Many illustrations were redrafted (with modifications) by John Klausmeyer, Kay Clahassey, or Margaret Van Bolt from drawings or photographs in earlier publications by other authors. These authors include Alfonso Caso (ills. 206, 252, 267–8); Alfonso Caso and Ignacio Bernal (ills. 5, 10, 12, 176–8, 247); Ignacio Bernal (ills. 210, 222); Jorge Acosta (ill. 265); Caso, Bernal, and Acosta (ills. 253, 285); Jorge Acosta and Javier Romero (ills. 183, 185–8); Ignacio Marquina (ills. 184, 204); Román Piña Chan (ill. 220); Luis Aveleyra Arroyo de Anda (ill. 25); René Millon (ills. 283–4); Michael Spence (ills. 282), Gareth W. Lowe (ills. 227–8); Pierre Agrinier (ills. 229–231); Marcus C. Winter (ill. 263); John Doebley (ill. 55); Paul Mangelsdorf, Richard S. MacNeish, and Walton Galinat (ills. 58, 60); Jonathan Friedman (ill. 85); Samuel K. Lothrop (ill. 97); Richard B. Woodbury and James A. Neely (ill. 152); Philip Drucker (ill. 154); Nancy Demand (ill. 156); Patrick V. Kirch (ill. 205); Michael J. O'Brien (ill. 167); Gregory A. Johnson (ill. 195); John Clark and Michael Blake (ills. 82–4); Michael F. Whalen (ills. 89, 93, 189–190); Robert D. Drennan (ills. 120, 149–150); Charles S. Spencer and Elsa M. Redmond (ill. 241); Richard E. Blanton (ills. 169, 272); Stephen A. Kowalewski (ill. 182); Kowalewski, Feinman, Finsten, Blanton, and Nicholas (ills. 70, 111, 128, 157, 193, 271, 274, 277). Illustration 136 was redrawn from the Codex Mendoza, and ills. 76–7 were done by Klausmeyer from specimens in the Museo Regional de Oaxaca. References to the publications of the authors mentioned above can be found either in our Bibliography or in Notes to the Text.

Index